WEHRMACHT PANZER DIVISIONS
1939–45

THE ESSENTIAL TANK IDENTIFICATION GUIDE

WEHRMACHT PANZER DIVISIONS
1939–45

amber
BOOKS

First published in 2005

Reprinted in 2006

Published by
Amber Books Ltd
Bradley's Close
74–77 White Lion Street
London N1 9PF
United Kingdom
www.amberbooks.co.uk

Copyright © Amber Books Ltd 2005

All rights reserved. No part of this publication may be reproduced, stored in a retrieval system, or transmitted in any form or by any means, electronic, mechanical, photocopying, recording, or otherwise, without prior permission in writing from the publishers.

Project Editor: Michael Spilling
Design: Hawes Design

ISBN-13: 978-1-904-687-46-7
ISBN-10: 1-904687-46-6

PICTURE CREDITS:
Art-Tech/Mars: 6, 81, 88, 106, 115, 169;
TRH Pictures: 10, 12, 13, 23, 60, 62, 73, 97, 118, 128, 137, 142, 174, 182, 185;
Ukrainian State Archive/Amber Books: 123;
Will Fowler: 149.

All illustrations supplied by Jorge Rosado.

Printed in Italy

Contents

Introduction — 6

Chapter 1
Pre-War Panzer Divisions — 10
(1st–5th Panzer Divisions)

Chapter 2
1939 Panzer Divisions — 60
(6th–10th Panzer Divisions)

Chapter 3
1940–41 Panzer Divisions — 106
(11th–23rd Panzer Divisions)

Chapter 4
Later Wartime Panzer Divisions — 174
(24th–26th, 116th and 130th Panzer Divisions)

Index — 188

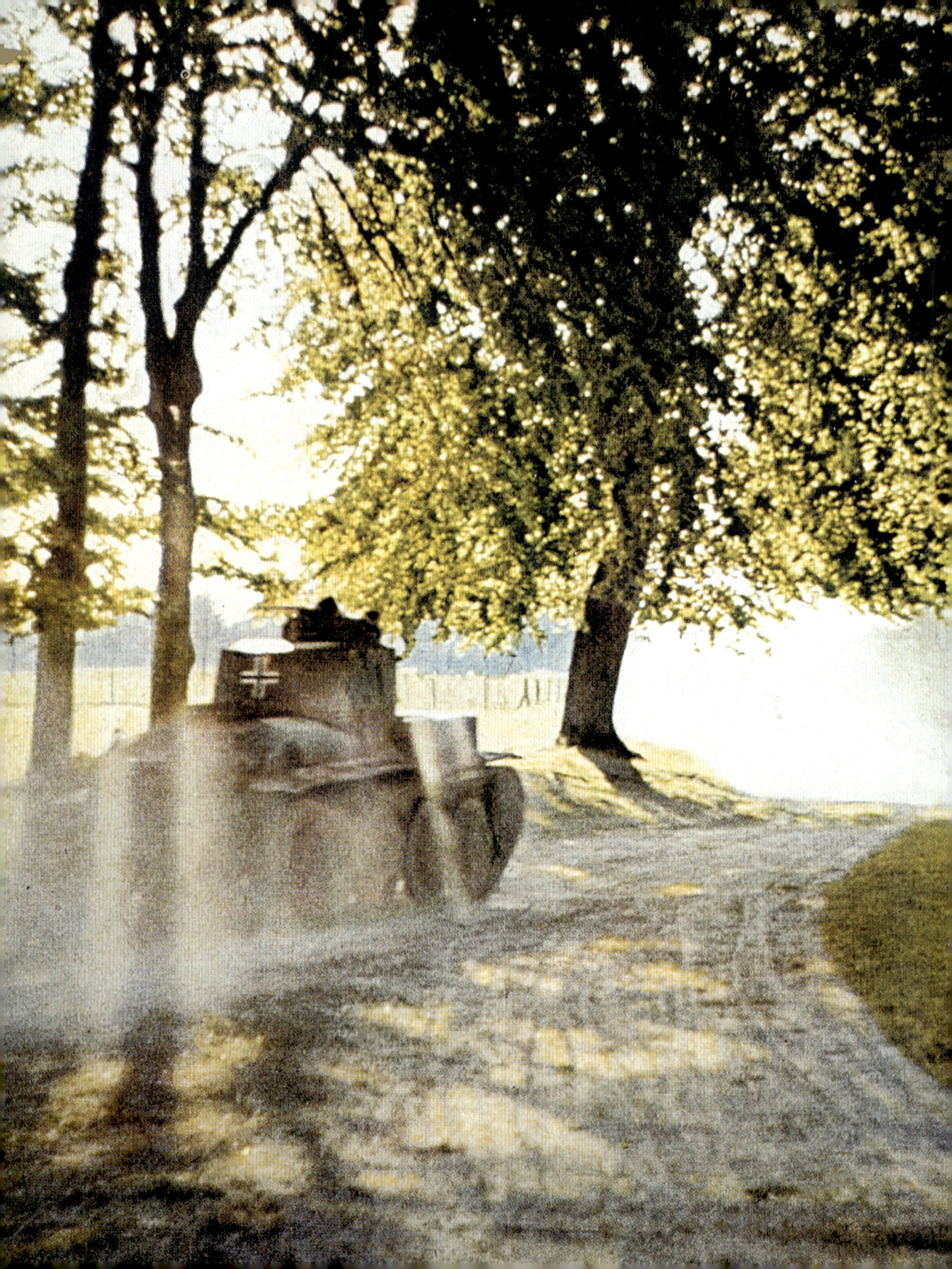

Introduction

Although they existed for less than a decade from the foundation of the first units in 1935, the Panzer Divisions of the *Wehrmacht* changed the face of modern warfare.

THROUGH A SERIES OF RAPID and sharp campaigns the German army was able to demonstrate to the whole world that it was master of a new form of warfare. *Blitzkrieg* enabled the *Wehrmacht* to overcome the bloody attritional strategies of World War I, and to humble enemy after enemy at minimum cost to the German nation and at maximum cost to its opponents.

The roots of *Blitzkrieg* lay in the German infiltration tactics of 1918. Special assault divisions with heavily-armed 'storm troopers' broke through weak points in the Allied lines. The troops carried heavy loads of grenades, machine guns and trench mortars, giving them superior firepower at the point of contact. They were supported by precision artillery fire and ground attack aircraft. Isolated pockets of defenders were dealt with by follow-up units: the storm troopers raged on through the Allied rear areas.

After the war, a few military theorists realized that armoured vehicles would add an extra dimension to the new German tactics. Most armies in the 1920s saw tanks purely as a means of supporting the infantry, but men like Liddell Hart, Fuller and Martel advocated the establishment of a much more mobile armoured force for use in future wars.

Balanced force

British theories regarding a balanced armoured force were examined in great detail by the *Truppenamt*, the clandestine General Staff of the *Reichswehr*. One of the most important of the officers involved was Colonel Heinz Guderian. Guderian took the ideas of Liddell Hart, Martel and Fuller and expanded them, proposing that any future armoured force had to be a balance of all arms, with the main striking force being provided by a mobile spearhead of tanks, mechanised infantry and artillery.

Guderian had to fight some opposition within the German army, but much of the General Staff looked on his ideas with favour. When the Nazis came to power, he found an even greater supporter in Hitler, who encouraged the efforts of the panzer troops at every stage. As a result, he was able to put some of his ideas into practice as the first experimental tank formations appeared in 1934, and the first true panzer divisions were formed a year later.

◀ **Czech-built Tank**
A Panzer 38(t) from General Erwin Rommel's 7th Panzer Division moves along a road in northern France as part of the *Fall Gelb* campaign of May 1940.

INTRODUCTION

Panzer Division Organization

The organization of the standard panzer division changed greatly during World War II. The rapid evolution of armoured formations was inspired by combat experience, and by the massive increase in the capabilities of tanks and other armoured vehicles.

IN A MANUAL WRITTEN soon after the establishment of the *Panzerwaffe*, the function of the new German panzer arm was defined as 'the creation of rapid concentrations of considerable fighting power, obtaining quick decisions by breakthroughs, deep penetration on wide fronts and the destruction of the enemy'. This policy was being advocated at a time when other armies were still slowing their armour to move at the pace of the marching soldier. The Germans preferred to increase the speed of their infantry, initially by carrying them on trucks and later by mounting them in specialized half-tracks.

Although the tanks were to be the spearhead, the first panzers were primarily training machines. They were small, lightly armed and armoured, and had definite tactical limitations; production of better designs was slow and expensive. But they were highly mobile, which was vital since speed was the essence of the newly emerging concept of *Blitzkrieg*.

The spearhead of the early panzer divisions was provided by a panzer brigade of two panzer regiments. The regiment in turn was divided into two light companies operating Panzer Is and IIs, and a medium company with Panzer IIs and IVs. This was matched by a motorized infantry or *Schützen* brigade. Typically, a panzer division would have a strength of some 300 armoured fighting vehicles.

Organization of 1st Panzer Division
1939
1. *Schützen-Brigade*
   Schützen-Regiment 1 (two battalions)
   Kradschützen-Bataillon 1 (motorcyle battalion)
1. *Panzer-Brigade*
   Panzer-Regiment 1 (two abteilungen)
   Panzer-Regiment 2 (two abteilungen)
73. *Artillerie-Regiment* (two abteilungen)
Aufklärungs-Abteilung 4
Panzerjäger-Abteilung 37
Pionier-Bataillon 37
Nachrichten-Abteilung 37
37th Divisional Support Unit

1940
Experience in Poland had shown that the panzer brigade formation was too large and unwieldy for tactical use, so after the invasion of France most divisions were reduced to a single panzer regiment, and the armoured and infantry brigade headquarters were dissolved. Total tank strength was typically 150.
   Schützen-Regiment 1 (two battalions)
   Schützen-Regiment 113 (two battalions)
   Panzer-Regiment 1 (two abteilungen)
   Artillerie-Regiment 73 (three abteilungen)
   Kradschützen-Abteilung 1
   Aufklärungs-Abteilung 4
   Panzerjäger-Abteilung 37
   Pionier-Bataillon 37
   Nachrichten-Abteilung 37
   37th Divisional Support Unit

1943
The organisation of panzer divisions was continually changing as new weapons became available. By the time of the battle of Kursk, nearly all of the early, light armoured vehicles had been withdrawn from service apart from a few Panzer IIs used for reconnaissance and security, and the 1st Panzer Division was almost exclusively equipped with around 160 long-barrelled Panzer IVs.
   Panzergrenadier-Regiment 1 (two battalions)
   Panzergrenadier-Regiment 113 (two battalions)
   Panzer-Regiment 1 (two abteilungen)
   Panzer-Artillerie-Regiment 73 (four abteilungen)
   Panzer-Aufklärungs-Abteilung 1
   Panzerjäger-Abteilung 37
   Panzer-Pionier-Bataillon 37
   Panzer-Nachrichten-Bataillon 37
   Heeres-Flak-Abteilung 299
   37th Divisional Support Unit

1944
In August 1944 a new divisional structure (see opposite) was created as the entire *Panzerwaffe* was reorganized after the loss of Normandy to the Allies.

INTRODUCTION

Type 44 Panzer Division (Nominal strength 14,691)

Divisional Headquarters (520 men)

Panzer Regiment (2006 men)
   Regimental Staff Company (5 x Pz.IV, 3 x PzBfWg.V)
      Flak Platoon (8 x 37-mm Flak 43 on Pz IV)
   1st Panzer Battalion (76-94 Pz.V Panther)
      Staff Company (5 x Pz.V, 3 x PzBfWg.V,
         3 x Flakvierling 20mm SP Guns)
      Four tank companies (each with 17 or 22 Pz.V Panther)
      Armoured maintenance company
      Armoured Supply Company
   2nd Panzer Battalion (76-94 Pz.IV)
      Staff Company (5 x Pz.IV, 3 x PzBfWg.IV,
         3 x Flakvierling 20mm SP Guns)
      Four tank companies (each with 17 or 22 Pz.IV)
      Armoured Maintenance Company
      Armoured Supply Company

1st Armoured Panzergrenadier Regiment (2287 men)
   Regimental Staff Company
   1st Panzergrenadier Battalion
      Battalion Staff
      Three Panzergrenadier Companies (half track)
      Heavy Company (half track)
         Infantry Gun Platoon
         Mortar Platoon
      Panzergrenadier Supply Company
   2nd Panzergrenadier Battalion
      Battalion Staff
      Three Panzergrenadier Companies (motorized)
      Heavy Company (motorised)
         Engineer Platoon
         Panzerjäger Platoon
         Infantry Gun Platoon
         SP Gun Battery
      Pioneer Company (motorized)

1st Motorised Panzergrenadier Regiment (2219 men)
   Regimental Staff Company
   Two Motorised Panzer Grenadier Battalions, each with
      Battalion Staff
      Three Panzergrenadier companies (Motorised)
      Motorised Heavy Company
      Supply Company
   Heavy Infantry Gun Company
   Pioneer Company

Self-propelled Panzerjäger battalion (475 men)
   Staff Company (3 PzJg IV)
   Motorised PanzerJäger Company (12 x 7.5cm PaK 40)
   Two self-propelled PanzerJäger Companies (14 PzJg IV)
   Supply Company

Armoured Reconnaissance Battalion (945 men)
   Staff Company (10 x Sd Kfz 251, 16 x Armoured cars)
   Armoured Reconnaissance Company (16 x Luchs Light
     Tanks) or Armoured Car Company (25 Armoured cars
     and Sd Kfz 250)
   Light Armoured Reconnaissance Company
     (30 Sd Kfz 250)
   Panzer Grenadier Company Company (23 Sd Kfz 251))
   Armoured Heavy Company
      Heavy Gun Platoon (6 x Sd Kfz 251/9)
      Mortar Platoon (6 x Sd Kfz 251/2)
      Pioneer Platoon
   Supply Company

Panzer Artillery Regiment (1315 men)
   Regimental Staff Battery
   1st self-propelled battalion
      2 light batteries (12 x leFH Sd Kfz 124 Wespe)
      1 heavy battery (6 x sFH Sd Kfz 165 Hummel)
   2nd Battalion (motorized)
      Staff Battery
      2 light batteries (12 x 10.5cm leFH 18)
   3rd Battalion (motorized)
      Staff Battery
      2 heavy batteries (8 x 15cm sFH 18)
      Gun Battery (4 x 10cm K 18)

Army Flak Battalion (635 men)
Armoured Pioneer Battalion (874 men)
Armoured Signals Battalion (463 men)
Field Replacement Battalion (973 men)
   Including 800 replacement troops
Panzer Supply Troop (781 men)
Vehicle Maintenance Troop (417 men)
Medical and Ambulance Companies (530 men)
Administration, Military Police and Other units (251 men)

KEY TO TACTICAL SYMBOLS USED IN ORGANIZATION CHARTS

Tactische Fernzeiche or Map Symbol for Regiment or larger-sized formation

Map Symbol for Battalion or *Abteilung*

St — *Stab* or Staff companies of Panzer Regiments

m — *Mittlerer* or Medium as applied to a Panzer Company

l — *Leichte* or light as applied to a Panzer Company

Sturmgeschütz or Assault Gun Company

Flammpanzer or Flamethrower Troop

Heavy self-propelled artillery battalion

Panzer *Abteilung* in *Leichte* motorised division 1938-1939

Self-propelled 2cm (0.8in) Flak detachment

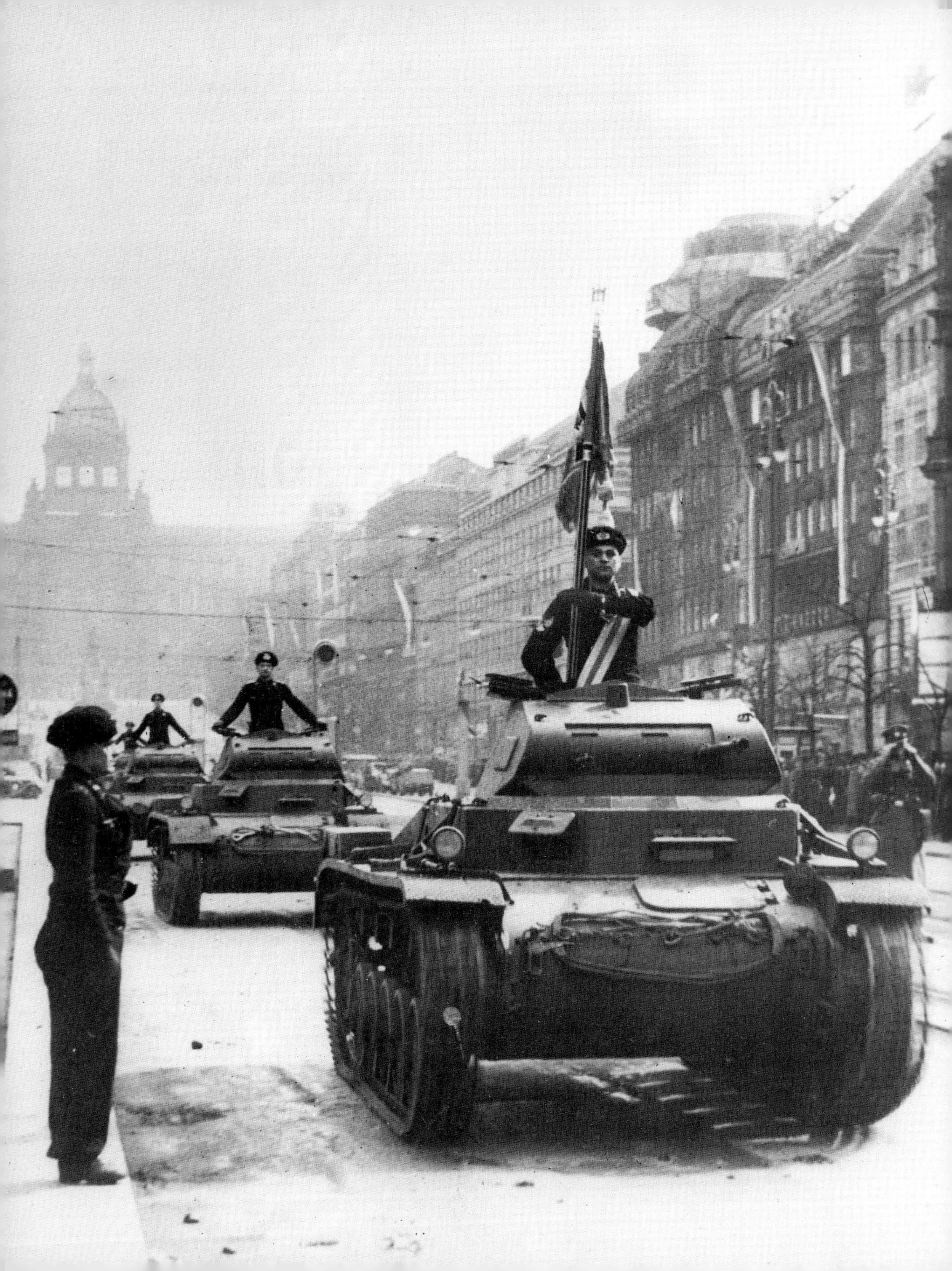

Chapter 1

Pre-War Panzer Divisions

In the years after World War I, tank enthusiasts in the German Army faced considerable resistance from the conservative cavalry and artillery officers who dominated the senior ranks of the *Reichswehr*. Nevertheless, new theories of armoured warfare were developed, and with Hitler's accession to power in 1933, the Panzer men gained the support of the one man who could see their ideas into practice. With the *Führer's* support, the *Wehrmacht* established its first Panzer units in 1934, and in 1935 the first true Panzer divisions were created.

◀ **Early triumphs**
Panzerkampfwagen IIs of the 3rd Panzer Division parade in triumph through Wenceslas Square in Prague just days after Germany occupied Czechoslovakia in March 1939.

1st Panzer Division

At its foundation in 1935, the 1st Panzer Division was a shadow of the mighty fighting machine that it was to become, but with the 2nd and 3rd Divisions it allowed the *Wehrmacht* to work out the new rules of armoured warfare.

THE FIRST PANZER DIVISIONS were established in 1935, after Hitler repudiated the Treaty of Versailles and brought into the open the massive expansion of the *Wehrmacht*, which he had secretly begun soon after coming to power. The 1st Panzer Division was formed in Weimar from elements of the 3rd *Kavallerie-Division,* and was placed under the command of *General der Kavellerie* Maximilian von Weichs. 1st Panzer Division, known initially as the 1st Panzer Brigade, included the 1st Panzer Regiment which was stationed at Erfurt, and the 2nd Panzer Regiment located in Eisenach. Other units attached to the division included the 1st *Schützen* Brigade (a motorized infantry unit with two battalions together with a motor-cycle battalion), 4th Reconnaissance Company, 37th Artillery Regiment and 37th Communications Company.

▼ **Battle Tank**
The Panzerkampfwagen III was intended to be the mainstay of Germany's Panzer forces, but few were in service at the start of World War II.

INSIGNIA

The original tactical symbol for the 1st Panzer Division was introduced on its formation in 1935. It was used until 1940.

Several variants of the original oak leaf design were used in the pre-war period and into the first campaigns of World War II.

During the second half of 1940, a simpler system of divisional identification was introduced. They were usually very simple outlines in white or yellow and were designed to be instantly recognizable.

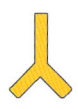

Late in 1940 an even simpler system was introduced, using straight lines that were easy to apply, remember and recognize.

1ST PANZER DIVISION

Each Panzer *Abteilung* included four light companies. Each company had a commander's platoon (with five tanks – one Pz.Kpfw II and four Pz.Kpfw I, which later became three Pz.Kpfw II and two Pz.Kpfw I). Each company had three more platoons with a similar structure. The tiny machine-gun armed Pz.Kpfw I was never intended to be more than a stopgap until the more battleworthy PzKpfw III and Pz.Kpfw IV medium tanks could be introduced.

Early in 1938, new commanders took over existing divisions, and the 1st Panzer Division was now commanded by *General* Rudolf Schmidt. Soon afterwards, the German army occupied Austria as that country was incorporated into the Reich. Only the 2nd Panzer Division was involved. In March 1939, German troops occupied the remaining part of Czechoslovakia, after the earlier takeover of the Sudetenland, but the only Panzer unit involved was the 3rd Panzer Division.

The 1st Panzer Division had to wait until the invasion of Poland to see its operational debut. By that time, each Panzer Regiment had 150–156 tanks, including 12 command tanks.

▶ **Training tank in combat**
The tiny Panzerkampfwagen I, armed only with machine guns, served in frontline units during the campaigns in Poland and France.

Commanders

Generaloberst R. Schmidt
(1 Sept 1939 – 2 Nov 1939)

General der Panzertruppen F. Kirchner
(2 Nov 1939 – 17 July 1941)

General der Panzertruppen W. Kruger
(17 July 1941 – 1 Jan 1944)

Generalleutnant R. Koll
(1 Jan 1944 – 19 Feb 1944)

Generalleutnant W. Marcks
(19 Feb 1944 – 25 Sept 1944)

Generalleutnant E. Thunert
(25 Sept 1944 – 8 May 1945)

⚜ *Fall Weiss*: the invasion of Poland
1 SEPTEMBER 1939

The invasion of Poland saw five German armies, a total of 42 divisions, cross the border. Most were infantry on foot, but the *Wehrmacht* fielded six Panzer and four *Leichte* Divisions.

For the invasion of Poland, the 1st Panzer Division served with Army Group South, where it formed part of Hoeppner's XVI *Panzerkorps* in von Reichenau's 10th Army. The Panzers were the spearhead of the German drive on Warsaw, reaching the outskirts of the city within a week. A counterattack by the Polish Pomoroze and Poznan Armies, bypassed in the earlier fighting, forced the Germans to detach motorized units, including 1st Panzer, from Warsaw to deal with the threat. The German tanks closed a ring of steel around the Poles, and in the Battle of Bzura 19 Polish divisions were destroyed or captured, and over 52,000 prisoners were taken by the *Wehrmacht*. In December 1939, the division returned to Germany.

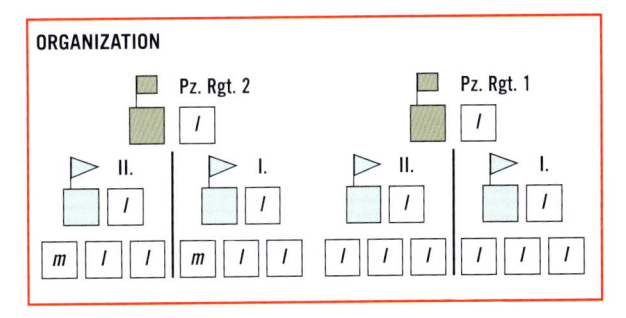

Panzer Unit	Pz. I	Pz. II	Pz. III	Pz. IV	Pz. Bef.
1st Pz. Rgt.	39	60	20	28	6
2nd Pz. Rgt.	54	62	6	28	6

ORGANIZATION

1ST PANZER DIVISION

▶ **Panzerkampfwagen I Ausf B (Sd Kfz 101)**
Pz. Rgt 1 / II Battalion / 5th Company / 2nd Zug / tank number 4
This vehicle was destroyed in combat in an action that took place south of Petrikau during the Polish campaign.

Specifications
Crew: 2	Engine: Maybach NL38TR
Weight: 6.4 tonnes (5.8 tons)	Speed: 40km/hr (24.9mph)
Length: 4.42m (14.5ft)	Range: 170km (105.6 miles)
Width: 2.06m (6.8ft)	Radio: FuG2
Height: 1.72m (5.6ft)	

The Germans used the white cross as their national insignia for the 1939 Poland campaign, but it was later changed because it provided an excellent target for enemy antitank gunners.

▶ **Panzerkampfwagen IV Ausf B (Sd Kfz 161)**
Pz. Rgt 1 / II Battalion / 8th Company / Company HQ tank of Hptm Von Kockeritz
This vehicle participated in the battle of Bzura, 16 September 1939. Two stripes on the turret rear were the unit's marks of recognition.

Specifications
Crew: 5	Engine: Maybach HL120TR
Weight: 20.7 tonnes (18.8 tons)	Speed: 40km/hr (24.9mph)
Length: 2.92m (9.6ft)	Range: 200km (124.3 miles)
Width: 2.83m (9.3ft)	Radio: FuG5
Height: 2.68m (8.8ft)	

✕ *Fall Gelb*: the French campaign
10 MAY 1940

In February 1940, the 1st Panzer Division under its new commander, *General der Panzertruppen* Friedrich Kirchner, was deployed to the *Westwall* to prepare for the campaign in the West.

THE 1ST PANZER DIVISION came under the command of Guderian's XIX *Panzerkorps*, which also included the 7th and 10th Divisions, for the surprise German attack through the Ardennes on 10 May. Breaking through at Sedan, Guderian's corps raced for the Channel, cutting off the bulk of the Allied field army in Belgium. After the British evacuation from Dunkirk, the Germans reorganized to strike southwards.

The 1st Panzer Division took part in the initial attack on the Aisne, on 5 June. After some hard fighting, the French defensive lines were breached, and the Panzers fanned out through France. The final French capitulation came on 22 June.

ORGANIZATION

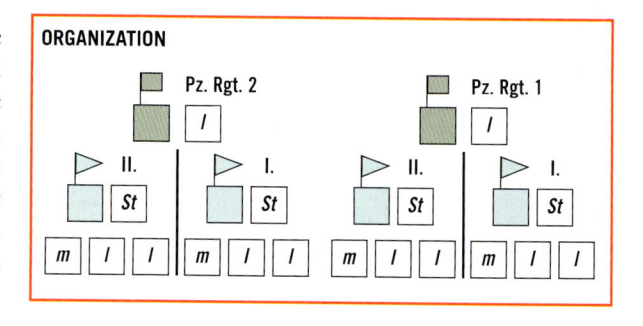

Pz. Rgt. 2 — I — II. / I. (St) — m / l — Pz. Rgt. 1 — I — II. / I. (St) — m / l

Panzer Unit	Pz. I	Pz. II	Pz. III	Pz. IV	Pz. Bef.
1st Pz. Rgt.	26	49	28	20	4
2nd Pz. Rgt.	26	49	30	20	4

1ST PANZER DIVISION

▶ Panzerbefehlswagen III Ausf E (Sd Kfz 266-267-268)
Pz. Rgt 2 / II Battalion / Stabskompanie / Signal Platoon / Commander's command tank

Although it looks like a standard tank, the turret was fixed and a dummy gun was fitted in an attempt to avoid drawing enemy attention to the command tank.

Specifications
Radio:
FuG6 + FuG2 (Sd Kfz 266)
FuG6 + FuG8 (Sd Kfz 267)
FuG6 + FuG7 (Sd Kfz 268)

▶ Panzerkampfwagen II Ausf C (Sd Kfz 121)
Pz. Rgt 1 / II Battalion / 5th Company / 1st Zug / tank number 4

The PzKpfw II formed the backbone of the Panzer divisions during the Polish and French campaigns. Although its armour and armament were inferior to other tanks of the day, its speed of 40km/h (24.9mph) allowed it to outmanoeuvre most Allied tanks. The white dot after the number 514 was used to indicate that this tank belonged to the 1st Regiment of the Division.

Specifications
Crew: 3
Weight: 9.8 tonnes (8.9 tons)
Length: 4.81m (15.8ft)
Width: 2.22m (7.3ft)
Height: 1.99m (6.5ft)
Engine: Maybach HL62TR
Speed: 40km/hr (24.9mph)
Range: 200km (124.3 miles)
Radio: FuG5

▶ Panzerkampfwagen II Ausf C (Sd Kfz 121)
Pz. Rgt 2 / II Battalion / 5th Company / 2nd Zug / tank number 2

The 2nd Regiment differentiated its tanks from those of the 1st Regiment by underlining the turret numbers with a white band. This PzKpfw II C is armed with a 20mm (0.78in) KwK30 L/55 cannon and a 7.92 MG34. The tank carries 18 ten-round magazines for the cannon, and 1425 rounds for the belt-fed machine gun.

Specifications
Crew: 3
Weight: 9.8 tonnes (8.9 tons)
Length: 4.81m (15.8ft)
Width: 2.22m (7.3ft)
Height: 1.99m (6.5ft)
Engine: Maybach IIL62TR
Speed: 40km/hr (24.9mph)
Range: 200km (124.3 miles)
Radio: FuG5

▶ Panzerfunkwagen (Sd Kfz 263) 8-Rad
37th Nachrichten Abteilung (Signal Battalion)

The Heavy Armoured Radio Vehicle was not intended as a fighting machine, and was armed with a single MG34 for self-defence. Its main function was to serve as a mobile communications station for Panzer unit commanders. The vertical antenna behind the fighting compartment was extendable to 9m (29.5ft) height.

Specifications
Crew: 5
Weight: 8.9 tonnes (8.1 tons)
Length: 5.85m (19.2ft)
Width: 2.2m (7.3ft)
Height: 2.9m (9.5ft)
Engine: Büssing-NAG L8V
Speed: 100km/hr (62.1mph)
Range: 300km (186.4 miles)
Radio: 1 Satz Funkgerat für Pz Funktrupp

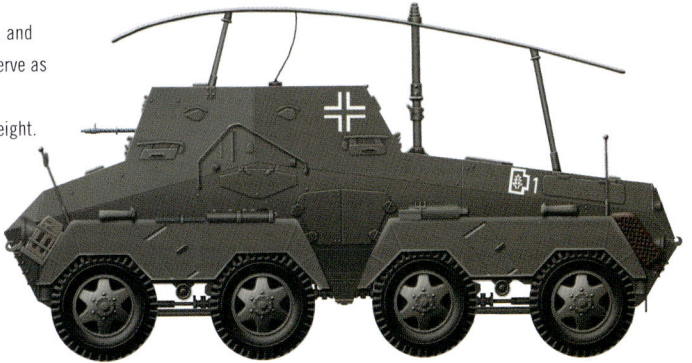

1ST PANZER DIVISION

▶ Mittlerer Schützenpanzerwagen Ausf A (Sd Kfz 251/1)

1st Schützen Brigade / II Battalion / 10th Company

Lessons learned in Spain taught the *Wehrmacht* that tanks needed infantry protection when operating in restricted terrain. Armoured half-tracks allowed infantry to accompany tanks in the advance, where they would be used to 'mop up' pockets of enemy resistance.

Specifications
- Crew: 2 plus 10 troops
- Weight: 8.8 tonnes (8 tons)
- Length: 5.98m (19.6ft)
- Width: 2.1m (6.9ft)
- Height: 1.75m (5.7ft)
- Engine: Maybach HL42TUKRM
- Speed: 53km/hr (32.9mph)
- Range: 300km (186.4 miles)
- Radio: FuG Spr Ger 1

▶ Panzerkampfwagen III Ausf E (Sd Kfz 141)

Pz. Rgt 2 / II Battalion / 7th Company / 2nd Zug / tank number 3

96 Ausf E model Panzer IIIs were built for the German Army between December 1938 and October 1939. Later models were built in much greater numbers.

Specifications
- Crew: 5
- Weight: 21.5 tonnes (19.5 tons)
- Length: 5.38m (17.7ft)
- Width: 2.91m (9.5ft)
- Height: 2.44m (8ft)
- Engine: Maybach HL120TR
- Speed: 40km/hr (24.9mph)
- Range: 165km (102.5 miles)
- Radio: FuG5

Barbarossa: the attack on Russia
22 JUNE 1941

The 1st Panzer Division saw extensive combat in the invasion of the Soviet Union, on both the Northern and Central sectors of the Eastern Front.

AFTER THE FRENCH CAMPAIGN, the 1st Panzer Division was transferred to XVI *Panzerkorps*, attached to the 18th Army in East Prussia. In March 1941, it became a reserve unit for 4th *Panzergruppe*, where it was brought up to strength for the impending invasion of the USSR.

Operation *Barbarossa* saw Germany amass seven armies and four *Panzergruppe* – which were armoured armies in all but name – into three main Army Groups. The 1st Panzer

Panzer Unit	Pz. I	Pz. II	Pz. III	Pz. IV	Pz. Bef.
1st Pz. Rgt.	15	43	75	28	8

Division, as part of General Hoeppner's 4th *Panzergruppe*, was attached to von Leeb's Army Group North. Striking through the Baltic States out of East Prussia on 22 June 1941, Army Group North was targeted on Leningrad, and in the next months 1st Panzer saw intensive action at Dunaberg and on the approaches to Leningrad.

On the Central Front

In October 1941, the Division was transferred to Hoth's 3rd *Panzergruppe*, part of Army Group Centre.

ORGANIZATION
- Pz. Rgt. 1
  - I
  - II.
    - St
    - m / l / m / l
  - I.
    - St
    - m / l

1ST PANZER DIVISION

▶ Panzerkampfwagen III Ausf F (Sd Kfz 141)
Pz. Rgt 1 / I Battalion / Stabskompanie / Signal Platoon / tank number 3

The Pz.Kpfw III Ausf F differed from the Ausf E model in having an additional 30mm (1.2in) of armour plate bolted to the turret and hull front. Other minor changes were made to the turret, the commander's cupola and the engine.

Specifications

Crew: 5	Engine: Maybach HL120TRM
Weight: 21.8 tonnes (19.8 tons)	Speed: 40km/hr (24.9mph)
Length: 5.38m (17.7ft)	Range: 165km (102.5 miles)
Width: 2.91m (9.5ft)	Radio: FuG5
Height: 2.44m (8ft)	

▶ Panzerkampfwagen IV Ausf D (Sd Kfz 161)
Pz. Rgt 1 / I Battalion / 4th Company / 2nd Zug / tank number 3

The fundamental mission of the *Mittlerer Panzer Kompanie*, or Medium Panzer Company, was to support the attack of the *Leichte Panzer Kompanien*. These would attack while the heavier tanks like this Panzer IV provided close support, engaging enemy tanks, field fortifications and antitank weapons.

Specifications

Crew: 5	Engine: Maybach HL120TRM
Weight: 22 tonnes (20 tons)	Speed: 40km/hr (24.9mph)
Length: 5.92m (19.4ft)	Range: 200km (124.3 miles)
Width: 2.84m (9.3ft)	Radio: FuG5
Height: 2.68m (8.8ft)	

Stabskompanie einer Panzer-Abteilung K.St.N.1150

The *Stabs* – 'Staff', or headquarters – Company of a Panzer Battalion early in the war was equipped in much the same as one of the light companies, with the addition of extra command and communication capacity in the shape of two or three Panzerbefehlswagen, or command tanks.

Signal Platoon: 2 Bef.Pz. III, Pz.Kpfw III

Light Platoon: 5 Pz.Kpfw II

Engineer Platoon: 3 Pz.Kpfw II

17

1ST PANZER DIVISION

Specifications
Crew: 5
Weight: 24 tonnes (21.8 tons)
Length: 5.41m (17.7ft)
Width: 2.95m (9.7ft)
Height: 2.44m (8ft)
Engine: Maybach HL120TRM
Speed: 40km/hr (24.9mph)
Range: 165km (102.5 miles)
Radio: FuG5

◀ **Panzerkampfwagen III Ausf H (Sd Kfz 141)**
Pz. Rgt 1 / II Battalion / 7th Company / 1st Zug / Zug Commander Leutnant Fromme
On 7 July 1941, Lt. Fromme destroyed nine Soviet tanks in this vehicle. The Ausf H had new sprocket and idler wheels and extra armour to protect against antitank guns like the British 2-pdr (37mm), the American 37mm (1.5in) M5 and the Soviet 45mm (1.8in) model 1937.

▼ **Ladungsleger auf Panzerkampfwagen I Ausf B**
37th Pioneer Battalion / 3rd Armoured Engineers Company
Demolition charge-laying tank. This version used a cable-operated arm, which pivoted over the tank to place a 50kg (110lb) explosive charge.

Specifications
Crew: 2
Weight: c. 6.6 tonnes (6 tons)
Length: 4.42m (14.5ft)
Width: 2.06m (6.8ft)
Height: 1.72m (5.6ft)
Engine: Maybach NL38TR
Speed: 40km/hr (24.9mph)
Range: 170km (105.6 miles)
Radio: FuG2

▶ **15cm sIG33 (Sf) auf Panzerkampfwagen I Ausf B**
702th schwere Infanteriegeschutz abteilung
This vehicle mounts the well proven 15cm (6in) sIG33 L/11 howitzer, which was carried on an early Pz.Kpfw I chassis. The howitzer could provide both direct and indirect artillery fire support.

Specifications
Crew: 4
Weight: 9.4 tonnes (8.5 tons)
Length: 4.67m (15.3ft)
Width: 2.06m (6.8ft)
Height: 2.8m (9.2ft)
Engine: Maybach NL38TR
Speed: 40km/hr (24.9mph)
Range: 140km (87 miles)
Armament: One 15cm (6in) sIG33 L/11

▶ **Leichter Gepanzerter Beobachtungswagen (Sd Kfz 253)**
73rd Artillery Regiment
Semi-tracked light armoured artillery observation post.

Specifications
Crew: 4
Weight: 6.3 tonnes (5.73 tons)
Length: 4.7m (15.4ft)
Width: 1.95m (6.4ft)
Height: 1.8m (6.2ft)
Engine: Maybach HL42TRKM
Speed: 65km/hr (40.4mph)
Range: 320km (198.8 miles)
Radio: FuG15 and/or FuG16

1ST PANZER DIVISION

⛋ *Fall Blau*: the Eastern Front
28 June 1942

With the failure to capture Moscow in the winter of 1941, the German Army had to implement major organizational changes to respond to the arrival at the front of 90 new Russian tank brigades in the spring of 1942.

AFTER A YEAR OF COMBAT around Rshev, the 1st Panzer Division was pulled out of the front and sent to France for refitting. It had suffered a considerable reduction in strength aside from combat losses: *Panzer-Abteilung* I of Panzer Regiment 1 was detached from the division, being sent to the newly formed 16th *Panzergrenadier* Division, where it was renamed *Panzer-Abteilung* 116.

With the loss of *Panzer-Abteilung* I, the Division had only one battalion of Panzers on strength, that being *Panzer-Abteilung* II/Panzer-Regiment 1. For six months, the tank strength of the Division was limited to seven Panzer IVs, 26 Panzer IIIs, and 12 light Panzer IIs and Czech-built Panzer 38(t)s.

ORGANIZATION

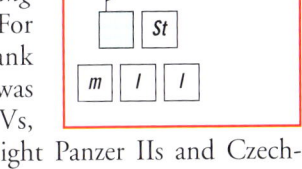

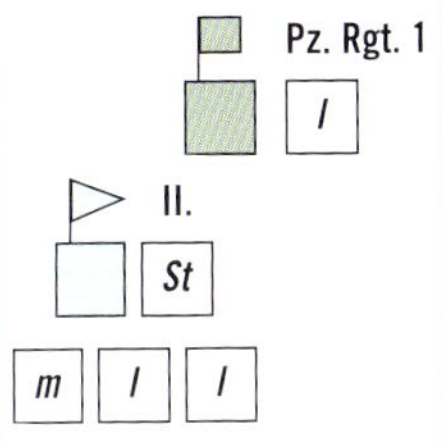

Panzer Unit	Pz. II	Pz. 38t	Pz. III	Pz. IV	Pz. Bef.
1st Pz. Rgt.	2	10	26	10	4

▶ Panzerkampfwagen IV Ausf E (Sd Kfz 161)
Pz. Rgt 1 / II Battalion / 4th Company / 2nd Zug / tank number 4

The Ausf E was a major improvement over the Ausf D. It had additional armour plate, with a thickness ranging from 20mm (0.8in) to 50mm (2in). All Pz.Kpfw IVs at this time were still armed with the short-barrelled 75mm (3in) L24 gun.

Specifications
- Crew: 5
- Weight: 23.2 tonnes (21 tons)
- Length: 5.92m (19.4ft)
- Width: 2.84m (9.3ft)
- Height: 2.68m (8.8ft)
- Engine: Maybach HL120TRM
- Speed: 42km/hr (26mph)
- Range: 200km (124.3 miles)
- Radio: FuG5

▶ Panzerjäger 38(t) fur 7.62cm PaK36(r) (Sd Kfz 139)
37th Panzerjäger Battalion / 1st Company / tank number 1

The Sd Kfz139 was an interim tank-destroyer design. It mounted the powerful Russian 76.2mm (3in) FK296 antitank gun, great numbers of which had been captured during the 1941 summer offensive.

Specifications
- Crew: 4
- Weight: 11.76 tonnes (10.67 tons)
- Length: 5.85m (19.2ft)
- Width: 2.16m (7ft)
- Height: 2.5m (8.2ft)
- Engine: Praga EPA or EPA/2
- Speed: 42km/hr (26mph)
- Range: 185km (115 miles)
- Radio: FuG Spr d

1ST PANZER DIVISION

▶ Panzerkampfwagen KV Ia 753(r)
Pz. Rgt 1 / Captured Russian tank

The Model 1939 was the first standard production version of the Soviet KV-1 heavy tank. Much more heavily armoured than any German tank, it mounted a powerful 76mm (3in) L-11 cannon in a low-slung gun mantlet. The Germans often added a commander's cupola to captured tanks pressed into *Wehrmacht* service.

Specifications
Crew: 5
Weight: 46.6 tonnes (42.3 tons)
Length: 6.68m (21.9ft)
Width: 3.32m (10.9ft)
Height: 2.71m (8.9ft)
Engine: V-2K
Speed: 35km/hr (21.7mph)
Range: 180km (111.8 miles)
Radio: 10R

▶ Panzerkampfwagen KV Ia 753(r)
Pz. Rgt 1 / Captured Russian tank

The KVs were impervious to the fire of German 37mm (1.5in) antitank guns, which prompted Russian tank commanders to roll over such guns instead of wasting ammo on them. This is a KV-1 model 1940, which is armed with the new longer-barrelled F-32 76mm (3in) cannon.

Specifications
Crew: 5
Weight: 46.6 tonnes (42.3 tons)
Length: 6.68m (21.9ft)
Width: 3.32m (10.9ft)
Height: 2.71m (8.9ft)
Engine: V-2K
Speed: 35km/hr (21.7mph)
Range: 180km (111.8 miles)
Radio: 10R

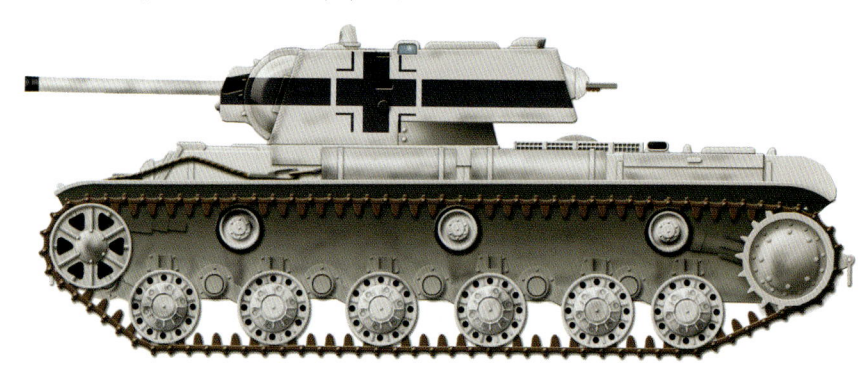

▶ Panzerkampfwagen KV Ia 753(r)
Pz. Rgt 1 / Captured Russian tank

The heavy fighting around Rshev saw the 1st Panzer Division losing tanks faster than they could be replaced. To maintain its fighting strength, the division was forced to press into service any available tank. This is a KV-1 model 1942, which has a cast-metal turret that was stronger than those used on earlier variants.

Specifications
Crew: 5
Weight: 45.7 tonnes (41.5 tons)
Length: 6.68m (21.9ft)
Width: 3.32m (10.9ft)
Height: 2.71m (8.9ft)
Engine: V-2K
Speed: 35km/hr (21.7mph)
Range: 160km (99.4 miles)
Radio: 10R

1ST PANZER DIVISION

▶ **Panzerkampfwagen IV Ausf F2 (Sd Kfz 161/1)**
Pz. Rgt 1 / II Battalion / 4th Company / 1st Zug / tank number 2

With the arrival of the long-barrelled Ausf F2 in the summer of 1942, the Germans now had a tank that could match the heavy Soviet tanks, and which was superior to all other Allied tanks then in service.

Specifications
Crew: 5
Weight: 25.4 tonnes (23 tons)
Length: 5.62m (18.4ft)
Width: 2.84m (9.3ft)
Height: 2.68m (8.8ft)
Engine: Maybach HL120TRM
Speed: 40km/hr (24.9mph)
Range: 200km (124.3 miles)
Radio: FuG5

Year of retreat
NOVEMBER 1943

The 1st Panzer Division was transferred to Germany and then to France in January 1943 for refitting. In June, it was sent to the Balkans, moving on to Greece for coastal defence duty.

IT REMAINED IN GREECE until November, when the Division returned to the Eastern Front, to the Ukraine. In December 1943, it was attached to XLVII *Panzerkorps* at Zhitomir. It took part in the counteroffensive at Kiev attached to 4th *Panzer-Armee* and later took part in defensive actions near Berdichev. Following the massive Soviet summer offensive in June 1944, which saw the destruction of Army Group Centre, 1st Panzer played its part in the German counteroffensive, attached to XLVIII *Panzerkorps*. However, following the failure to hold the southern flank, it was forced to retreat back across the Vistula.

In October, it was sent to Hungary. In May 1945, it was in Austria, where the 1st Panzer Division surrendered to the US Army.

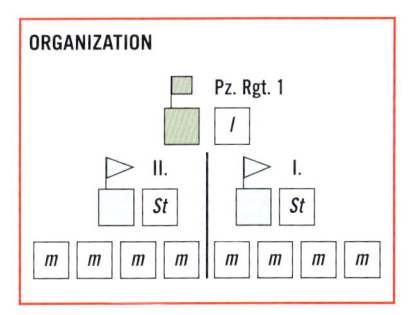

ORGANIZATION

Pz. Rgt. 1 / I / II. / I. / St / St / m m m m m m m m

Panzer Unit	VK 1801	Pz. IV	Pz. V	Flammpz	Pz. Bef.
1st Pz. Rgt.	8	95	76	7	8

▶ **Panzerkampfwagen I Ausf F**
Pz. Rgt 1 / Special Regiment Platoon

The VK 1801 was an experimental heavily armoured small infantry assault tank. In 1942, eight were issued to the 1st Panzer Division for combat evaluation. The tank was armed with two 7.92mm (0.3in) MG34 machine guns.

Specifications
Crew: 2
Weight: 23.2 tonnes (21 tons)
Length: 4.38m (14.4ft)
Width: 2.64m (8.7ft)
Height: 2.05m (8.2ft)
Engine: Maybach HL45p
Speed: 25km/hr (15.5mph)
Range: 150km (93.2 miles)
Radio: FuG5

2ND PANZER DIVISION

▶ Mittlerer Flammpanzerwagen Gerat 916 Ausf C (Sd Kfz 251/16)
Unknown formation

Based on the versatile Sd Kfz 251 half-track, this flamethrowing vehicle carried 700 litres (739.7 quarts) of inflammable fuel, which was enough for 80 bursts of up to two seconds.

Specifications

Crew: 5
Weight: 9.5 tonnes (8.62 tons)
Armament: two 1.4cm (0.6in) Flammenwerfer, two 7.62mm (0.3in) MG34 or MG42, earlier models also carried a single 0.7cm (0.3in) man-portable Flammenwerfer 42

▶ Panzerjäger 38(t) mit 7.5cm PaK40/3 Ausf M (Sd Kfz 138)
37th Panzerjäger Battalion

With 975 units produced between April 1943 and May 1944, the Marder III was readily available to Panzerjäger battalions of both Panzer and infantry divisions on all fronts. This example was used in the heavy fighting that took place in the unsuccessful defence of Budapest, Hungary, during the winter of 1944 and into 1945, when the city fell to the Soviets.

Specifications

Crew: 4
Weight: 11.6 tonnes (10.5 tons)
Length: 4.95m (16.2ft)
Width: 2.15m (7ft)
Height: 2.48m (8.1ft)
Engine: Praga AC
Speed: 42km/hr (26mph)
Range: 190km (118 miles)
Radio: FuG Spr d

Specifications

Crew: 5
Weight: 50.2 tonnes (45.5 tons)
Length: 8.86m (29ft)
Width: 3.4m (11.2ft)
Height: 2.98m (9.8ft)
Engine: Maybach HL230P30
Speed: 46km/hr (28.6mph)
Range: 200km (124.3 miles)
Radio: FuG5

▲ Panzerkampfwagen V Ausf G (Sd Kfz 171)
Pz. Rgt 1 / I Battalion / 4th Company / 3rd Zug / tank number 3

The Panther entered service in large numbers in 1944, but by 15 March 1945 the Division had only 10 operational Pz.Kpfw V tanks. The 1st Panzer Division surrendered to US forces in May 1945.

2nd Panzer Division

The 2nd Panzer Division fought from the beginning of World War II to the end, seeing action on both Eastern and Western Fronts as well as in the Balkans.

▲ **Preparing for War**
The German army mounted large-scale armoured exercises from 1936, using the light Panzer I to develop many of the techniques of *Blitzkrieg*, or 'Lightning War'.

INSIGNIA

2nd Panzer Division tactical recognition symbol, used in 1939 and 1940.

Alternative recognition symbol used by the 2nd Panzer Division during the invasion of Poland in 1939.

In the simplified system introduced at the end of 1940, 2nd Panzer Division's symbol was the same as the 1st Division, with the addition of a short line next to the upright of the inverted 'Y'.

2nd Panzer used a Trident symbol in the last year of the war, when it fought in Normandy and in the Ardennes.

A *Zusatzsymbol*, or additional mark, carried by panzers of the 2nd Panzer Division was the arms of the City of Vienna.

ESTABLISHED IN OCTOBER 1935, the 2nd Panzer Division differed from the 1st and 3rd Divisions in that it was commanded by an *Oberst,* or Colonel, rather than a General. However, that *Oberst* was Heinz Guderian, the inspiration behind Germany's *Panzerwaffe.*

Headquartered at Wurzburg, the tank component of the 2nd Panzer Division was provided by the 3rd Panzer Regiment, located at Kamenz, and the 4th Panzer Regiment at Ohrdruf. Other units in the table of organization included the 2nd *Schützen* Brigade with two battalions, the 2nd Motorcycle Battalion, the 5th Reconnaissance Company, the two battalions of the 74th Artillery Regiment and various signals, antitank and pioneer battalions.

Commanders

General der Panzertruppen R. Veiel
(1 Sep 1939 – 17 Feb 1942)

General der Panzertruppen H. Esebeck
(17 Feb 1942 – 1 June 1942)

Generalleutnant A. Lenski
(1 June 1942 – 5 Sept 1942)

Generalleutnant V. Lubbe
(5 Sept 1942 – 1 Feb 1944)

General der Panzertruppen H. Luttwitz
(1 Feb 1944 – 5 May 1944)

Generalleutnant F. Westhoven
(5 May 1944 – 27 May 1944)

General der Panzertruppen H. Luttwitz
(27 May 1944 – 31 Aug 1944)

Generalmajor H. Schonfeld
(31 Aug 1944 – 15 Dec 1944)

Generalmajor M. Lauchert
(14 Dec 1944 – 20 Mar 1945)

Generalmajor O. Munzel
(20 Mar 1945 – 1 Apr 1945)

Oberst C. Stollbrock
(1 Apr 1945 – 8 May 1945)

In February and March of 1936, the three Panzer Divisions deployed in an extensive series of training exercises on proving grounds at Staumuhlen. In fact, they were being used as a reserve force for the German operation to take control of the Rhineland. Following the reoccupation on 7 March 1936, all units, including the Panzer Divisions, returned to their home bases.

Austrian Anschluss

On 12 March 1938, German forces occupied Austria. 2nd Panzer Division, together with the SS Regiment *Leibstandarte Adolf Hitler* (selected because it was fully motorized) were placed under Guderian's overall command. In the bloodless occupation, the 2nd Panzer Division covered 700 km (435 miles) in 48 hours. Valuable lessons were learned about rapid, long-distance movement in the process, since the division lost about a third of its tanks en route because of mechanical failure. The division remained in Austria, which was to be its new home base.

2ND PANZER DIVISION

✠ *Fall Weiss*: the invasion of Poland
1 SEPTEMBER 1939

The 2nd Panzer Division was a key part of the fast-moving German mechanized spearhead force that outmanoeuvred and destroyed the Polish Army in September 1939.

IN SEPTEMBER 1939, the 2nd Panzer Division was assigned to Army Group South, being part of XVIII *Panzerkorps* in General List's 14th Army. This force was the southernmost of Germany's armies, tasked with smashing through the Polish Krakow Army before racing deep into Poland as the outer arm of a vast pincer movement. It was then to destroy Polish reserves massing to the south of Warsaw, before linking up with Guderian's *Panzerkorps,* which had attacked out of East Prussia. The 2nd Panzer Division suffered relatively heavy losses in Poland when compared with the other Panzer divisions, and in January 1940 it was sent to the Eifel region to refit.

ORGANIZATION

Panzer Unit	Pz. I	Pz. II	Pz. III	Pz. IV	Pz. Bef.
3rd Pz. Rgt.	62	78	3	8	9
4th Pz. Rgt.	62	77	3	9	11

▲ Panzerkampfwagen I Ausf B (Sd Kfz 101)
Pz. Rgt 4 / II Battalion / 3rd Company

The vehicle depicted was a survivor of the Polish campaign. The crew had toned down the side turret crosses but left the one in the rear to aid recognition from the air. The divisional rhomboid symbol was painted onto the hull rear and on the lower left front armour plate.

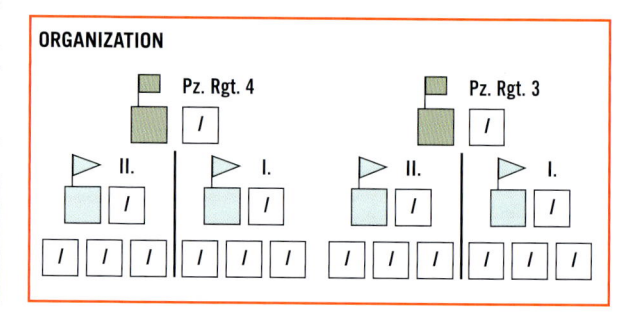

Specifications
Crew: 2
Weight: 6.4 tonnes (5.8 tons)
Length: 4.42m (14.5ft)
Width: 2.06m (6.8ft)
Height: 1.72m (5.6ft)
Engine: Maybach NL38TR
Speed: 40km/hr (24.9mph)
Range: 170km (105.6 miles)
Radio: FuG2

▶ Panzerkampfwagen III Ausf A (Sd Kfz 141)
Unknown formation

Early Panzer IIIs were armed with a 3.7cm (1.5in) KwK L46.5 gun, and carried 150 rounds of explosive and armour-piercing ammunition. The suspension proved unsatisfactory and all Ausf As had been withdrawn by February 1940.

Specifications
Crew: 5
Weight: 17 tonnes (15.4 tons)
Length: 5.69m (18.7ft)
Width: 2.81m (9.2ft)
Height: 2.34m (7.7ft)
Engine: Maybach HL108TR
Speed: 35km/hr (21.7mph)
Range: 165km (102.5 miles)
Radio: FuG5

2ND PANZER DIVISION

•• *Fall Gelb*: the French campaign
10 May 1940

The German offensive in the Low Countries tempted the Allies northwards out of their defensive positions into Belgium. This left them vulnerable to a Panzer attack through the Ardennes.

BURSTING THROUGH the supposedly impassible Ardennes on 10 May, von Rundstedt's Army Group A caught the Allies totally by surprise. The attack was spearheaded by Guderian's XIX *Panzerkorps*, comprising the 1st, 2nd and 10th Panzer Divisions. Guderian's corps was across the Meuse at Sedan by 14 May. It reached Abbeville by the 20th, and a battalion of the 2nd Panzer Division was the first German unit to reach the sea. However, after taking Calais, Hitler ordered the Panzers to halt, allowing the British to escape from Dunkirk.

After the Allied defeat at Dunkirk, Guderian's newly renamed *Panzergruppe* raced with equal speed through France, with the 2nd Panzer Division reaching the Swiss border on 17 June.

ORGANIZATION

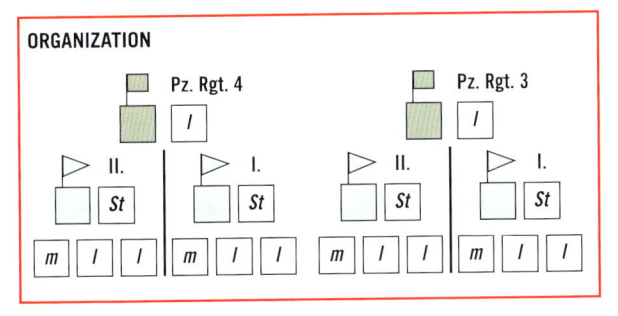

Panzer Unit	Pz. I	Pz. II	Pz. III	Pz. IV	Pz. Bef.
3rd Pz. Rgt.	22	55	29	16	8
4th Pz. Rgt.	23	60	29	16	8

▶ **Panzerkampfwagen II Ausf C (Sd Kfz 121)**
Pz. Rgt 3 / II Battalion / 5th Company / 2nd Zug / tank number 4

Although the Pz.Kpfw II was used in combat with enemy tanks early in the war, its 2cm (0.8in) gun was really too small for the role. With the entry into service of larger, more heavily gunned tanks after 1940, the light Panzer IIs were used for reconnaissance until phased out of service with the *Panzerwaffe* late in 1943.

Specifications
Crew: 3
Weight: 9.8 tonnes (8.9 tons)
Length: 4.81m (15.8ft)
Width: 2.22m (7.3ft)
Height: 1.99m (6.5ft)
Engine: Maybach HL62TR
Speed: 40km/hr (24.9mph)
Range: 200km (124.3 miles)
Radio: FuG5

▶ **Schwerer Panzerspahwagen (Sd Kfz 231) 6-Rad**
5th Reconnaissance Battalion

This heavy armoured car bears the name of 'Salzburg' next to the divisional symbol, reflecting the 2nd Panzer Division's Austrian connections.

Specifications
Crew: 4
Weight: 5.9 tonnes (5.35 tons)
Length: 5.57m (18.3ft)
Width: 1.82m (6ft)
Height: 2.25m (7.4ft)
Speed: 70km/hr (43.5mph)
Range: 300km (186.4 miles)
Radio: FuG Spr Ger 'a'

2ND PANZER DIVISION

War in the Balkans
6 April 1941

In the spring of 1941, Germany was forced to come to the assistance of Italy in the Balkans.

FOLLOWING THE FALL OF FRANCE, the 2nd Panzer Division transferred to Poland, where it was used for occupation duties. At the same time, it lost the 4th Panzer Regiment, which was used as the Panzer nucleus of the newly formed 13th Panzer Division.

Balkan campaign
The Italian fiasco in Greece forced Hitler to send troops to save his fellow dictator, Benito Mussolini. An invasion of Greece was planned, together with the conquest of Yugoslavia, where a military coup had overturned the pro-German Government. 2nd Panzer Division was assigned to Field Marshal List's 12th Army, tasked with attacking Greece through Macedonia. The Division made one of the key manoeuvres of the whole campaign, outflanking the Greek positions along the Metaxas Line.

The 2nd helped take Athens in Greece, along with the 6th *Gebirgs* Division. After the campaign, the wheeled units entrained in Croatia for Germany. The tracked elements of the division returned by sea from the Greek port of Patras, but most were lost when two transports were sunk by British mines.

Panzer Unit	Pz. II	Pz. III(37)	Pz. III(50)	Pz. IV	Pz. Bef.
3rd Pz. Rgt.	45	27	44	20	6

ORGANIZATION

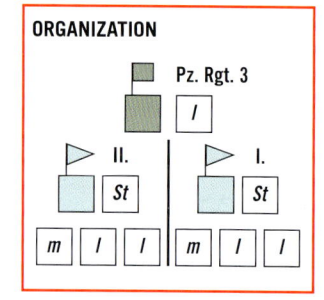

▶ **15cm sIG33 (Sf) auf Panzerkampfwagen I Ausf B**
703rd Schwere Infanteriegeschütz Abteilung
As a horse-drawn howitzer, the 15cm (6in) sIG33 L/11 was too slow to follow the Panzers, so it was mounted onto a Pz.Kpfw I chassis, wheels and trail included. It could be dismounted and used as a conventional towed gun. This example carried the name 'Alte Fritz' on the front shield beneath the gun.

Specifications
Crew: 4
Weight: 9.4 tonnes (8.5 tons)
Length: 4.67m (15.3ft)
Width: 2.06m (6.8ft)
Height: 2.8m (9.2ft)
Engine: Maybach NL38TR
Speed: 40km/hr (24.9mph)
Range: 140km (87 miles)
Armament: One 15cm (6in) sIG33 L/11

◀ **Kleiner Panzerbefehlswagen (Sd Kfz 265)**
Pz. Rgt 3 / Regiment Staff Signal Platoon
The Sd Kfz 265 was a variant of the Pz.Kpfw I with a built-up fixed superstructure, making room for a map board and a powerful radio. As a command tank, it had two radios, a FuG2 listening receiver and a FuG6 ultra shortwave transmitter/receiver with 3–6km (1.9–3.7 miles) voice or 4–8km (2.5–5 miles) range.

Specifications
Crew: 3
Weight: 6.5 tonnes (5.9 tons)
Length: 4.42m (14.5ft)
Width: 2.06m (6.8ft)
Height: 1.99m (6.5ft)
Engine: Maybach NL38TR
Speed: 40km/hr (24.9mph)
Range: 170km (105.6 miles)
Radio: FuG2 and FuG6

2ND PANZER DIVISION

Fall Blau: the Eastern Front
28 June 1942

The 3rd Regiment, 1st Battalion was detached to the 33rd Panzer Regiment, 9th Panzer Division.

THE LOSS OF MUCH of its armour returning from Greece meant that the 2nd Panzer Division could play no part in the early stages of Operation *Barbarossa*. It was building up its manpower in Germany when the invasion of the Soviet Union began, but soon afterwards, in July of 1941, it was transferred to Poland. In August 1941, it was sent to the south of France to re-equip before entraining for Russia, arriving at the front in October 1941.

ORGANIZATION
Pz. Rgt. 3 / II. / St / m / l / I

Drive on Moscow

The 2nd Panzer Division was assigned to XXXX *Korps*, 4th *Panzergruppe*, Army Group Centre, arriving at the front to play its part on the drive on Moscow. After fighting through Roslavl and Vyazma, it reached the outskirts of Moscow at the onset of the bitter Russian winter. Along with the rest of Germany's forces in the region, 2nd Panzer Division was pushed back from the gates of Moscow by the massive Soviet winter counteroffensive.

Panzer Unit	Pz. II	Pz. 38t	Pz. III	Pz. IV	Pz. Bef.
3rd Pz. Rgt.	22	33	20	5	2

▶ **Panzerkampfwagen III Ausf J (Sd Kfz 141)**
Pz. Rgt 3 / II Battalion / 6th Company / Company HQ

The German flag was often used as an air recognition aid, but only during those times that the *Luftwaffe* was able to maintain air superiority. This Headquarters Panzer III displays a winged serpent in a shield, one of a series of non-standard markings used by the 6th Company to identify its tank platoons.

Specifications
Crew: 5
Weight: 24 tonnes (21.5 tons)
Length: 6.28m (20.6ft)
Width: 2.95m (9.7ft)
Height: 2.5m (8.2ft)
Engine: Maybach HL120TRM
Speed: 40km/hr (24.9mph)
Range: 155km (96.3 miles)
Radio: FuG5

▶ **Panzerkampfwagen III Ausf J (Sd Kfz 141)**
Pz. Rgt 3 / II Battalion / 6th Company / 2nd Zug / tank number 4

The entire production run of 1549 J model Pz.Kpfw IIIs was taken up in replacing the 1400 examples of Panzer IIIs lost during the first years of the war – almost the entire inventory of earlier Ausf E, F, G and H models. Note the diamond outline used by the 2nd Platoon contrasting with the shield used by Company Headquarters above.

Weapons Specifications
Main Gun: 5cm (2in) KwK39 L/60
Ammunition: 92 rounds
Traverse: 360° (manual)
Elevation: -10° to +20°
Sight: TZF5e
Co-axial MG: 7.92mm (0.3in) MG 34
Hull MG: 7.92mm (0.3in) MG34
Ammunition: 4950 rounds Patr SmK
MG sight: KgZF2

2ND PANZER DIVISION

▶ **Panzerkampfwagen III Ausf J (Sd Kfz 141)**
Pz. Rgt 3 / II Battalion / 6th Company / 3rd Zug / tank number 1

The Pz.Kpfw III Ausf J was armed with a 5cm (2in) KwK L/42 with 84 rounds and two 7.92mm (0.3in) MG34 machine guns with 4950 rounds. This example is from the 3rd Platoon of the same company as the previous examples, and uses a triangle outline around the winged serpent. A Panzer rhomboid and the '6' are painted on the vision slit.

Specifications
Crew: 5
Weight: 24 tonnes (21.5 tons)
Length: 6.28m (20.6ft)
Width: 2.95m (9.7ft)
Height: 2.5m (8.2ft)
Engine: Maybach HL120TRM
Speed: 40km/hr (24.9mph)
Range: 155km (96.3 miles)
Radio: FuG5

Stabskompanie einer Panzer-Abteilung K.St.N.1150

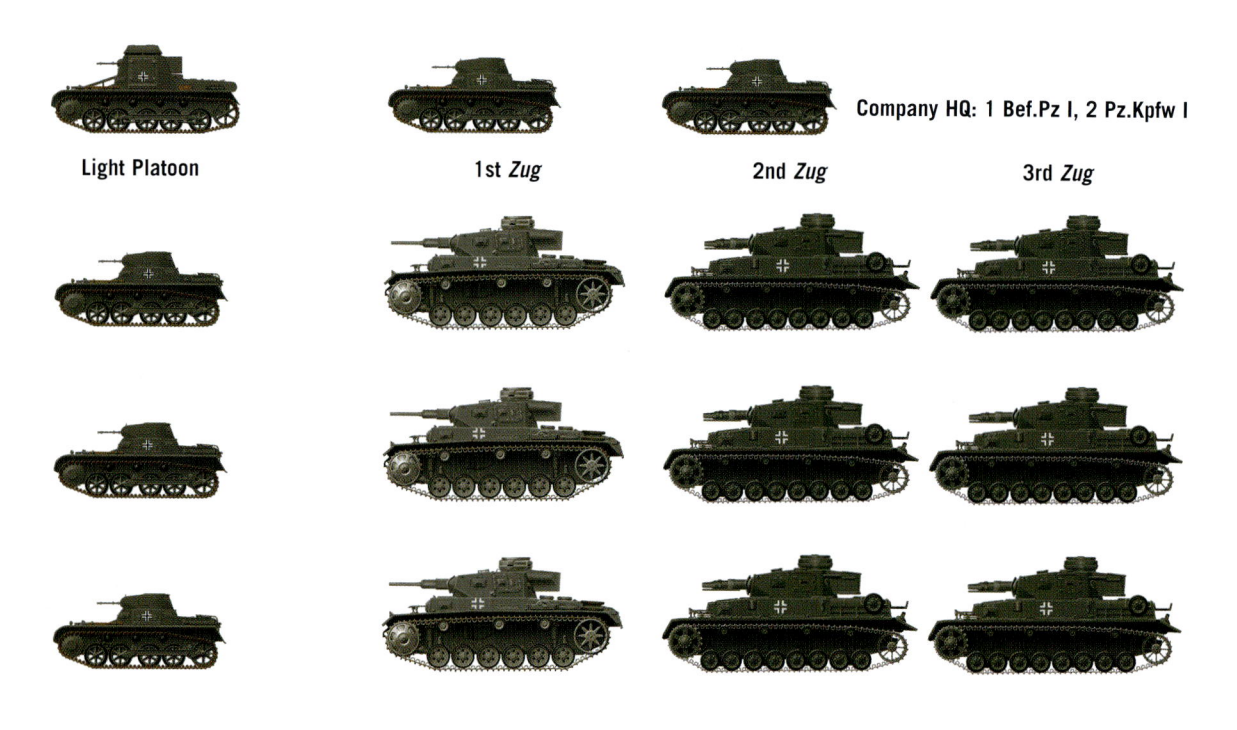

Light Platoon | **1st *Zug*** | **2nd *Zug*** | **3rd *Zug***

Company HQ: 1 Bef.Pz I, 2 Pz.Kpfw I

Organization of a Light Company type 'a' effective March 1939

Until 1939, the standard light Panzer companies in Panzer battalions were exclusively equipped with Panzer Is and IIs in four platoons – 1st, 2nd and 3rd *Zugen*, or platoons, with two Panzer Is and three Panzer IIs, the 4th *Zug* being equipped with five Panzer IIs. However, the new Medium Panzer IIIs and IVs were now entering service. Until enough had been delivered to form medium companies, they were deployed in 'Light Panzer Company Type A' formations, with the command troop operating seven Panzer Is and IIIs while the 1st, 2nd and 3rd platoons, three tanks strong, were equipped with Panzer IIIs and Panzer IVs.

2ND PANZER DIVISION

The last summer offensive
1 July 1943

The Division had authorized the formation of a *Flammpanzer* platoon early in 1943, but none of the flame-throwing tanks were in service at the time of the Kursk offensive.

Following the retreat from Moscow, the 2nd Panzer Division was heavily engaged in the actions to blunt the Soviet counteroffensive on the central front. For most of 1942, it was attached to XXXXI *Panzerkorps*, initially with 3rd *Panzerarmee* at Karmanovo, but from February under the control of the 9th Army. After months of heavy fighting around Rzhev and Byeloye, the Division was withdrawn in August, forming part of 9th Army's reserve while being brought back up to strength. In 1942, *Panzer-Abteilung* I of Panzer Regiment 3 was transferred to the 33rd Panzer Regiment, leaving the division with only a single *Abteilung* of Panzers. *Aufklärungs-Abteilung* 5 was converted into a motorcycle battalion, and as *Kradschützen-Abteilung* 24 was transferred to the 24th Panzer Division.

Divisional Organization

In 1943, the main fighting units in the divisional organization included the 2/3rd Panzer Regiment, the 2nd *Panzergrenadier* Regiment, the 304th *Panzergrenadier* Regiment, the 2nd Reconnaissance Battalion, the 74th Panzer Artillery Regiment, the 18th *Panzerjäger* Battalion and the 273rd Army Flak Battalion. During the year, the 276th *Sturmgeschütz*, or Assault Gun Battalion, was assigned to the Division.

In 1942, the division still had a dozen Panzer IIs and more than 40 Panzer IIIs in its vehicle park, but by the summer of 1943 these had all been replaced. At the time of the Battle of Kursk, 2/3rd Panzer Regiment had four companies, each with 22 Panzer IVs. It also received seven Panzer III flamethrower tanks, but these were not yet operational at Kursk.

Some of the Division's artillery units still used towed guns, but the 1st Battalion of the 74th Panzer Artillery Regiment had by now re-equipped with two batteries each of six Wespe 10.5cm (4.1in) self-propelled guns, and a battery of six Hummel 15cm (6in) self-propelled guns. The division's tank hunter regiment began to re-equip with self-propelled

Panzer Unit	Pz. II	Pz. III(50)	Pz. III(75)	Pz. IV	Pz. Bef.
3rd Pz. Rgt.	12	20	20	60	6

systems at the same time. The divisional Flak battalion included two batteries of four towed 8.8cm (3.5in) weapons, which could be used against both aircraft and tanks.

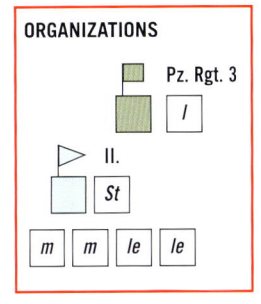

Kursk and After

In May 1943, 2nd Panzer Division was pulled back from the frontline, going into 2nd Panzer Army's reserve at Smolensk as the *Wehrmacht* High Command built up strength for the offensive against the Kursk Salient. For this, launched in July 1943, it was attached to XXXXVII *Panzerkorps* in Model's 9th Army. This was the main strike force of the northern prong of the giant pincer movement designed to destroy the Soviet forces located in the bulge in the frontlines around Kursk.

The attack was launched on 5 July 1943. Several delays had given the Soviets time to reinforce the salient, and progress was slow. As resistance stiffened, the German advance was stopped. In 10 days of fighting, 4th Panzer Army in the south had advanced just 32km (19.9 miles), and in the north Model's 9th Army, including 2nd Panzer, had penetrated just 19km (11.8 miles) into Soviet-held territory.

The end came when the Soviets launched a major counteroffensive in the north, forcing 9th Army to withdraw. In all, the Kursk battle had cost the *Wehrmacht* 50,000 dead, and had seen the loss of more than 1000 tanks.

Over the next months, 2nd Panzer Division was all but used up in the series of costly defensive battles around Kiev and along the Dnieper River. By the end of 1943, the division was in reserve, supporting the 2nd Army around Gomel.

2ND PANZER DIVISION

▶ **Panzerkampfwagen III Ausf M (Sd Kfz 141/1)**
Pz. Rgt 3 / II Battalion

For much of the war, the 2nd Panzer Division continued to recruit most of its personnel from Austria. As a result, the Viennese coat of arms was used to adorn many of the formation's vehicles.

Specifications
Crew: 5
Weight: 25 tonnes (22.7 tons)
Length: 6.41m (21ft)
Width: 2.95m (9.7ft)
Height: 2.5m (8.2ft)
Engine: Maybach HL120TRM
Speed: 40km/hr (24.9mph)
Range: 155km (96.3 miles)
Radio: FuG5

▶ **Panzerkampfwagen III Ausf N (Sd Kfz 141/2)**
Pz. Rgt 3 / II Battalion

20 Ausf N were operational with the Division in time for the summer offensive of 1943. Armed with a short-barrelled 7.5cm (3in) gun, the type was used for close support against infantry positions and enemy strongpoints.

Specifications
Crew: 5
Weight: 25.4 tonnes (23 tons)
Length: 5.52m (18.1ft) Ausf L or 5.65m (18.5ft) Ausf M conversion
Width: 2.95m (9.7ft)
Height: 2.5m (8.2ft)
Engine: Maybach HL120TRM
Speed: 40km/hr (24.9mph)
Range: 155km (96.3 miles)
Radio: FuG5

▶ **Panzerkampfwagen IV Ausf H (Sd Kfz 161/2)**
Pz. Rgt 3 / II Battalion

The Ausf H model was armed with a long-barelled 7.5cm (3in) KwK40 L/48 cannon, and provided much of the strike power of the Panzer divisions in 1943 and 1944. The tank could carry 87 rounds of ammunition, divided between high explosive, armour-piercing and smoke shells. This Panzer Regiment 3 vehicle does not display the unit tactical number on the turret.

Specifications
Crew: 5
Weight: 27.6 tonnes (25 tons)
Length: 7.02m (23ft)
Width: 2.88m (9.4ft)
Height: 2.68m (8.8ft)
Engine: Maybach HL120TRM
Speed: 38km/hr (23.6mph)
Range: 210km (130.5 miles)
Radio: FuG5

2ND PANZER DIVISION

⇑ The Western Front
JUNE 1944

On 15 January 1944, the remains of the 2nd Panzer Division were withdrawn from combat on the Eastern Front, and the formation was sent to France to be rebuilt.

FROM FEBRUARY 1944, *Panzer-Abteilung* I of Panzer Regiment 3 was rebuilt with Pz.Kpfw V Panther tanks, providing the division with two *Abteilungen* of Panzers for the first time in two years. On 7 May 1944, *Panzer-Abteilung* I/*Panzer-Regiment* 3 became *Panzer-Abteilung* 507, an independent unit equipped with Tiger tanks. Later, on 30 June 1944, the unit was returned to the 2nd Panzer Division, again becoming *Panzer-Abteilung* I/*Panzer-Regiment* 3, exchanging its Tigers for Panthers in the process.

Normandy Battles
After a period of rest in France, the Division was deployed to Amiens as part of the reserve force for Army Group B. It was ordered to the Normandy Front after the invasion, but destroyed bridges and constant air attack meant that it took more than a week to reach the battle zone. Attached to XXXXVII Corps of *Panzergruppe* West, it saw heavy fighting against the British before being detached for the abortive Mortain offensive designed to split the American forces threatening to break through the German defences. As the Americans broke out from the bridgehead, the German Panzers were pushed back to their starting points and beyond. The 2nd Panzer Division was caught and nearly destroyed in the Falaise pocket. It managed to break out through the Falaise Gap, suffering staggering losses in men and materiel while doing so.

Panzer Unit	Pz. IV	Pz. V	FlkPz	StuG	B IV
3rd Pz. Rgt.	98	79	12	10	36

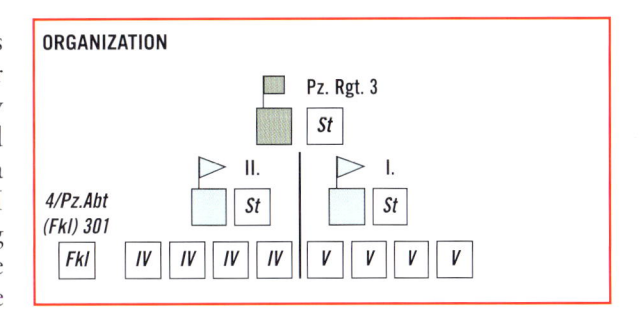

ORGANIZATION

Pz. Rgt. 3
4/Pz.Abt (Fkl) 301 — II. — I.
Fkl | IV IV IV IV | V V V V

Specifications
Crew: 5
Weight: 49.4 tonnes (44.8 tons)
Length: 8.86m (29ft)
Width: 3.42m (11.2ft)
Height: 2.98m (9.8ft)
Engine: Maybach HL230P30
Speed: 46km/hr (28.6mph)
Range: 200km (124.3 miles)
Radio: FuG5

▼ **Panzerkampfwagen V Ausf A (Sd Kfz 171)**
Pz. Rgt 3 / I Battalion / 3rd Company / 1st Zug / tank number 1
After heavy losses on the Eastern Front, the division was sent to Amiens, France at the beginning of 1944 to be refitted. While there, the *I Abteilung* of Panzer Regiment 3 was reformed and equipped with the Pz.Kpfw V Panther.

2ND PANZER DIVISION

▶ **Panzerkampfwagen IV Ausf H (Sd Kfz 161/2)**
Pz. Rgt 3 / II Battalion / 8th Company / 2nd Zug / tank number 1

By 1944, the Division had consolidated all Pz.Kpfw IV tanks into the II *Abteilung*. German commanders usually assigned their best crews to older model tanks; the reasoning was that their experience would compensate for any mechanical inferiority.

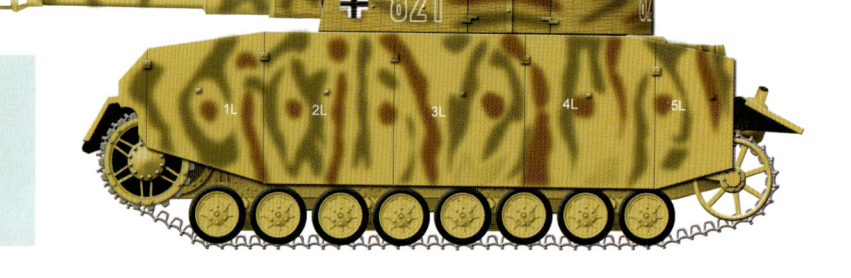

Specifications
Crew: 5
Weight: 27.6 tonnes (25 tons)
Length: 7.02m (23ft)
Width: 2.88m (9.4ft)
Height: 2.68m (8.8ft)
Engine: Maybach HL120TRM
Speed: 38km/hr (23.6mph)
Range: 210km (130.5 miles)
Radio: FuG5

▶ **Panzerkampfwagen IV Ausf H (Sd Kfz 161/2)**
Pz. Rgt 3 / II Battalion / 8th Company / 2nd Zug / tank number 5

After heavy losses fighting in the area of Villers-Bocage, the 2nd Panzer Division was ordered to take part in the counterattack at Mortain, designed to drive a wedge between the Allied armies. The offensive failed, and the division was later trapped in the Falaise pocket.

Weapons Specifications
Main Gun: 7.5cm (3in) KwK40 L/48
Ammunition: 87 rounds
Traverse: 360° (electric)
Elevation: -8° to +20°
Sight: TZF5f/1
Co-axial MG: 7.92mm (0.3in) MG 34
Hull MG: 7.92mm (0.3in) MG34
Ammunition: 3150 rounds
Patr SmK
MG sight: KgZF2

▶ **15cm Schweres Infanteriegeschütz 33 (Sf)**
auf Panzerkampfwagen 38(t) Ausf H (Sd Kfz 138/1)
2nd Panzergrenadier Regiment / II Battalion / Self-propelled Infantry Gun Company

Ninety examples of this heavy infantry gun, based in the chassis of the Czech-built Panzer 38(t), were produced between February and April 1943, and the equipment was still in service with the 2nd Panzer Division in Normandy in June 1944.

Specifications
Crew: 5
Weight: 12.7 tonnes (11.5 tons)
Length: 4.61m (15.1ft)
Width: 2.16m (7ft)
Height: 2.4m (7.9ft)
Engine: Praga EPA/2
Speed: 35km/hr (21.7mph)
Range: 185km (115 miles)
Radio: FuG16

2ND PANZER DIVISION

▼ Leichter Schützenpanzerwagen (Sd Kfz 250/9)
2nd Reconnaissance Battalion / 2nd Reconnaissance Company

With the urgent need for a better reconnaissance vehicle to replace ineffective armoured cars and vulnerable motorcycles, the Sd Kfz250 was selected as a replacement. Mounting the turret of the Sd Kfz 222 light armoured car, it was so successful that production of the Sd Kfz 222 was terminated in favour of the half-track.

Specifications
Crew: 3
Weight: 6.6 tonnes (6.02 tons)
Length: 4.61m (15.1ft)
Width: 1.95m (6.4ft)
Height: 2.16m (7ft)
Engine: Maybach HL42TUKRM
Speed: 60km/hr (37.3mph)
Range: 300km (186.4 miles)
Radio: FuG 12

▶ Schwerer Panzerspähwagen (5cm) (Sd Kfz 234/2)
2nd Reconnaissance Battalion / 4th Reconnaissance Company 'Puma'

This was one of the most capable armoured cars built during World War II, and 25 Pumas were issued to one of the companies in the 2nd Panzer Division's reconnaissance battalion. Its main armament consisted of one 5cm (2in) KwK 39/1 L60 cannon, for which it carried 55 rounds of ammunition.

Specifications
Crew: 4
Weight: 12.9 tonnes (11.74 tons)
Length: 6.8m (22.3ft)
Width: 2.4m (7.9ft)
Height: 2.28m (7.5ft)
Engine: Tatra 103
Speed: 80km/hr (49.7mph)
Range: 900km (559.2 miles)
Radio: Fu Spr Ger 'a'

▼ Mittlerer Schützenpanzerwagen I Ausf D (Sd Kfz 251/9)
2nd Reconnaissance Battalion / 5th Heavy Reconnaissance Company

The mission of the Sd Kfz 251/9 was to provide fire support to the other companies of the 2nd Reconnaissance Battalion. This vehicle was also known by the unofficial designation of 'Stummel', in reference to the short 7.5cm (3in) KwK L/24 mounted in the superstructure. The gun became available when the Panzer IVs that had originally carried it were upgunned, and when mounted on the half-track, it was redesignated as the K51(Sf). The vehicle could carry 52 rounds for the gun.

Specifications
Crew: 3
Weight: 9.4 tonnes (8.53 tons)
Length: 5.98m (19.6ft)
Width: 2.1m (6.9ft)
Height: 2.07m (6.8ft)
Engine: Maybach HL42TUKRM
Speed: 53km/hr (32.9mph)
Range: 300km (186.4 miles)
Radio: FuG Spr Ger f

2ND PANZER DIVISION

▶ Mittlerer Pionierpanzerwagen Ausf D (Sd Kfz 251/7)
38th Panzer Pioneer Battalion

This vehicle was built to carry a *Sturmpionier* squad of combat engineers into battle, along with all of their equipment. It was fitted with racks for demolition charges, flamethrowers and mines, and it carried a small assault bridge.

Specifications
Crew: 7/8
Weight: 8.9 tonnes (8.07 tons)
Length: 0m (0ft)
Width: 0m (0ft)
Height: 2.7m (8.9ft)
Engine: Maybach HL42TUKRM
Speed: 53km/hr (32.9mph)
Range: 300km (186.4 miles)
Radio: FuG5 when operating with a Panzer HQ company

▶ 7.5cm Sturmgeschütz 40 Ausf G (Sd Kfz 142/1)
Panzer-Abteilung (FkI) 301 / 4th Company / 2nd Zug / tank number 2 (Attached)

The Radio Control Armoured Unit, (FkI) 301, detached its 4th Company for service with the 2nd Panzer Division, and it saw combat against the Allies in Normandy. The box behind the armoured fighting compartment housed a powerful command radio transmitter used to detonate explosive charges remotely.

Specifications
Crew: 4
Weight: 26.3 tonnes (23.9 tons)
Length: 6.77m (22.2ft)
Width: 2.95m (9.7ft)
Height: 2.16m (7ft)
Engine: Maybach HL120TRM
Speed: 40km/hr (24.9mph)
Range: 155km (96.3 miles)
Radio: FuG 15 and FuG 16

▶ Schwerer Ladungstrager (Sd Kfz 301) Ausf A
Panzer-Abteilung (FkI) 301 / 4th Company (Attached)

The remote control tracked demolition charge layer was desgned to carry a 500kg (1100lb) demolition charge to a target. The driver would drop the charge and get clear before the explosives were detonated. Alternatively, the vehicle could be remotely controlled by radio. The unit's mission was to use the charges to clear paths through minefields and to destroy enemy fortifications.

Specifications
Crew: 1
Weight: 4 tonnes (3.6 tons)
Length: 3.65m (12ft)
Width: 1.8m (6.2ft)
Height: 1.19ft (3.9ft)
Engine: Borgward 6M RTBV
Speed: 38km/hr (23.6mph)
Range: 212km (131.7 miles)
Radio: EP3 with UKE6

2ND PANZER DIVISION

The Battle of the Bulge
14 December 1944

The Division was wrecked in the Falaise Pocket, with only a small personnel cadre being able to escape. On rebuilding, the 1st Battalion was equipped with Panthers while the 2nd Battalion was a mixed unit with two companies of Pz.Kpfw IV and two *Sturmgeschütz* companies.

AFTER ITS DESTRUCTION in Normandy, the remaining cadre of the 2nd Panzer Division was withdrawn to Wittlich in the Eifel area of Germany, where the division was reformed and reequipped. To make up numbers, it absorbed the remains of the 352nd Infantry Division. At the end of 1944, it was attached to Hasso von Manteuffel's 5th *Panzerarmee*, for use in the surprise winter attack to be launched against the Allies in the Ardennes. It was a massive operation, and 2nd Panzer advanced further than any other formation. However, the offensive failed and the division suffered heavily.

At the end of March 1945, what remained of 2nd Panzer was absorbed by the scraped together Thuringen Panzer Brigade in the Mosel region and at Fulda. With little fuel or equipment left, the unit surrendered to US troops at Plauen in May, 1945.

ORGANIZATION

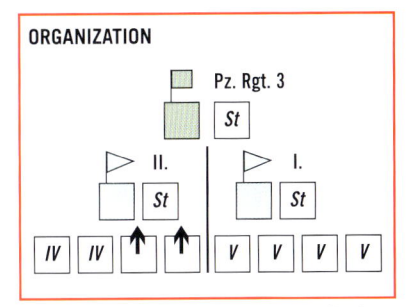

Panzer Unit	Pz. IV	Pz. V	StuG	FlkPz(20)	FlkPz(37)
3rd Pz. Rgt.	28	64	24	7	4

▼ **Sturmgeschütz neuer Art mit 7.5cm PaK L/48 auf Fahrgestell Panzerkampfwagen IV (Sd Kfz 162)**
38th Panzerjäger Battalion
The *Jagdpanzer* IV was also commonly known as 'Guderian's Duck', because the Inspector General of Panzer Troops had played a large part in its development.

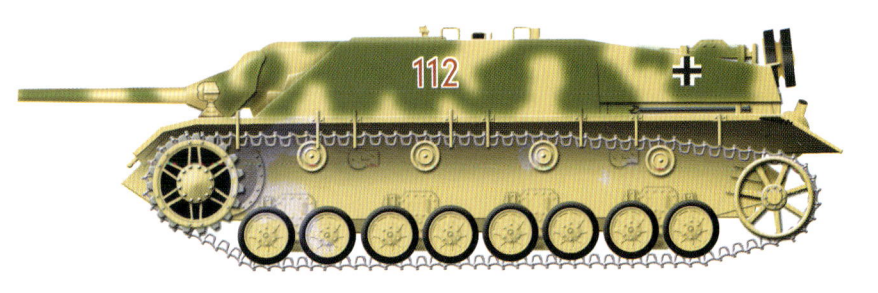

Specifications
Crew: 4
Weight: up to 27.6 tonnes (25 tons)
Length: 6.85m (22.5ft)
Width: 6.7m (22ft)
Height: 1.85m (6ft)
Engine: Maybach HL120TRM
Speed: 38km/hr (23.6mph)
Range: 210km (130.5 miles)
Radio: FuG 15 and FuG 160

▶ **Flakpanzer IV / 2cm Vierling**
Pz. Rgt 3
Air defence assets became vital to the *Panzerwaffe* as Allied air superiority began to tell. The Flakpanzer IV, also known as *Wirbelwind* (or 'Whirlwind'), was armed with a quadruple 2cm (0.8in) *Flakvierling* mount.

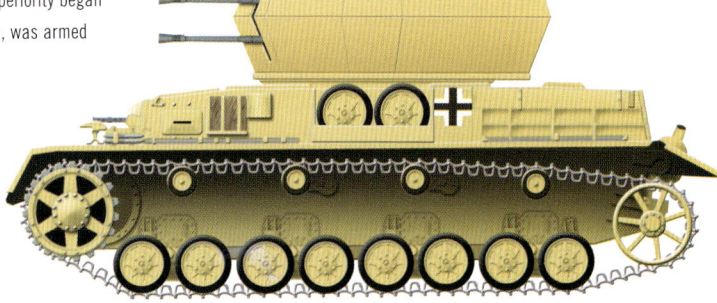

Specifications
Crew: 5
Weight: 24.3 tonnes (22 tons)
Length: 5.92m (19.4ft)
Width: 2.9m (9.5ft)
Height: 2.76m (9ft)
Engine: Maybach HL120TRM
Speed: 38km/hr (23.6mph)
Range: 200km (124.3 miles)
Radio: FuG2 and FuG5

3rd Panzer Division

The third of the original Panzer divisions was established, like the 1st and 2nd Panzer Divisions, on 15 October 1935. It was commanded by *Generalmajor* Ernst Fessmann.

THE 3RD PANZER DIVISION was headquartered at Berlin. In September 1937, the Division, along with the 1st Panzer Brigade, took part in a series of manoeuvres around Neusterlitz. Soon afterwards, Fessman was succeeded as divisional commander by *Generalmajor* Geyr von Schweppenburg. In March 1939, Germany took over the remaining part of Czechoslovakia after the occupation of the Sudetenland. Elements of the 3rd Panzer Division reached Prague at 8.20am on 13 March 1939, followed by the 6th Panzer Regiment in the afternoon. Two days later, the tanks led the first German parade through the Czech capital.

Commanders

General der Panzertruppen L. Schweppenburg
(1 Sep 1939 – 7 Oct 1939)

General der Panzertruppen H. Stumpff
(7 Oct 1939 – Sept 1940)

General der Panzertruppen F. Kuhn
(Sept 1940 – 4 Oct 1940)

General der Panzertruppen H. Stumpff
(4 Oct 1940 – 13 Nov 1940)

Generalfeldmarschall W. Model
(13 Nov 1940 – 1 Oct 1941)

General der Panzertruppen H. Breith
(1 Oct 1941 – 1 Oct 1942)

Generalleutnant F. Westhoven
(1 Oct 1942 – 25 Oct 1943)

Generalleutnant F. Bayerlein
(25 Oct 1943 – 5 Jan 1944)

Oberst R. Lang
(5 Jan 1944 – 25 May 1944)

Generalleutnant W. Philipps
(25 May 1944 – 1 Jan 1945)

Generalmajor W. Soth
(1 Jan 1945 – 19 Apr 1945)

Oberst V. Schone
(19 Apr 1945 – 8 May 1945)

INSIGNIA

3rd Panzer originated in Berlin, and its first tactical symbol represented the Brandenburg Gate. The symbol was later used by the 20th Panzer Division.

In the system introduced in 1940, 3rd Panzer's symbol followed in sequence from the 1st and 2nd Divisions.

Tactical symbol used by 6th Panzer Regiment of the 3rd Panzer Division.

The symbol of the city of Berlin is the bear. Since the 3rd Division was established in Berlin, it used a bear as a *Zusatz*, or additional symbol.

Variant of the Divisional bear insignia.

Another bear variant used by the Division was a shield containing the heraldic bear of the city of Berlin.

Fall Weiss: the invasion of Poland
1 SEPTEMBER 1939

On 17 August 1939, Germany's Panzer units were given their war orders. On 25 August, they began moving towards the eastern borders of the Reich.

ON 1 SEPTEMBER 1939, World War II began as German Armies poured over the Polish border. The 3rd Panzer Division was attached to General Heinz Guderian's XIX *Panzerkorps*, based in Pomerania. As hostilities started, Guderian's corps seized the Polish Corridor, cutting Poland off from the Baltic. Racing through northern Poland, led by the tanks of the 3rd Panzer Division, Guderian's corps formed the outer ring of the massive pincer that would encircle and defeat the Polish army.

Panzer Unit	Pz. I	Pz. II	Pz. III	Pz. IV	Pz. Bef.
5th Pz. Rgt.	63	77	3	9	8
6th Pz. Rgt.	59	79	3	9	8
Pz.Lehr Abt	0	20	37	14	2

3RD PANZER DIVISION

Victory in Poland

On 18 September, 3rd Panzer made contact south of Brest-Litovsk with the XXII *Panzerkorps* advancing from the south. With the closing of the pincers, the fate of Poland's field army was sealed. Warsaw fell on 27 September, and the last Polish troops still fighting surrendered on 6 October.

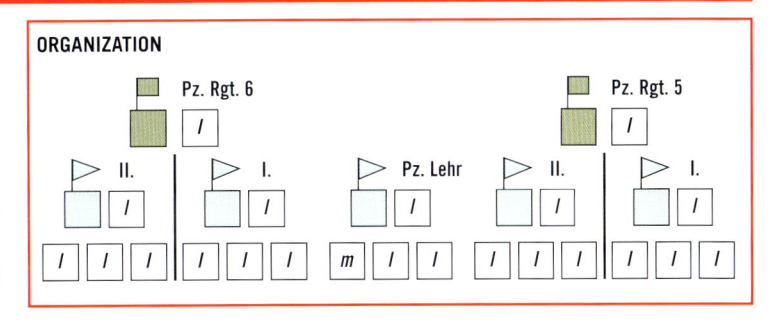

ORGANIZATION

Company HQ: 1 Bef.Pz. I, 1 Pz.Kpfw II, 2 Pz.Kpfw I

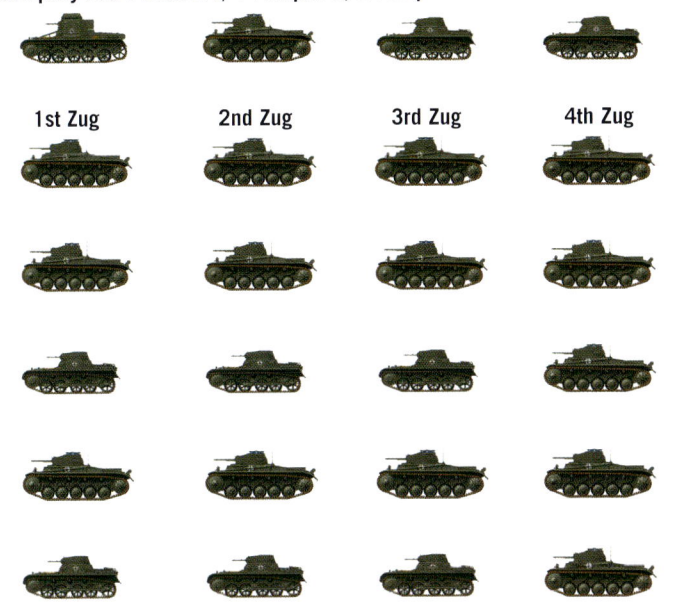

1st Zug 2nd Zug 3rd Zug 4th Zug

Leichte Panzerkompanie K.St.N.1171

Theoretical organization of a light company effective March 1939. When the Panzer divisions were created, the official table of organization of a light panzer company included one light *Zug*, or platoon, of five Panzer IIs, and the remaining three platoons were intended to be equipped with five Panzer IIIs each. However, production was slow. Early variants had too little armour protection and unsatisfactory suspension. Fewer than 150 Panzer IIIs had been manufactured by the outbreak of war, and only 98 tanks were actually operational.

Plans had been modified to reduce the number of Panzer IIIs to just three tanks to equip a single *Zug* in one of the regiment's 'a'-type light company, giving a division a total Panzer III strength of between six and 12 tanks.

However, supplies were so short that some of the panzer divisions in Poland were exclusively equipped with Panzer Is and Panzer IIs. These were deployed in five-tank platoons as illustrated, with three further gun tanks and a command tank assigned to company headquarters.

Fall Gelb: the French campaign
10 MAY 1940

The 3rd Panzer Division was attached to Army Group B during the Western campaign, and did not take part in the surprise attack through the Ardennes.

3RD PANZER DROVE into Holland and Belgium as part of the force intended to pull the Allies out of France and into the Low Countries. When the attack on France started, 3rd Panzer advanced west of Paris.

Panzer Unit	Pz. I	Pz. II	Pz. III	Pz. IV	Pz. Bef.
5th Pz. Rgt.	22	55	29	16	8
6th Pz. Rgt.	23	60	29	16	8

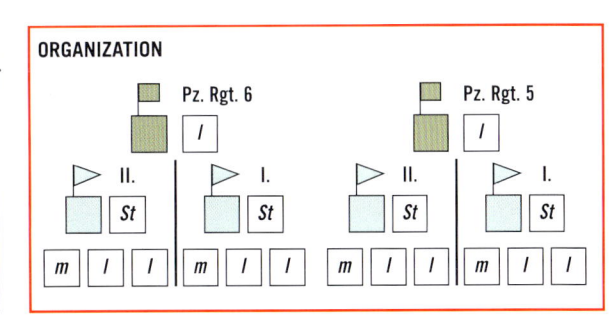

ORGANIZATION

37

3RD PANZER DIVISION

▶ **Panzerkampfwagen IV Ausf D (Sd Kfz 161)**
Unknown formation
The Pz.Kpfw IV's short-barrelled 7.5cm (3in) L/24 gun was not designed as an antitank weapon, but was powerful enough to deal with most Allied tanks in 1940.

Specifications
Crew: 5
Weight: 22 tonnes (20 tons)
Length: 5.92m (19.4ft)
Width: 2.84m (9.3ft)
Height: 2.68m (8.8ft)
Engine: Maybach HL120TRM
Speed: 40km/hr (24.9mph)
Range: 200km (124.3 miles)
Radio: FuG5

▶ **Panzerkampfwagen II Ausf C (Sd Kfz 121)**
Unknown formation
The 3rd Panzer Division claimed 87 enemy tank kills in 1940. Actions in France included a major engagement with the French 3rd Mechanized Division.

Specifications
Crew: 3
Weight: 9.8 tonnes (8.9 tons)
Length: 4.81m (15.8ft)
Width: 2.22m (7.3ft)
Height: 1.99m (6.5ft)
Engine: Maybach HL62TR
Speed: 40km/hr (24.9mph)
Range: 200km (124.3 miles)
Radio: FuG5

▶ **Munitionsschlepper auf Panzerkampfwagen I Ausf A (Sd Kfz 111)**
Unknown formation
A number of early Pz.Kpfw I Ausf As were converted into ammunition carriers. The Sd Kfz 111 was developed to supply ammunition to frontline units under fire and served during the invasion of Poland and France. This example carries a standard Panzer Death's Head insignia, which differed from that used by the SS.

Specifications
Crew: 2
Weight: 5.5 tonnes (5 tons)
Length: 4.02m (13.2ft)
Width: 2.06m (6.8ft)
Height: 1.4m (4.6ft)
Engine: Krupp M305
Speed: 37km/hr (23mph)
Range: 95km (59 miles)
Radio: None

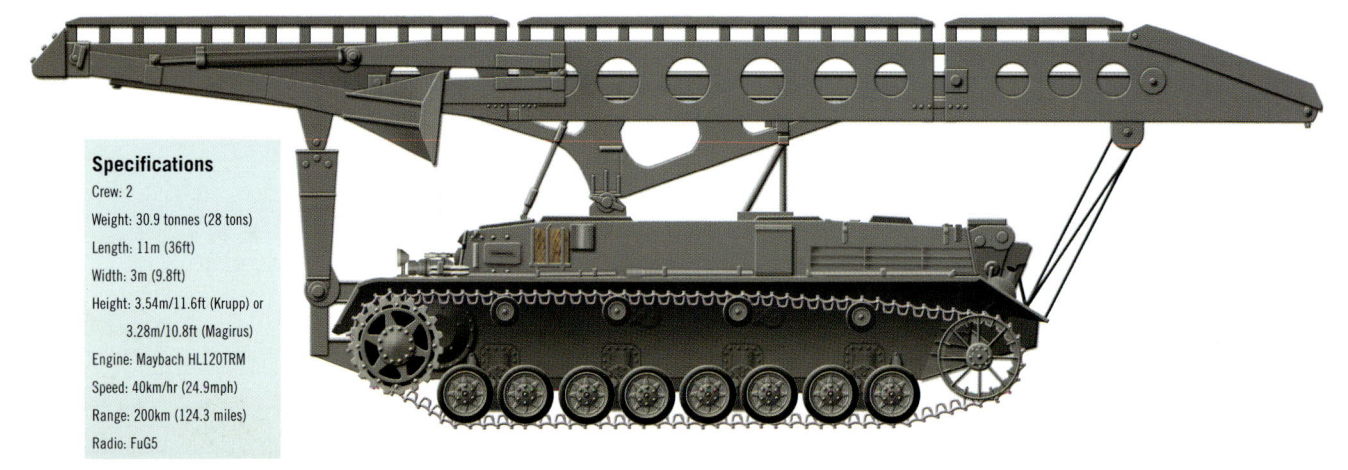

▼ **Infanterie Sturmsteg auf Fahrgestell Panzerkampfwagen IV**
39th Panzer Pioneer Battalion
Four assault bridges were delivered to each full Panzer division in 1940.

Specifications
Crew: 2
Weight: 30.9 tonnes (28 tons)
Length: 11m (36ft)
Width: 3m (9.8ft)
Height: 3.54m/11.6ft (Krupp) or 3.28m/10.8ft (Magirus)
Engine: Maybach HL120TRM
Speed: 40km/hr (24.9mph)
Range: 200km (124.3 miles)
Radio: FuG5

3RD PANZER DIVISION

▶ **Panzerkampfwagen I Ausf B (Sd Kfz 101)**
Unknown formation
It has been suggested that 3rd Panzer's Divisional symbol, a lopsided 'E', was a stylized representation of the famous Brandenburg Gate in Berlin.

Specifications

Crew: 2	Engine: Maybach NL38TR
Weight: 6.4 tonnes (5.8 tons)	Speed: 40km/hr (24.9mph)
Length: 4.42m (14.5ft)	Range: 170km (105.6 miles)
Width: 2.06m (6.8ft)	Radio: FuG2
Height: 1.72m (5.6ft)	

Barbarossa: the attack on Russia
22 JUNE 1941

Panzer Regiment 5 was detached along with other divisional units in January 1941 to reinforce the 5th *Leichte* Panzer Division, which was to form part of the newly created *Afrika Korps*.

After refitting in Germany, the 3rd Panzer Division formed part of Guderian's 2nd *Panzergruppe* in Russia in July 1941. By September, hard use meant that its tank strength had fallen from nearly 200 to about 50, most of which were Panzer IIs.

Panzer Unit	Pz. II	Pz. III(37)	Pz. III(50)	Pz. IV	Pz. Bef.
6th Pz. Rgt.	58	29	81	20	15

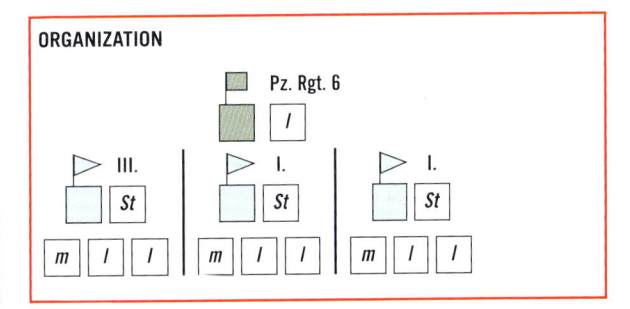

ORGANIZATION

Pz. Rgt. 6
I
III. / I. / I.
St / St / St
m l l / m l l / m l l

▶ **Panzerkampfwagen III Ausf J (Sd Kfz 141)**
Pz. Rgt 6 / I Battalion / 1st Company / 2nd Zug / tank number 2
The Pz.Kpfw III's three-man turret reduced crew workloads considerably.

Specifications

Crew: 5	Engine: Maybach HL120TRM
Weight: 24 tonnes (21.5 tons)	Speed: 40km/hr (24.9mph)
Length: 5.52m (18.1ft)	Range: 155km (96.3 miles)
Width: 2.95m (9.7ft)	Radio: FuG5
Height: 2.5m (8.2ft)	

▶ **Panzerkampfwagen III Ausf H (Sd Kfz 141)**
Pz. Rgt 6 / II Battalion / 5th Company / 3rd Zug / tank number 1
Two-colour tactical numbers improved poor-weather identification.

Specifications

Crew: 5	Engine: Maybach HL120TRM
Weight: 24 tonnes (21.8 tons)	Speed: 40km/hr (24.9mph)
Length: 5.41m (17.7ft)	Range: 165km (102.5 miles)
Width: 2.95m (9.7ft)	Radio: FuG5
Height: 2.44m (8ft)	

3RD PANZER DIVISION

Fall Blau: the Eastern Front
28 June 1942

The Soviet winter offensive petered out in March 1942, and the *Wehrmacht* began planning its summer offensive. The main German attack was to be switched from Moscow to the south.

In March 1943, the 3rd Panzer Division transferred from Army Group Centre to the 6th Army at Kharkhov. After taking part in von Manstein's masterly victory there, it was again transferred, to von Kleist's 1st *Panzerarmee*, part of Army Group A. Kleist's Panzers raced southeast towards the Caucasus mountains and the vital oilfields beyond, while the German 6th Army was directed at the Volga.

The stalemate and eventual annihilation of the 6th Army at Stalingrad over the winter of 1942/43 threatened to cut off Army Group A in the Caucasus, but von Kleist managed a superb fighting retreat. The 3rd Panzer Division was again transferred at the beginning of 1943, being assigned to Army Group Don at Rostov.

ORGANIZATION

Panzer Unit	Pz. II	Pz. III(kz)	Pz. III(lg)	Pz. IV(kz)	Pz. IV(lg)
6th Pz. Rgt.	25	66	40	21	12

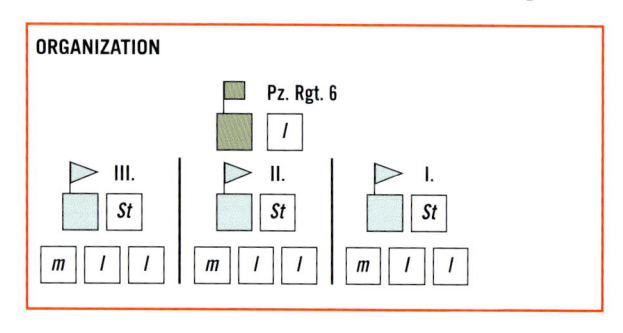

▶ **Mittlerer Schützenpanzerwagen Ausf C (Sd Kfz 251/1)**
3rd Schutzen Regiment

This troop-carrying half-track is depicted as it was when the 3rd Panzer Division was serving with Army Group South before the advance into the Caucasus that summer. It is armed with a captured Soviet PTRD-41 antitank rifle, which could penetrate the side armour of a Pz.Kpfw III.

Specifications

Crew: 2 plus 12 troops
Weight: 9.9 tonnes (9 tons)
Length: 5.98m (19.6ft)
Width: 2.1m (6.9ft)
Height : 1.75m (5.7ft) or 2.16m (7ft) with MG shield
Engine: Maybach HL42TUKRM
Speed: 53km/hr (32.9mph)
Range: 300km (186.4 miles)
Radio: FuG Spr Ger f

▶ **Mittlerer Kommandopanzerwagen Ausf B (Sd Kfz 251/6)**
Unknown formation

The 2.8cm (1.1in) *Panzerbuchse* 41 was not a standard weapon for the Sd Kfz 251/6 armoured command post. It fired a high-velocity round through a barrel which tapered from 28mm (1.1in) at the chamber to 20mm (0.8in) at the muzzle.

Specifications

Crew: 8
Weight: 9.4 tonnes (8.5 tons)
Length: 5.98m (19.6ft)
Width: 2.1m (6.9ft)
Height: 2.4m (7.9ft)
Engine: Maybach HL42TUKRM
Speed: 53km/hr (32.9mph)
Range: 300km (186.4 miles)
Radio: FuG11 plus FuG Tr

3RD PANZER DIVISION

The last summer offensive
1 July 1943

The 3rd Panzer Battalion was disbanded in May 1943. The 1st Battalion was refitted as a Pz.Kpfw V Panther *Abteilung* and was combat-ready by August 1943.

THE MASSIVE SOVIET offensives launched after the *Wehrmacht*'s failure at Kursk meant that Army Group South, which included 3rd Panzer Division, was forced to withdraw through the Ukraine.

3rd Panzer was commanded by Fritz Bayerlein, a veteran of the Desert War, and was at Kirovograd when the town was surrounded by a surprise Soviet offensive in December 1943. 3rd Panzer led the breakout from the pocket, finally meeting up with a relief force led by the elite *Grossdeutschland* Division.

The *Wehrmacht*'s retreats continued through 1944 and 1945 through the Ukraine. The 3rd Panzer Division fought its way back through Uman, across the Bug and into Poland.

Briefly transferred to the remnants of Army Group Centre as the *Wehrmacht* tried to stabilize the front following its destruction, the division was moved to Hungary in January 1945. 3rd Panzer fought in Hungary until April 1945, when it retreated to Austria where it later surrendered to the US Army.

ORGANIZATION

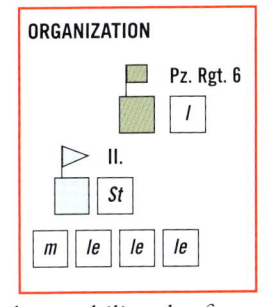

Pz. Rgt. 6 / I / II. / St / m / le / le / le

Panzer Unit	Pz. II	Pz.III(50)	Pz.III(75)	Pz. IV	Pz. Bef.
6th Pz. Rgt.	7	42	17	23	1

Black and pink are the colours of the Panzer troops, black uniforms being worn with pink *Waffenfarbe*, or piping.

▶ **Mittlerer Funkpanzerwagen Ausf D (Sd Kfz 251/3)**
Pz. Rgt 6 / Regimental Staff Company
The Iron Cross in the corner of 6th Regiment's command standard shows the regimental commander was a Knight's Cross holder. Variants of this radio vehicle were used by several command levels, with radio fit depending on the role.

Specifications (Radio)
Crew: 7
Divisional: FuG8, FuG5, FuG4
Division to Artillery: FuG8, FuG4
Division to Panzer: FuG8, FuG5
Ground-to-air: FuG7, FuG1
Command post: FuG12, FuG11, plus Kdo FuG Tr.
The Kdo FuG Tr was deployed with a variety of transmitters with powers from 15 to 100 Watts

▶ **Panzerkampfwagen IV Ausf H (Sd Kfz 161/2)**
Pz. Rgt 6 / II Battalion / 2nd Company / 2nd Zug / tank number 1
This vehicle took part in 3rd Panzer's long defensive retreat through 1944. The *Schürzen,* or side skirts, provided protection against shaped-charge antitank rounds or grenades.

Specifications
Crew: 5
Weight: 27.6 tonnes (25 tons)
Length: 7.02m (23ft)
Width: 2.88m (9.4ft)
Height: 2.68m (8.8ft)
Engine: Maybach HL120TRM
Speed: 38km/hr (23.6mph)
Range: 210km (130.5 miles)
Radio: FuG5

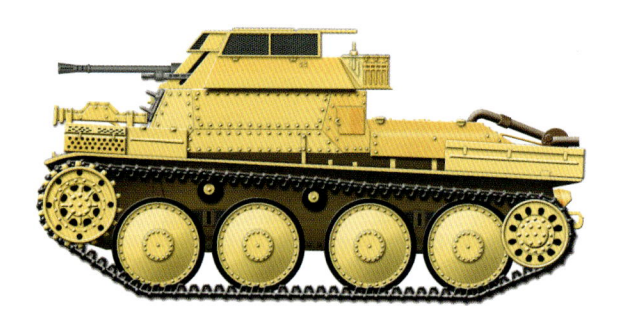

3RD PANZER DIVISION

◀ **Aufklärungspanzerwagen 38 (2cm) (Sd Kfz 140/1)**
3rd Reconnaissance Battalion / 1st Company

The Sd Kfz 140/1 was one of the last variants of the Panzer 38(t) chassis. It is armed with a 2cm (0.8in) KwK38 L/55 cannon. In September 1944, the 1st Company received 25 vehicles, nine of which carried FuG12 long-range radios.

Specifications
Crew: 2	Engine: Praga EPA/2
Weight: 10.7 tonnes (9.75 tons)	Speed: 42km/hr (26mph)
Length: 4.51m (14.8ft)	Range: 210km (130.5 miles)
Width: 2.14m (7ft)	Radio: FuG12
Height: 2.17m (7.1ft)	

▶ **Panzerkampfwagen IV Ausf H (Sd Kfz 161/2)**
Pz. Rgt 6

By 1944, the Pz.Kpfw IV was showing its age. Even though the long-barrelled KwK40 L/48 could penetrate the armour of a T-34 from a distance of up to 1200m (3973ft) when using Pz.gr 39 ammunition, the tank could no longer match the capabilities of the latest T-34/85 and JS-122 tanks.

Specifications
Crew: 5	Engine: Maybach HL120TRM
Weight: 27.6 tonnes (25 tons)	Speed: 38km/hr (23.6mph)
Length: 7.02m (23ft)	Range: 210km (130.5 miles)
Width: 2.88m (9.4ft)	Radio: FuG5
Height: 2.68m (8.8ft)	

Specifications
Crew: 5	Engine: Maybach HL230P30
Weight: 49.4 tonnes (44.8 tons)	Speed: 46km/hr (28.6mph)
Length: 8.86 m (29ft)	Range: 200km (124.3 miles)
Width: 3.42m (11.2ft)	Radio: FuG5
Height: 2.98m (9.8ft)	

▼ **Panzerkampfwagen V Ausf A (Sd Kfz 171)**
Kampfgruppe / Pz. Rgt 6

By December 1944, the 3rd Panzer Division had been reorganized as a Panzer *Kampfgruppe* with a mixed tank company of Pz.Kpfw IVs and Pz.Kpfw Vs. It had a total of 20 operational tanks.

4th Panzer Division

Further expansion of the *Panzerwaffe* meant that by the autumn of 1938, six new Panzer brigades had been formed. The 7th Brigade was to be the nucleus of a new Panzer division.

THE 4TH PANZER DIVISION was raised at Wurzburg on 10 October 1938. The division's Panzer brigade included the 35th and 36th Panzer Regiments. In August 1939, the first three panzer divisions were identical in size and organization, but the 4th Panzer Division still lacked some of its motorized infantry and antitank units.

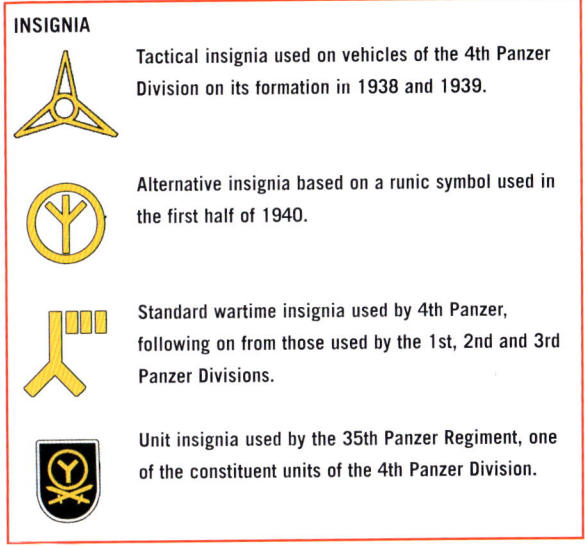

Commanders

Generaloberst G. Reinhardt
(1 Sept 1939 – 5 Feb 1940)

Generalleutnant L. von Radlmeier
(5 Feb 1940 – 8 June 1940)

Generalleutnant J. Stever
(8 June 1940 – 24 July 1940)

Generalleutnant H. Boineburg-Lengsfeld
(24 July 1940 – 8 Sept 1940)

General der Panzertruppen W. von Langermann
(8 Sept 1940 – 27 Dec 1941)

General der Panzertruppen D. Saucken
(27 Dec 1941 – 2 Jan 1942)

General der Panzertruppen W. von Langermann
(2 Jan 1942 – 6 Jan 1942)

General der Panzertruppen H. Eberbach
(6 Jan 1942 – 2 Mar 1942)

Generalleutnant O. Heidkamper
(2 Mar 1942 – 4 Apr 1942)

General der Panzertruppen H. Eberbach
(4 Apr 1942 – 14 Nov 1942)

Generalleutnant E. Schneider
(14 Nov 1942 – 31 May 1943)

General der Panzertruppen D. von Saucken
(31 May 1943 – Jan 1944)

Generalleutnant H. Junck
(Jan 1944 – Feb 1944)

General der Panzertruppen D. von Saucken
(Feb 1944 – 1 May 1944)

Generalleutnant C. Betzel
(1 May 1944 – 27 Mar 1945)

Oberst E. Hoffmann
(27 Mar 1945 – 8 May 1945)

INSIGNIA

Tactical insignia used on vehicles of the 4th Panzer Division on its formation in 1938 and 1939.

Alternative insignia based on a runic symbol used in the first half of 1940.

Standard wartime insignia used by 4th Panzer, following on from those used by the 1st, 2nd and 3rd Panzer Divisions.

Unit insignia used by the 35th Panzer Regiment, one of the constituent units of the 4th Panzer Division.

Fall Weiss: the invasion of Poland
1 SEPTEMBER 1939

For the Polish campaign, the 4th Panzer Division was attached to General Hoeppner's XVI *Panzerkorps*, serving alongside the 1st Panzer Division.

HOEPPNER'S CORPS PROVIDED the striking power for General von Reichenau's 10th Army, which was tasked with driving towards Warsaw. From the start of the invasion on 1 September, the Division advanced at breakneck pace. 4th Panzer units reached the outskirts of Warsaw on 8 September, and entered the city the next day. However, the *Wehrmacht* learned a valuable lesson about fighting in built-up areas: tanks are extremely vulnerable in such terrain, and the division lost 50 of its 120 tanks in the action before it was replaced by infantry units.

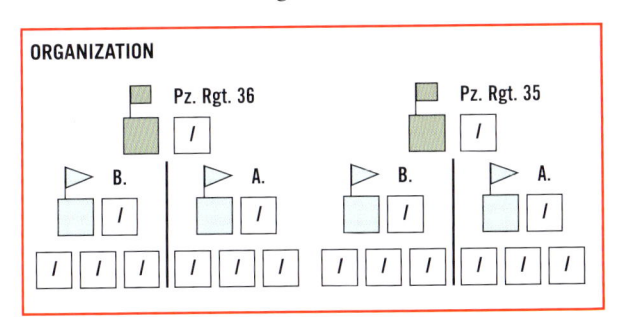

Panzer Unit	Pz. I	Pz. II	Pz. III	Pz. IV	Pz. Bef.
35th Pz. Rgt.	99	64	0	6	8
36th Pz. Rgt.	84	66	0	6	8

4TH PANZER DIVISION

During the Polish campaign, a low visibility cross was created by painting it completely yellow or painting the centre yellow and leaving a white border.

Specifications
Crew: 2
Weight: 6.4 tonnes (5.8 tons)
Length: 4.42m (14.5ft)
Width: 2.06m (6.8ft)
Height: 1.72m (5.6ft)
Engine: Maybach NL38TR
Speed: 40km/hr (24.9mph)
Range: 170km (105.6 miles)
Radio: FuG2

▲ **Panzerkampfwagen I Ausf B (Sd Kfz 101)**
Pz. Rgt 35 / A Battalion / Stabskompanie / Light Platoon / tank number 5
This vehicle participated in the battle of Bzura, 16 September 1939.

▶ **Panzerbefehlswagen III Ausf D1 (Sd Kfz 267-268)**
Pz. Rgt 36 / B Battalion / Stabskompanie / Signal Platoon
Thirty Ausf D1 tanks were produced between June 1938 and March 1939. The turret was bolted into place, and a dummy gun was fitted to make this command tank look like a standard gun tank.

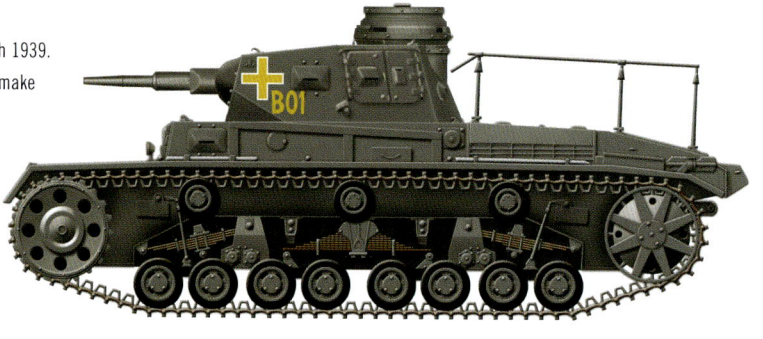

Specifications
Crew: 5
Weight: 20 tonnes (18.2 tons)
Length: 5.98m (19.6ft)
Width: 2.87m (9.4ft)
Height: 2.42m (7.9ft)
Engine: Maybach HL 108TR
Speed: 40km/hr (24.9mph)
Range: 165km (102.5 miles)
Radio: FuG6 plus FuG7 or FuG8

▶ **Panzerkampfwagen II Ausf B (Sd Kfz 121)**
Pz. Rgt 35 / I Battalion / 1st Company / 4th Zug / tank number 5
This early Panzer II was one of 50 Panzers destroyed during the fight for Warsaw.

Specifications
Crew: 3
Weight: 8.7 tonnes (7.9 tons)
Length: 4.76m (15.6ft)
Width: 2.14m (7ft)
Height: 1.96m (6.4ft)
Engine: Maybach HL62TR
Speed: 40km/hr (24.9mph)
Range: 200km (124.3 miles)
Radio: FuG5

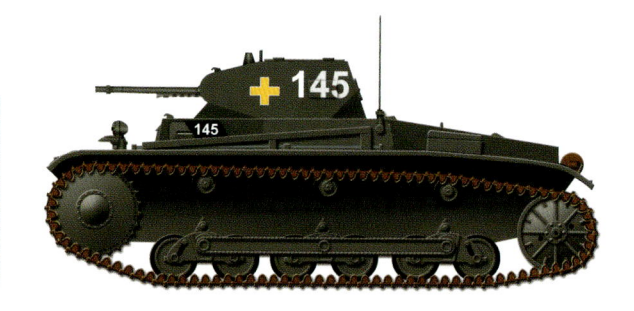

Fall Gelb: the French campaign
10 May 1940

Following the conquest of Poland, 4th Panzer Division returned to Germany. Based in the Niederrhein, it formed part of 6th Army's reserve in Army Group B.

IN MAY 1940, 4TH PANZER remained with General Hoeppner's XVI *Panzerkorps*, which was taking up positions on the Belgian/Dutch border. Together with 3rd Panzer, the Division would provide the

Panzer Unit	Pz. I	Pz. II	Pz. III	Pz. IV	Pz. Bef.
35th Pz. Rgt.	69	50	20	12	5
36th Pz. Rgt.	66	55	20	12	5

4TH PANZER DIVISION

armoured punch for von Bock's Army Group B attacking Holland and Belgium. Serving as a 'Matador's cape' to draw the attention of the Anglo-French High Command, the Panzers attacked towards Brussels and Liege. The plan worked perfectly. As the Allies rushed into Belgium, the main German attack erupted out of the Ardennes.

Following Dunkirk, 4th Panzer was redeployed with all the rest of Germany's armour along the line of the Somme. Launching the battle for France on 5 June, the Division advanced through the centre of the country, reaching as far south as Grenoble in the Alps by the time the Armistice was signed at Compiègne on 22 June.

Following the victory, 4th Panzer remained on occupation duties in France until March 1941.

ORGANIZATION

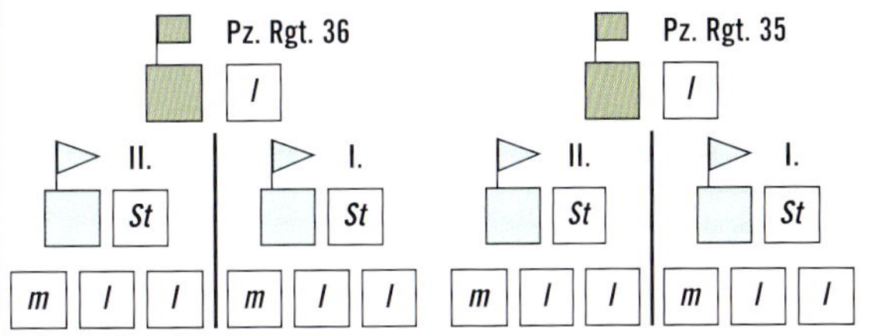

Specifications
Crew: 2
Weight: 6.4 tonnes (5.8 tons)
Length: 4.42m (14.5ft)
Width: 2.06m (6.8ft)
Height: 1.72m (5.6ft)
Engine: Maybach NL38TR
Speed: 40km/hr (24.9mph)
Range: 170km (105.6 miles)
Radio: FuG2

▶ **Panzerkampfwagen I Ausf B (Sd Kfz 101)**
Pz. Rgt 36 / I Battalion / 1st Company / 3rd Zug / tank number 3
The Pz.Kpfw I Ausf B mounted two 7.92mm (0.3in) MG13 machine guns for which it carried 2250 rounds of ammunition. The small dot after the turret number was an identification mark carried by Panzer Regiment 36 vehicles.

▶ **Panzerbefehlswagen III Ausf E (Sd Kfz 266-267-268)**
Pz. Rgt 36 / Regimental Staff Company / HQ tank of Hptm Jesse
'RN1' stands for *Regiment Nachrichten-1* (Regimental Signal Platoon – 1). The German National Flag draped across the command radio antenna supplemented the white rectangular air recognition sign painted on the engine deck.

Specifications
Crew: 5
Weight: 21.5 tonnes (19.5 tons)
Length: 5.38m (17.7ft)
Width: 2.91m (9.5ft)
Height: 2.44m (8ft)
Engine: Maybach HL120TR
Speed: 40km/hr (24.9mph)
Range: 165km (102.5 miles)
Radio: FuG6 plus FuG2 or FuG7 or FuG8

▶ **Panzerkampfwagen III Ausf F (Sd Kfz 141)**
Pz. Rgt 36 / I Battalion / 1st Company / 5th Zug / tank number 6
The Ausf F model of the Panzer III was armed with a 3.7cm (1.5in) KwK L/46.5 cannon. This was ineffective against tanks like the French Somua and the Char D2, since at combat ranges most of the shots just bounced off the enemy armour.

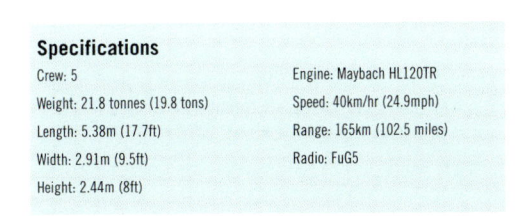

Specifications
Crew: 5
Weight: 21.8 tonnes (19.8 tons)
Length: 5.38m (17.7ft)
Width: 2.91m (9.5ft)
Height: 2.44m (8ft)
Engine: Maybach HL120TR
Speed: 40km/hr (24.9mph)
Range: 165km (102.5 miles)
Radio: FuG5

4TH PANZER DIVISION

▶ Panzerkampfwagen III als Tauchpanzer
Pz. Rgt 35 / I Battalion / 2nd Company / 2nd Zug / tank number 1

In preparation for the planned invasion of England, 168 tanks were converted into 'diving tanks' to operate in up to 15m (49.2ft) of water. This tank belonged to the 3rd Panzer Division before it was transferred.

Specifications
Crew: 5
Weight: 21.8 tonnes (19.8 tons)
Length: 5.38m (17.7ft)
Width: 2.91m (9.5ft)
Height: 2.44m (8ft)
Engine: Maybach HL120TR
Speed: 40km/hr (24.9mph)
Range: 165km (102.5 miles)
Radio: FuG5

▶ Kleiner Panzerbefehlswagen (Sd Kfz 265)
Unknown formation

Although not an official variant, the Sd Kfz 265 command tank was pressed into service as an armoured ambulance, room for casualties being made by removing the command radios.

Specifications
Crew: 2/3
Weight: 6.5 tonnes (5.9 tons)
Length: 4.42m (14.5ft)
Width: 2.06m (6.8ft)
Height: 1.99m (6.5ft)
Engine: Maybach NL38TR
Speed: 40km/hr (24.9mph)
Range: 170km (105.6 miles)
Radio: None, or FuG2

Barbarossa: the attack on Russia
22 June 1941

In this period, the 36th Regiment was detached to form the core of the 14th Panzer Division.

IN APRIL 1941, THE DIVISION was sent from occupation duties in France to refit in reserve with Army Group B in East Prussia. In June 1941, it was returned to combat status with XXIV *Panzerkorps*. This formed part of Guderian's *Panzergruppe* 2, the tank army that was to lead Army Group Centre's drive into the Soviet Union. After smashing through the Red Army at Gomel and Smolensk, Guderian's panzers were diverted to assist Army Group South at Kiev. In the largest battle of encirclement in history, more than half a million Soviet soldiers were taken prisoner.

When the advance towards Moscow resumed at the end of September, 4th Panzer led Guderian's *Panzergruppe*, reaching Orel on 3 October after driving through 200 km (124.3 miles) of woodlands in two days. However, as autumn set in, the road towards Tula turned to a river of mud, which froze as winter arrived. In December, in an assault on Tula, 4th Panzer reached the outskirts of the city, but was forced to pull back by new Soviet counterattacks.

Panzer Unit	Pz. II	Pz. III(37)	Pz. III(50)	Pz. IV	Pz. Bef.
35th Pz. Rgt.	44	31	74	20	8

ORGANIZATION

Pz. Rgt. 35
I
II.   I.
St   St
m / / /   m / / /

4TH PANZER DIVISION

▲ **Panzerkampfwagen II Ausf B (Sd Kfz 121)**
Pz. Rgt 35 / I Battalion / Stabskompanie / Light Platoon / tank number 6

The Panzer II's 2cm (0.8in) *Panzergranate* (armour-piercing) round was ineffective against Russian armour. Crews usually loaded *Sprenggranate* (high-explosive fragmentation) shells, which were very effective against live targets and soft-skin vehicles. This particular tank had a memorial inscription in honour of Frank Lott, a crewman killed in action, painted in the turret.

Specifications
Crew: 3
Weight: 9.8 tonnes (8.9 tons)
Length: 4.81m (15.8ft)
Width: 2.22m (7.3ft)
Height: 1.99m (6.5ft)
Engine: Maybach HL62TR
Speed: 40km/hr (24.9mph)
Range: 200km (124.3 miles)
Radio: FuG5

Fall Blau: the Eastern front
28 June 1942

A Panzer battalion from the Division was renamed 3/15th Panzer Regiment and was sent to reinforce the 11th Panzer Division.

THE SOVIET COUNTEROFFENSIVES around Moscow were mounted by fresh troops from Siberia, with full winter equipment and training. Already suffering from the harsh conditions for which they were not prepared, 2nd *Panzerarmee* was forced back towards Orel. The Soviet offensives continued through the winter, but lost momentum by the end of March.

The German High Command decided that the *Wehrmacht*'s 1942 summer offensive would take place in the south, pushing towards the Volga and the Caucasus oil fields. The 4th Panzer Division was to play no part in it, remaining with 2nd *Panzerarmee* on the Orel Front for the next 18 months.

Panzer Unit	Pz. II	Pz. III	Pz. IV	Pz. Bef.
35th Pz. Rgt.	13	28	5	2

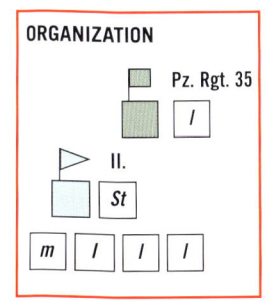

Mittlerer Panzerkompanie K.St.N.1175

The standard organization of a Panzer division at the outbreak of war in 1939 included two Panzer regiments operating as a Panzer brigade. Combat operations showed the brigade to be slightly unwieldy, and by the end of 1941 most Panzer divisions had a single Panzer regiment. This was divided into two or three battalions, each consisting of a staff company, a medium company and two or three light companies. All Panzer companies had a light platoon with five Panzer IIs: the other platoons of the light companies operated with five Panzer IIIs, while the medium company had three platoons of four Panzer IVs, as illustrated here.

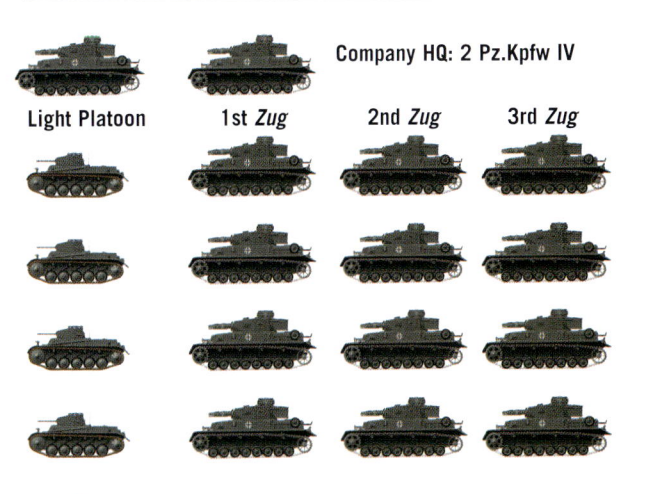

47

4TH PANZER DIVISION

The last summer offensive
1 July 1943

The 35th Panzer Regiment was reinforced in February 1943, when the independent 700th *Panzer Verband* was disbanded and its remnants were absorbed into the 4th Panzer Division.

THE 4TH PANZER DIVISION played a supporting role in the great battle at Kursk in July 1943. The 2nd *Panzerarmee* was supposed to guard the flank of Model's 9th Army, but was attacked itself by Soviet forces bursting out from the Kursk salient.

After Kursk, the German armies in the East were on the defensive. 4th Panzer remained with Army Group Centre for the next year, being driven back through Desna, Gomel and the Pripjet Marshes. In May 1944, it was moved to Army Group North in the Ukraine for refitting – which meant that it avoided the annihilation of Army Group Centre in June 1944. In July 1944, the Division was sent northwards as the High Command tried to stabilize the line. From August 1944, it saw combat in the Baltic states, being forced out of Latvia and Lithuania in October. It fought in the Courland pocket until January 1945, eventually retreating to West Prussia, where it surrendered to the Red Army.

ORGANIZATION
- Pz. Rgt. 35 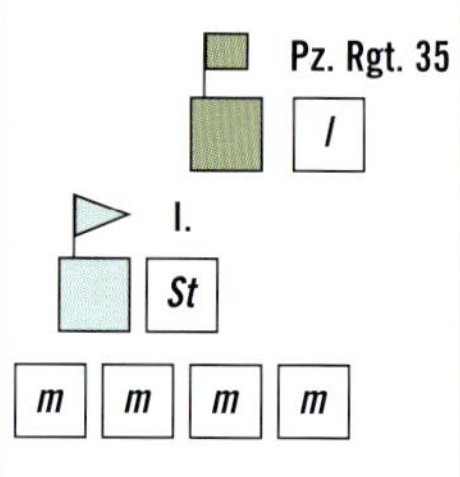
- I
- I.
- St
- m m m m

Panzer Unit	Pz. III	Pz. IV(kz)	Pz. IV(lg)	Pz. Bef
35th Pz. Rgt.	15	1	79	6

▶ **Panzerfunkwagen (Sd Kfz 263) 8-Rad**
79th Nachtrichten Abteilung (Signal Battalion)
The Sd Kfz 263 was an extremely capable communications vehicle issued to the signal battalions of both motorized and Panzer divisions, as well as being used to provide mobile signal capacity to corps and army headquarters.

Specifications
Crew: 5
Weight: 8.9 tonnes (8.1 tons)
Length: 5.85m (19.2ft)
Width: 2.2m (7.2ft)
Height: 2.9m (9.5ft)
Engine: Büssing-NAG L8V
Speed: 100km/hr (62.1mph)
Range: 300km (186.4 miles)
Radio: 1 Sätz Funkgerät für (m) Pz Funktruppe b

▶ **Panzerkampfwagen II Ausf L (Sd Kfz 123)**
4th Reconnaissance Battalion / 2nd Company (Luchs)
100 of the redesigned Pz.Kpfw II Ausf L Luchs, or 'Lynx', were built between September 1943 and January 1944. 4th Panzer was one of two units to receive a full company. In October 1943, the division reported 27 'Lynx' ready for combat.

Specifications
Crew: 4
Weight: 14.3 tonnes (13 tons)
Length: 4.63m (15.2ft)
Width: 2.48m (8.1ft)
Height: 2.21m (7.3ft)
Engine: Maybach HL66P
Speed: 60km/hr (37.3mph)
Range: 290km (180.2 miles)
Radio: FuG12 plus FuG Spr a

48

4TH PANZER DIVISION

▶ **Panzerkampfwagen IV Ausf G (Sd Kfz 161/1 und 161/2)**
Pz. Rgt 35 / I Battalion
After the abortive German offensive at Kursk, the 4th Panzer Division was involved in a series of very costly defensive battles protecting the retreat of Army Group Centre.

Specifications
Crew: 5
Weight: 25.9 tonnes (23.5 tons)
Length: 6.62m (21.7ft)
Width: 2.88m (9.4ft)
Height: 2.68m (8.8ft)
Engine: Maybach HL120TRM
Speed: 40km/hr (24.9mph)
Range: 210km (130.5 miles)
Radio: FuG5

▶ **Panzerkampfwagen II Ausf L (Sd Kfz 123)**
4th Reconnaissance Battalion / 2nd Company (Luchs)
Based on the Panzer II but with a completely new suspension and a new, larger turret, the Luchs also had a wider hull and tracks.

Armament Specifications
Main gun: 2cm (0.8in) KwK38 L/55
Ammunition: 330 rounds
Turret traverse: 360° (manual)
Elevation: -9° to +18°
Sights: TZF6/38
Secondary armament: 7.92mm (0.3in) MG 34
Ammunition: 2250 rounds
Sights: KgZF2

▶ **Schwerer Panzerspähwagen (7.5cm) (Sd Kfz 233)**
4th Reconnaissance Battalion / 3rd Armoured Car Company
A late version of the Sd Kfz 233, this has 30mm (1.2in) frontal armour. A six-sided armour shield protected the short-barrelled 7.5cm (3in) gun.

Specifications
Crew: 3
Weight: 9.6 tonnes (8.7 tons)
Length: 5.85m (19.2ft)
Width: 2.2m (7.2ft)
Height: 2.25m (7.4ft)
Engine: Büssing-NAG L8V
Speed: 80km/hr (49.7mph)
Range: 300km (186.4 miles)
Radio: FuG Spr Ger 'a'

▶ **Leichter Schützenpanzerwagen (3.7cm PaK) (Sd Kfz 250/10)**
4th Reconnaissance Battalion
The Sd Kfz 250/10 provided heavy support fire for reconnaissance units. The obsolete 3.7cm (1.5in) PaK36 was not highly regarded: it was nicknamed the 'door knocker', because of its inability to penetrate the armour of Soviet tanks.

Specifications
Crew: 4
Weight: 6.3 tonnes (5.67 tons)
Length: 4.56m (15ft)
Width: 1.95m (6.4ft)
Height: 1.97m (6.5ft)
Engine: Maybach KL42TRKM
Speed: 60km/hr (37.3mph)
Range: 320km (198.8 miles)
Radio: FuG Spr Ger 1

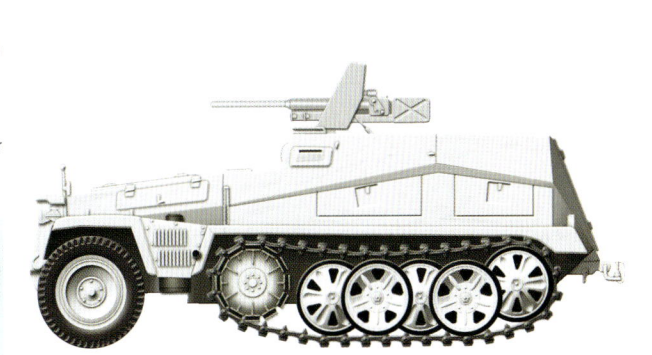

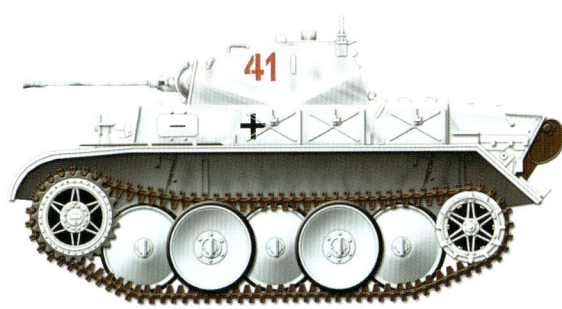

49

4TH PANZER DIVISION

▶ **7.5cm PaK40/2 auf Fahrgestell Panzerkampfwagen II (Sf) (Sd Kfz 131)**
49th Panzerjäger Battalion
The Marder II was a tank hunter that mounted a powerful antitank gun on a modified Panzer II chassis. Six kill rings are painted on the barrel of this example.

Specifications
Crew: 3
Weight: 11.9 tonnes (10.8 tons)
Length: 6.36m (20.9ft)
Width: 2.28m (7.5ft)
Height: 2.2m (7.2ft)
Engine: Maybach HL62TRM
Speed: 40km/hr (24.9mph)
Range: 190km (118 miles)
Radio: FuG Spr 'd'

Specifications
Crew: 6
Weight: 26.5 tonnes (24 tons)
Length: 7.17m (23.5ft)
Width: 2.97m (9.7ft)
Height: 2.81m (9.2ft)
Engine: HL120TRM
Speed: 42km/hr (26mph)
Range: 215km (133.6 miles)
Radio: FuG Spr 1

▲ **15cm Schwere Panzerhaubitze auf Fahrgestell Panzerkampfwagen III/IV (Sf) (Sd Kfz 165)**
103rd Panzer Artillery Regiment / 3rd (mot) Battalion
The SdKfz 165 first saw action at Kursk in 1943. This example belongs to one of the two heavy batteries assigned to the 4th Panzer Division's Artillery Regiment.

▶ **Mittlerer Kommandopanzerwagen Ausf B (Sd Kfz 251/6)**
4th Panzer Division / Division Staff / command vehicle of Gen Lt Deitrich von Saucken
The SdKfz 251/6 was a command and control vehicle for senior officers. It carried the same radios as the similar 251/3, but its equipment fit also included the 'Enigma' cryptographic machine.

Specifications
Crew: 8
Weight: 9.4 tonnes (8.5 tons)
Length: 5.98m (19.6ft)
Width: 2.1m (6.9ft)
Height: 1.75m (5.7ft)
Engine: Maybach HL42TUKRM
Speed: 53km/hr (32.9mph)
Range: 300km (186.4 miles)
Radio: FuG11 plus FuG Tr 100W; later FuG19 plus FuG12

▶ **Mittlerer Schützenpanzerwagen Ausf C (Sd Kfz 251/1)**
12th Panzergrenadier Regiment
Kurland, 1944. The Sd Kfz 251/1 crew consisted of a driver, co-driver and a 10-man grenadier squad.

Specifications
Crew: 0 plus 10 infantrymen
Weight: 8.8 tonnes (8 tons)
Length: 5.98m (19.6ft)
Width: 2.1m (6.9ft)
Height: 1.75m (5.7ft)
Engine: Maybach HL42TUKRM
Speed: 53km/hr (32.9mph)
Range: 300km (186.4 miles)
Radio: FuG Spr Ger 1

4TH PANZER DIVISION

▶ **Panzerkampfwagen V Ausf A (Sd Kfz 171)**

Pz. Rgt 35 / I Battalion / 1st Company / 1st Zug / tank number 3

In June 1944, the Division was reinforced with a Panther *Abteilung* of 79 tanks. The old 1st Battalion, equipped with Pz.Kpfw IVs, was renamed the 2nd Battalion while the Panther unit became the 1st Battalion.

Specifications

Crew: 5
Weight: 49.4 tonnes (44.8 tons)
Length: 8.86m (29ft)
Width: 3.42m (11.2ft)
Height: 2.98m (9.8ft)
Engine: Maybach HL230P30
Speed: 46km/hr (28.6mph)
Range: 200km (124.3 miles)
Radio: FuG5

▶ **Panzerkampfwagen IV Ausf H (Sd Kfz 161/2)**

Pz. Rgt 35 / II Battalion / 5th Company / Company HQ tank

In July 1944, 4th Panzer was sent to the Warsaw area where it clashed with the Soviet 2nd Tank Army.

Specifications

Crew: 5
Weight: 27.6 tonnes (25 tons)
Length: 7.02m (23ft)
Width: 2.88m (9.4ft)
Height: 2.68m (8.8ft)
Engine: Maybach HL120TRM
Speed: 38km/hr (23.6mph)
Range: 210km (130.5 miles)
Radio: FuG5

▼ **Schützenpanzerwagen I Ausf D (Sd Kfz 251/3)**

33rd Panzergrenadier / Regimental Staff Company

By the end of 4 July, Panzer Division had been divided into two *kampfgruppen*.

Black and green are the colours of the *Panzergrenadiers*.

Specifications

Crew: 8
Weight: 9.4 tonnes (8.5 tons)
Length: 5.98m (19.6ft)
Width: 2.1m (6.9ft)
Height: 1.75m (5.7ft)
Engine: Maybach HL42TUKRM
Speed: 53km/hr (32.9mph)
Range: 300km (186.4 miles)
Radio: Various, depending upon mission

◀ **Leichter Panzerspähwagen (2cm) (Sd Kfz 222)**

Kampfgruppe Christen / 4th Reconnaissance Battalion

The 4th Panzer Division fought back through the Baltic states in the last months of the war. The division surrendered to the Soviets in West Prussia in April 1945.

Specifications

Crew: 3
Weight: 5.3 tonnes (4.8 tons)
Length: 4.8m (15.7ft)
Width: 1.95m (6.4ft)
Height: 2m (6.6ft)
Engine: Horch 3.5 or 3.8
Speed: 85km/hr (52.8mph)
Range: 300km (186.4 miles)
Radio: FuG Spr Ger 'a'

51

5th Panzer Division

The 5th Panzer Division came into being on 24 November 1938, two weeks after 4th Panzer Division was set up. Its first commander was *Generalleutnant* Heinrich von Viettinghoff-Scheel.

THE MAIN COMPONENTS of the 5th Panzer Division, which was established at Oppeln (now Opole in Poland), included the 5th *Schützen* Brigade, which provided the motorized infantry strength, and the 8th Panzer Brigade, which included the 31st and 15th Panzer Regiments. Each regiment had two battalions, consisting of an armoured signals platoon, a staff platoon with light tanks, three light Panzer companies, one motorized infantry platoon, one supply unit and a maintenance company.

INSIGNIA

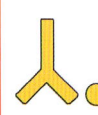

Standard tactical symbol used by the 5th Panzer Division in 1940, following on from the first four panzer divisions.

From 1941, 5th Panzer Division changed its tactical symbol to a cross. It would continue to use the symbol until 1945.

Variants of standard tactical symbols were often used. In this instance, the 5th Panzer cross is painted onto a black panel.

Additional insignia painted onto vehicles of the 31st Panzer Regiment, 5th Panzer Division, in 1941 and 1942

Commanders

Generaloberst H. Viettinghoff-Scheel
(1 Sept 1939 – 8 Oct 1939)

Generalleutnant M. Hartlieb-Walsporn
(8 Oct 1939 – 29 May 1940)

General der Panzertruppen J. Lemelsen
(29 May 1940 – 25 Nov 1940)

General der Panzertruppen G. Fehn
(25 Nov 1940 – 10 Aug 1942)

Generalleutnant E. Metz
(10 Aug 1942 – 1 Feb 1943)

Generalmajor J. Nedtwig
(1 Feb 1943 – 20 June 1943)

Generalleutnant E. Fackenstedt
(20 June 1943 – 7 Sept 1943)

General der Panzertruppen K. Decker
(7 Sept 1943 – 15 Oct 1944)

Generalmajor R. Lippert
(16 Oct 1944 – 5 Feb 1945)

Generalmajor G. Hoffmann-Schonborn
(5 Feb 1945 – Apr 1945)

Oberst der Reserve H. Herzog
(Apr 1945 – 8 May 1945)

Fall Weiss: the invasion of Poland
1 SEPTEMBER 1939

Although it had been in existence for less than a year, the 5th Panzer Division was ready for action when German forces invaded Poland on 1 September 1939.

ATTACKING OUT OF SILESIA, the 5th Panzer Division formed part of VIII *Panzerkorps* in General List's 14th Army. Controlled by von Rundstedt's Army Group South, the mission of the corps was to defeat the Polish armies on the Vistula, before driving towards Warsaw and Brest Litovsk.

The mobile forces of 14th Army, made up from two *Panzerkorps*, formed the southern prong of the massive, fast-moving pincer movement that was to meet Guderian's panzers at Brest-Litovsk and which sealed the fate of Poland.

ORGANIZATION

Pz. Rgt. 31 — II., I.
Pz. Rgt. 15 — II., I.

Panzer Unit	Pz. I	Pz. II	Pz. III	Pz. IV	Pz. Bef.
15th Pz. Rgt.	72	81	3	8	11
31st Pz. Rgt.	80	63	0	6	11

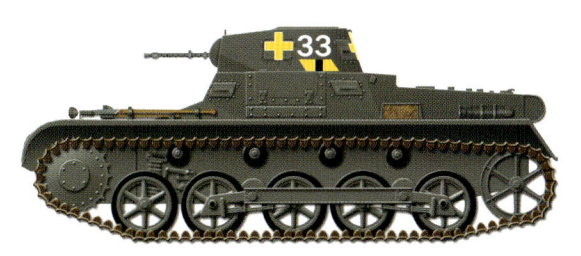

5TH PANZER DIVISION

▲ Panzerkampfwagen II Ausf C (Sd Kfz 121)
Unknown formation

The 5th Panzer Division used a two-digit tactical number system (platoon and tank number) during the invasion of Poland. Their tanks were recognizable by the use of a yellow tank rhomboid painted on the turret sides.

Specifications
Crew: 3
Weight: 9.8 tonnes (8.9 tons)
Length: 4.81m (15.8ft)
Width: 2.22m (7.3ft)
Height: 1.99m (6.5ft)
Engine: Maybach HL62TR
Speed: 40km/hr (24.9mph)
Range: 200km (124.3 miles)
Radio: FuG5

▲ Panzerkampfwagen I Ausf B (Sd Kfz 101)
Unknown formation

In combat, the Pz.Kpfw I's task was to conduct reconnaissance. It was also used to protect the flanks of an advance from enemy infantry. This particular vehicle was knocked out at Pszczyna, fighting the 6th Polish Infantry Division.

Specifications
Crew: 2
Weight: 60.4 tonnes (5.8 tons)
Length: 4.42m (14.5ft)
Width: 2.06m (6.8ft)
Height: 1.72m (5.6ft)
Engine: Maybach NL38TR
Speed: 40km/hr (24.9mph)
Range: 170km (105.6 miles)
Radio: FuG2

▶ Panzerkampfwagen IV Ausf B (Sd Kfz 161)
Unknown formation

Small numbers of the Pz.Kpfw IV Ausf B reached service in time for the Polish campaign. They were issued to the 4th *Zugen* of *Leichte Panzerkompanies*.

Specifications
Crew: 5
Weight: 20.7 tonnes (18.8 tons)
Length: 5.92m (19.4ft)
Width: 2.83m (9.3ft)
Height: 2.68m (8.8ft)
Engine: Maybach HL120TR
Speed: 40km/hr (24.9mph)
Range: 200km (124.3 miles)
Radio: FuG5

⚔ *Fall Gelb*: the French campaign
10 May 1940

The 5th Panzer Division was withdrawn from Poland in December 1939.

Panzer Unit	Pz. I	Pz. II	Pz. III	Pz. IV	Pz. Bef.
15th Pz. Rgt.	51	61	24	16	15
31st Pz. Rgt.	46	59	28	16	11

ORGANIZATION

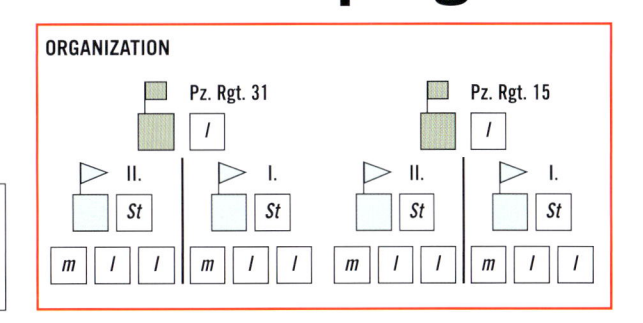

Pz. Rgt. 31 — II. St, I. St — m l l / m l l

Pz. Rgt. 15 — II. St, I. St — m l l / m l l

THE DIVISION MOVED towards the Ardennes in April 1940, where it formed part of General Herman Hoth's XV *Panzerkorps*. Crossing the Meuse at Dinant with Rommel's 7th Panzer Division, it was part of the tank force that swept towards the coast, cutting off the Allied armies at Dunkirk.

53

5TH PANZER DIVISION

▶ **Panzerkampfwagen IV Ausf D (Sd Kfz 161)**
4th Panzer Division, 1940

The Ausf D variant of the Pz.Kpfw IV was introduced in October 1939. The main improvements over earlier variants were the provision of thicker armour and the fitting of an external mantlet or gun shield for the 7.5cm (3in) KwK. Some 229 examples of this model were produced between October 1939 and May 1941.

Specifications
Crew: 5
Weight: 22 tonnes (20 tons)
Length: 5.92m (19.4ft)
Width: 2.84m (9.3ft)
Height: 2.68m (8.8ft)
Engine: Maybach HL120TRM
Speed: 40km/hr (24.9mph)
Range: 200km (124.3 miles)
Radio: FuG5

✕ War in the Balkans
6 APRIL 1941

Early in 1941, 5th Panzer Division was transferred to Field Marshal List's 12th Army in Romania and Bulgaria. The Division played a key part in Germany's conquest of the Balkans.

Crossing the Yugoslav border on 6 April, the 5th Panzer Division drove towards Skopje as part of *Panzergruppe* Kleist before turning northwards to seize Nis in company with the 11th Panzer Division. By 17 April, the Germans had captured Belgrade, and the Yugoslav government was forced to surrender.

Turning southwards, 5th Panzer drove through the centre of Greece. After passing through Lamia, the Division encountered a stubborn British rearguard on the ancient battlefield of Thermopylae. Forced to attack in single file, the division lost 20 Panzers in quick succession, and the delay allowed the British to withdraw safely.

Chasing the retreating British southwards, 5th Panzer crossed the Corinth canal on 28 April. The panzers headed for the beaches at Kalamata where an evacuation was taking place, and after a vicious fight captured the last 7000 British soldiers on the beach.

Panzer Unit	Pz. I	Pz. II	Pz. III	Pz. IV	Pz. Bef.
31st Pz. Rgt.	9	40	51	16	5

ORGANIZATION

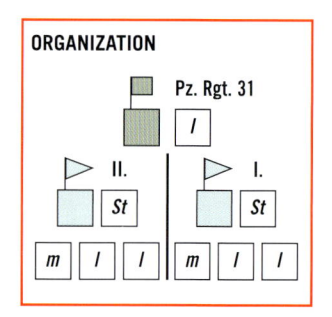

Pz. Rgt. 31

▶ **Panzerkampfwagen III Ausf E (Sd Kfz 141)**
Pz. Rgt 31 / I Battalion / 1st Company / 2nd Zug / tank number 3

Nineteen Pz.Kpfw III armed with the 3.7cm (1.5in) cannon were listed operational at the time of 5th Panzer's attack through the centre of Greece.

Specifications
Crew: 5
Weight: 21.5 tonnes (19.5 tons)
Length: 5.38m (17.7ft)
Width: 2.91m (9.5ft)
Height: 2.44m (8ft)
Engine: Maybach HL120TR
Speed: 40km/hr (24.9mph)
Range: 165km (102.5 miles)
Radio: FuG5

5TH PANZER DIVISION

▶ **Panzerkampfwagen IV Ausf F (Sd Kfz 161)**
Pz. Rgt 31 / I Battalion / 4th Company / 5th Zug / tank number 1
The rapid German attack in the Balkans eventually forced the Greeks to surrender, while the British fought a series of stubborn rearguard actions.

Specifications
Crew: 5	Engine: Maybach HL120TRM
Weight: 24.6 tonnes (22.3 tons)	Speed: 42km/hr (26mph)
Length: 5.92m (19.4ft)	Range: 200km (124.3 miles)
Width: 2.84m (9.3ft)	Radio: FuG5
Height: 2.68m (8.8ft)	

▶ **Schwere Panzerspähwagen (Fu) 8-rad (Sd Kfz 232)**
Unknown unit
The SdKfz 232 had driving controls at both front and rear, allowing for rapid manoeuvring of the vehicle in reverse.

Specifications
Crew: 4	Engine: Büssing-NAG L8V
Weight: 9.1 tonnes (8.3 tons)	Speed: 85km/hr (52.8mph)
Length: 5.85m (19.2ft)	Range: 300km (186.4 miles)
Width: 2.2m (7.2ft)	Radio: FuG12 plus
Height (no aerial): 2.35m (7.7ft)	fuG Spr Ger 'a'

The 704th was the last of the six *Infanteriegeschütz Abteilung* to still be listed in service in 1943.

Specifications
Crew: 4	Engine: Maybach NL38TR
Weight: 9.4 tonnes (8.5 tons)	Speed: 40km/hr (24.9mph)
Length: 4.67m (15.3ft)	Range: 140km (87 miles)
Width: 2.06m (6.8ft)	Armament: One 15cm (6in) sIG33 L/11
Height: 2.8m (9.2ft)	

▲ **15cm sIG33 (Sf) auf Panzerkampfwagen I Ausf B**
704th Schwere Infanteriegeschütz Abteilung
The 15cm (6in) sIG howitzer could be dismounted and used as towed artillery.

▶ **Mittlerer Schützenpanzerwagen I Ausf B (Sd Kfz 251/1)**
5th Schützen Regiment / II Battalion / 9th Company
The Sd Kfz 251/1 Ausf B eliminated the vision ports in the side of the vehicle. Early vehicles like this had unprotected machine gun mounts; armoured shields would become standard in new models, and were retrofitted to earlier variants.

Specifications
Crew: 2 plus 12 troops	2.16m (7ft) with MG shield
Weight: 9.9 tonnes (9 tons)	Engine: Maybach HL42TUKRM
Length: 5.98m (19.6ft)	Speed: 53km/hr (32.9mph)
Width: 2.1m (6.9ft)	Range: 300km (186.4 miles)
Height : 1.75m (5.7ft) or	Radio: FuG Spr Ger f

55

5TH PANZER DIVISION

▶ Panzerkampfwagen III Ausf J (Sd Kfz 141)
Pz. Rgt 31

The 5th Panzer Division was expecting to join the *Afrika Korps* in 1941. Its tanks had already been painted in desert colours when orders came to proceed immediately to Russia to compensate for the heavy losses in Panzers experienced by the *Wehrmacht*. The crew of this tank had added an improvised stowage rack on the tailplate.

Specifications
Crew: 5
Weight: 24 tonnes (21.5 tons)
Length: 6.28m (20.6ft)
Width: 2.95m (9.7ft)
Height: 2.5m (8.2ft)
Engine: Maybach HL120TRM
Speed: 40km/hr (24.9mph)
Range: 155km (96.3 miles)
Radio: FuG5

▶ Panzerkampfwagen III Ausf J (Sd Kfz 141)
Pz. Rgt 31

By December 1941, 5th Panzer was with Army Group Centre advancing towards Moscow. Like the rest of the *Wehrmacht*, its tank crews were ill-prepared for freezing temperatures and atrocious weather.

Weapons Specifications

Main Gun: 5cm (2in) KwK39 L/60	Co-axial MG: 7.92mm (0.3in) MG 34
Ammunition: 92 rounds	Hull MG: 7.92mm (0.3in) MG34
Traverse: 360° (manual)	Ammunition: 4950 rounds Patr
Elevation: -10° to +20°	SmK
Sight: TZF5e	MG sight: KgZF2

▶ Panzerkampfwagen III Ausf J (Sd Kfz 141)
Pz. Rgt 31

The Germans were unprepared for the Russian winter. Tanks and weapons froze, while winter clothing was in short supply. Even white paint was lacking: this tank has an improvised disruptive camouflage scheme using broad stripes of lime whitewash.

Armour Thickness
Turret: 57mm (2.2in) front, 30mm (1.2in) side, rear 30mm (1.2in), top 10mm (0.4in)
Superstructure: 50–70mm (2–2.8in) front, 30mm (1.2in) side; 50mm (2in) rear
Hull: 50mm (2in) front, 30mm (1.2in) side, 50mm (2in) rear, 16mm (0.6in) bottom
Mantlet: 50–70mm (2–2.8in)

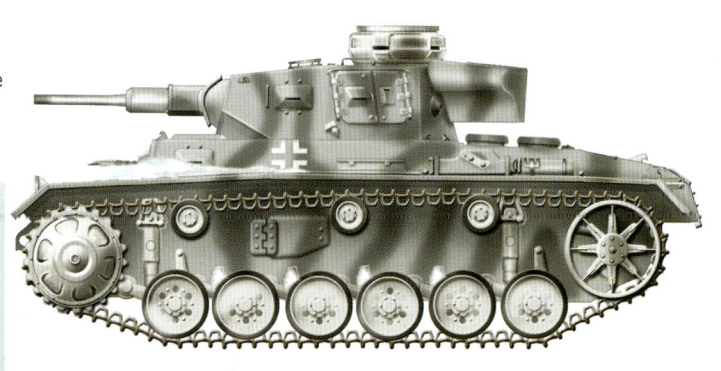

5TH PANZER DIVISION

▶ **Panzerkampfwagen III Ausf F (Sd Kfz 141)**
Pz. Rgt 31 / I Battalion / 3rd Company / 2nd Zug / tank number 1
The last 100 Pz.Kpfw III Ausf F had the 50mm (2in) KwK L/42 cannon, in place of the 37mm (1.5in) KwK L/46.5 . The 'Rommel Kit' stowage box, standard from the Ausf G onwards, was a retro-fit to this vehicle.

Specifications
Crew: 5
Weight: 21.8 tonnes (19.8 tons)
Length: 5.38m (17.7ft)
Width: 2.91m (9.5ft)
Height: 2.44m (8ft)
Engine: Maybach HL120TRM
Speed: 40km/hr (24.9mph)
Range: 165km (102.5 miles)
Radio: FuG5

Fall Blau: the Eastern Front
28 JUNE 1942

The 5th Panzer Division arrived on the Eastern Front just in time for Army Group Centre's unsuccessful drive on Moscow.

AFTER THE RETREAT from Moscow, 5th Panzer remained with 4th *Panzerarmee* around Gshatsk until May. In the summer of 1942, it was transferred to the control of 9th Army, taking part in the series of battles around Rshev. It remained in the region until the winter, when it was transferred to 3rd *Panzerarmee* at Vyasma.

In 1942, Army Group Centre, while far from being a sideshow, was no longer the main area of German operations. The High Command's attention was primarily on the Summer Offensive in the South, *Fall Blau*, and on the bid to seize Leningrad. Ordered to hold its positions, Army Group Centre spent most of 1942 trying to pinch off strips of Soviet-held territory which were interspersed with German fortified areas, or 'Hedgehogs'.

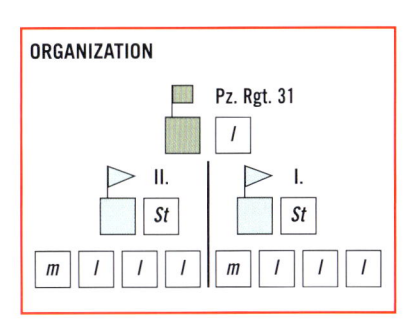

ORGANIZATION

Pz. Rgt. 31

Panzer Unit	Pz. II	Pz. III(kz)	Pz. IV(kz)	Pz. Bef.
31st Pz. Rgt.	26	55	13	9

▶ **Panzerbefehlswagen III Ausf E (Sd Kfz 266-267-268)**
Pz. Rgt 31 / I Battalion / Stabskompanie / Signal Platoon / tank number 2
The Russians became adept in locating and knocking out command tanks, which were easy to recognize by their frame antennae. As a result, Panzer commanders were forced to travel in normal Panzers, with signal officers riding in a second tank close by.

Specifications
Crew: 5
Weight: 21.5 tonnes (19.5 tons)
Length: 5.38m (17.7ft)
Width: 2.91m (9.5ft)
Height: 2.44m (8ft)
Engine: Maybach HL120TRM
Speed: 40km/hr (24.9mph)
Range: 185km (115 miles)
Radio: FuG6 plus FuG 2 (266) or FuG 8 (267) or FuG7 (268)

5TH PANZER DIVISION

The last offensive
1 JULY 1943

In the six months prior to the Battle of Kursk, the 5th Panzer Division had been involved in heavy fighting as part of Army Group Centre in Vyasma and Demjansk.

IN MARCH 1943, THE DIVISION was transferred to the 2nd *Panzerarmee* in the Orel sector. For the Kursk Offensive, the army was tasked with providing flank security to the attack by 9th Army, but it came under heavy Soviet attack and was forced to withdraw as the offensive was called off by Hitler.

Over the next year, 5th Panzer Division retreated through Bryansk, Gomel and the Pripjet Marshes to Poland, where it had started three years before. After surviving the massive Soviet offensives of 1944, it ended the war fighting in Latvia, in the Courland pocket and in East Prussia, where it finally surrendered to the Red Army in April 1945 near Danzig.

ORGANIZATION

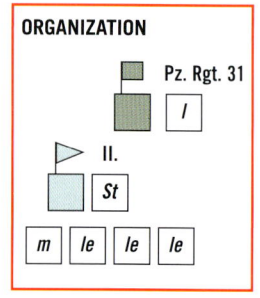

Panzer Unit	Pz. II	Pz. III(75)	Pz. IV(lg)	Pz. Bef.
31st Pz. Rgt.	0	17	76	9

▶ **Leichter Panzerspähwagen (Fu) (Sd Kfz 261)**
77th Panzer Signal Battalion
The Sd Kfz 261 was identical to the Sd Kfz 223 light armoured car, except that it lacked a turret. The vehicle had an FuG10 radio capable of transmitting signals up to 40km (24.9 miles) using key or 10km (6.2 miles) using voice. A second set, the FuG Spr, was used for inter-vehicle communication.

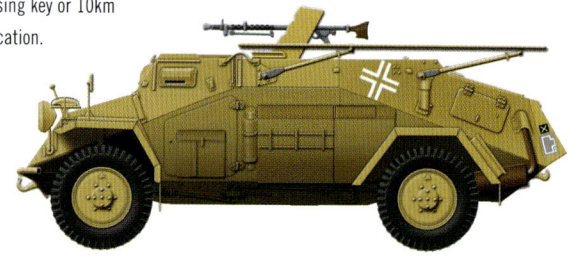

Specifications
Crew: 4
Weight: 4.7 tonnes (4.3 tons)
Length: 4.83m (15.8ft)
Width: 1.99m (6.5ft)
Height: 1.78m (5.8ft)
Engine: Horch 3.5l or 3.8l
Speed: 85km/hr (52.8mph)
Range: 310km (192.6 miles)
Radio: FuG Spr Ger 'a' plus FuG7 or FuG12

The standard military map symbol for self-propelled artillery was used to identify Hummels of the 3rd Battalion, 103rd Panzer Artillery Regiment.

▼ **15cm (6in) Schwere Panzerhaubitze auf Fahrgestell Panzerkampfwagen III/IV (Sf) (Sd Kfz 165)**
116th Panzer Artillery Regiment / 1st (self-propelled) Battalion
The Hummel self-propelled howitzer was based on a modified Panzer IV hull.

Specifications
Crew: 6
Weight: 26.5 tonnes (24 tons)
Length: 7.17m (23.5ft)
Width: 2.97m (9.7ft)
Height: 2.81m (9.2ft)
Engine: HL120TRM
Speed: 42km/hr (26mph)
Range: 215km (133.6 miles)
Radio: FuG Spr 1

5TH PANZER DIVISION

◀ **Fiat-Ansaldo Carro Armato L 6/40**
3rd Italian Armoured Battalion (Attached)
From November 1943 to September 1944, an Italian battalion was listed in the Division order of battle. The L6/40 was armed with one 2cm (0.8in) Breda cannon. Secondary armament consisted of one 8mm (0.3in) Breda machine gun.

Specifications
Crew: 2
Weight: 7.5 tonnes (6.8 tons)
Length: 3.78m (12.4ft)
Width: 1.92m (6.3ft)
Height: 2.03m (6.7ft)
Engine: SPA 18 D
Speed: 42km/hr (26mph)
Range: 200km (124.3 miles)
Radio: RF 1 CA

This version of the National Insignia was standard between 1940 and 1945.

Specifications
Crew: 5
Weight: 50.2 tonnes (45.5 tons)
Length: 8.86 m (29ft)
Width: 3.4m (11.2ft)
Height: 2.98m (9.8ft)
Engine: Maybach HL230P30
Speed: 46km/hr (28.6mph)
Range: 200km (124.3 miles)
Radio: FuG5

▲ **Panzerkampfwagen V Ausf G (Sd Kfz 171)**
Pz. Rgt 31 / I Battalion / 1st Company / 3rd Zug / tank number 5
Although a superb tank, the complex and expensive Panther was built in much smaller numbers than the American M4 Sherman or the Soviet T-34, both of which were available in huge quantities.

▶ **Panzerkampfwagen IV Ausf H (Sd Kfz 161/2)**
Pz. Rgt 31 / II Battalion / 8th Company / 3rd Zug / tank number 1
This vehicle was in action in West Prussia in March 1945. A month later, the 5th Panzer Division surrendered to the Soviets near Danzig.

Specifications
Crew: 5
Weight: 27.6 tonnes (25 tons)
Length: 7.02m (23ft)
Width: 2.88m (9.4ft)
Height: 2.68m (8.8ft)
Engine: Maybach HL120TRM
Speed: 38km/hr (23.6mph)
Range: 210km (130.5 miles)
Radio: FuG5

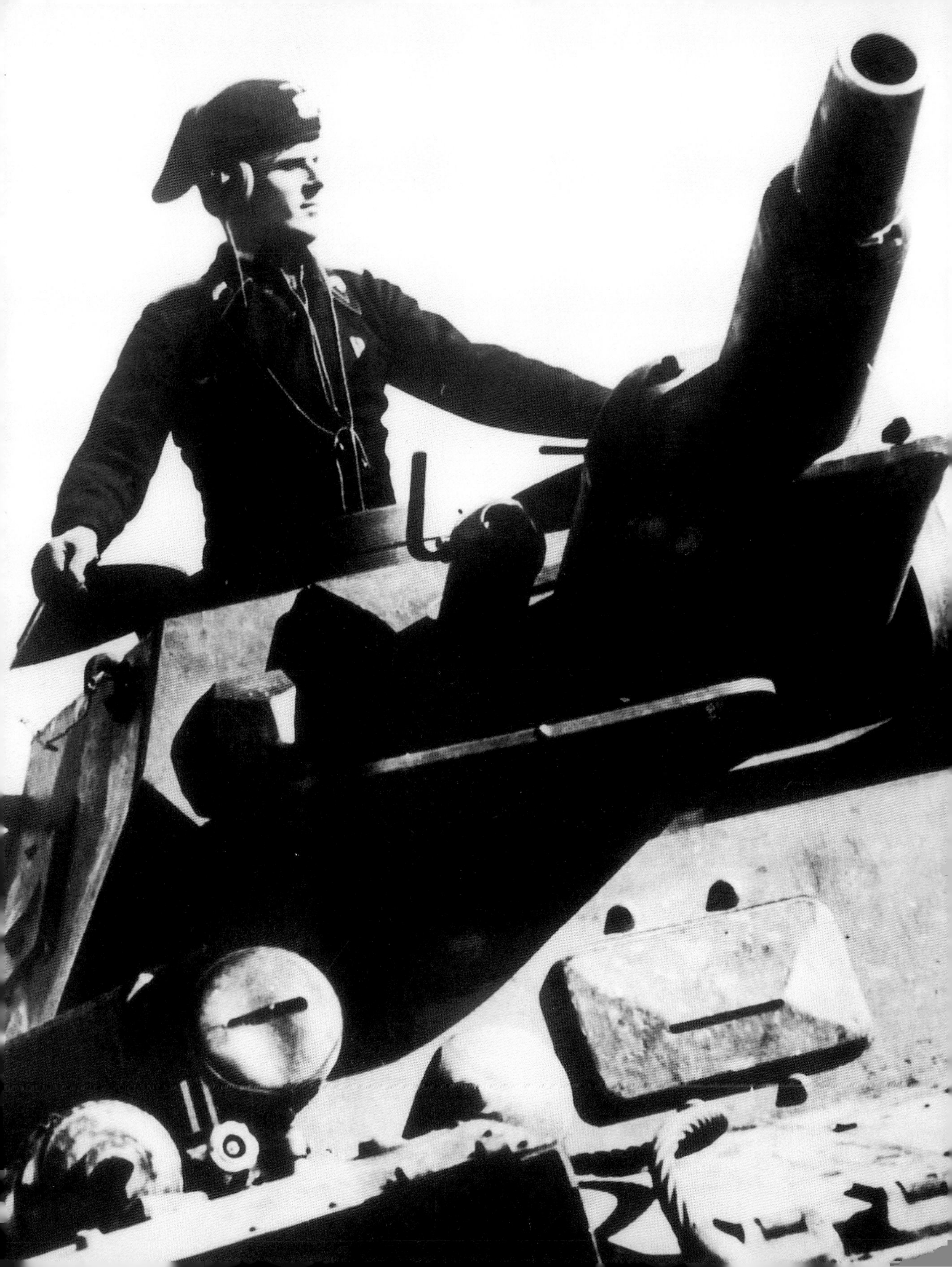

Chapter 2

1939 Panzer Divisions

The initial growth of Germany's *Panzerwaffe* came to a brief halt in the late 1930s. However, as war loomed, even the most reactionary officers in the General Staff realized that armoured formations were the way of the future, and the expansion of the Panzer arm continued at an even greater pace. The first new Panzer divisions were formed in 1939 from the so-called '*Leichte*', or Light, divisions, which had been created by the cavalry, and which were now converted into fully-fledged armoured divisions.

◀ **Growth of the *Panzerwaffe***
Although powerful fighting vehicles like the Panzer IV were in service with the German Army by 1939, the small tanks with which the *Panzerwaffe* had learned its trade served far longer than expected.

6th Panzer Division

The 6th Panzer Division was formed at Wuppertal in October 1939, by converting the 1st *Leichte Division*, which had fought in the Polish campaign.

THE LIGHT DIVISIONS were a product of the internal politics of the *Wehrmacht*. For centuries, the cavalry had been the premier arm of the German Army, officered almost exclusively by aristocrats. Senior cavalrymen had been most vocal in their opposition to the Panzers, fearing that the new arm would detract from their own standing. That opposition had almost crippled the early *Panzerwaffe*, since the cavalry insisted on controlling reconnaissance units. Similarly, the infantry controlled the *Schützen* units, and the artillery controlled the guns of the early Panzer divisions.

In 1938, the *Wehrmacht* underwent a major upheaval. Hitler dismissed the War Minister, General von Blomberg, and the Commander-in-Chief, General von Fritsch. The *Führer* took direct control of the Armed Forces, and Hitler was a Panzer enthusiast.

Cavalry Panzers

Clearly, Panzers were the way of the future. The cavalrymen formed four *Leichte*, or Light, Divisions. These were essentially motorized infantry units with four rifle battalions, to which was added a single tank battalion (which by the outbreak of war in 1939 had been increased to two battalions in a Panzer regiment). The rifle battalions were called *Kavallerieschützen*, or Cavalry Rifle units. Finding tanks for these new units stretched Germany's limited tank-building capability. Some tanks were taken from those destined for new Panzer units, but more than half came from newly acquired Czech stocks.

As it crossed the Polish border on 1 September 1939, the 1st *Leichte* Division, commanded by *Generalleutnant* Friedrich-Wilhelm von Löper, had 65 Pz.Kpfw IIs, 41 Pz.KpfW IVs, 112 Czech-built Pz.Kpfw 35(t)s and eight Panzer 35 command tanks, for a total of 226 Panzers.

INSIGNIA

Standard tactical insignia used on vehicles of the 6th Panzer Division in 1940.

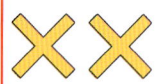

As more divisions formed, the similarity of the standard tactical symbols became confusing. 6th Panzer adopted this new insignia in 1941.

An additional tactical symbol applied to vehicles of the 6th Panzer Division during the advance on Moscow in 1941.

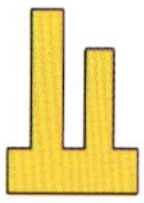

6th Panzer, June 1943. A completely new set of symbols were introduced for divisions taking part in the Battle of Kursk.

▼ **Armoured Artillery**
As the war progressed, the Panzers were joined on the frontline by armoured and self-propelled artillery pieces and assault guns like the *Sturmgeschütz*.

Commanders

General der Panzertruppen W. Kempf
(18 Oct 1939 – 6 Jan 1941)

Generalleutnant F. Landgraf
(6 Jan 1941 – June 1941)

General der Panzertruppen W. Ritter von Thoma
(June 1941 – 15 Sept 1941)

Generalleutnant F. Landgraf
(15 Sept 1941 – 1 Apr 1942)

Generaloberst E. Raus
(1 Apr 1942 – 7 Feb 1943)

Generalleutnant W. von Hunersdorff
(7 Feb 1943 – 16 July 1943)

Generalmajor W. Crisolli
(16 July 1943 – 21 Aug 1943)

Generalleutnant R. Freiherr von Waldenfels
(21 Aug 1943 – 8 Feb 1944)

Generalleutnant W. Marcks
(8 Feb 1944 – 21 Feb 1944)

Generalleutnant R. Freiherr von Waldenfels
(21 Feb 1944 – 13 Mar 1944)

Generalleutnant W. Denkert
(13 Mar 1944 – 28 Mar 1944)

Generalleutnant R. Freiherr von Waldenfels
(28 Mar 1944 – 23 Nov 1944)

Oberst F. Jurgens
(23 Nov 1944 – 20 Jan 1945)

Generalleutnant R. Freiherr von Waldenfels
(20 Jan 1945 – 8 May 1945)

6TH PANZER DIVISION

Fall Weiss: the invasion of Poland
1 SEPTEMBER 1939

Although relatively lightly equipped with tanks, 1st *Leichte Division* was used as a regular Panzer division during the Invasion of Poland.

THE 1ST *LEICHTE* DIVISION was assigned with the 3rd *Leichte* Division to General von Reichenau's 10th Army, part of General von Rundstedt's Army Group South. In the initial stages of the invasion, 1st *Leichte* was part of the 10th Army reserve as the Germans drove to encircle the Polish armies at Radom. By 5 September, they were already halfway to Warsaw. The Poles launched a counterattack out of the Pomorze pocket, but the Germans encircled the Poles on the Bzura, using 1st Panzer together with 1st, 2nd and 3rd *Leichte* Divisions.

After the fall of Poland, the *Leichte* divisions were reorganized as full Panzer divisions.

Panzer Unit	Pz. II	Pz. 35(t)	Pz. IV	Pz.Bef.35(t)
11st Pz. Rgt.	45	75	27	6
Pz.Abt.65	2	37	14	2

▶ **Panzerkampfwagen 35(t)**
1 Leichte Division Pz. Rgt 11 / I Battalion / 2nd Company / Company HQ tank of Hptm Mecke

When Germany occupied the Czech Republic, it immediately pressed into service all their war material, which included 219 Pz.Kpfw 35(t) light tanks. It was much more powerful than the PzKpfw I or II, with a 37mm (1.5in) gun renowned for its accuracy. In German service, the tank was modified to accept two radio sets and an extra crewman – a loader – was added.

Specifications
Crew: 4
Weight: 11.6 tonnes (10.5 tons)
Length: 4.9m (16ft)
Width: 2.1m (6.9ft)
Height: 2.35m (7.7ft)
Engine: Skoda T11
Speed: 35km/hr (21.7mph)
Range: 190km (118 miles)
Radio: FuG37(t)

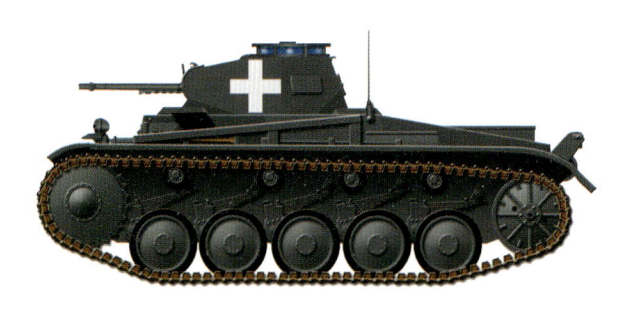

▼ **Panzerkampfwagen II Ausf C (Sd Kfz 121)**
1 Leichte Division

The cavalry branch of the German Army, which claimed descent from the Teutonic Knights of medieval times, fought tenaciously for its place in twentieth-century warfare. The creation of the *Leichte* Divisions was a political compromise to allow the aristocrat *Kavallerie* to play its part in mechanized warfare. The cavalrymen considered their mechanized infantry units to be dragoons or mounted infantry, who had simply replaced their horses with trucks and tanks.

Specifications
Crew: 3
Weight: 9.8 tonnes (8.9 tons)
Length: 4.81m (15.8ft)
Width: 2.22m (7.3ft)
Height: 1.99m (6.5ft)
Engine: Maybach HL62TR
Speed: 40km/hr (24.9mph)
Range: 200km (124.3 miles)
Radio: FuG5

6TH PANZER DIVISION

⚐ *Fall Gelb*: the French campaign
10 May 1939

Experience in Poland had shown the *Leichte* Divisions had not been a success. On 10 October, they were reorganized, and 1st *Leichte* Division became 6th Panzer Division.

AFTER REORGANIZING as a full Panzer Division (though still operating with a large number of Czech tanks), 6th Panzer Division was assigned to Reinhardt's XLI *Panzerkorps* for the assault on the west. Along with the corps commanded by Hoth and Guderian, XLI *Panzerkorps* formed the armoured spearhead of the German drive through the Ardennes. 6th Panzer met with some difficulties on the way to the Meuse, mainly caused by congestion. Finally crossing on 15 May, it raced through northern France, trying to catch up with Guderian's Panzers. In the process, it overran and largely destroyed the French 2nd *Division des Cuirassées Rapide*, which had been scattered by the German advance.

Panzer Unit	Pz. II	Pz. 35(t)	Pz. IV	Pz.Bef.35(t)
6th Pz. Div.	60	118	31	14

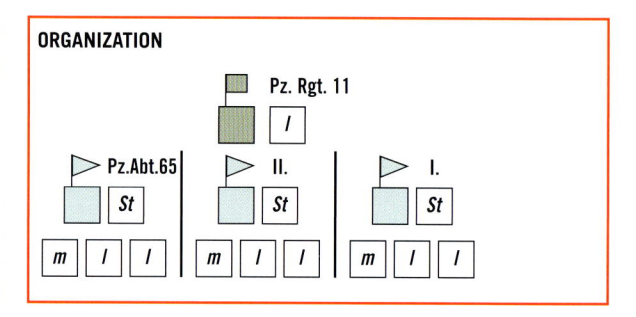

ORGANIZATION

▶ Panzerkampfwagen IV Ausf D (Sd Kfz 161)
Unknown formation

In October 1939, the *Leichte* Division was reorganized as the 6th Panzer Division. In the early stages of the war, each tank's tactical number was painted onto a black metal plate shaped like the rhomboid used as the map symbol for armour.

Specifications

Crew: 5	Engine: Maybach HL120TRM
Weight: 22 tonnes (20 tons)	Speed: 40km/hr (24.9mph)
Length: 5.92m (19.4ft)	Range: 200km (124.3 miles)
Width: 2.84m (9.3ft)	Radio: FuG5
Height: 2.68m (8.8ft)	

▶ Panzerkampfwagen 35(t)
Pz. Rgt 11 / II Battalion / 5th Company / Company HQ

Between 1935 and 1938, 424 Panzer 35(t)s were produced and the *Wehrmacht* pressed 219 into service. The Pz.Kpfw 35(t) was armed with one 37mm (1.5in) KwK34(t) L/40 cannon and carried a mix of 72 high explosive and antitank rounds.

Weapons Specifications

Main armament: 3.7cm (1.4in) KwK34(t) L/34	Co-axial MG: 7.92mm (0.3in) MG37(t)
Ammunition: 72 rounds	Hull MG: 7.92mm (0.3in) MG37(t)
Traverse: 360° (manual)	Ammunition: 1800 rounds
Elevation: -10° to +25°	MG sight: MGZF(t)
Sight: TZF(t)	

6TH PANZER DIVISION

▶ Panzerkampfwagen IV Ausf E (Sd Kfz 161)

Unknown formation

The invasion of the Low Countries caused the reaction planned for by the German High Command: it drew the French and British armies north into Belgium. The powerful German armoured thrust though the Ardennes, followed by a race for the coast, then came as a surprise, cutting through Allied lines of communication like a sickle cutting through long grass.

Specifications
Crew: 5
Weight: 23.2 tonnes (21 tons)
Length: 5.92m (19.4ft)
Width: 2.84m (9.3ft)
Height: 2.68m (8.8ft)
Engine: Maybach HL120TRM
Speed: 42km/hr (26mph)
Range: 200km (124.3 miles)
Radio: FuG5

▶ Panzerkampfwagen 35(t)

65th Battalion / Stabskompanie / Signal Platoon / HQ tank of Oberstleutnant Schenk

The 65th Tank Battalion was an independent unit within the 6th Panzer Division, and had a different set of tactical numbers. A01 indicates the first tank of the command company. The crew consisted of a driver, machine gunner/radioman, loader and the tank commander, who also had to operate the main gun.

Armour Specifications
Turret: 25mm (1in) front, 15mm (0.6in) side, 15mm (0.6in) rear, 8mm (0.3in) top
Superstructure: 25mm (1in) front, 16mm (0.6in) side, 15mm (0.6in) rear, 8mm (0.3in) top
Hull: 25mm (1in) front, 16mm (0.6in) side 16mm (0.6in) back, 8mm (0.3in) underside
Gun mantlet: 25mm (1in)

▶ Panzerbefehlswagen 35(t)

65th Battalion / Stabskompanie / Signal Platoon / tank of Oberstleutnant Marquart

The *stabskompanie* of the 65th Battalion operated Panzer 35(t) command tanks. These were equipped with two-way radios in addition to the receive-only sets carried by all German tanks. The 10-watt FuG37(t) transmitter/receiver had a voice range of about 1 km (0.6 miles).

Specifications
Crew: 4
Weight: 11.6 tonnes (10.5 tons)
Length: 4.9m (16ft)
Width: 2.1m (6.9ft)
Height: 2.35m (7.7ft)
Engine: Skoda T11
Speed: 35km/hr (21.7mph)
Range: 190km (118 miles)
Radio: FuG37(t)

65

6TH PANZER DIVISION

✖✖ *Barbarossa*: the attack on Russia
22 JUNE 1941

Initially assigned to Army Group North's reserve during Operation *Barbarossa*, 6th Panzer Division went into action with XLI *Panzerkorps*, part of the 4th *Panzergruppe*.

FIGHTING WITH GREAT FEROCITY, the division was one of the first to pierce the Stalin Line and reach Leningrad, where it took part in the early stages of the siege of the city. In October 1941, the division was transferred to LVI *Panzerkorps*, part of the 3rd *Panzergruppe* with Army Group Centre. Suffering heavy losses in the drive on Moscow and in the Soviet counterattack that followed, the 6th Panzer Division was transferred to the 9th Army, where it took part in the fighting around Rzhev. As the Soviet winter offensive petered out, the division was transferred to France for rest and rebuilding.

ORGANIZATION

Panzer Unit	Pz. II	Pz. 35(t)	Pz. IV	Pz.Bef35(t)	Pz. Bef.
6th Pz. Div.	47	155	30	5	8

▶ **Panzerbefehlswagen III Ausf E (Sd Kfz 266-267-268)**
Pz. Rgt 11 / I Battalion / Stabskompanie / Signal Platoon / signal officer tank
45 Pz. Bef Ausf E were produced between July 1939 and February 1940.

Specifications
Crew: 5
Weight: 21.5 tonnes (19.5 tons)
Length: 5.38m (17.7ft)
Width: 2.91m (9.5ft)
Height: 2.44m (8ft)
Engine: Maybach HL120TR
Speed: 40km/hr (24.9mph)
Range: 165km (102.5 miles)
Radio: FuG6 plus FuG2 or FuG7 or FuG8

▶ **Panzerkampfwagen 35(t)**
Pz. Rgt 11 / II Battalion / Stabskompanie / Signal Platoon / commander's command tank

The 6th Panzer Division served with Army Group North. By August 1941, the Division had lost 35 Panzers. Damaged tanks could be repaired only by cannibalizing others, as parts for older Czech tanks were no longer being made. By the end of the winter, most Pz.Kpfw 35(t) were lost or out of action.

Specifications
Crew: 4
Weight: 11.6 tonnes (10.5 tons)
Length: 4.9m (16ft)
Width: 2.1m (6.9ft)
Height: 2.35m (7.7ft)
Engine: Skoda T11
Speed: 35km/hr (21.7mph)
Range: 190km (118 miles)
Radio: FuG37(t)

6TH PANZER DIVISION

▶ **4.7cm PaK(t) (Sf) auf Panzerkampfwagen I Ausf B**
41st Panzerjäger Battalion

The Czech 4.7cm (1.9in) antitank gun mounted on an obsolete Pz.Kpfw I chassis proved to be an effective weapon until confronted with the Russian T-34 and KV tanks, which started to appear in numbers at the end of 1941. The five-sided gun shield is characteristic of an early production model.

Specifications

Crew: 3	Engine: Maybach NL38TR
Weight: 7 tonnes (6.4 tons)	Speed: 40km/hr (24.9mph)
Length: 4.42m (14.5ft)	Range: 140km (87 miles)
Width: 2.06m (6.8ft)	Radio: FuG2
Height: 2.25m (7.4ft)	

▶ **Panzerkampfwagen II Ausf F (Sd Kfz 121)**
Unknown formation

The Ausf F was a version of the Panzer II with extra armour. This variant had 30mm (1.2in) of armour plate protecting all front areas of the tank, which was more than double the thickness of armour carried by the earlier Ausf C.

Specifications

Crew: 3	Engine: Maybach HL62TR
Weight: 10.5 tonnes (9.5 tons)	Speed: 40km/hr (24.9mph)
Length: 4.81m (15.8ft)	Range: 200km (124.3 miles)
Width: 2.28m (7.5ft)	Radio: FuG5
Height: 2.15m (7ft)	

▶ **Panzerkampfwagen 35(t)**
Pz. Rgt 11 / II Battalion / 7th Company / 2nd Zug / tank number 2

Designed to be manoeuvrable and able to travel great distances, the Pz.Kpfw 35(t) used a pneumatically-operated transmission. This should have been ideal for operations in Russia, but it proved to be a great weakness when confronted by the harsh conditions of the Russian winter.

Specifications

Crew: 4	Engine: Skoda T11
Weight: 11.6 tonnes (10.5 tons)	Speed: 35km/hr (21.7mph)
Length: 4.9m (16ft)	Range: 190km (118 miles)
Width: 2.1m (6.9ft)	Radio: FuG37(t)
Height: 2.35m (7.7ft)	

6TH PANZER DIVISION

▶ **Mittlerer Gepanzerter Beobachtungskraftwagen (Sd Kfz 254)**
76th Panzer Artillery Regiment / 76th (mot) Observation Battery

Designed for the Austrian army, the SdKfz 254 was a wheel-cum-track medium armoured observation post. This example served at Leningrad in 1941.

Specifications
Crew: 7
Weight: 7 tonnes (6.4 tons)
Length: 4.56m (15ft)
Width: 2.02m (6.6ft)
Height: 1.88m (6.2ft)
Engine: Saurer CRDv diesel
Speed: 60km/hr (37.3mph)
Range: 500km (310.7 miles)
Radio: FuG8, FuG4, FuG Spr Ger 1

▶ **Gepanzerter Selbstfahrlafette für Sturmgeschütz 7.5cm Kanone Ausf B (Sd Kfz 142)**
Unknown formation

6th Panzer was transferred to 3.*Pz.Gruppe*, Army Group Centre, in October 1941, and was nearly wiped out during the winter of 1941–42. It was re-equipped in France in 1942, acquiring a battalion of assault guns in the process.

Specifications
Crew: 4
Weight: 21.6 tonnes (19.6 tons)
Length: 5.38m (17.7ft)
Width: 2.92m (9.6ft)
Height: 1.95m (6.4ft)
Engine: Maybach HL120TR
Speed: 40km/hr (24.9mph)
Range: 160km (99.4 miles)
Radio: FuG15 or FuG16

During the assault on Moscow, September–October 1941, the Division used a yellow war hatchet as a temporary divisional insignia.

▼ **Panzerbefehlswagen III Ausf H (Sd Kfz 266-267-268)**
Pz. Rgt 11 / I Regimental Staff Company

By November 1942, the bulk of 6th Panzer's tanks were Pz.Kpfw IIIs.

Specifications
Crew: 5
Weight: 24 tonnes (21.8 tons)
Length: 5.4m (17.7ft)
Width: 2.95m (9.7ft)
Height: 2.44m (8ft)
Engine: Maybach HL120TRM
Speed: 40km/hr (24.9mph)
Range: 165km (102.5 miles)
Radio: FuG6 plus FuG2 or FuG7 or FuG8

6TH PANZER DIVISION

▶ **Schwerer Panzerfunkwagen (Sd Kfz 263) 6-Rad**
82nd Nachtrichen Abteillung (Signal Battalion)

Syscheva, March 1942. This armoured car bears the name of 'Peterle' next to the division symbol. Although similar to the Sd Kfz 231, the Sd Kfz 263 had a fixed turret and it was not intended as a scout car. It was primarily a command post, equipped with long-range radios, and it was issued to signals units within most armoured formations.

Specifications
Crew: 5
Weight: 6.6 tonnes (6 tons)
Length: 5.57m (18.3ft)
Width: 1.82m (6ft)
Height: 2.25m/7.4ft (no aerial)
Engine: Büssing-NAG G or DB M09 or Magirus s88
Speed: 70km/hr (43.5mph)
Range: 300km (186.4 miles)
Radio: FuG Spr Ger 'a'

✕✕ The last summer offensive
1 July 1943

The Division returned from France after refitting at the end of 1942. It arrived on the Eastern Front to join Army Group South just in time for the attempt to rescue the 6th Army at Stalingrad.

While refitting, the division lost the 65th Battalion, which was merged with the 11th Panzer Regiment. Assigned to Hoth's 4th *Panzerarmee*, it led the attack on the Soviets encircling Stalingrad, penetrating to the Tschir river less than 21 km (13 miles) from the city before being stopped. During the Battle of Kursk, it served with Army Detachment *Kempf*, supporting 4th *Panzerarmee* in the southern sector. Afterwards, the Division was heavily engaged around Kharkov and in the retreat to the Dnieper, fighting back through the Southern Ukraine. In 1945, it saw action at Budapest, then retreated through Austria to Moravia, surrendering there to the Red Army.

ORGANIZATION
Pz. Rgt. 11 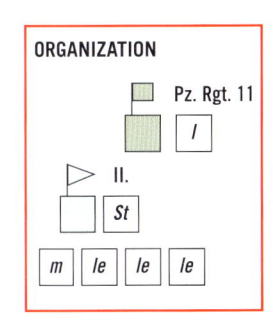
I
II.
St
m le le le

Panzer Unit	Pz. II	Pz. III	Pz. IV	Pz. Bef.	Flmmpz
11th Pz. Rgt.	13	52	32	6	14

▶ **Panzerkampfwagen III Ausf M (Sd Kfz 141/1)**
Pz. Rgt 11 / II Battalion / 6th Company / HQ tank

In 1943, 6th Panzer listed 34 Pz.Kpfw III armed with the long 5cm (2in) KwK39 L/60 as operational. The 6th participated in the retaking of the city of Kharkov that year and formed part of the southern pincer attack at Kursk during Operation *Zitadelle*.

Specifications
Crew: 5
Weight: 25 tonnes (22.7 tons)
Length: 6.41m (21ft)
Width: 2.95m (9.7ft)
Height: 2.5m (8.2ft)
Engine: Maybach HL120TRM
Speed: 40km/hr (24.9mph)
Range: 155km (96.3 miles)
Radio: FuG5

69

6TH PANZER DIVISION

▶ **Panzerkampfwagen III Ausf M (Sd Kfz 141/1)**
Pz. Rgt 11 / II Battalion / 6th Company / Company HQ tank number 2

The second tank in the Company HQ section was usually assigned to the unit's adjutant. In the event that the company commander's tank was damaged, he could use this tank to continue in control of the battle.

Weapons Specifications

Main gun: 5cm (2in) KwK39 L/60
Ammunition: 92 rounds
Traverse: 360° (manual)
Elevation: -10° to +20°
Sight: TZF5e
Co-axial MG: 7.92mm (0.3in) MG34
Hull MG: 7.92mm (0.3in) MG34
Ammunition: 3750 rounds of Patr SmK
MG sight: KgZF2

▶ **Panzerkampfwagen III Ausf N (Sd Kfz 141/2)**
Pz. Rgt 11 / II Battalion / 7th Company / 3rd Zug / tank number 1

The Ausf N was armed with a short 7.5cm (3in) KwK L/24, which fired a much more powerful high explosive round than the gun it replaced, the 5cm (2in) L/60. The letters 'OP' in the side of the tank may refer to the 11th Regiment commander, *Oberst* von Oppein-Bronikowski.

Specifications

Crew: 5
Weight: 25.4 tonnes (23 tons)
Length: 5.65m (18.5ft)
Width: 2.95m (9.7ft)
Height: 2.5m (8.2ft)
Engine: Maybach HL120TRM
Speed: 40km/hr (24.9mph)
Range: 155km (96.3 miles)
Radio: FuG5

Panzer-Flamm-Zug K.St.N.1190

Infantry flamethrowers had been in use since World War I, and were horribly effective in close-range combat dealing with enemy fortifications and in built-up areas. Mounting a flamethrower in an armoured vehicle meant that larger weapons and much more incendiary fuel could be carried. In 1942, it was decided to equip each panzer division with a flamethrower platoon, and in 1943 the theoretical establishment of such platoons was to include seven Panzerkampfwagen III (Fl) tanks. One hundred tanks were produced between February and April 1943, and three divisions had operational *Flamm-Zugen* by the time of the Kursk battles.

6TH PANZER DIVISION

▶ **Panzerkampfwagen III (Fl) (Sd Kfz 141/3)**
Pz. Rgt 11 / II Battalion / 8th Company / 5th Flamm Zug / tank number 1

The 8th Company at Kursk had a *Panzer-Flamm-Zug* attached as its 5th Platoon. Experience in Stalingrad suggested the need for a dedicated Panzer armed with a flamethrower for use in close-range urban combat.

Specifications
Crew: 3
Weight: 25.4 tonnes (23 tons)
Length: 6.41m (21ft)
Width: 2.95m (9.7ft)
Height: 2.5m (8.2ft)
Engine: Maybach HL120TRM
Speed: 40km/hr (24.9mph)
Range: 155km (96.3 miles)
Radio: FuG5 (plus FuG2 in platoon commander's tank)

PanzerKompanie 'Panther'

The arrival of the Panzerkampfwagen V Panther in increasing numbers at the end of 1943 brought about a major reorganization of the armoured component of a Panzer division. It now consisted of a single panzer regiment of two battalions, the first equipped with Panthers and the second with Panzer IVs. The Panther battalion deployed one staff company with five Panthers and three command tanks, and four tank companies, each with a two-tank company HQ and three or four five-tank platoons, for a battalion total of between 72 and 91 tanks. In January 1944, the 1st Battalion of the 11th Panzer Regiment was converted to a Panther unit.

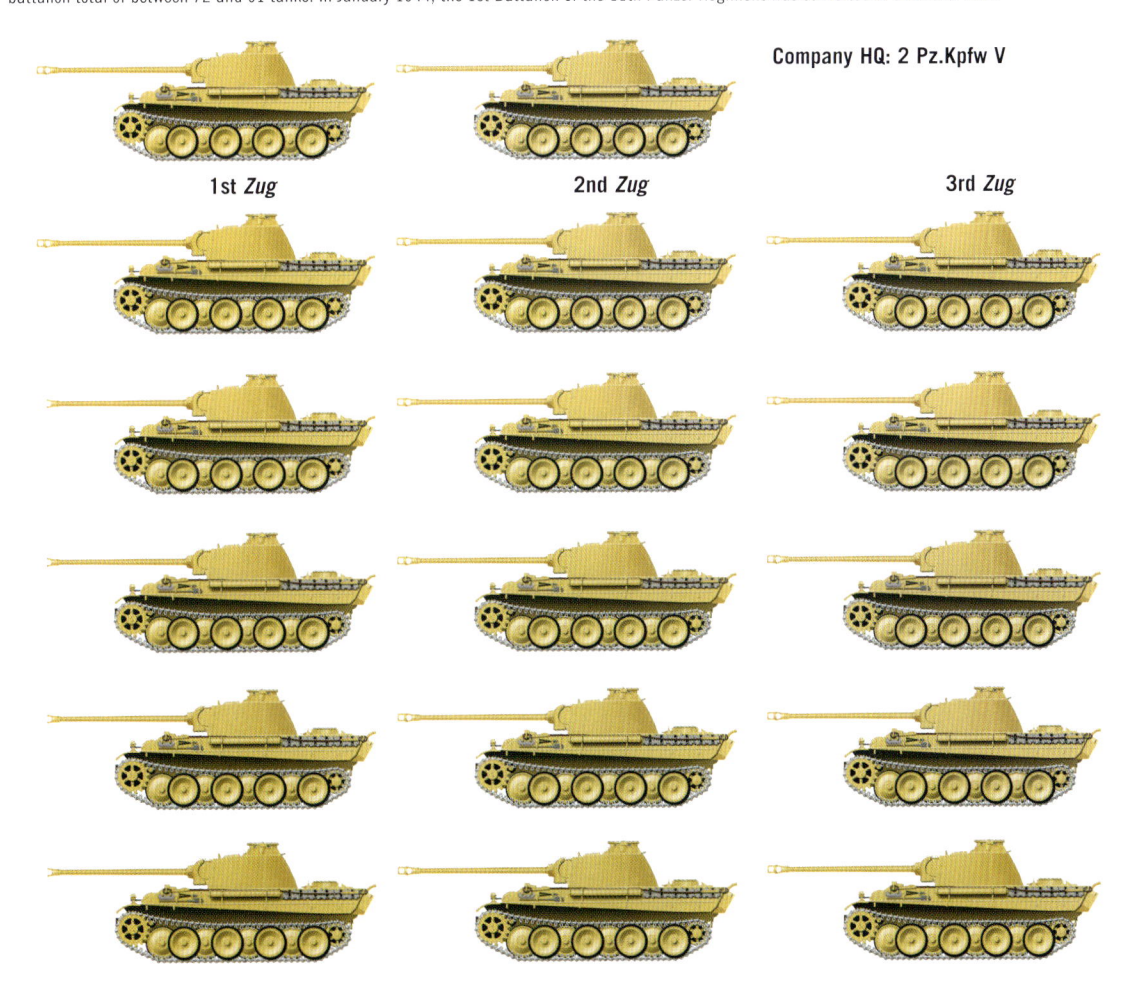

Company HQ: 2 Pz.Kpfw V

1st *Zug*   2nd *Zug*   3rd *Zug*

6TH PANZER DIVISION

✖✖ Schwer Panzergruppe Bake
1943–1945

Early in 1944, *Oberstleutnant* Dr. Franz Bake of the 6th Panzer Division was assigned to command a special heavy Panzer unit bearing his own name.

FRANZ BAKE was one of the outstanding tank commanders of World War II. An infantry corporal during World War I, he qualified as a dentist in the 1920s, before joining the reserves in the 1930s. Called up for World War II, he served as an antitank platoon leader in France in 1940. He became a tank commander before the invasion of the Soviet Union, rising through the command ranks to lead Panzer Regiment 11 of 6th Panzer Division in November 1943.

Panzer Regiment Bake

Early in 1944, Bake was assigned to command a special armoured unit that would serve as a 'Fire Brigade'. Incorporating the 503rd Heavy Panzer *Abteilung*, Panzer Regiment Bake included 34 Tiger Is, 123 Panthers and a number of Hummel self-propelled guns from 1st Battalion, 88th Artillery Division. The Fire Brigade concept was intended to encourage enemy armour to penetrate the German front and then to cut them off from their supporting infantry. The German infantry would seal the gap while the Panzer force would attack from the flank and rear, destroying the Soviet tanks.

Bake's personal heroism was rewarded when Swords were added to the Knight's Cross with Oakleaves he already held. He was also awarded four 'Individual Tank Destruction Badges', each given for the single-handed destruction of five enemy tanks. Bake left 6th Panzer later in 1944. In 1945, after transferring to the regular army from the reserves (as a reserve officer he could not be promoted beyond *Oberst*), he was appointed commander of 13th Panzer Division *Feldherrnhalle* 2.

▼ **Panzerkampfwagen VI Ausf E (Sd Kfz 181)**

Schwere Panzergruppe Bake / Pz. Abt. 503 / 1st Company / 3rd Zug / tank number 2

Early in 1944 at the Balabonowka Pocket, *Panzer-Regiment Bake* engaged the III Soviet Tank Corps in a five-day battle. Tigers formed the centre of Bake's formation while the faster Panthers in two wedge formations outflanked the enemy. By the end, 268 enemy tanks and 156 guns had been destroyed for the loss of one Tiger and four Panthers.

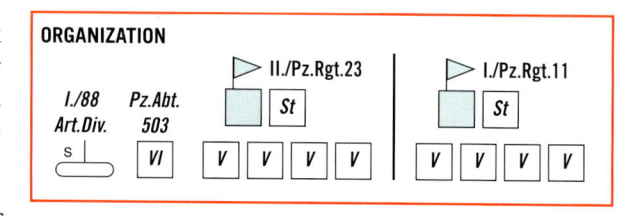

Specifications

Crew: 5
Weight: 62.8 tonnes (57 tons)
Length: 8.45m (27.7ft)
Width: 3.7m (12.1ft)
Height: 2.93m (9.6ft)
Engine: Maybach HL210P45
Speed: 38km/hr (23.6mph)
Range: 140km (87 miles)
Radio: FuG5

7th Panzer Division

Like the 6th Panzer Division, 7th Panzer Division was formed in October 1939 by the conversion of one of the *Wehrmacht*'s *Leichte* Divisions to full Panzer Division status.

▲ Battle of France
Panzer IIs of Rommel's 7th Panzer Division cross a pontoon bridge in 1940. The 'R' on the turret indicates that it is from the regimental staff company.

THE 2ND *LEICHTE* DIVISION was officially formed on 10 November 1938 at Gera, to the south of Leipzig. Despite the fact that Germany had very little cavalry strength, the cavalry arm was the most prestigious in the German armed forces, and the light divisions had been formed primarily as a sop to the few but highly influential cavalry officers who dominated the high command.

In 1939, the 2nd *Leichte* Division was under the command of *General de Kavallerie* Stumme. At full strength, the division comprised 457 officers and warrant officers leading 11,000 NCOs and men.

Panzer strength

The Division was organized and equipped into a tank-light, infantry-heavy unit. The 6th and 7th *Kavallerie Schützen* Regiments each consisted of two battalions of motorized infantry. Other divisional units included a reconnaissance regiment, an artillery regiment, an antitank battalion, a pioneer or combat engineer battalion, a signals battalion and other service and support units.

Divisional armoured strength was provided by a single Panzer unit, the 33rd Panzer Battalion. This included one motorized signals platoon, one staff platoon, three light panzer companies, one motorized reserve platoon, one motorized maintenance platoon, and one light supply column. At the outbreak of war, the Panzer *Abteilung* had 62 tanks available, mostly Pz.Kpfw Is and IIs, with a few Pz.Kpfw IIIs and IVs becoming operational.

The support units included more supply, maintenance and fuel columns, a divisional administration unit, a field bakery, a butcher detachment, various medical and veterinary units, a military police troop and a field post office.

Commanders

General der Kavallerie G. Stumme
(18 Oct 1939 – 5 Feb 1940)

Generalmajor E. Rommel
(5 Feb 1940 – 14 Feb1941)

General der Panzertruppen H. Freiherr von Funck
(14 Feb1941 – 17 Aug 1943)

Oberst W. Glasemer
(17 Aug 1943 – 20 Aug 1943)

General der Panzertruppen H. von Manteuffel
(20 Aug 1943 – 1 Jan 1944)

Generalmajor A. Schulz
(Jan 1944 – 28 Jan 1944)

Oberst W. Glasemer
(28 Jan 1944 – 30 Jan 1944)

General der Panzertruppen Dr. K. Mauss
(30 Jan 1944 – 2 May 1944)

Generalmajor G. Schmidhuber
(2 May 1944 – 9 Sept 1944)

General der Panzertruppen Dr. K. Mauss
(9 Sept 1944 – 31 Oct 1944)

Generalmajor H. Mader
(31 Oct 1944 – 30 Nov 1944)

General der Panzertruppen Dr. K. Mauss
(30 Nov 1944 – 5 Jan 1945)

Generalmajor M. Lemke
(5 Jan 1945 – 23 Jan 1945)

General der Panzertruppen Dr. K. Mauss
(23 Jan 1945 – 22 Mar 1945)

Oberst H. Christern
(23 Mar 1945 – 8 May 1945)

INSIGNIA

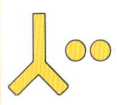

Standard tactical symbol for the 7th Panzer Division, introduced in the second half of 1940.

New tactical symbol introduced in 1941, and generally carried by divisional vehicles to the end of the war.

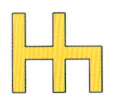

Alternative tactical symbol carried by 7th Panzer Division vehicles.

Special tactical symbol adopted by 7th Panzer for the Battle of Kursk.

7TH PANZER DIVISION

Fall Weiss: the invasion of Poland
1 SEPTEMBER 1939

Together with the 3rd *Leichte* Division, the 2nd *Leichte* Division formed the XV Motorized Corps in the 10th Army, attached to Army Group South for the Polish campaign.

THE BEGINNING OF THE INVASION of Poland saw the 2nd *Leichte* Division launching its attack from the area around Horneck in Silesia. As part of the armoured spearhead of von Reichenau's 10th Army, its mission was to take part in the elimination of Polish forces around the key cities of Kielce and Radom. The Division advanced without much in the way of fighting, reaching Radom by 9 September. However, fighting was harder elsewhere, and the Division was one of several diverted to deal with a Polish counterattack at Bzura, to the west of Warsaw.

After the battle, the Division advanced towards Modlin, continuing to encircle the south of the Polish capital. The Poles capitulated on 27 September 1939, and German units not needed for occupation duty were ordered home on 1 October.

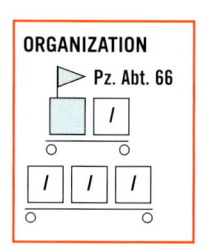

Arriving in Thuringia in mid-October, the 2nd *Leichte* prepared for radical change. As a result of combat experience in Poland, the *Wehrmacht* had learned some lessons about what kind of units were needed in large-scale combat. As a result, the four *Leichte* divisions were to be reorganized as fully-fledged Panzer divisions, to be numbered from 6 to 9. The 2nd *Leichte* Division was renamed the 7th Panzer Division on 18 October 1939.

ORGANIZATION
Pz. Abt. 66

Fall Gelb: the French campaign
10 MAY 1940

A command change in February 1940 brought an unknown General to lead the 7th Panzer Division, but Erwin Rommel's abilities would soon make him a household name in Germany.

COMMANDED BY *GENERALMAJOR* (later Field Marshal) Erwin Rommel from February 1940 to February 1941, the 7th Panzer Division played a key role in the invasion of France in May and June of 1940. It was assigned to Hoth's XV *Panzerkorps*, part of Army Group A's powerful armoured force which struck through the Ardennes.

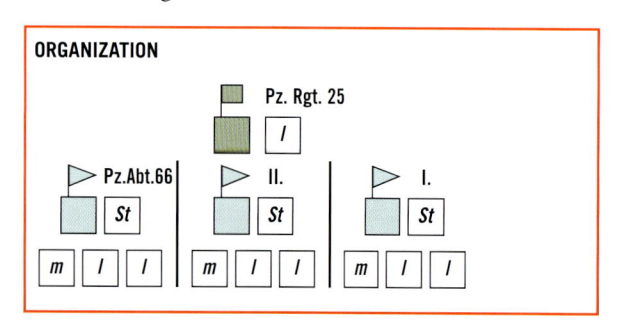

7th Panzer was one of the first armoured units across the Meuse at Dinant, and raced towards the Somme. The only check came when Rommel's division had to fight off a British counterattack at Arras, which had already rattled the 3rd SS Division *Totenkopf*.

Under Rommel's command, the 7th Panzer earned the sobriquet *Gespenster-Division*, or the 'Ghost Division' – the speed of its advance left the French uncertain when or where on the battlefield it would appear next. 7th Panzer was the first German unit to cross the Seine, and on 19 June Rommel's panzers took the key port of Cherbourg.

ORGANIZATION
Pz. Rgt. 25
Pz. Abt. 66

Panzer Unit	Pz. I	Pz. II	Pz. 38(t)	Pz. IV	Pz.Bef38(t)
7th Pz. Div.	34	68	91	24	8

7TH PANZER DIVISION

▶ **Panzerfunkwagen (Sd Kfz 263) 8-Rad**
Division Staff / Signal Platoon / Command car of Major-General Erwin Rommel

The 7th Panzer was called the 'Ghost Division' because the Allies never knew its exact location during the battle for France. Neither did the German High Command for much of the time, though Rommel could have used his communications vehicle to keep in touch. Rommel's command car carried the license plate WH 143149 painted on the vehicle's bow.

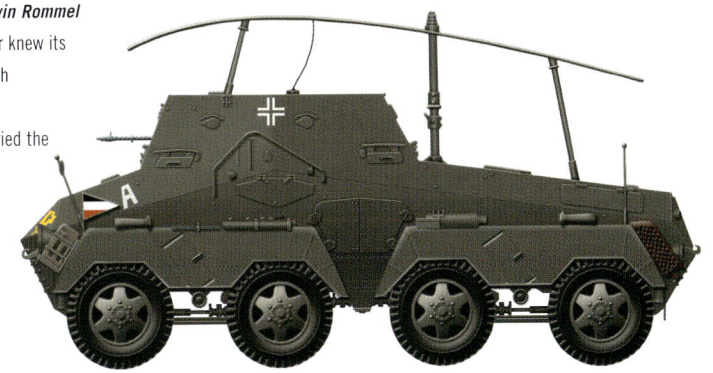

Specifications
Crew: 5
Weight: 8.9 tonnes (8.1 tons)
Length: 5.85m (19.2ft)
Width: 2.2m (7.2ft)
Height: 2.9m (9.5ft)
Engine: Büssing-NAG L8V
Speed: 100km/hr (62.1mph)
Range: 300km (186.4 miles)
Radio: 1 Sätz Funkgerät für (m) Pz Funktruppe b

▶ **Panzerbefehlswagen 38(t) Ausf B**
Pz. Rgt 25 / Regimental Staff Company / Signal Platoon / tank number 2

The British armoured attack near Arras caught the SS *Totenkopf* (mot) Division by surprise. The British force was composed of 74 vehicles, including thickly armoured Matilda infantry tanks. The British gave the Germans a major scare, until Rommel used the *Luftwaffe* 88mm (3.5in) anti-aircraft guns attached to his division to engage the otherwise invulnerable Matilda. Other *Luftwaffe* assistance came from Ju-87 Stuka attacks called in by Rommel's 7th Panzer.

Specifications
Crew: 4
Weight: 10.5 tonnes (9.5 tons)
Length: 4.61m (15.1ft)
Width: 2.14m (7ft)
Height: 2.4m (7.9ft)
Engine: Praga EPA
Speed: 42km/hr (26mph)
Range: 250km (155.3 miles)
Radio: FuG37(t)

▶ **Panzerkampfwagen 38(t) Ausf B**
Pz. Rgt 25 / I Battalion / 1st Company / 2nd Zug / tank number 3

The Czech-built Pz.Kpfw 38(t) was used in place of the Pz.Kpfw III in the table of organization of the 7th Panzer Division. The large red tactical number was characteristic of 7th Panzer vehicles in the early years of the war.

Weapons Specifications
Main gun: 3.7cm (1.5in) KwK38(t) L/47.8
Ammunition: 42 rounds
Traverse: 360° (manual)
Elevation: -10° to +14°
Sight: TZF(t)
Co-axial MG: 7.92mm (0.3in) MG37(t)
Hull MG: 7.92mm (0.3in) MG37(t)
Ammunition: 2400 rounds
MG sight: MGZF(t)

7TH PANZER DIVISION

▶ Panzerkampfwagen I Ausf B (Sd Kfz 101)
Pz. Rgt 25 / I Battalion / 1st Company / 4th Zug / tank number 1

675 Ausf B variants of the Panzer I were manufactured from August 1935 to June 1937. The Ausf B is easily distinguishable from the Ausf A; it had five road wheels, four return rollers and a longer chassis. The armour was unchanged, being 13mm (0.5in) thick on the front and sides and only 6mm (0.2in) at the top.

Specifications
Crew: 2
Weight: 6.4 tonnes (5.8 tons)
Length: 4.42m (14.5ft)
Width: 2.06m (6.8ft)
Height: 1.72m (5.6ft)
Engine: Maybach NL38TR
Speed: 40km/hr (24.9mph)
Range: 170km (105.6 miles)
Radio: FuG2

▶ Schwerer Panzerspähwagen (Sd Kfz 231) 6-Rad
37th Reconnaissance Battalion

The Sd Kfz 231 was armed with one 20mm (0.8in) KwK30 L/55 cannon and carried 200 rounds of ammunition. Secondary armament consisted of one MG13 machine gun with 1500 rounds of ammunition.

Specifications
Crew: 4
Weight: up to 6.6 tonnes (6 tons)
Length: 5.57m (18.3ft)
Width: 1.82m (6ft)
Height: 2.25m (7.4ft)
Engine: Büssing-NAG G or Daimler-Benz M09 or Magirus s88
Speed: 70km/hr (43.5mph)
Range: 300km (186.4 miles)
Radio: FuG Spr Ger 'a'

▶ 15cm sIG33 (Sf) auf Panzerkampfwagen I Ausf B
705th Schwere Infanteriegeschütz Abteilung

Mounting a standard 15cm (6in) field gun onto the chassis of a Panzer I allowed the German Army to provide Panzer and motorized divisions with heavyweight artillery support at all times. This particular vehicle had the name 'Berta' painted on the front shield under the gun barrel.

Specifications
Crew: 4
Weight: 9.4 tonnes (8.5 tons)
Length: 4.67m (15.3ft)
Width: 2.06m (6.8ft)
Height: 2.8m (9.2ft)
Engine: Maybach NL38TR
Speed: 40km/hr (24.9mph)
Range: 140km (87 miles)
Radio: Name

▶ Ladungsleger auf Panzerkampfwagen I Ausf B
58th Pioneer Battalion / 3rd Armoured Engineers Company

Demolition charge-laying tank. Each Pioneer Panzer Battalion had ten *Ladungsleger* in its organization chart. This vehicle was equipped with a rear deck demolition charge mounted on a special sledge, and was used to clear obstacles in the path of the assault troops.

Specifications
Crew: 2
Weight: 6.6 tonnes (6 tons)
Length: 4.42m (14.5ft)
Width: 2.06m (6.8ft)
Height: 1.72m (5.6ft)
Engine: Maybach NL38TR
Speed: 40km/hr (24.9mph)
Range: 170km (105.6 miles)
Radio: FuG2

7TH PANZER DIVISION

Barbarossa: the attack on Russia
22 JUNE 1941

After the victory in France, 7th Panzer remained there on occupation duties until early in 1941. Then Rommel left for Africa, and the Division returned to Germany to prepare for Russia.

As part of *Generaloberst* Hermann Hoth's 3rd *Panzergruppe* on the northern flank of Army Group Centre, the 7th Panzer Division attacked across the Memel River in Lithuania and, after taking Vilnius, crossed into Russia proper. The division continued its advance through Minsk and Vitebsk before taking part in the capture of Smolensk in July 1941. In the battle for Moscow, a regiment of the Division captured the bridge across the Volga-Moscow Canal at Yakhroma on 28 November 1941.

However, with no German reserves available to exploit the bridgehead, its troops had reluctantly to withdraw back across the canal. In January, the retreat continued back to the defensive lines at Rzhev.

ORGANIZATION

Panzer Unit	Pz. II	Pz. 38(t)	Pz. IV	Pz.Bef38(t)	Pz. Bef.
25th Pz. Rgt.	53	167	30	7	8

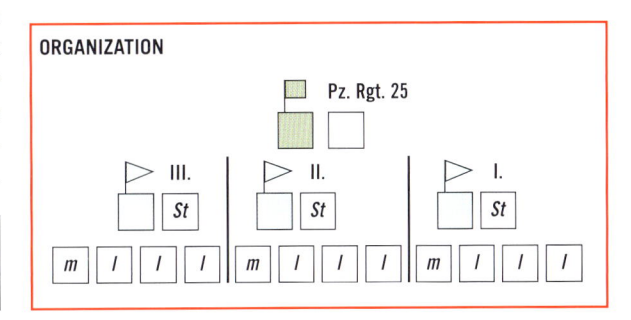

▶ **Panzerkampfwagen IV Ausf E (Sd Kfz 161)**
Pz. Rgt 25 / I Battalion / 4th Company / 2nd Zug / tank number 1

Although Germany deployed 5264 tanks during the invasion of the USSR, they faced 20,000 and 24,000 tanks of the Red Army. However, German tactics enabled them to defeat this far more numerous force.

Specifications
Crew: 5
Weight: 23.2 tonnes (21 tons)
Length: 5.92m (19.4ft)
Width: 2.84m (9.3ft)
Height: 2.68m (8.8ft)
Engine: Maybach HL120TRM
Speed: 42km/hr (26mph)
Range: 200km (124.3 miles)
Radio: FuG5

▶ **Panzerkampfwagen II Ausf C (Sd Kfz 121)**
Pz. Rgt 25 / II Battalion / Stabskompanie / Light Platoon / tank number 8

The Light Platoon was used by Panzer battalion commanders to perform reconnaissance missions ahead of their main combat units.

Specifications
Crew: 3
Weight: 9.8 tonnes (8.9 tons)
Length: 4.81m (15.8ft)
Width: 2.22m (7.3ft)
Height: 1.99m (6.5ft)
Engine: Maybach HL62TR
Speed: 40km/hr (24.9mph)
Range: 200km (124.3 miles)
Radio: FuG5

7TH PANZER DIVISION

▶ Panzerkampfwagen II Ausf C (Sd Kfz 121)
Pz. Rgt 25 / III Battalion / Stabskompanie / Light Platoon / tank number 14

Although long replaced as a frontline battle tank, the Panzer II continued to serve as a reconnaissance vehicle as late as the Kursk battles in 1943.

Specifications

Crew: 3
Weight: 9.8 tonnes (8.9 tons)
Length: 4.81m (15.8ft)
Width: 2.22m (7.3ft)
Height: 1.99m (6.5ft)

Engine: Maybach HL62TR
Speed: 40km/hr (24.9mph)
Range: 200km (124.3 miles)
Radio: FuG5

The 7th Panzer Division continued to use simple tactical symbols until the end of the war: this was a variant symbol used from 1941 to 1945.

Specifications

Crew: 9
Weight: 22 tonnes (20 tons)
Length: 7.35m (24.1ft)
Width: 2.5m (8.2ft)
Height: 2.8m (9.2ft)

Engine: Maybach HL85TUKRM
Speed: 50km/hr (31mph)
Range: 260km (161.6 miles)
Radio: FuG Spr Ger 'a' or none

▼ 8.8cm FlaK 18 (Sf) auf Zugkraftwagen 12t (Sd Kfz 8)
19th Heavy Panzerjäger Battalion (Attached)

Although specialized antitank variants of the famous 'acht-acht' existed, the 8.8cm (3.5in) FlaK 18 L/56 anti-aircraft gun was a dual-purpose weapon that could destroy any Soviet tank.

▶ Panzerkampfwagen 38(t) Ausf E/F
Pz. Rgt 25 / III Battalion / 10th Company / Company HQ

525 Ausf E/F variants of the Pz.Kpfw 38(t) were produced between November 1940 and October 1941. Although protection had been increased, it was too lightly armoured for the Eastern Front and its gun was too small. By September 1941, the last vehicles were being withdrawn from the frontline by the 7th Panzer Division.

Specifications

Crew: 4
Weight: 10.9 tonnes (9.85 tons)
Length: 4.61m (15.1ft)
Width: 2.14m (7ft)
Height: 2.4m (7.9ft)

Engine: Praga EPA
Speed: 42km/hr (26mph)
Range: 250km (155.3 miles)
Radio: FuG37(t)

7TH PANZER DIVISION

🪖 The last summer offensive
1 July 1943

1943 saw the turning point of World War II, as for the first time the Soviets stopped a German summer offensive in its tracks, and then took the initiative on the Eastern Front.

AFTER SERVING IN THE DEFENSIVE lines near Rzhev for the first months of 1942, the 7th Panzer Division transferred to France in May 1942 for a much-needed rest and refit. After a period in the South of France, the division returned to the Eastern Front in December, where it was assigned to the reserve of Army Group Don. Attached to III *Panzerkorps* of 1st *Panzerarmee*, the division took part in Operation *Zitadelle* at Kursk, fighting in the Biglerons sector with Army Detachment *Kempf*. After the retreat from Kursk, 7th Panzer Division fought at Kiev and Zhitomir, forming part of the XXXXVIII Corps with 4th *Panzerarmee* and Army Group South. Hard fighting in the autumn of 1943 saw the division once again suffering heavy losses.

Panzer Unit	Pz. II	Pz. III(50)	Pz. III(75)	Pz. IV	Pz. Bef.
25th Pz. Rgt.	12	43	12	38	5

ORGANIZATION

Pz. Rgt. 25
  I
    II. — St (m, le, m, le, le)
    I. — St (m, le, m, le, le)

▶ **Panzerbefehlswagen mit 5cm KwK39 L/60**
Pz. Rgt 25 / I Battalion / Stabskompanie / Signal Platoon / tank number 2

The Ausf K command tank was based on the Ausf L or M chassis. Fifty were produced between December 1942 and February 1943. It was armed with one 5cm (2in) L/60.

Specifications
Crew: 5
Weight: 25.4 tonnes (23 tons)
Length: 6.41m (21ft)
Width: 2.95m (9.7ft)
Height: 2.51m (8.2ft)
Engine: Maybach HL120TRM
Speed: 40km/hr (24.9mph)
Range: 155km (96.3 miles)
Radio: FuG5 plus FuG7 or FuG8

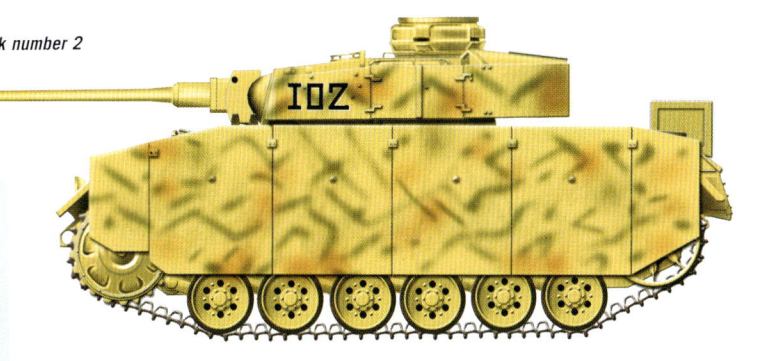

🪖 The last year on the Eastern front
1944

The Division had re-equipped the 1st Battalion with 79 Panthers by May 1944; the 2nd Battalion was still operating Pz.Kpfw IVs. In January 1945, near Deutsch-Eylau, the 7th Panzer Division, at that time reduced to 20 operational tanks, engaged a much larger Russian force. Facing odds of more than ten to one, the division was destroyed, but it was quickly re-built.

IN NOVEMBER 1943, 7th Panzer Division was one of the units assigned to the Zhitomir campaign. Under the command of General Hermann Balck, the XLVIII *Panzerkorps* advanced northwards to Zhitomir, smashing an armoured fist through the Soviet line on 15 November. The Russian Third

7TH PANZER DIVISION

ORGANIZATION
▷ I. Pz. Rgt. 25
St
V V V V

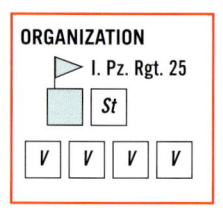

Guards Tank Army mounted counterattacks east of Zhitomir, and Balck promptly took the decision to entrap the enemy army within a pocket. By 24 November, the Soviet forces in the pocket had been eliminated.

Tarnopol break out

In March 1944, the 7th Panzer Division was encircled in a pocket around Kamenez-Podolsk, and the Germans were forced to attempt another break out towards Tarnopol. 7th Panzer played a major part in the break-out.

After 21 June, 7th Panzer was raced to the front in an attempt to stem the flood of Red Army tanks after the destruction of Army Group Centre. In July, 7th Panzer was transferred to Lithuania. Engaged on the Vistula over the winter, 7th Panzer Division was used to delay Soviet attacks on Danzig. Some elements of the Division fought at Berlin, before surrendering to the British in May 1945.

▸ **Mittlerer Schützenpanzerwagen Ausf D (Sd Kfz 251/3)**
Kampfgruppe / 78th Panzer Artillery Regiment
East Pomerania, March 1945. By this time, the 7th Panzer Division had been reduced to a *Kampfgruppe* with a mixed battalion (10 Pz.Kpfw V and 13 Pz.Kpfw IV) and an assortment of units attached as available.

Specifications
Crew: 2 plus 12 troops
Weight: 9.9 tonnes (9 tons)
Length: 5.98m (19.6ft)
Width: 2.1m (6.9ft)
Height: 2.16m (7ft)
Engine: Maybach HL42TUKRM
Speed: 53km/hr (32.9mph)
Range: 300km (186.4 miles)
Radio: FuG Spr Ger 'f'

◂ **15cm Panzerwerfer 42 auf Sf (Sd Kfz 4/1)**
Kampgruppe / 78th Panzer Artillery Regiment
In service in East Pomerania in March 1945. A *Nebelwerfer* Battery consists of six launchers and each vehicle was armed with a 10-tube rocket launcher.

Specifications
Crew: 3
Weight: 7.8 tonnes (7.1 tons)
Length: 6.0m (19.7ft)
Width: 2.2m (7.2ft)
Height: 2.5m (8.2ft)
Engine: Opel 3.6l 6-cyl
Speed: 40km/hr (24.9mph)
Range: 130km (80.8 miles)
Radio: FuG Spr Ger 'f'

Specifications
Crew: 4
Weight: 9.9 tonnes (9 tons)
Length: 5.98m (19.6ft)
Width: 2.1m (6.9ft)
Height: 2.16m (7ft)
Engine: Maybach HL42TUKRM
Speed: 53km/hr (32.9mph)
Range: 300km (186.4 miles)
Radio: FuG Spr Ger 'f'

▴ **Mittlerer Schützenpanzerwagen Ausf D (Sd Kfz 251/22)**
Kampfgruppe / 7th Reconnaissance Battalion / 5th Heavy Company / Panzerjäger Platoon
As Soviet tanks approached the borders of the Reich, orders were issued to produce as many vehicles equipped with antitank weapons as possible. The PaK 40 antitank gun was mounted onto a half-track, using its standard field carriage but minus the wheels.

8th Panzer Division

The 8th Panzer Division came into existence in October 1939, when the 3rd *Leichte* Division was upgraded and renamed following service in the invasion of Poland.

THE 3RD *LEICHTE* DIVISION was originally formed on 10 November 1938 at Cottbus, a small garrison town northeast of Dresden. It was one of the four 'Light' Divisions formed by the cavalry in competition with the new armoured divisions being formed by the *Panzerwaffe*.

At the time of the invasion of Poland, the division was commanded by *Generalmajor* Kuntzen. Divisional strength was 438 officers and around 10,300 NCOs and men. The division was organized and equipped as follows:

8th *Kavallerie Schützen* Regiment with two motorized infantry battalions, one motorcycle platoon and one heavy company with machine guns, mortars and PAK antitank guns;

9th *Kavallerie Schützen* Regiment with one motorized infantry battalion and one motorcycle infantry battalion;

1st Battalion, 8th Reconnaissance Regiment with one motorcycle company, two armoured car companies and one heavy company with two 7.5cm (3in) infantry guns and three 3.7cm (1.5in) PAK 36 antitank guns;

67th Panzer Battalion, equipped with Panzer IIs, and Panzer 38(t)s in three light panzer companies;

80th Artillery Regiment of two motorized battalions, each three batteries of truck-towed 10.5cm (4.1in) leFH field howitzers;

43rd *Panzerabwehr* Battalion, made up from three companies each with 12 3.7-cm (1.5-in) PAK 36 antitank guns;

59th Pioneer Battalion with two Pioneer (combat engineer) companies, one motorized pioneer company, one bridging company and one engineering supply column;

4th Battalion, 3rd Signals Regiment;

58th Divisional Service units, operating supply, fuels and maintenance columns;

59th Divisional Administration unit;

59th Motorized Field Bakery;

59th Motorized Field Hospital;

1st and 2nd Motorized Medical companies;

59th Veterinary company;

59th Motorized Field Police Troop;

59th Motorized Field Post Office.

INSIGNIA

Standard tactical symbol used by the 8th Panzer Division in 1940.

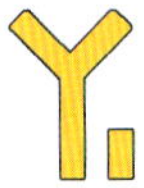

Modified variant of 8th Panzer's tactical insignia, used by the division from 1941 to 1945.

Commanders

General der Panzertruppen A. Kuntzen
(16 Oct 1939 – 20 Feb 1941)

General der Panzertruppen E. Brandenberger
(20 Feb 1941 – 21 Apr 1941)

Generalleutnant W. Neumann-Silkow
(21 Apr 1941 – 26 May 1941)

General der Panzertruppen E. Brandenberger
(26 May 1941 – 8 Dec 1941)

Generalleutnant W. Huhner
(8 Dec 1941 – 20 Mar 1942)

General der Panzertruppen E. Brandenberger
(20 Mar 1942 – 6 Aug 1942)

Generalleutnant J. Schrotter
(6 Aug 1942 – 10 Nov 1942)

General der Panzertruppen E. Brandenberger
(10 Nov 1942 – 17 Jan 1943)

Generalleutnant S. Fichtner
(17 Jan 1943 – 20 Sept 1943)

Generalmajor G. Frolich
(20 Sept 1943 – 1 Apr 1944)

Generalmajor W. Friebe
(1 Apr 1944 – 21 July 1944)

Generalmajor G. Frolich
(21 July 1944 – 5 Jan 1945)

Generalmajor H. Hax
(5 Jan 1945 – 8 May 1945)

▲ **Panzerkampfwagen 38(t)**
The growth of the *Panzerwaffe* coincided with the occupation of Czechoslovakia, and Czech factories provided much of the tank strength for the new divisions.

8TH PANZER DIVISION

Fall Weiss: the invasion of Poland
1 September 1939

At full strength, the 3rd *Leichte* Division had 332 officers, 105 warrant officers, 1616 NCOs and 8719 soldiers. The 67th Panzer Battalion had 45 Pz.Kpfw II, 59 Pz.Kpfw 38(t) and 2 Pz.Bef 38(t). In October 1939, the Division was reorganized as the 8th Panzer Division.

From its base at Gera in Thuringia, where it had been formed under the supervision of *Wehrkreis* (Military Administrative District) IX, the 3rd Light Division was mobilized for the invasion of Poland on 28 August 1939. It was moved to Horneck in Silesia, where along with the 2nd Light Division it became part of *Generalleutnant* Stumme's XV Motorized Corps of von Reichenau's 10th Army assigned to Army Group South.

XV Corps advanced rapidly towards Kielce on the outbreak of war, going on to reach the key city of Radom on 9 September. It was then diverted with other armoured and motorized formations by a serious Polish counterattack on the Bzura river, to the west of Warsaw. The Germans won the largest battle of encirclement up to that time, before pressing on to surround the Polish capital.

After the Polish capitulation, the Division was pulled back to Germany, where it was reorganized and strengthened to become the 8th Panzer Division. There it went into Army Group B's reserve until called on for the Western campaign.

ORGANIZATION
Pz. Abt. 67

◀ **Panzerkampfwagen 38(t) Ausf A**
3 Leichte Division / Pz.Abt. 67 / 3rd Company / 1st Zug / tank number 3
150 Ausf A were produced from May to November 1939. The original Czech LT Vz 38 was armed with a semi-automatic SKODA A7 gun and carried a crew of three. Its ammunition consisted of 5 spring-loaded magazines with 18 rounds each and 2400 rounds for both machine guns. The tank had no intercom, the commander communicating with the driver using a coloured lights system.

Specifications
Crew: 4	Engine: Praga EPA
Weight: 10.5 tonnes (9.5 tons)	Speed: 42km/hr (26mph)
Length: 4.61m (15.1ft)	Range: 250km (155.3 miles)
Width: 2.14m (7ft)	Radio: FuG37(t)
Height: 2.4m (7.9ft)	

▶ **Panzerkampfwagen II Ausf D (Sd Kfz 121)**
3 Leichte Division / Pz.Abt. 67 / 3rd Company / 1st Zug / tank number 4
Forty-three Ausf D were produced between May 1938 and August 1939. They were issued only to the *Leichte* Divisions. The Pz.Kpfw II Ausf D was developed to replace horse-mounted German Cavalry units. With a speed of 55km/hr (34.2mph), it was well suited to the pursuit and reconnaissance missions for which it was designed.

Specifications
Crew: 3	Engine: Maybach HL62TRM
Weight: 11 tonnes (10 tons)	Speed: 55km/hr (34.2mph)
Length: 4.65m (15.3ft)	Range: 200km (124.3 miles)
Width: 2.3m (7.5ft)	Radio: FuG5
Height: 2.06m (6.8ft)	

8TH PANZER DIVISION

Y° *Fall Gelb*: the French campaign
10 May 1940

8th Panzer Division was assigned to General Reinhardt's XLI *Panzerkorps*, in the centre of Army Group A's armoured thrust through the supposedly impassable Ardennes.

REINHARDT'S CORPS MADE SLOWER progress than those of Guderian and Hoth, being caught up in a monumental traffic jam as three *Panzerkorps* tried to funnel through the narrow, twisting roads passing through the heavily forested Ardennes.

Leichte PanzerKompanie

The light panzer companies of the former *Leichte* divisions began to re-equip after the Polish campaign, replacing many of their Panzer IIs with the Czech-built Panzer 38(t). The companies themselves operated mixed *Zugen*, or platoons, with four Panzer 38(ts) and a single Panzer II.

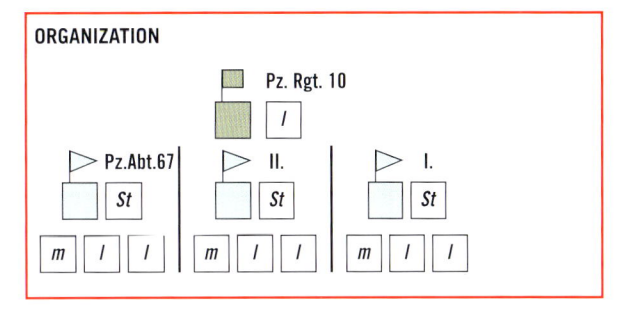

ORGANIZATION

Panzer Unit	Pz. II	Pz. 38(t)	Pz. IV	Pz.Bef.38(t)
8th Pz. Div.	58	116	23	15

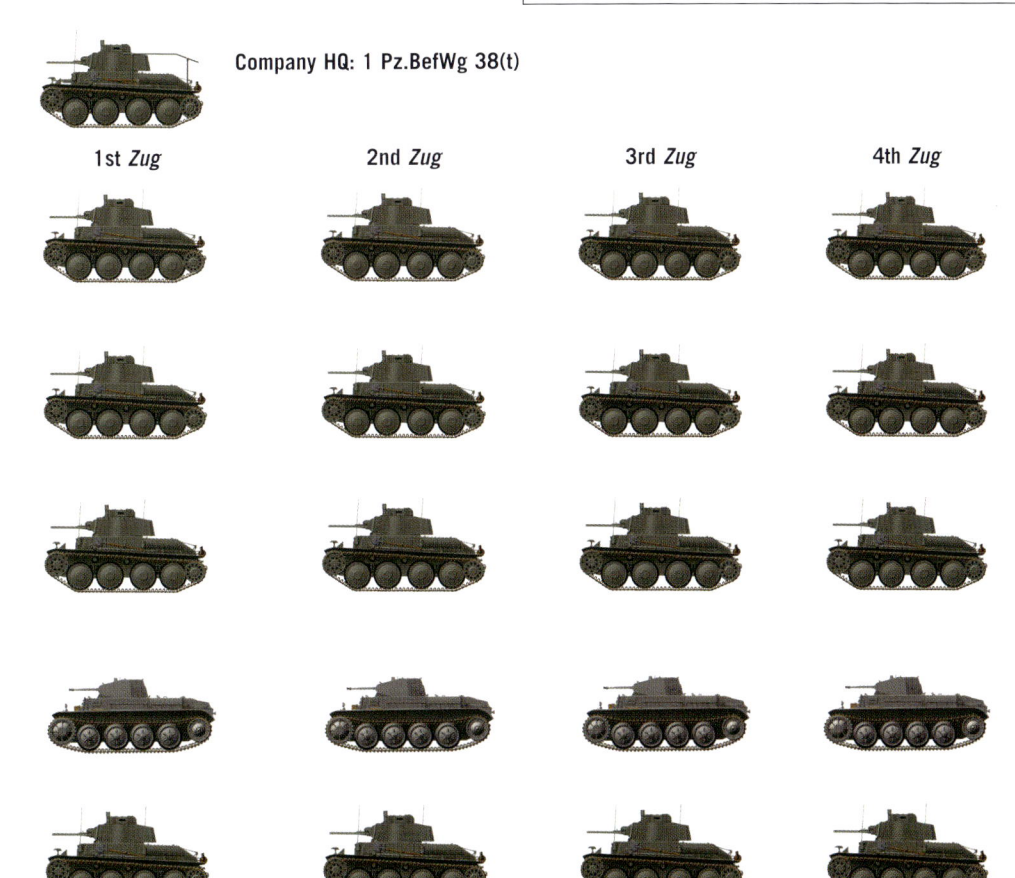

Company HQ: 1 Pz.BefWg 38(t)

1st *Zug*   2nd *Zug*   3rd *Zug*   4th *Zug*

8TH PANZER DIVISION

War in the Balkans
6 April 1941

The last thing Hitler wanted was a war in the Balkans, diverting forces from his planned strike on Russia. However, he had to help fellow fascist dictator Mussolini, who was in trouble.

THE 8TH PANZER DIVISION was attached to General Maximilian von Weichs' 2nd Army in Hungary, which was tasked with taking the northern half of Yugoslavia in a lightning assault. The 8th Panzer Division crossed the Hungarian border on 6 April 1941, outflanking Yugoslavian defensive positions and driving rapidly towards Belgrade. By 15 April, Belgrade, Zagreb and Sarajevo had been taken, and the Yugoslav government surrendered two days later.

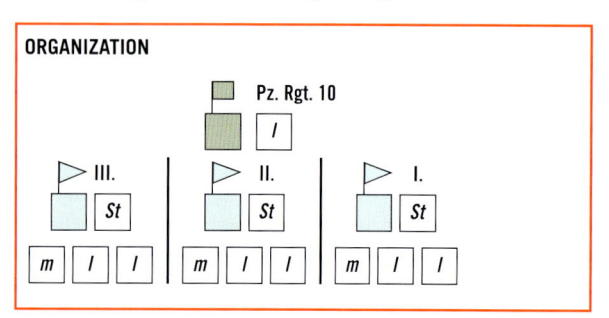

The campaign was described by some German officers as a parade: less than 600 German casualties were recorded. However, much harder days were to follow as a bitter partisan war began.

Panzer Unit	Pz. II	Pz. 38(t)	Pz. IV	Pz.Bef.38(t)
10th Pz. Reg.	49	125	30	not known

Barbarossa: the attack on Russia
22 June 1941

After the conquest of Yugoslavia, the 8th Panzer Division was sent by train to the Reich Protectorate of Bohemia for refitting, ready for the invasion of the USSR.

THE 8TH PANZER DIVISION was assigned to General Hoeppner's 4th *Panzergruppe* of Army Group North for Operation *Barbarossa*. Its main target was Leningrad. Driving rapidly through the Baltic states, the Panzers outpaced their supporting infantry. After fighting through Dvinsk, the Panzers were already approaching Pskov when their infantry units were just clearing Daugavpils, more than 100 km (62 miles) back. In spite of the anguished pleas of the Panzer commanders, who wanted to continue the drive through the demoralized Soviet armies towards Leningrad, the Panzers were ordered to wait for their infantry. This gave the Soviets a little time to regroup, which meant that resistance was much stiffer by the time the offensive resumed.

By the time 8th Panzer reached Leningrad, the chances of taking the city had gone, and the Germans settled in for a siege. 8th Panzer continued to serve on the Leningrad Front for the next year, being moved to Army Group Centre in December 1942.

Panzer Unit	Pz. II	38(t)	Pz. IV	Pz.Bef38(t)	Pz.Bef
10th Pz. Rgt.	49	118	30	7	8

8TH PANZER DIVISION

▶ Panzerbefehlswagen 38(t) Ausf B
Pz. Rgt 10 / II Battalion / Stabskompanie / Signal Platoon

This command tank variant used rod antennae instead of the large frame antenna characteristic of other command tanks. To make space for extra radios in the cramped interior, the bow machine gun and its ammunition were removed. A rounded plate would usually be bolted over the empty MG position.

Specifications
Crew: 4
Weight: 10.5 tonnes (9.5 tons)
Length: 4.61m (15.1ft)
Width: 2.14m (7ft)
Height: 2.4m (7.9ft)
Engine: Praga EPA
Speed: 42km/hr (26mph)
Range: 250km (155.3 miles)
Radio: FuG37(t) plus FuG6

▶ Panzerkampfwagen II Ausf C (Sd Kfz 121)
Pz. Rgt 10 / II Battalion / Stabskompanie / Light Platoon

8th Panzer was part of the 4th *Panzergruppe*, Army Group North. The Pz.Kpfw II Ausf D was withdrawn from service after the invasion of France was completed. Its chassis was used for conversion to Pz.Kpfw II (*Flamm*) flamethrowers, while it was replaced in frontline service by the earlier but more numerous Ausf C.

Specifications
Crew: 3
Weight: 9.8 tonnes (8.9 tons)
Length: 4.81m (15.8ft)
Width: 2.22m (7.3ft)
Height: 1.99m (6.5ft)
Engine: Maybach HL62TR
Speed: 40km/hr (24.9mph)
Range: 200km (124.3 miles)
Radio: FuG5

▶ Panzerkampfwagen 38(t) Ausf C
Pz. Rgt 10 / II Battalion / 7th Company / 3rd Zug / tank number 1

110 Ausf C models were produced between May and August 1940. At the start of Operation *Barbarossa*, four Panzer divisions used the Pz.Kpfw 38(t) as their main battle tank. Six months later, losses of this model would reach 796 units. Too small to be upgraded further, the Germans started passing them to other Axis allies or assigning them to anti-partisan duties.

Specifications
Crew: 4
Weight: 10.5 tonnes (9.5 tons)
Length: 4.61m (15.1ft)
Width: 2.14m (7ft)
Height: 2.4m (7.9ft)
Engine: Praga EPA
Speed: 42km/hr (26mph)
Range: 250km (155.3 miles)
Radio: FuG37(t)

8TH PANZER DIVISION

Specifications
Crew: 5
Weight: 46.6 tonnes (42.3 tons)
Length: 6.68m (21.9ft)
Width: 3.32m (10.9ft)
Height: 2.71m (8.9ft)
Engine: V-2K
Speed: 35km/hr (21.7mph)
Range: 180km (111.8 miles)
Radio: 10R

▲ **Panzerkampfwagen KV Ia 753(r)**
Pz. Rgt 10
A captured Russian KV-1 model 1940, armed with a 76mm (3in) F-32 cannon. The Panzer divisions encountered several of these heavy tanks in their drive towards Leningrad, and only the 8.8cm (3.5in) anti-aircraft gun was capable of knocking out the thickly armoured Soviet vehicle.

Fall Blau: the Eastern Front
28 JUNE 1942

In May 1942, the 2nd Panzer Battalion was detached to form part of a new Panzer division, becoming the 3rd Battalion, 2nd Regiment, 16th Panzer Division.

AFTER THE FAILURE to take Leningrad at the end of 1941, 8th Panzer Division fought around the small Russian town of Cholm, on the Lovat River in the Kalinin sector. German troops had entered the Leningrad suburbs of Slutsk and Pushkin, and had seized the Summer Palace of the Tsars at Krasnoye Selo. A Soviet counteroffensive in January aimed at relieving Leningrad failed, but the bitter fighting had isolated numerous pockets of the German invaders.

One of those pockets was at Cholm, where the Red Army had cut off some 6000 German troops in the town. For the next four months, they would conduct an epic defence, withstanding over 100 infantry assaults and more than 40 armoured attacks.

The German defenders were eventually relieved on 5 May, but the area around Cholm remained a major combat area, since it could serve as a springboard for a campaign to relieve the even larger German pocket at Demjansk, where the bulk of the German II Corps was trapped.

Although the German High Command continued in its desire to take Leningrad, Hitler's obsession with Stalingrad and the Caucasus oilfields meant that Army Group South carried the full weight of German power, and that Army Groups Centre and North were simply expected to hold the line while the summer offensive in the south went ahead.

Panzer Unit	Pz. II	38(t)	Pz. IV	Pz.Bef.38(t)
10th Pz. Rgt.	1	65	2	0

ORGANIZATION
Pz. Rgt. 10
I
III.   I.
St   St
m le le   m le le

The 8th Panzer Division continued to operate around Cholm through the summer and the autumn. From March through to July, it was attached to XXXIX Corps of the 15th Army. In August, 8th Panzer would have been involved in Operation *Lichtschlag*, a German plan to break the deadlock around Leningrad by mounting a major offensive north of Cholm to the Lovat River. However, the division was transferred to Army Group Centre in December of 1942.

The last summer offensive
1 July 1943

The 3rd Battalion was disbanded in October 1942 and its remnants were absorbed by the 1st Battalion. In the summer of 1943, the Division was assigned to Army Group Centre, where it formed part of the north pincer attack at Kursk.

In December 1942, 8th Panzer was attached to LIX Corps of Army Group Centre, and it took part in operations around Smolensk and Bryansk over the next two months. In April 1943, it was again moved to become part of the XXIII *Panzerkorps*, attached to 2nd *Panzerarmee* on the Orel sector.

2nd *Panzerarmee* was intended to play a supporting role during the Battle of Kursk, providing flank protection for the main Northern strike force, Model's 9th Army. In the event, a Soviet counter-attack out of the Kursk Salient brought the army into more direct action than it had expected.

Following the rebuff at Kursk, the 8th Panzer Division played its part in the long retreat through the Ukraine, taking part in the fighting around Kiev and being used in the German tactical victory at Zhitomir. By January 1944, however, it was fighting to avoid encirclement and destruction in the Kamenez-Podolsk pocket near Tarnopol.

Panzer Unit	Pz. II	Pz. 38(t)	Pz. III	Pz. IV	Pz. Bef.
10th Pz. Rgt.	14	3	59	22	14

The last year on the Eastern Front
1944

By September 1944, 8th Panzer had been reorganized as a 'Type 44' division: the 2nd and 4th companies of the divisional Panzer battalion were re-equipped with the Pz.Kpfw V Panther.

During the retreat through the Ukraine, the 8th Panzer Division had been in continuous action, taking part in major battles at Zhitomir and Tarnopol. In May 1944, it was placed into Army Group North Ukraine's reserve, before being called into action in the retreat through Brody and Lemberg and back into Poland.

The German Army Groups in the southern sectors of the Eastern Front avoided the fate of Army Group Centre, wiped out by the Soviet Operation *Bagration* in the summer of 1944, but they were placed under considerable pressure by the southern Soviet fronts, which launched their own series of offensives in August 1944.

The 8th Panzer Division fought back through the Carpathian mountains and into Slovakia as Germany's allies Romania, Slovakia and Hungary either changed sides or were occupied by German troops to prevent their switch to the Allies.

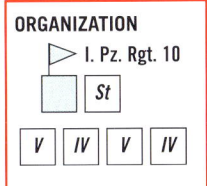

In December 1944, the Division found itself under the control of Army Group South at Budapest. Hitler's determination to hold the Hungarian capital cost the *Wehrmacht* dearly. After failing to relieve the city with the last of its first line panzer forces, the German High Command transferred what was left of the 8th Panzer Division to Army Group Centre, where it was attached to the 17th Army in Moravia. The 8th Panzer Division eventually surrendered to the Red Army at Brno.

9th Panzer Division

The last of the pre-war *Leichte* divisions to be brought up to full Panzer Division status, the 9th Panzer Division came into existence on 1 March 1940.

THE 4TH *LEICHTE* DIVISION was formed at Vienna on 1 April 1938, soon after the *Anschluss* between Austria and Germany. Manpower was provided by the former Austrian army. In March 1939, it took part in the occupation of Czechoslovakia. As with the other Light divisions, its fighting strength was provided by two motorized infantry regiments and a single understrength Panzer battalion, the 33rd.

Commanders

General der Panzertruppen A. Ritter von Hubicki
(3 Jan 1940 – 15 Apr 1942)

Generalleutnant J. Baßler
(15 Apr 1942 – 27 July 1942)

Generalmajor H. von Hulsen
(27 July 1942 – 4 Aug 1942)

Generalleutnant W. Scheller
(4 Aug 1942 – 22 July 1943)

Generalleutnant E. Jolasse
(22 July 1943 – 1 Oct 1943)

Generalmajor Dr. J. Schulz
(1 Oct 1943 – 27 Nov 1943)

Generalleutnant E. Jolasse
(27 Nov 1943 – 10 Aug 1944)

Oberst M. Sperling
(10 Aug 1944 – 3 Sept 1944)

Generalmajor G. Muller
(3 Sept 1944 – 16 Sept 1944)

Generalleutnant H. von Elverfeldt
(16 Sept 1944 – 6 Mar 1945)

Oberst H. Zollenkopf
(6 Mar 1945 – 26 Apr 1945)

INSIGNIA

One of the earliest of the simplified tactical symbols, applied to 4th Light Division vehicles in 1939.

Tactical symbol used by 9th Panzer Division after the French Campaign in the summer of 1940.

Modified tactical symbol, used by the 9th Panzer Division from 1941 to 1945.

▶ **Balkans Interlude**
Motorized infantry pass in review in Athens after the victory in the Balkans in 1941. The 9th Panzer Division played a key part in the campaign.

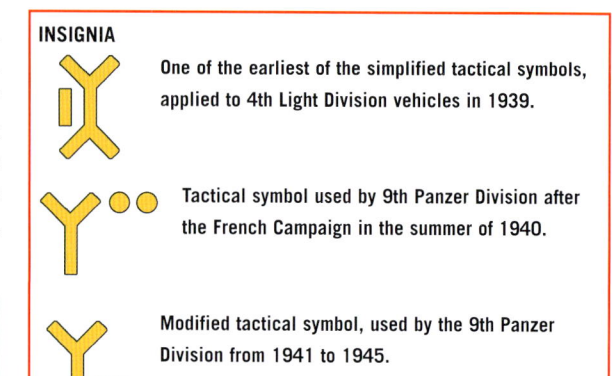

Fall Weiss: the invasion of Poland
1 SEPTEMBER 1939

With just 57 fighting tanks, the 4th Light Division was the weakest armoured formation that took part in the German invasion of Poland in September 1939.

THE INVASION OF POLAND saw the 4th Light Division assigned to XVIII Army Corps of General List's 14th Army, part of Army Group South. On 19 August, the division received its war orders to move to forming up points in the Tatra Mountains.

Commanded by *General der Panzertruppen* Dr. Alfred Ritter von Hubicki, 4th Light was part of the drive to encircle and defeat the Polish Krakow Army, a mission that was completed in just over a week. At the end of the campaign the Division was located at Tomaszow, facing westward after outflanking the Poles.

The Division remained in Poland until 25 October, when it returned to Germany. On 3 January 1940, the Division was reorganized and upgraded to become the 9th Panzer Division.

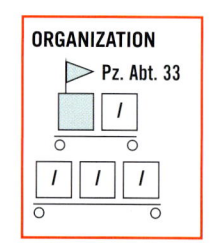

ORGANIZATION
▷ Pz. Abt. 33

88

9TH PANZER DIVISION

Y∵ *Fall Gelb*: the French campaign
10 May 1940

On January 1940, the 4th Light Division was reorganized as the 9th Panzer Division.

THE NEWLY FORMED 9th Panzer Division was one of the few armoured formations assigned to von Bock's Army Group B for the attack on the west in May 1940. After driving towards Rotterdam, the Division moved southward following the Belgian capitulation, and formed the northern flank of the German forces that surrounded Dunkirk. Transferring to *Panzergruppe Kleist* for the Battle of France, it drove through the centre of the country, reaching Lyon by the time of the Armistice at the end of June.

9th Panzer remained in France for two months, eventually being ordered back to Germany and then on to occupation duties in Poland in September 1940.

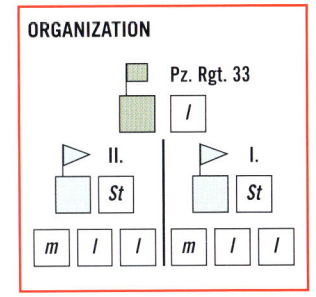

Panzer Unit	Pz. I	Pz. II	Pz. III	Pz. IV	Pz. Bef.
33rd Pz. Rgt.	30	54	41	16	12

ORGANIZATION
Pz. Rgt. 33

▶ Panzerkampfwagen IV Ausf E (Sd Kfz 161)
Pz. Rgt 33 / I Battalion / 4th Company / 2nd Zug / tank number 1

The 9th Panzer Division was the only armoured unit assigned to the invasion of the Low Countries. The defensive postures adopted by the Belgians and Dutch around their canal systems were inadequate to stop a three-dimensional attack composed of fast mechanized units and paratroops.

Specifications
Crew: 5
Weight: 23.2 tonnes (21 tons)
Length: 5.92m (19.4ft)
Width: 2.84m (9.3ft)
Height: 2.68m (8.8ft)
Engine: Maybach HL120TRM
Speed: 42km/hr (26mph)
Range: 200km (124.3 miles)
Radio: FuG5

▶ 15cm sIG33 (Sf) auf Panzerkampfwagen I Ausf B
701st Schwere Infanteriegeschütz Abteilung

The sIG33 was an awkward design, and its tall shape made the vehicle a good target. The high centre of gravity and overloaded chassis hindered its cross-country capability. However, vehicles armed with a 15cm (6in) howitzer provided effective close fire support to *Panzergrenadier* Regiments on all fronts. The 701st Abteilung was disbanded in June 1943.

Specifications
Crew: 4
Weight: 9.4 tonnes (8.5 tons)
Length: 4.67m (15.3ft)
Width: 2.06m (6.8ft)
Height: 2.8m (9.2ft)
Engine: Maybach NL38TR
Speed: 40km/hr (24.9mph)
Range: 140km (87 miles)
Radio: FuG5

9TH PANZER DIVISION

Y.. *Barbarossa*: the attack on Russia
22 JUNE 1941

9th Panzer Division would have been with Army Group Centre for the invasion of Russia, had it not been diverted south to take part in the Balkans campaign.

ATTACHED TO XXXX CORPS of 12th Army, 9th Panzer along with the elite *Leibstandarte* SS brigade attacked Yugoslavia through Macedonia. Cutting the Yugoslavs off from any British or Greek assistance, the Division seized Skopje before Yugoslavia fell.

Withdrawn from the Balkans, the Division was rested and refitted for *Barbarossa*, the invasion of the Soviet Union. In July, 9th Panzer was attached to XIV *Panzerkorps* of the 1st *Panzergruppe*, fighting with Army Group South. It saw action at Uman, Kiev, where it played an important part in the encirclement and capture of more than 600,000 Soviet troops, and in the continuing German drive on to the Dnieper River.

On 9 October, Panzer was transferred to LXVIII *Panzerkorps* of Guderian's 2nd *Panzergruppe* in time for Operation *Typhoon*, Army Group Centre's delayed assault on Moscow. In November, it was fighting at Briansk, and at the end of the year it was involved in fighting off the Soviet winter offensive.

ORGANIZATION

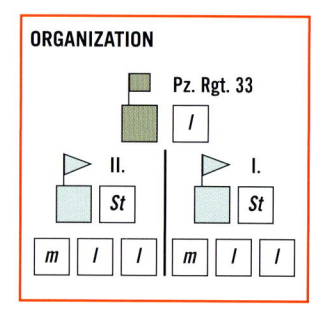

Pz. Rgt. 33
- I
- II.
  - St
  - m / l / m / l
- I.
  - St

Panzer Unit	Pz. I	Pz. II	Pz. III	Pz. IV	Pz. Bef.
33rd Pz. Rgt.	8	32	71	20	12

▼ Panzerkampfwagen I Ausf B (Sd Kfz 101)
Pz. Rgt 33 / I Battalion / 3rd Company / 2nd Zug / tank number 1

By 1941, the Pz.Kpfw I was obsolete. Orders were issued to convert all the models at hand into *Munitionsschlepper*, or ammunition carriers. This was originally to be accomplished by building a wooden box on the top of the chassis, but in most cases the removal of the turret provided sufficient space to carry cargo.

Specifications
- Crew: 2
- Weight: 6.4 tonnes (5.8 tons)
- Length: 4.42m (14.5ft)
- Width: 2.06m (6.8ft)
- Height: 1.72m (5.6ft)
- Engine: Maybach NL38TR
- Speed: 40km/hr (24.9mph)
- Range: 170km (105.6 miles)
- Radio: FuG2

▶ Panzerkampfwagen III Ausf H (Sd Kfz 141)
Pz. Rgt 33 / I Battalion / 3rd Company / 2nd Zug / tank number 3

A total of 308 Ausf H variants of the Panzer III were produced between October 1940 and April 1941. This model was armed with one 5cm (2in) KwK L/42 cannon and carried 99 *Panzergranate* and *Sprenggranaten*.

Specifications
- Crew: 5
- Weight: 24 tonnes (21.8 tons)
- Length: 5.41m (17.7ft)
- Width: 2.95m (9.7ft)
- Height: 2.44m (8ft)
- Engine: Maybach HL120TRM
- Speed: 40km/hr (24.9mph)
- Range: 165km (102.5 miles)
- Radio: FuG5

9TH PANZER DIVISION

▶ Panzerkampfwagen II Ausf C (Sd Kfz 121)
Pz. Rgt 33 / I Battalion / 4th Company / 1st Zug / tank number 3

Medium Panzer companies usually had five Pz.Kpfw II assigned for reconnaissance. The tactical number on this example may indicate that the light platoon was designated 1st *Zug* and that the other Pz.Kpfw IV *Zug* were renumbered accordingly.

Specifications

Crew: 3	Engine: Maybach HL62TR
Weight: 9.8 tonnes (8.9 tons)	Speed: 40km/hr (24.9mph)
Length: 4.81m (15.8ft)	Range: 200km (124.3 miles)
Width: 2.22m (7.3ft)	Radio: FuG5
Height: 1.99m (6.5ft)	

▶ Mittlerer Kommandopanzerwagen Ausf C (Sd Kfz 251/6)
Unknown formation

This command vehicle had a FuG11 radio with a range of 50km (31 miles) using key and 10km (6.2 miles) transmitting voice. It used a frame antenna.

Specifications

Crew: 8	Engine: Maybach HL42TUKRM
Weight: 9.4 tonnes (8.5 tons)	Speed: 53km/hr (32.9mph)
Length: 5.98m (19.6ft)	Range: 300km (186.4 miles)
Width: 2.1m (6.9ft)	Radio: FuG11 plus FuG Tr 100W;
Height: 1.75m (5.7ft)	later FuG19 plus FuG12

Fall Blau: the Eastern Front
28 June 1942

In 1942, Hitler abandoned plans to take Moscow as his eyes turned southward with plans to cross the Volga and to seize the Caucasus region and its oilfields.

THE EFFECT OF *FALL BLAU*, the plan for Germany's summer offensive in the south, was to leave Army Groups Centre and North in limbo. Denied the resources to mount any major offensives, Army Group Centre in particular was left to hold the line against an increasingly strong Soviet army. At the beginning of 1942, 9th Panzer was on the line near Kursk. Along with the rest of XLVIII Corps, it was transferred to Army Group South, though it remained in the Kursk sector. When *Fall Blau* opened, forces on the northern flank of the offensive were used to attack past Kursk towards Voronezh, which was reached after a month of fighting across the steppes. In August, the Division was placed in reserve before being pulled back to Army Group Centre at Orel.

ORGANIZATION

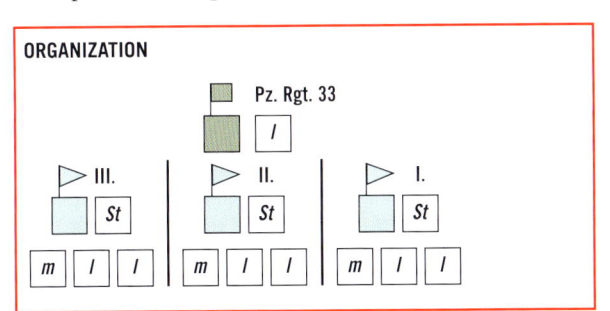

Pz. Rgt. 33 — I
- III. — St — m / l
- II. — St — m / l
- I. — St — m / l

Panzer Unit	Pz. II	Pz. III	Pz. IV(kz)	Pz. IV(lg)	Pz. Bef.
33rd Pz. Rgt.	22	99	9	12	2

9TH PANZER DIVISION

The last summer offensive
1 July 1943

The 9th Panzer Division's armoured strength was halved in 1943, when the 3rd Battalion was disbanded and the 2nd Battalion was detached to become the 51st Panzer Battalion.

AT THE BEGINNING OF 1943, the 9th Panzer Division had been returned from Army Group South to Army Group Centre, serving with XXVII Corps of the 9th Army at Rshev. In February, it was transferred to Army Corps *Burdach*, and in March it moved on to Army Corps *Scheele*, part of the 2nd *Panzerarmee* that was located in the Orel sector of the front.

In April 1943, the 9th Panzer Division was placed in the Army Group Reserve before being attached to 2nd *Panzerarmee* Reserve. Over the next two months, the Division was brought up to strength ready for Operation *Zitadelle*, the German offensive at Kursk.

In July 1943, the division was assigned to XLVII Corps of 9th Army. Commanded by General Model, 9th Army was the main strike force of the northern pincer that was intended to isolate and destroy the huge bulge in the frontline around the city of Kursk.

Kursk offensive

When the German offensive at Kursk opened in the early hours of 5 July, 9th Panzer Division could field a single battalion of 14 Panzer IIs, 59 Panzer IIIs and 20 Panzer IVs to cut the Soviet salient. The 2nd Battalion had been detached to become an independent Tiger battalion.

Panzer Unit	Pz. II	Pz. III	Pz. IV(kz)	Pz. IV(lg)	Pz. Bef.
33rd Pz. Rgt.	1	38	8	30	6

9th Army's assault could make little headway against the Soviet defences. In two days of fierce fighting in sweltering heat, Model's army lost 10,000 men and more than 200 armoured vehicles. Over the next eight days, the Germans advanced less than 20 km (12.4 miles), before being forced to retreat by a Soviet counteroffensive.

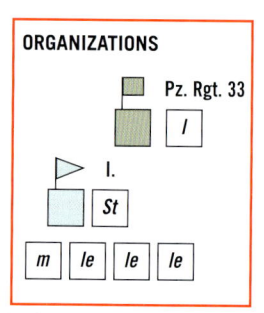

The operation at Kursk was the last major German offensive in the East as the *Wehrmacht* lost the initiative to the Red Army. For the rest of the year, 9th Panzer continued to retreat, taking heavy losses in the murderous fighting on the Dnieper River.

In August, 9th Panzer was again transferred, becoming part of XLI Corps of the 2nd *Panzerarmee* at Briansk. In September, it was moved south to join the reconstituted 6th Army at Mius and Stalino. In October, it was fighting with 1st Panzer Army at Zaporozhe, and at the end of the year it was in action at Krivoi Rog.

ORGANIZATIONS

▶ **7.5cm PaK40/3 auf Panzerkampfwagen 38(t) Ausf H (Sd Kfz 138)**
50th Panzerjäger Battalion
Nine kills rings are painted on the barrel of this vehicle. After the failure of the Kursk offensive, the 9th Panzer was heavily involved in the defensive battles that drove the *Wehrmacht* back to the Dneipr River, and suffered serious losses in the winter of 1943–44.

Specifications
Crew: 4
Weight: 11.9 tonnes (10.8 tons)
Length: 5.77m (18.9ft)
Width: 2.16m (7ft)
Height: 2.51m (8.2ft)

Engine: Praga EPA/2
Speed: 35km/hr (21.7mph)
Range: 250km (155.3 miles)
Radio: FuG5

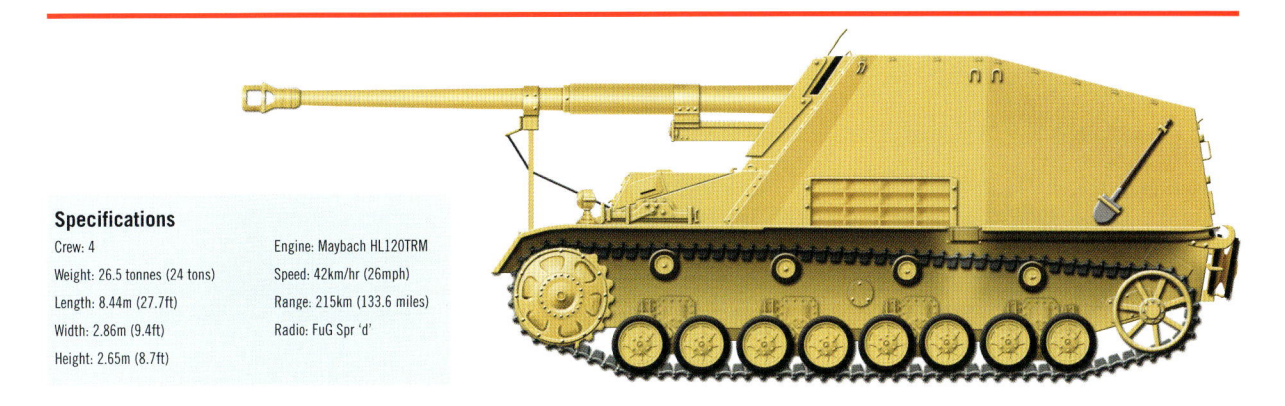

9TH PANZER DIVISION

Specifications
Crew: 4
Weight: 26.5 tonnes (24 tons)
Length: 8.44m (27.7ft)
Width: 2.86m (9.4ft)
Height: 2.65m (8.7ft)
Engine: Maybach HL120TRM
Speed: 42km/hr (26mph)
Range: 215km (133.6 miles)
Radio: FuG Spr 'd'

▲ **8.8cm PaK43/1 (L/71) auf Fahrgestell Panzerkampfwagen III/IV (Sf)**
50th Panzerjäger Battalion
A total of 30 'Nashorn' was listed as operational in 1943. When employed from defensive positions, the 'Nashorn' was a formidable weapon. It was able to defeat any armour with its 8.8cm (3.5in) cannon, and several instances were recorded of a single tank destroyer annihilating a whole company of Russian tanks.

Panzer-Jäger-Kompanie 'Nashorn' (8.8cm PaK43) K.St.N 1148b

Introduced in 1943, the Nashorn, or 'Rhinoceros', was a powerful self-propelled tank-hunter mounting the PaK variant of the 8.8cm (3.5in) FlaK gun onto a modified Panzer IV. This was lengthened, and the motor was moved forward from the rear to the centre of the vehicle. The Nashorns were issued to independent *schwere Panzerjäger abteilungen*, attached to formations at corps or army level. Typically, a heavy *Panzerjäger* battalion would include a staff battery with three Nashorns and three *Flakvierling* quad 2cm (0.8in) air defence guns, and three *Panzerjäger* companies arranged as seen here.

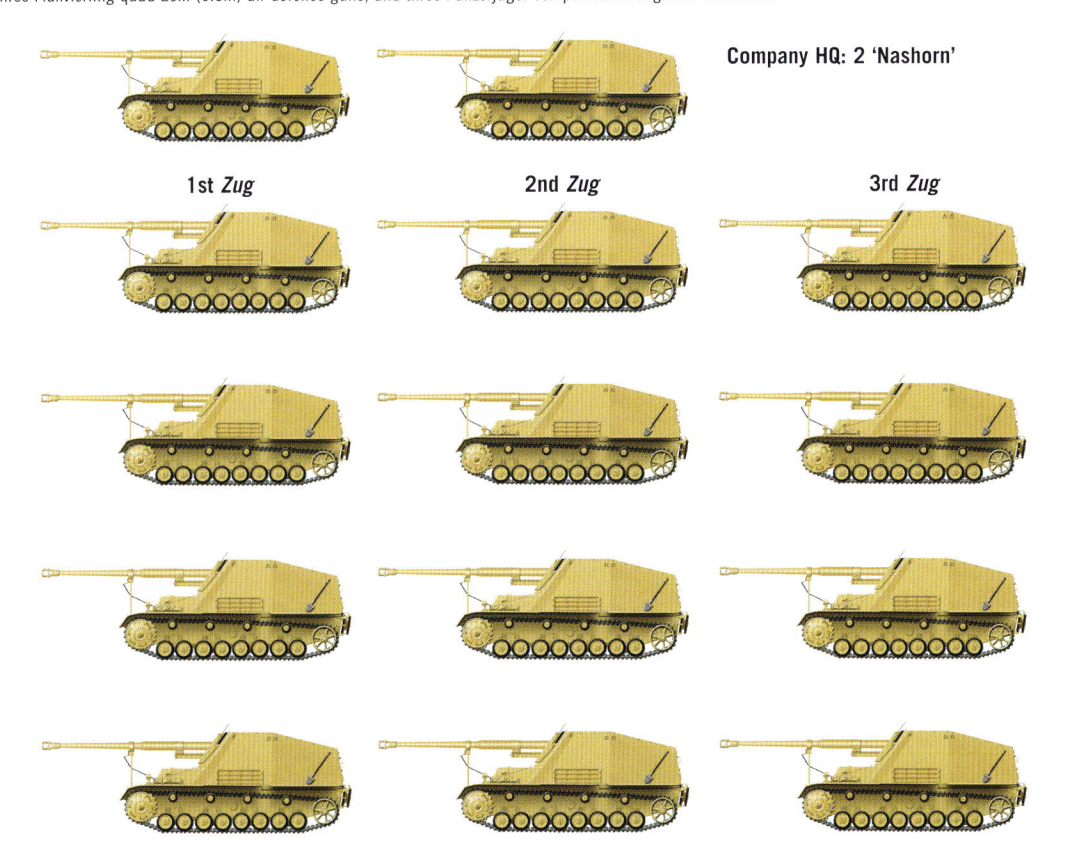

Company HQ: 2 'Nashorn'

1st *Zug*   2nd *Zug*   3rd *Zug*

93

9TH PANZER DIVISION

The Western Front
JUNE 1944

Early in 1944, the 9th Panzer Division arrived in Carcassonne in southern France, where it was to be refitted. It absorbed the 155th Reserve Panzer Division in the process.

THE 51ST BATTALION had traded in its Tigers for Panthers, and rejoined the division as the 2nd Battalion, 33rd Panzer Regiment. The 1st Battalion was now equipped with long-barrelled Panzer IVs. Based in the South of France, it was in no position to intervene when the Allies landed in Normandy in June 1944. Ordered north in July, it took weeks to cover the distance. *Maquis* attacks and sabotaged bridges delayed matters, and as they got closer to Normandy, Allied air attacks meant that they were only able to travel during the short summer nights. By the time the unit arrived in Normandy, the Americans had already broken out of the beachhead, and the British were pressing southward from Caen. The Division arrived on the battle front just in time to be caught in the Falaise Pocket, escaping only after most of its men were killed or captured, and with only 12 tanks.

ORGANIZATION

Pz. Rgt. 33 / St
II. St — I. St
IV IV IV IV | V V V V

Panzer Unit	Pz. IV	Pz. V	Flk.Pz
33rd Pz. Rgt.	79	79	8

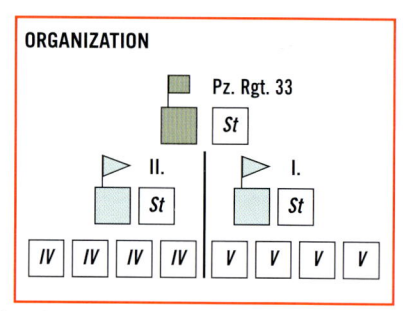

▶ **Jagdpanzer 38(t) Hetzer (Panzerjäger 38(t)) fur 7.5cm PaK39**
50th Panzerjäger Battalion

Some 2584 Hetzers were produced from April 1944 to May 1945. The MG34 or MG42 machine gun was internally controlled. This effective tank-destroyer was armed with one 7.5cm (3in) PaK39 L/48 cannon, and carried 41 rounds of ammunition.

Specifications
Crew: 4
Weight: 17.4 tonnes (15.75 tons)
Length: 6.38m (20.9ft)
Width: 2.63m (8.6ft)
Height: 2.17m (7.1ft)
Engine: Praga AC/2
Speed: 42km/hr (26mph)
Range: 177km (110 miles)
Radio: FuG5 plus FuG Spr 1

▶ **Panzerkampfwagen II Ausf L (Sd Kfz 123)**
9th Reconnaissance Battalion / 1st Company (Luchs)

With the invasion of Normandy, the Division was ordered north. Only able to travel at night because of Allied air superiority over the invasion front, it arrived after the American breakout, Operation *Cobra*, and was caught in the Falaise Pocket. A full company with 29 of these modernized Panzer IIs was in the divisional inventory in August 1943.

Specifications
Crew: 4
Weight: 14.3 tonnes (13 tons)
Length: 4.63m (15.2ft)
Width: 2.48m (8.1ft)
Height: 2.21m (7.3ft)
Engine: Maybach HL66P
Speed: 60km/hr (37.3mph)
Range: 290km (180.2 miles)
Radio: FuG12 plus FuG Spr 'a'

9TH PANZER DIVISION

▶ **Leichte Feldhaubitze 18/2 auf Fahrgestell Panzerkampfwagen II (Sf)**
102nd Panzer Artillery Regiment / 2nd Battalion

The need to provide artillery support to the fast-moving Panzer divisions led to the development of many new examples of self-propelled artillery. 676 Wespe, or 'Wasp', SP guns were produced between February 1943 and July 1944. The Wespe mounted the LeFH 18M L/28 10.5cm (4.1in) howitzer, and was built on the production lines of the now obsolete Pz.Kpfw II.

Specifications
Crew: 5
Weight: 12.1 tonnes (11 tons)
Length: 4.81m (15.8ft)
Width: 2.28m (7.5ft)
Height: 2.3m (7.5ft)
Engine: Maybach HL62TR
Speed: 40km/hr (24.9mph)
Range: 220km (136.7 miles)
Radio: FuG Spr 1

The Battle of the Bulge
14 December 1944

Only 2000 men and 12 tanks escaped from the Falaise Pocket, but a major refit brought the Division up to combat strength in time for the winter offensive in the Ardennes in 1944.

THE ARDENNES OFFENSIVE was Hitler's last gamble in the West. Manteuffel's 5th *Panzerarmee* achieved some success, but was fought to a standstill after penetrating more than 100 km (62 miles) into the Allied lines. Manteuffel called for reinforcements, and 9th Panzer was one of the Panzer divisions that were sent to his assistance, when it was attached to the XLVII Corps. However, even before it arrived, the American 1st and 3rd Armies had begun to roll the German spearheads back. When an Allied counteroffensive began on 3 January, the Germans had nothing left to fight it.

ORGANIZATION
Pz. Rgt. 33
1/Pz.Abt (Tiger/Fkl) 301
II. — St / V / V / V
I. — St / V / IV / IV
Fkl

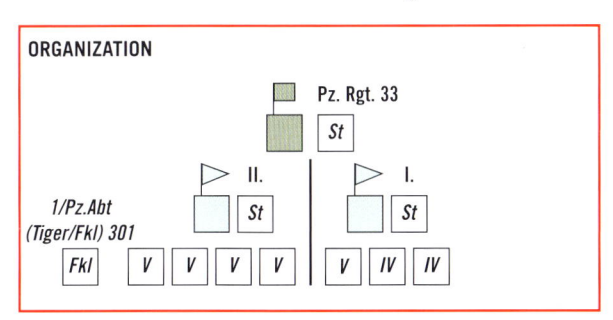

Panzer Unit	Pz. IV	Pz. V	StuG	FlkPz(20)	FlkPz(37)
33rd Pz. Rgt.	28	57	14	4	4

▼ **Schwerer Ladungstrager (Sd Kfz 301) Ausf B**
I Battalion / Schwere Panzer Abteilung (Tiger-Fkl) 301 (Attached)

The *Ladungstrager* was a remote-controlled tracked demolition charge layer. Once the enemy realized that demolition charge layers were being used against them, their first action was to identify and knock out their control vehicle. By using the Tiger I heavy tank as a control vehicle, the 301st had a weapon with enough armour and firepower to keep the enemy at bay and to enable the unit to complete its mission.

Specifications
Crew: 1 (or 0 when remote-controlled)
Weight: 4 tonnes (3.6 tons)
Length: 3.65m (12ft)
Width: 1.8m (6.2ft)
Height: 1.19m (3.9ft)
Engine: Borgward 6M RTBV
Speed: 38km/hr (23.6mph)
Range: 212km (131.7 miles)
Radio: EP3 mit UKE6

9TH PANZER DIVISION

▲ Panzerkampfwagen VI Ausf E (Sd Kfz 181)
I Battalion / Schwere Panzer Abteilung (Tiger-Fkl) 301 / 1st Company / tank number 1 (Attached to 9th Panzer)
No fewer than 70 Allied tanks were claimed as kills by the guns of the Tigers of the 301st Heavy Battalion while it operated with the 9th Panzer Division in the last months of the war. This is a late version of the Tiger I, with all-steel wheels.

Specifications
Crew: 5
Weight: 62.8 tonnes (57 tons)
Length: 8.45m (27.7ft)
Width: 3.7m (12.1ft)
Height: 2.93m (9.6ft)
Engine: Maybach HL210P45
Speed: 38km/hr (23.6mph)
Range: 140km (87 miles)
Radio: FuG5

▶ Panzerkampfwagen IV Ausf H (Sd Kfz 161/2)
Kampfgruppe / Pz. Rgt 33
As deployed in the Harz Region in 1945. During February 1945, the Division unsuccessfully mounted an attack on the US forces in possession of the Remagen Bridge.

Specifications
Crew: 5
Weight: 27.6 tonnes (25 tons)
Length: 7.02m (23ft)
Width: 2.88m (9.4ft)
Height: 2.68m (8.8ft)
Engine: Maybach HL120TRM
Speed: 38km/hr (23.6mph)
Range: 210km (130.5 miles)
Radio: FuG5

▶ Panzerjäger 38(t) mit 7.5cm PaK40/3 Ausf M (Sd Kfz 138)
Kampfgruppe / 50th Panzerjäger Battalion
One of the Division's last operational vehicles, in action in the Cologne region in 1945. The 9th Panzer Division was trapped in the Ruhr Pocket in April 1945, where it surrendered to US forces.

Specifications
Crew: 4
Weight: 11.6 tonnes (10.5 tons)
Length: 4.95m (16.2ft)
Width: 2.15m (7ft)
Height: 2.48m (8.1ft)
Engine: Praga AC
Speed: 42km/hr (26mph)
Range: 190km (118 miles)
Radio: FuG Spr d

10th Panzer Division

The last of the pre-war armoured divisions to be formed, the 10th Panzer Division was also to have the shortest life of all of them.

THE 10TH PANZER DIVISION was created primarily as an occupation force in Czechoslovakia after the final takeover of that country early in 1939. Components of the new Division were provided by other formations, including the 4th Panzer Brigade.

Commanders
General der Panzertruppen F. Schaal
(1 Sept 1939 – 2 Aug 1941)
General der Panzertruppen W. Fischer
(2 Aug 1941 – 1 Feb 1943)
Generalleutnant F. von Broich
(1 Feb 1943 – 12 May 1943)

INSIGNIA

Possibly the simplest of all tactical symbols, the single oblique line was used by the 10th Panzer Division in 1939 and 1940.

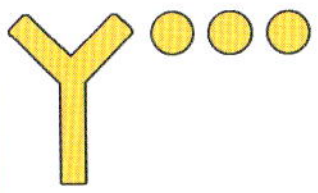

Standard tactical symbol used by 10th Panzer in 1940.

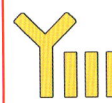

Modified version of the standard 10th Panzer tactical insignia, used by the Division between 1941 and 1943.

Buffalo symbol used by 7th Panzer Regiment, and adopted by some other 10th Panzer units as a *Zusatzsymbol* between 1941 and 1943.

◀ **Defeat in Tunisia**
The men of the 10th Panzer Division were among 150,000 Axis troops who went into captivity in Tunisia following the Allied victory in 1943.

Fall Weiss: the invasion of Poland
1 SEPTEMBER 1939

Newly formed, the 10th Panzer Division was held in reserve for Army Group North during the early days of the Invasion of Poland.

WHEN HEINZ GUDERIAN needed reinforcement for his lightning assault through northern Poland, 10th Panzer was assigned to his XIX Army Corps. The division's first major action was at Wizna, where the Poles had fortified a position to cover the crossings of the Narev and the Biebrza Rivers, and to protect the roads from Bialystock and to Brest-Litovsk.

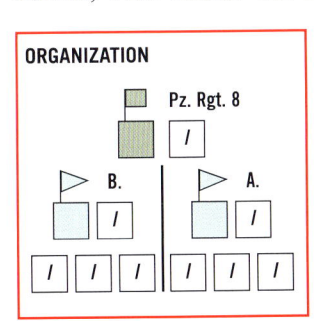

The fortifications were quickly smashed, and Guderian's Panzers advanced towards Wysokie Mazowieckie, encircling and destroying the Polish Narew Corps. After removing these obstacles, Guderian's panzers advanced to Brest Litovsk. Lead units made contact with XXII *Panzerkorps*, advancing from the south on 18 September, one day after the Red Army moved in from the east. The two conquerors then ruthlessly divided Poland.

ORGANIZATION
Pz. Rgt. 8
B.   A.

Panzer Unit	Pz. I	Pz. II	Pz. III	Pz. IV	Pz. Bef.
8th Pz. Rgt.	57	74	3	7	9

10TH PANZER DIVISION

▶ **Panzerkampfwagen II Ausf B (Sd Kfz 121)**
Pz. Rgt 8 / A Battalion / 2nd Company / 3rd Zug / tank number 4
25 Ausf B models were produced between February and March 1937. Succeeding variants had a revised and much more effective suspension and tracks.

Specifications
Crew: 3
Weight: 8.7 tonnes (7.9 tons)
Length: 4.76m (15.6ft)
Width: 2.14m (7ft)
Height: 1.96m (6.4ft)
Engine: Maybach HL62TR
Speed: 40km/hr (24.9mph)
Range: 200km (124.3 miles)
Radio: FuG5

▶ **Panzerfunkwagen (Sd Kfz 263) 8-Rad**
90th Nachrichten Kompanie (Signal Company)
Not intended as a combat vehicle, the Sd Kfz 263 served as a communications hub for Panzer divisions as well as at Corps and Army level. Some 240 examples were manufactured between April 1938 and April 1943.

Specifications
Crew: 5
Weight: 8.9 tonnes (8.1 tons)
Length: 5.85m (19.2ft)
Width: 2.2m (7.2ft)
Height: 2.9m (9.5ft)
Engine: Büssing-NAG L8V
Speed: 100km/hr (62.1mph)
Range: 300km (186.4 miles)
Radio: 1 Satz Funkgerat fur (m) Pz.Funktrupp b

Fall Gelb: the French campaign
10 MAY 1940

After the fall of Poland, 10th Panzer Division was assigned to Army Group A in the Eifel Mountains, as the *Wehrmacht* redeployed its forces westward.

FOR THE CAMPAIGN IN THE WEST, 10th Panzer was once again assigned to Guderian's *Panzerkorps*. Bursting through the Ardennes on 10 May, the corps was through Sedan and across the Meuse by 14 May. 10th Panzer, along with the elite *Grossdeutschland* infantry regiment, provided flank protection while 1st and 2nd Panzer Divisions raced westward. Guderian's corps reached the Channel a week later, cutting off the best of the Allied field armies.

Guderian was rewarded with a two-corps *Panzergruppe* for the next stage of the Battle of France, which saw the Germans strike south on a broad front on 5 June. By the time of the Armistice, Guderian's Panzers had reached the Swiss border and had cut off the French armies on the Maginot Line.

ORGANIZATION

Panzer Unit	Pz. I	Pz. II	Pz. III	Pz. IV	Pz. Bef.
7th Pz. Rgt.	22	58	29	16	9
8th Pz. Rgt.	22	55	29	16	9

10TH PANZER DIVISION

▶ Panzerkampfwagen III Ausf E (Sd Kfz 141)
Pz. Rgt 7 / A Battalion / 1st Company / 2nd Zug / tank number 2

The 10th Panzer Division was part of *Panzergruppe* von Kleist during the Western campaign, advancing through Belgium to the Meuse.

Specifications

Crew: 5
Weight: 24 tonnes (21.8 tons)
Length: 5.41m (17.7ft)
Width: 2.95m (9.7ft)
Height: 2.44m (8ft)
Engine: Maybach HL120TRM
Speed: 40km/hr (24.9mph)
Range: 165km (102.5 miles)
Radio: FuG5

▼ Panzerkampfwagen I Ausf A (Sd Kfz 101)
Pz. Rgt 7 / A Battalion / 1st Company / 3rd Zug / tank number 4

The early Ausf A had four road wheels, with the idler wheel touching the ground. The suspension was satisfactory at low speeds, but it pitched badly when moving faster. The turret was all welded, and was armed with two 7.92mm (0.3 in) MGs, which were operated by the commander who had to perform as the gunner as well.

Specifications

Crew: 2
Weight: 6 tonnes (5.4 tons)
Length: 4.02m (13.2ft)
Width: 2.06m (6.8ft)
Height: 1.72m (5.6ft)
Engine: Krupp M305
Speed: 37km/hr (23mph)
Range: 145km (90 miles)
Radio: FuG2

▶ Panzerkampfwagen IV Ausf B (Sd Kfz 161)
Pz. Rgt 7 / B Battalion / 4th Company / 3rd Zug / tank number 2

The Ausf B had a straight front hull. It was fitted by a more powerful engine, the 300hp Maybach HL 120 T engine with a new ZF six-speed SSG 76 transmission.

Specifications

Crew: 5
Weight: 20.7 tonnes (18.8 tons)
Length: 5.92m (19.4ft)
Width: 2.83m (9.3ft)
Height: 2.68m (8.8ft)
Engine: Maybach HL120TR
Speed: 40km/hr (24.9mph)
Range: 200km (124.3 miles)
Radio: FuG5

▶ Panzerkampfwagen II Ausf b (Sd Kfz 121)
Pz. Rgt 7 / B Battalion / 5th Company / 4th Zug / tank number 2

The Ausf B variant of the Panzer II incorporated numerous modifications to improve the vehicle compared to the first series. The main improvements involved a larger motor and strengthening the drive mountings and transmission.

Armament Specifications

Main gun: 2cm (0.8 in) KwK30 L/55 in left of turret
Ammunition: 180 rounds
Traverse: 360° (manual)
Elevation: -9.5° to +20°
Sight: TZF4
Secondary: 7.92mm (0.3in) MG34 in right of turret
Ammunition: 2250 rounds
MG sight: As for main armament

10TH PANZER DIVISION

▼ 15cm sIG33 (Sf) auf Panzerkampfwagen I Ausf B
706th Schwere Infanteriegeschütz Abteilung

Heavy Infantry Gun detachments were assigned to six of the Panzer divisions engaged in the Western campaign in 1940.

The letter 'K' is used to identify units assigned to *Panzergruppe von Kleist*, which included the three panzer corps spearheading Germany's surprise attack through the Ardennes.

Specifications
Crew: 4
Weight: 9.4 tonnes (8.5 tons)
Length: 4.67m (15.3ft)
Width: 2.06m (6.8ft)
Height: 2.8m (9.2ft)
Engine: Maybach NL38TR
Speed: 40km/hr (24.9mph)
Range: 140km (87 miles)
Radio: Name

Barbarossa: the attack on Russia
22 JUNE 1941

While 10th Panzer remained on occupation duties in France until February 1941, the 8th Panzer Regiment was detached and assigned to the 15th Panzer Division, destined for Africa.

THE 10TH PANZER DIVISION returned to Germany in March 1941, and was assigned to Army Group Centre for Operation *Barbarossa*. As part of Hoth's 3rd *Panzergruppe*, the division fought through Minsk, Smolensk and Vyasma before joining 4th *Panzerarmee* for the assault on Moscow.

Driven back from the gates of the Soviet capital, 10th Panzer remained with Army Group Centre until May 1942, when it was transferred to Army Group D in France. It was one of the units used to respond to the British and Canadian forces that raided Dieppe.

Panzer Unit	Pz. II	Pz. III(50)	Pz. IV	Pz. Bef
7th Pz. Rgt.	45	105	20	12

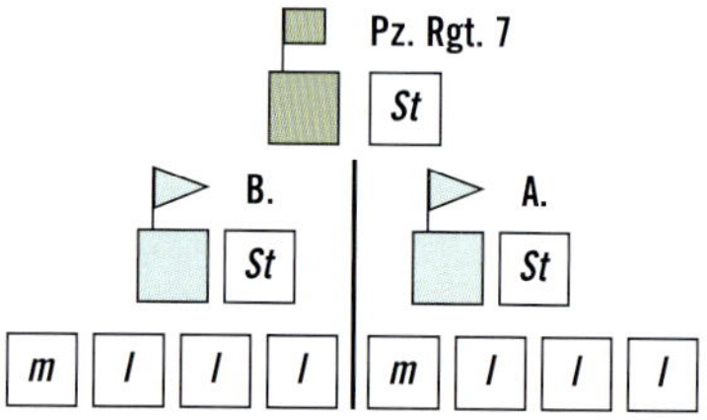

▶ Panzerbefehlswagen III Ausf E (Sd Kfz 266-267-268)
Pz. Rgt 7 / B Battalion / Stabskompanie / Signal Platoon / signal officer tank

The 7th Panzer Regiment used the letters 'A' and 'B' to identify its battalions, instead of the roman numerals used by other units.

Specifications
Crew: 5
Weight: 21.5 tonnes (19.5 tons)
Length: 5.38m (17.7ft)
Width: 2.91m (9.5ft)
Height: 2.44m (8ft)
Engine: Maybach HL120TR
Speed: 40km/hr (24.9mph)
Range: 165km (102.5 miles)
Radio: FuG6 plus FuG2 or FuG7 or FuG8

10TH PANZER DIVISION

▶ Panzerkampfwagen III Ausf G (Sd Kfz 141)
Pz. Rgt 7 / A Battalion / 3rd Company / 4th Zug / tank number 3

For Operation *Barbarossa*, the 10th Panzer was part of Army Group Centre, assigned to *Panzergruppe Guderian*.

Specifications
Crew: 5
Weight: 22.4 tonnes (20.3 tons)
Length: 5.41m (17.7ft)
Width: 2.95m (9.7ft)
Height: 2.44m (8ft)
Engine: Maybach HL120TRM
Speed: 40km/hr (24.9mph)
Range: 165km (102.5 miles)
Radio: FuG5

▶ Panzerkampfwagen T-34 747 (r)
Pz. Rgt 7

A Captured Russian T-34 model 1941. General Guderian requested that German industry copy this tank, but the Panther which emerged was a much more sophisticated vehicle.

Specifications
Crew: 4
Weight: 34.6 tonnes (31.39 tons)
Length: 6.58m (21.6ft)
Width: 2.98m (9.8ft)
Height: 2.57m (8.4ft)
Engine: V-2-34
Speed: 40km/hr (24.9mph)
Range: 430km (267 miles)
Radio: 10R

▶ Panzerkampfwagen III Ausf H (Sd Kfz 141)
Pz. Rgt 7 / B Battalion / 6th Company / 2nd Zug / tank number 1

By October 1941, the 10th Panzer was 60km (37.3 miles) from Moscow. By December, temperatures of -35°C (-31° F) had frozen it in place.

Specifications
Crew: 5
Weight: 24 tonnes (21.8 tons)
Length: 5.41m (17.7ft)
Width: 2.95m (9.7ft)
Height: 2.44m (8ft)
Engine: Maybach HL120TRM
Speed: 40km/hr (24.9mph)
Range: 165km (102.5 miles)
Radio: FuG5

▶ Panzerjäger 38(t) fur 7.62cm PaK36 (r) (Sd Kfz 139)
90th Panzerjäger Battalion / 1st Self-propelled Battery / 1st Zug / tank number 3

The 1st Self-propelled Battery was equipped with nine 'Marder III' armed with a Russian 76.2mm (3in) gun.

Specifications
Crew: 4
Weight: 11.76 tonnes (10.67 tons)
Length: 5.85m (19.2ft)
Width: 2.16m (7ft)
Height: 2.5m (8.2ft)
Engine: Praga EPA or EPA/2
Speed: 42km/hr (26mph)
Range: 185km (115 miles)
Radio: FuG Spr d

10TH PANZER DIVISION

Defeat in North Africa
NOVEMBER – DECEMBER 1942

Rommel and the *Afrika Korps* had been fighting their own war in North Africa since February 1941. It was now in trouble, after the Battle of Alamein and the Allied landings in Algeria.

ROMMEL HAD LONG BEGGED for reinforcements and now, when it was almost too late, they were being poured into North Africa. The reinforcements included the 10th Panzer Division and the Tigers of sPzAbt 501 and 1/sPzAbt 504.

Rommel conducted a fighting retreat from Libya in the face of Montgomery's vastly more powerful 8th Army. Before leaving North Africa on sick leave, Rommel showed one more spark of his old genius, smashing the inexperienced American II Corps at Kasserine. However, Allied materiel superiority could not be stopped, and Tunisia fell on 12 May 1943.

Survivors of the 10th Panzer Division went into captivity along with the 15th and 21st Panzer Divisions and over 150,000 troops. The 10th Panzer Division was stricken on 30 June 1943. It was never to be reformed.

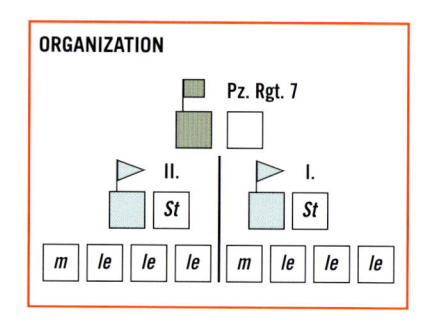

ORGANIZATION

Pz. Rgt. 7

Panzer Unit	Pz. II	Pz. III	Pz. IV(kz)	Pz. IV(lg)	Pz. Bef.
7th Pz. Rgt.	21	105	4	16	9

◀ **Panzerkampfwagen II Ausf F (Sd Kfz 121)**
Pz. Rgt 7 / Regiment Company / Light Platoon

The 10th Panzer was transferred to Tunis in response to Operation *Torch*, the Allied invasion of North Africa. It formed part of the newly created 5th *Panzerarmee* under the command of General von Arnim.

Specifications
Crew: 3
Weight: 10.5 tonnes (9.5 tons)
Length: 4.81m (15.8ft)
Width: 2.28m (7.5ft)
Height: 2.15m (7ft)
Engine: Maybach HL62TR
Speed: 40km/hr (24.9mph)
Range: 200km (124.3 miles)
Radio: FuG5

▶ **Panzerkampfwagen III Ausf L (Sd Kfz 141/1)**
Pz. Rgt 7 / II Battalion / 7th Company

653 Ausf L variants of the Panzer III were produced between June and December 1942. The Ausf L was armed with a long-barrelled 5cm (2in) KwK L/60, and its front turret armour had been increased from 30mm (1.2in) to 57mm (2.2in) thickness.

Specifications
Crew: 5
Weight: 22.7 tons (25 tonnes)
Length: 6.28m (20.6ft)
Width: 2.95m (9.7ft)
Height: 2.5m (8.2ft)
Engine: Maybach HL120TRM
Speed: 40km/hr (24.9mph)
Range: 155km (96.3 miles)
Radio: FuG5

10TH PANZER DIVISION

Specifications
Crew: 5
Weight: 25.9 tonnes (23.5 tons)
Length: 6.62m (21.7ft)
Width: 2.88m (9.4ft)
Height: 2.68m (8.8ft)
Engine: Maybach HL120TRM
Speed: 40km/hr (24.9mph)
Range: 210km (130.5 miles)
Radio: FuG5

▲ **Panzerkampfwagen IV Ausf G (Sd Kfz 161/1 und 161/2)**
Pz. Rgt 7 / II Batalion / 8th Company / 2nd Zug / tank number 3
The Ausf G variant of the Panzer IV had one 7.5cm (3in) KwK40 L/48 cannon and carried a total of 87 antitank, high-explosive and smoke rounds. This is a late version of the Ausf G, with the vision port in the turret side removed. The cannon had the new-style muzzle brake and the turret carried a new cupola with thicker armour.

▶ **Schwerer Panzerspähwagen (7.5cm) (Sd Kfz 233)**
10th Motorcycle Battalion / 5th Heavy Company
In spite of its name, the 10th Motorcycle Battalion included the 1st Armoured Car Company, the 2nd Half-track Company and the 5th Heavy Company, as well as the 3rd and 4th Motorcycle Companies. The license plate carried by this close-support armoured car was WH 240815.

Specifications
Crew: 3
Weight: 9.6 tonnes (8.7 tons)
Length: 5.85m (19.2ft)
Width: 2.2m (7.2ft)
Height: 2.25m (7.4ft)
Engine: Büssing-NAG L8V
Speed: 80km/hr (49.7mph)
Range: 300km (186.4 miles)
Radio: FuG Spr Ger 'a'

▶ **7.5cm Sturmgeschütz 40 Ausf F/8 (Sd Kfz 142/1)**
I Battalion / Sturmgeschütz Abteilung 242 (Attached to division)
The Ausf F/8 variant of the StuG III was armed with one 7.5cm (3in) StuK40 L/48 cannon, and it carried 44 rounds of ammunition. Only one battery of the 242nd Battalion made it to North Africa; the rest of the unit was sent to the Eastern Front.

Specifications
Crew: 4
Weight: 25.6 tonnes (23.2 tons)
Length: 6.77m (22.2ft)
Width: 2.92m (9.6ft)
Height: 2.15m (7ft)
Engine: Maybach HL120TRM
Speed: 40km/hr (24.9mph)
Range: 140km (87 miles)
Radio: FuG15 or FuG16

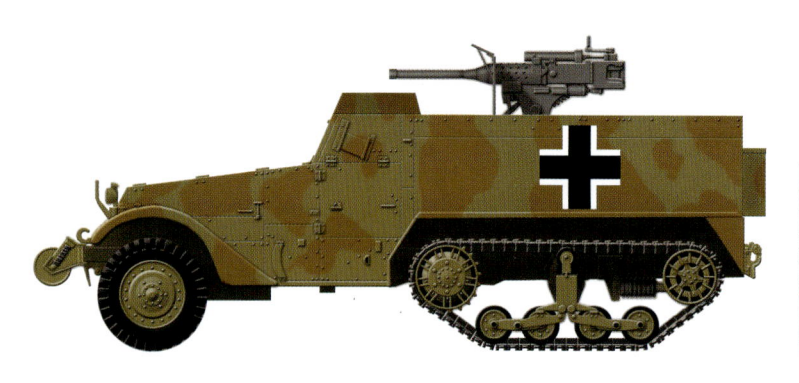

10TH PANZER DIVISION

Specifications
Crew: 6
Weight: c. 9.9 tonnes (9 tons)
Length: 6.2m (20.3ft)
Width: 2.24m (7.3ft)
Height: 2.28m (7.5ft)
Engine: White 160AX
Speed: 72km/hr (44.7mph)
Range: 290km (180.2 miles)
Radio: (if fitted) FuG Spr Ger 1

▲ **Mittlerer Schützenpanzerwagen M3(a)**
Unknown formation
The 10th Panzer Division captured several American vehicles in North Africa and pressed them into service immediately against their former owners. This example is a self-propelled anti-aircraft gun, with a French 3.7cm (1.5in) M1925 gun mounted onto an American M3 half-track. The M1925 was the primary light AA weapon in French warships. Its rate of fire was 30–42 rounds per minute.

▶ **Infanterie Panzerkampfwagen Mk III 749(e)**
Pz. Rgt 7
A Captured British Valentine Mk III infantry tank, armed with one 2pdr (40mm) gun. Two Valentines were among the 16 German tanks lost at the Kasserine Pass, when the *Afrika Korps* inflicted inflicted a stinging reverse and severe losses to the inexperienced American forces who had landed in North Africa.

The National cross variant generally (but not always) used in North Africa was toned down to match the desert camouflage applied to vehicles in the theatre.

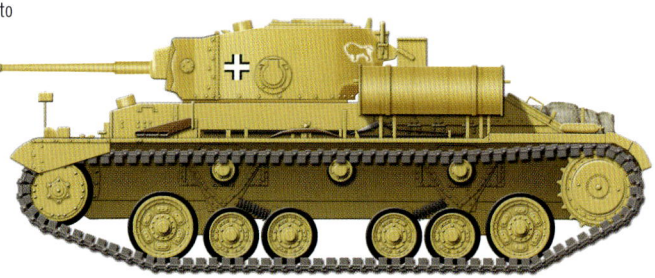

Specifications
Crew: 3
Weight: 18.7 tonnes (17 tons)
Length: 5.89m (19.3ft)
Width: 2.63m (8.6ft)
Height: 2.273m (7.5ft)
Engine: AEC or GMS 6-cyl diesel
Speed: 24km/hr (15mph)
Range: 145km (90 miles)
Radio: British No.9 set

▶ **Panzerkampfwagen III Ausf N (Sd Kfz 141/2)**
Pz. Rgt 7 / II Battalion / 7th Company / 2nd Zug / tank number 3
The light companies of the 501st Heavy Tank Battalion, the first Tiger tank unit, were absorbed by the 7th Regiment and incorporated into the 7th and 8th Companies. The Ausf N Panzer III issued to the 501st Heavy Panzer Battalion were converted from Ausf L chassis.

Specifications
Crew: 5
Weight: 25.4 tonnes (23 tons)
Length: 5.52m (18.1ft)
Width: 2.95m (9.7ft)
Height: 2.5m (8.2ft)
Engine: Maybach HL120TRM
Speed: 40km/hr (24.9mph)
Range: 155km (96.3 miles)
Radio: FuG5

10TH PANZER DIVISION

Schwere Panzer Kompanie

The first Heavy Panzer Companies were formed early in 1942, providing the cores of the first Heavy Panzer Battalions later that year. The early organization of the companies saw the massive Pz.Kpfw VI Tiger serving in mixed platoons with Pz.Kpfw IIIs. The mobile Panzer IIs provided flank protection for the ponderous Tigers. The 501st and 503rd Battalions were sent to North Africa at the end of 1942. In March 1943, the organization changed, with each battalion equipped only with Tigers.

1st *Zug*   2nd *Zug*   3rd *Zug*

Specifications

Crew: 5
Weight: 62.8 tonnes (57 tons)
Length: 8.45m (27.7ft)
Width: 3.7m (12.1ft)
Height: 2.93m (9.6ft)
Engine: Maybach HL210P45
Speed: 38km/hr (23.6mph)
Range: 140km (87 miles)
Radio: FuG5

▼ **Panzerkampfwagen VI Ausf E (Sd Kfz 181)**
Pz. Rgt 7 / II Battalion / 8th Company / 2nd Zug / tank number 3

Until their surrender, the Tigers and Ausf N of the 501st claimed to have destroyed 170 Allied tanks. The remnants of the 10th Panzer Division surrendered with the rest of the *Afrika Korps* in May 1943, and was never reformed.

105

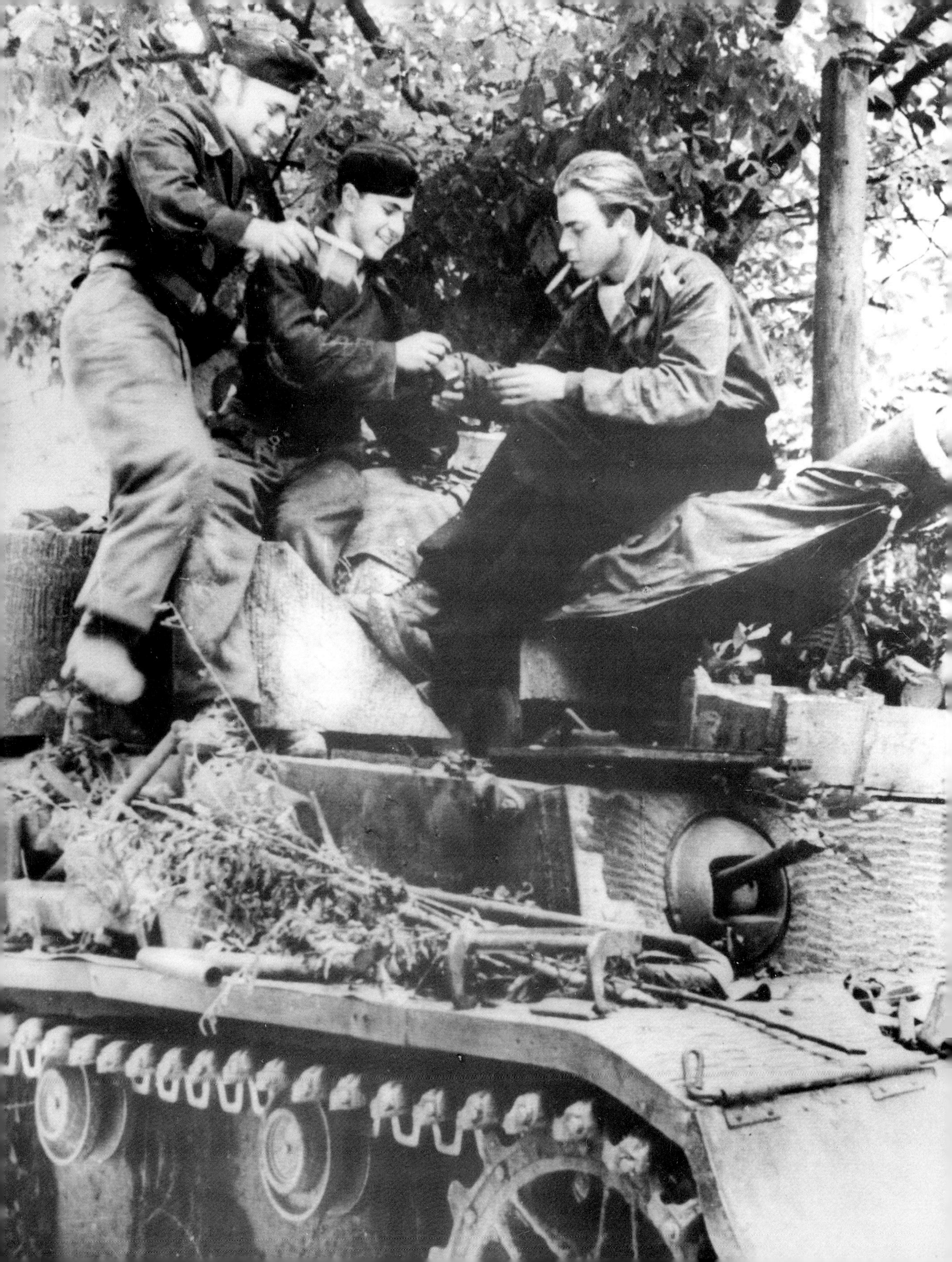

Chapter 3

1940–41 Panzer Divisions

The triumphant conquest of France and the Low Countries in May and June 1940 proved that the Panzer was the essential component of the modern, *Blitzkrieg*-style of warfare. Ten Panzer divisions had provided sufficient armoured power to complete the conquest of France, but even as the Battle of Britain commenced Hitler's eyes were looking eastwards. To win a war with the Soviet Union, the *Wehrmacht* was going to need more tanks, more motorized infantry and more tank divisions.

◀ **Panzer Professionals**
By the time of Operation *Barbarossa* – the Invasion of the Soviet Union in June 1941 – the German Panzerwaffe was the most experienced and most capable armoured force in the world.

11th Panzer Division

The massive expansion of the *Panzerwaffe*, which began after the Battle of France, placed a great strain on the *Wehrmacht*'s capacity to man the new Panzer formations.

THE 11TH PANZER DIVISION was established on 1 August 1940. The motorized infantry component of the formation was provided by the independent 11th *Schützen* Brigade, while the experienced 15th Panzer Regiment was transferred from the 5th Panzer Division to provide the armoured core. The motorcycle, reconnaissance and *Panzerjäger* battalions were newly formed, with men coming from the 231st Infantry Division.

INSIGNIA

The standard tactical symbol used by the 11th Panzer Division from its foundation to the end of the war in 1945.

An occasionally seen variant of the standard divisional insignia, with an interrupted outer circle.

A *Zusatzsymbol*, or additional mark, carried from 1941 to 1945. Derived from the 'ghost' nickname acquired by the 15th Panzer Regiment in 1940.

Commanders

General der Panzertruppen L. Cruwell
(1 Aug 1940 – 15 Aug 1941)

Generalleutnant G. Angern
(15 Aug 1941 – 24 Aug 1941)

General der Panzertruppen H. von Esebeck
(24 Aug 1941 – 20 Oct 1941)

Generalleutnant W. Scheller
(20 Oct 1941 – 16 May 1942)

General der Panzertruppen H. Balck
(16 May 1942 – 4 Mar 1943)

General der Infanterie D. von Choltitz
(4 Mar 1943 – 15 May 1943)

Generalleutnant J. Mickl
(15 May 1943 – 10 Aug 1943)

Generalleutnant W. von Wietersheim
(10 Aug 1943 – 10 Apr 1945)

Generalmajor H. Freiherr Treusch und Buttlar – Brandenfels
(10 Apr 1945)

Signals units were provided by the 311th Infantry Division, the Pioneers or combat engineers were transferred from the 209th Infantry Division, and another *Schützen* battalion was organized from a regiment of the 4th Infantry Division.

War in the Balkans
6 APRIL 1941

After working up in Germany, 11th Panzer was assigned to XIV Corps of 12th Army in Poland. Early in 1941, it went with 12th Army to Romania and Bulgaria for the invasion of Yugoslavia.

THE 11TH PANZER DIVISION was attached to Kleist's 1st *Panzergruppe* for the invasion of Yugoslavia, attacking across the Bulgarian border on 7 April. After driving towards Skopje, 5th and 11th Panzer Divisions were detached from Kleist's force and directed northwards towards Nis in Serbia. After taking the town, 11th Panzer pushed on towards Belgrade.

Racing north, 11th Panzer units aimed to be first to reach the Yugoslav capital, but were chagrined to discover once they had entered the suburbs that they were hours too late. They had been beaten to Belgrade by 10 men from the motorcycle reconnaissance company of SS Division *Reich* (later to become the SS Panzer Division *Das Reich*), who had taken the surrender of the city.

The fall of Belgrade brought the conventional war in Yugoslavia to an end, but it marked the beginning of four years of brutal partisan war.

ORGANIZATION

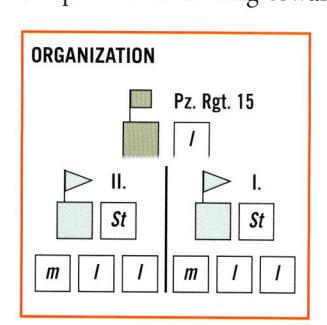

Pz. Rgt. 15

Panzer Unit	Pz. II	Pz. III(37)	Pz. III(50)	Pz. IV	Pz. Bef.
15th Pz. Rgt.	45	25	26	16	14

11TH PANZER DIVISION

▶ **Kleiner Panzerbefehlswagen (Sd Kfz 265)**

Pz. Rgt 15 / II Battalion / Stabskompanie / Signal Platoon / tank number 4

The yellow circle indicates that this small command vehicle belonged to the 2nd Battalion. A yellow tactical number '04' was painted on the front of the vehicle.

Specifications

Crew: 3
Weight: 6.5 tonnes (5.9 tons)
Length: 4.42m (14.5ft)
Width: 2.06m (6.8ft)
Height: 1.99m (6.5ft)
Engine: Maybach NL38TR
Speed: 40km/hr (24.9mph)
Range: 170km (105.6 miles)
Radio: FuG2 and FuG6

▶ **Panzerkampfwagen IV Ausf E (Sd Kfz 161)**

Pz. Rgt 15

The 11 Panzer Division used a two-digit tactical number (platoon/tank number). The 15th Regiment was also known as the *Gespenster,* or 'Ghost', Regiment after reports from prisoners taken during the invasion of France, to the effect that the 15th Regiment, then with the 5th Panzer Division, appeared from nowhere.

Specifications

Crew: 5
Weight: 23.2 tonnes (21 tons)
Length: 5.92m (19.4ft)
Width: 2.84m (9.3ft)
Height: 2.68m (8.8ft)
Engine: Maybach HL120TRM
Speed: 42km/hr (26mph)
Range: 200km (124.3 miles)
Radio: FuG5

Leichte Panzerkompanie 'Gliederung'

The organization of the Light Panzer Company changed considerably after the fall of France. The pause in the fighting after July 1940 gave German industry the chance to build up production of modern tanks, allowing the German army to replace many of the obsolete vehicles with which it had fought from the outbreak of war. The light companies, originally equipped with a mix of Pz.Kpf Is and Pz.Kpfw IIs, now took delivery of large numbers of Pz.Kpfw IIIs. By early 1941, the Command troop of the company was exclusively equipped with Panzer IIIs, as were the 1st, 2nd and 3rd *Zugen* or Platoons. One *Zug* in each company was designated as a Light Platoon, and these retained the lightweight Panzer II. These were more suited to reconnaissance than the Panzer IIIs.

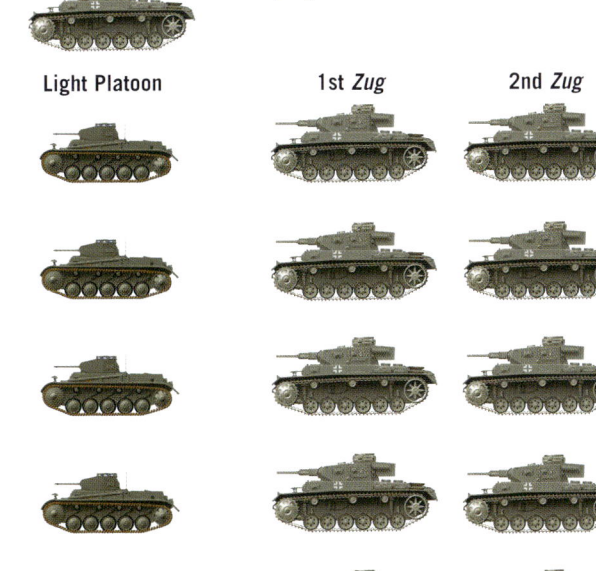

11TH PANZER DIVISION

▶ **Mittlerer Gepanzerter Beobachtungskraftwagen (Sd Kfz 254)**
119th Panzer Artillery Regiment

This artillery observation vehicle was assigned to the 3rd Battery of a towed artillery battalion operating in Yugoslavia in 1941. One of the few diesel-powered vehicles in German service, the SdKfz 254 chassis, with its unique wheel-cum-track arrangement, was originally designed by Saurer for the Austrian army.

Specifications
Crew: 7
Weight: 7 tonnes (6.4 tons)
Length: 4.56m (15ft)
Width (on wheels): 2.2m (7.2ft)
Height: 1.88m (6.2ft)
Engine: Saurer CRDv
Speed: 60km/hr (37.3mph)
Range (on wheels): 500km (310.7 miles)
Radio: FuG4 plus FuG8 and FuG Spr Ger 'f'

The vehicle carries the Divisional insignia and the military symbol for communications troops. Front plate licence plate WH-800920.

▶ **Mittlerer Schützenpanzerwagen Ausf B (Sd Kfz 251/1)**
11th Schützen Brigade / 110th Schützen Regiment

Markings on this standard troop carrier indicate that it was assigned to the Battalion's 2nd Motorized Infantry Company.

The vehicle carries the motorized infantry symbol on the left front mudguard, next to the shielded headlight.

Specifications
Crew: 2 plus 12 troops
Weight: 9.9 tonnes (9 tons)
Length: 5.98m (19.6ft)
Width: 2.1m (6.9ft)
Height: 1.75m (5.7ft) or 2.16m (7ft)
with MG shield
Engine: Maybach HL42TUKRM
Speed: 53km/hr (32.9mph)
Range: 300km (186.4 miles)
Radio: FuG Spr Ger f

Barbarossa: the attack on Russia
22 JUNE 1941

Following the Yugoslav campaign, 11th Panzer returned to Germany to refit, which meant that it missed the opening days of Operation *Barbarossa*.

ATTACHED TO ARMY GROUP SOUTH, the 11th Panzer Division entered combat in the Ukraine in July. After fighting through Zhitomir and Uman, it was in reserve for the great encirclement at Kiev. On 11 October, Panzer transferred to the 4th *Panzergruppe*, which was part of Army Group Centre, for the delayed assault on Moscow. The division remained active with Army Group Centre until well into the summer of 1942.

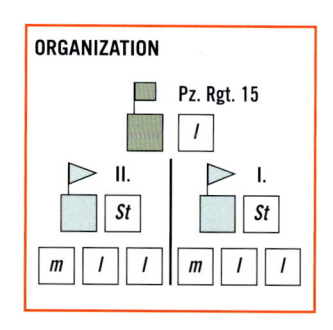

Panzer Unit	Pz. II	Pz. III(37)	Pz. III(50)	Pz. IV	Pz. Bef.
15th Pz. Rgt.	44	24	47	20	8

ORGANIZATION

Pz. Rgt. 15

11TH PANZER DIVISION

▶ **Panzerkampfwagen III Ausf H (Sd Kfz 141)**
Pz. Rgt 15 / I Battalion / 1st Company

The Ausf H variant of the Pz.Kpfw III was the first to be armed with the 5cm (2in) KwK L/42 gun. It was introduced to service in October 1940. 1st Company vehicles were recognizable by the use of a white tank rhomboid on the turret side. It was fitted with an extra storage box on the back of the turret, commonly known as a 'Rommel' kit.

Markings on the 'Rommel' kit – extra storage attached to the rear of the turret – indicated that this tank belonged to the Battalion's 1st Company.

Specifications
Crew: 5
Weight: 24 tonnes (21.8 tons)
Length: 5.41m (17.7ft)
Width: 2.95m (9.7ft)
Height: 2.44m (8ft)
Engine: Maybach HL120TRM
Speed: 40km/hr (24.9mph)
Range: 165km (102.5 miles)
Radio: FuG5

▶ **Panzerkampfwagen II Ausf F (Sd Kfz 121)**
Pz. Rgt 15 / II Battalion / 5th Company / 2nd Platoon

At the start of Operation *Barbarossa*, 11th Panzer still had 44 Panzer IIs in its inventory. The Ausf F was armed with one 2cm (0.8in) KwK30 L/55 automatic cannon and carried 180 PzGr and SpGr rounds. The white circle was used to identify units of the 2nd Platoon of one of the Light Panzer companies.

Specifications
Crew: 3
Weight: 10.5 tonnes (9.5 tons)
Length: 4.81m (15.8ft)
Width: 2.28m (7.5ft)
Height: 2.15m (7ft)
Engine: Maybach HL62TR
Speed: 40km/hr (24.9mph)
Range: 200km (124.3 miles)
Radio: FuG5

▶ **Panzerkampfwagen IV Ausf D (Sd Kfz 161)**
Pz. Rgt 15

The 11th Panzer Division was part of the 1st *Panzergruppe*, Army Group South during the drive on Kiev in the summer of 1941. The Division had 20 Panzer IVs, which operated with the Medium Panzer companies of each battalion.

Specifications
Crew: 5
Weight: 22 tonnes (20 tons)
Length: 5.92m (19.4ft)
Width: 2.84m (9.3ft)
Height: 2.68m (8.8ft)
Engine: Maybach HL120TRM
Speed: 40km/hr (24.9mph)
Range: 200km (124.3 miles)
Radio: FuG5

11TH PANZER DIVISION

⊕ *Fall Blau*: the Eastern Front
28 June 1942

In July 1942, the 11th Panzer Division transferred with 4th *Panzerarmee* from Army Group Centre to Army Group South, where it was to support the summer offensive in southern Russia.

4TH *PANZERARMEE* struck westwards towards Voronezh, before being moved 500 km (310.7 miles) south to guard the flank of Paulus' 6th Army advancing on Stalingrad. Coming under the command of Manstein's Army Group Don, 11th Panzer was detached once the Red Army encircled Stalingrad, being sent to support Romanian forces of the Chir River.

Under the command of one of the outstanding Panzer commanders of the war, Hermann Balck, 11th Panzer fought first to reach the forces trapped in Stalingrad, and then to counter the massive Soviet offensives which followed. The battles on the Chir saw the destruction of more than 700 Soviet tanks – but the understrength 11th Panzer Division was all but destroyed in the process.

Panzer Unit	Pz. II	Pz. III(kz)	Pz. III(lg)	Pz. IV	Pz. Bef.
15th Pz. Rgt.	15	14	110	13	3

ORGANIZATION

Pz. Rgt. 15 — I
- III. St / m / l
- II. St / m / l
- I. St / m / l

⊕ The last summer offensive
1 July 1943

11th Panzer Division's outstanding but costly performance in the Stalingrad campaign meant that Hitler ordered the Division's recreation almost immediately.

BY MAY OF 1943, the reconstituted 11th Panzer Division was working up to full strength at Kharkov. It fought at Belgorod, Kursk, Krivoj Rog and suffered heavy losses when it was encircled at Kresun, south of Kiev. In July 1943, it was attached to LXVIII *Panzerkorps* of the 4th *Panzerarmee* at Belgorod.

11th Panzer Division was one of Army Group South's lead formations during the Battle of Kursk. On 4 July, the division advanced, and after three days took the high ground around Butovo while the *Grossdeutschland Panzergrenadier* Division attacked the town. However, LXVIII Corps became bogged down in fighting its way through the multi-layered Soviet defences, and progress slowed to a crawl. By 10 July, the German advance had come to a halt. The massive tank battle at Prokorovka was a victory for neither side, but it left LXVIII *Panzerkorps* exposed. When the Soviets launched a massive counterattack, the Germans had to withdraw. By 23 July they were back at their original positions. 11th Panzer Division had lost heavily in the fighting and had fewer than 20 tanks left.

ORGANIZATION

Pz. Rgt. 15 — I
- II. St / m / le / le
- I. St / m / le / le

Panzer Unit	Pz. II	Pz. III	Pz. IV	Pz. Bef.	Flammpz
15th Pz. Rgt.	8	62	26	4	13

11TH PANZER DIVISION

▶ **Schwerer Panzerspähwagen (Sd Kfz 231)**
11th Reconnaissance Battalion / 1st Armoured Car Company

11th Panzer formed part of the southern pincer attack at Kursk in 1943, for which the *Wehrmacht* had concentrated 1035 older Panzers plus 45 Tigers and 200 Panthers. The Sd Kfz 231 seen here was armed with one 2cm (0.8in) cannon.

Specifications
Crew: 4
Weight: 9.1 tonnes (8.3 tons)
Length: 5.85m (19.2ft)
Width: 2.2m (7.2ft)
Height: 2.35m (7.7ft)
Engine: Büssing-NAG L8V
Speed: 85km/hr (52.8mph)
Range: 300km (186.4 miles)
Radio: FuG Spr Ger 'a'

The Western Front
JUNE 1944

The 11th Panzer was sent to Bordeaux for refitting in June 1944, where it absorbed the 273rd Reserve Panzer Division. It was equipped with 79 Panthers and eight 3.7cm (1.5in) FlaK Panzer.

AFTER A YEAR OF FIGHTING RETREATS on the Eastern Front, culminating in fighting free of the Cherkassy Pocket in February 1944, 11th Panzer was in need of serious reconstruction. The 1st Battalion, 15th Panzer Regiment re-equipped with Pz.Kpfw V Panthers, while the 2nd Battalion continued to operate with long-barrelled Panzer IVs.

The division would probably have been ordered to the Normandy invasion front, had it not been for the Allied landings in the South of France. In July 1944, the Division was shifted to Toulouse, where its major mission was in countering Resistance sabotage. In August, it took part in delaying actions after the Allied landings, and later in the withdrawal to Alsace. There, it participated in the defence of the Belfort Gap in September 1944, and subsequently withdrew north into the Saar region, where the Division was again rebuilt.

ORGANIZATION
Pz. Rgt. 15
St
I.
St
V V V V

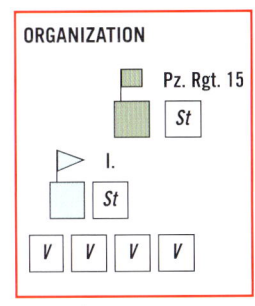

Leichte Panzerkompanie 'Gliederung'

By the last year of the war, there was no place for companies of light tanks in a Panzer division. However, there was a need for integrated air defence, given the superiority of Allied air power over the battlefield. Type 45 Divisions incorporated air defence into the Panzer units, each tank battalion having an armoured flak company of two platoons. One was armed with Flakvierling 2cm (0.8in) guns; the other, shown here, was equipped with the 3.7cm (1.5in) FlaK tanks nicknamed *Möbelwagens*.

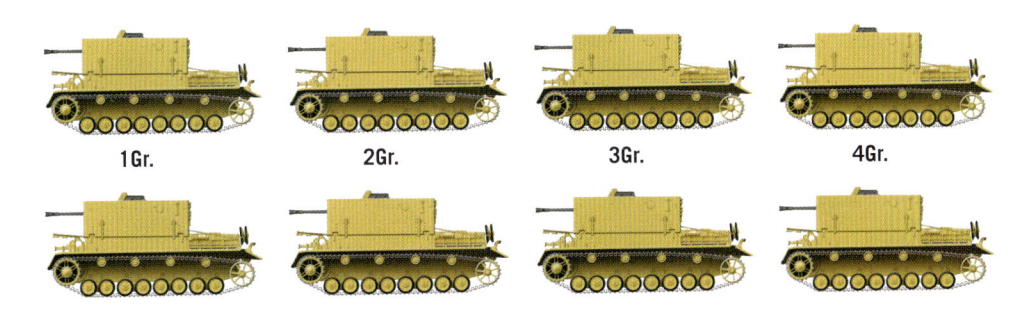

1Gr.   2Gr.   3Gr.   4Gr.

11TH PANZER DIVISION

The Battle of the Bulge
14 December 1944

The 11th Panzer Division conducted a fighting retreat through France, covering the escape of Army Group G from Provence, up the Rhone and into Alsace.

AFTER AGAIN REBUILDING from its base in the Belfort Gap, the 11th Panzer Division was placed in Army Group G's reserve in the Saarland. In December, the division was attached to XIII SS Corps, and was committed to action against the US Army near Biche. Based on the *Westwall* fortifications near Fort Simserhof and Fort Schiesseck, it fought alongside the 25th *Panzergrenadier* Division and the 361st *Volksgrenadier* Division.

Following the stalling of Operation *Wacht am Rhein* – the massive attack through the Ardennes, known now as the Battle of the Bulge – the 11th Panzer Division was pulled out of the line to be refitted. For this, there were only limited resources available, but the Division was then assigned as the mobile reserve of 7th Army, still embroiled on the southern flank of the Ardennes.

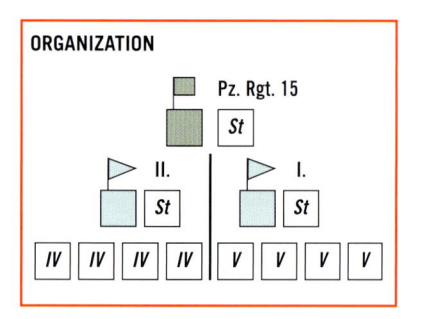

Panzer Unit	Pz. IV	Pz. V	FlkPz(20)	FlkPz(37)
15th Pz. Rgt.	31	47	8	7

Last Days

The division saw some action in the Ardennes, but was more heavily engaged in the 7th Army's defensive actions around the Trier area in January and February 1945. In March 1945, troops of the American 3rd Army seized the Ludendorff Bridge over the Rhine at Remagen before it could be blown. The 11th Panzer Division was attached to the 15th Army as it made an unsuccessful attempt to dislodge the Americans from this vital crossing. The remnants of the division retreated through Hesse and Thuringia, finally surrendering to the Americans in the Bavarian Forest on 4 May 1945.

ORGANIZATION
Pz. Rgt. 15 / St
II. / St / IV IV IV IV
I. / St / V V V V

▼ **Panzerkampfwagen V Ausf G (Sd Kfz 171)**
Pz. Rgt 15 / I Battalion / 2nd Company / 3rd Zug / tank number 1
11th Panzer participated in the Ardennes offensive at the end of 1944 and saw combat at Remagen before surrendering to US forces in Bavaria, May 1945. In the last months of the war, it was equipped with four Panther companies and four companies of Panzer IVs.

Specifications
Crew: 5
Weight: 45.5 tons (50.2 tonnes)
Length: 8.86 m (29ft)
Width: 3.4m (11.2ft)
Height: 2.98m (9.8ft)
Engine: Maybach HL230P30
Speed: 46km/hr (28.6mph)
Range: 200km (124.3 miles)
Radio: FuG5

12th Panzer Division

The 12th Panzer Division began forming at Stettin in northern Germany in October 1940, and its constituent units had been completely assembled by January 1941.

THE 2ND (MOT) INFANTRY DIVISION provided the structure for the new panzer formation. The 12 *Schützen* Brigade incorporated the 5th and 25th Infantry Regiments, while the three battalions of the 29th Panzer Regiment were new. Panzer strength in the spring of 1941 consisted of 40 Panzer Is, 33 Panzer IIs, 109 Panzer 38(t)s, 30 Panzer IVs and 8 Panzer 3(t) command tanks. The division was attached to the XLVI Corps of the 11th Army, part of Army Group C. The first divisional commander was *Generalmajor* (later *Generaloberst*) Josef Harpe, who had commanded the tank training school at Zossen.

Close support
The Panzer IVs of the 12th Panzer Division provided close support to the smaller fighting tanks which made up the bulk of the division's inventory.

Commanders

Generaloberst J. Harpe
(5 Oct 1940 – 15 Jan 1942)

Generalleutnant W. Wessel
(15 Jan 1942 – 1 Mar 1943)

Generalleutnant E. von Bodenhausen
(1 Mar 1943 – 28 May 1944)

Generalmajor G. Muller
(28 May 1944 – 16 July 1944)

Generalleutnant E. von Bodenhausen
(16 July 1944 – 12 April 1945)

Oberst von Usedom
(12 April 1945 – 8 May 1945)

INSIGNIA

The 12th Panzer Division's tactical insignia was carried by divisional vehicles from 1941 to the end of the war in 1945.

Barbarossa: the attack on Russia
22 JUNE 1941

In July 1941, the 12th Panzer Division was transferred to Army Group Centre on the Eastern Front, where it formed part of 3rd *Panzergruppe's* XXXIX Corps.

THE WEHRMACHT'S TRIUMPHANT advance into Russia saw 12th Panzer playing its part in the operations to encircle Minsk, cross the Dnieper and to take Smolensk. In September 1941, XXXIX Corps was moved to the 16th Army of Army Group North. 12th Panzer was engaged in the Battle of Mga, and then suffered heavy losses during the Soviet winter counteroffensive on the Leningrad Front.

12th Panzer Division was withdrawn to Estonia to refit. In February 1942, it returned to the Volkhov Front to fight in the many battles south of Leningrad. In November 1942, the 12th Panzer Division was transferred to Army Group Centre, near Roslavl.

Panzer Unit	Pz. I	Pz. II	Pz. 38(t)	Pz. IV	PzBef38(t)
29th Pz. Rgt.	40	33	109	30	8

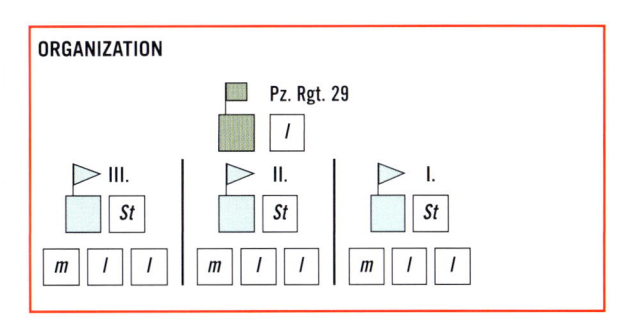

ORGANIZATION

Pz. Rgt. 29

III. — St — m l l
II. — St — m l l
I. — St — m l l

12TH PANZER DIVISION

▶ Panzerkampfwagen 38(t) Ausf C
Pz. Rgt 29 / I Battalion / 1st Company / 2nd Zug / tank number 2
The Ausf C variant of this Czech-designed tank was armed with one 3.7cm (1.5in) KwK38 (t) L/48.8 cannon and two 7.92 MG37 (t) machineguns. Note the set of *Nebel* (smoke) grenade launchers attached to the rear deck.

Specifications
Crew: 4
Weight: 10.5 tonnes (9.5 tons)
Length: 4.61m (15.1ft)
Width: 2.14m (7ft)
Height: 2.4m (7.9ft)
Engine: Praga EPA
Speed: 42km/hr (26mph)
Range: 250km (155.3 miles)
Radio: FuG37(t)

▼ Panzerkampfwagen II Ausf b (Sd Kfz 121)
12th Reconnaissance Battalion
A96 stands for *Aufklärungs* (Reconnaissance) Battalion, 9th Platoon, 6th vehicle. During the early phases of the invasion of the USSR, it was common for the *Panzertruppen* to carry extra fuel and supplies, necessary because of the vast distances that had to be covered in Russia.

Specifications
Crew: 3
Weight: 8.7 tonnes (7.9 tons)
Length: 4.76m (15.6ft)
Width: 2.14m (7ft)
Height: 1.96m (6.4ft)
Engine: Maybach HL62TR
Speed: 40km/hr (24.9mph)
Range: 200km (124.3 miles)
Radio: FuG5

▶ Panzerkampfwagen IV Ausf E (Sd Kfz 161)
Pz. Rgt 29
The 12th Panzer Division served initially with the 3rd *Panzergruppe*, Army Group Centre, before being transferred to the northern sector. The Panzer IV depicted here still used the old (1939–40) system of painting the tank tactical number in a black tank rhomboid on the hull.

Specifications
Crew: 5
Weight: 23.2 tonnes (21 tons)
Length: 5.92m (19.4ft)
Width: 2.84m (9.3ft)
Height: 2.68m (8.8ft)
Engine: Maybach HL120TRM
Speed: 42km/hr (26mph)
Range: 200km (124.3 miles)
Radio: FuG5

12TH PANZER DIVISION

🜨 The last summer offensive
1 July 1943

In 1942, the 3rd Panzer Battalion was transferred to the 13th Panzer Division. The 1st Battalion was redesignated as the 508th Panzer Battalion between May and July 1943.

From January 1943, the 12th Panzer Division was engaged in operations in and around Orel, Bryansk, Gomel and Zhlobin. During the Kursk battles of July 1943, 12th Panzer served with 2nd *Panzerarmee* on the northern sector. In the autumn of 1943, the Division was heavily engaged in defensive operations along the Dnieper.

In February 1944, the division was again moved north to take part in the desperate battles around Leningrad, but the *Wehrmacht* was not able to help stem the massive Soviet offensives against Army Group North. Over the next few months, 12th Panzer withdrew west along with the rest of the retreating German forces, until it was pushed into the Courland Pocket in September 1944.

Isolated until May 1945, the 12th Panzer Division surrendered to the Soviets early in that month, when *Festung Kurland* was forced to give in to the victorious Red Army.

Panzer Unit	Pz. II	Pz. III	Pz. III(75)	Pz. IV	Pz. Bef.
29th Pz. Rgt.	6	30	6	37	4

ORGANIZATION

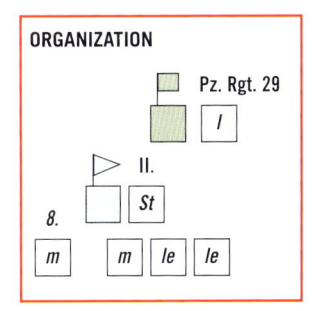

▸ Panzerkampfwagen I Ausf F
Unknown formation

The heavily armoured Ausf F variant of the Panzer I was designed as a support weapon for infantry assaults – rather like a mobile pillbox. It was loved by its crews for its ability to survive mine explosions.

Specifications
Crew: 2
Weight: 23.2 tonnes (21 tons)
Length: 4.38m (14.4ft)
Width: 2.64m (8.7ft)
Height: 2.05m (8.2ft)
Engine: Maybach HL45P
Speed: 25km/hr (15.5mph)
Range: 150km (93.2 miles)
Radio: FuG5

▸ Panzerkampfwagen IV Ausf H (Sd Kfz 161/2)
Pz. Rgt 29 / II Battalion / 5th Company / Company HQ tank

Late-war Panzer IVs in service with the 12th Panzer Division, with their long 7.5cm (3in) guns and extra armour, were immensely more powerful than the Panzer IVs of 1939.

Specifications
Crew: 5
Weight: 27.6 tonnes (25 tons)
Length: 7.02m (23ft)
Width: 2.88m (9.4ft)
Height: 2.68m (8.8ft)
Engine: Maybach HL120TRM
Speed: 38km/hr (23.6mph)
Range: 210km (130.5 miles)
Radio: FuG5

13th Panzer Division

The 13th Panzer Division was formed in Vienna on 11 October 1940, using elements of the 13th Infantry Division (mot.) and the 4th Panzer Regiment, detached from the 2nd Panzer Division.

In NOVEMBER 1940, 13th Panzer was sent to Romania as a *Lehrtruppe,* or demonstration unit, for the German military mission, nominally to teach Panzer tactics, but in fact to protect the Ploesti oil fields, which were vital to the German war effort. In May 1941, the Division was returned to Silesia for reinforcement and preparation for the war in Russia.

INSIGNIA

Like the 12th Panzer Division, vehicles of the 13th Panzer Division carried the same tactical insignia from 1941 to the end of the war.

Commanders

Generalleutnant F. von Rotkirch und Panthen
(11 Oct 1940 – 25 June 1941)

Generalleutnant W. Duvert
(25 June 1941 – 30 Nov 1941)

General der Panzertruppen T. Herr
(1 Dec 1941 – 1 Nov 1942)

Generalleutnant H. von der Chevallerie
(1 Nov 1942 – 1 Dec 1942)

Generalleutnant W. Crisolli
(1 Dec 1942 – 15 May 1943)

Generalleutnant H. von der Chevallerie
(15 May 1943 – 1 Sept 1943)

Generalleutnant E. Hauser
(1 Sept 1943 – 26 Dec 1943)

Generalleutnant H. Mikosch
(26 Dec 1943 – 18 May 1944)

Oberst F. von Hake
(18 May 1944 – 25 May 1944)

Generalleutnant H. Troger
(25 May 1944 – 9 Sept 1944)

Generalmajor G. Schmidhuber
(9 Sept 1944 – 11 Feb 1945)

◀ **Panzers across the Don**
During Germany's 1942 summer offensive, 13th Panzer provided the spearhead for Kleist's armoured thrust into the Caucasus.

⊕ *Barbarossa*: the attack on Russia
22 JUNE 1941

The 13th Panzer Division, commanded by *Generalmajor* Walther Düvert, was assigned to *Generaloberst* von Kleist's 1st *Panzergruppe* in Army Group South.

THE DIVISION CROSSED the river Bug on the Polish-Soviet frontier on 23 June 1941, behind the 44th Infantry Division. Advancing rapidly despite stiff Soviet resistance, it broke through the heavily fortified Stalin Line at Hulsk. The 13th Panzer Division captured Kremenchug, and on 25 August established the first bridgehead across the Dnieper river at Dniepropetrosvk. The advanced continued, reaching the Mius river by way of Mariopol and Taganrog, which had been taken by the SS-*Leibstandarte*.

On 13 November, 13th Panzer fought its way into Rostov-on-Don, but had to withdraw to the Mius Line, where it spent the next seven months over the severe winter of 1941/42. In the heavy defensive fighting that ensued, the Division was able to hold its own against repeated Soviet infantry assaults.

ORGANIZATION

Pz. Rgt. 4

II. / I.
St / St
m / l / m / l

Panzer Unit	Pz. II	Pz. III(37)	Pz. III(50)	Pz. IV	Pz. Bef.
4th Pz. Rgt.	45	27	44	20	13

13TH PANZER DIVISION

▶ Panzerkampfwagen II Ausf F (Sd Kfz 121)
Pz. Rgt 4 / II Battalion / Stabskompanie / Light Platoon / tank number 12

The Panzer II units were generally used for security patrols when the Division came to a halt. Their duties included blocking enemy reconnaissance patrols, repelling minor attacks and giving the main unit time to deploy in case of major attacks.

Specifications

Crew: 3	Engine: Maybach HL62TR
Weight: 10.5 tonnes (9.5 tons)	Speed: 40km/hr (24.9mph)
Length: 4.81m (15.8ft)	Range: 200km (124.3 miles)
Width: 2.28m (7.5ft)	Radio: FuG5
Height: 2.15m (7ft)	

▶ Panzerkampfwagen III Ausf F (Sd Kfz 141)
Pz. Rgt 4 / II Battalion / 8th Company / 3rd Zug / tank number 5

The 3.7cm (1.5in) gun could not penetrate the frontal armour of Soviet T-34s or KV-1s, even at point-blank range. But an expert crew could damage the enemy's gun barrel or turret ring at short ranges, forcing the Soviet tank to disengage.

Specifications

Crew: 5	Engine: Maybach HL120TR
Weight: 21.8 tonnes (19.8 tons)	Speed: 40km/hr (24.9mph)
Length: 5.38m (17.7ft)	Range: 165km (102.5 miles)
Width: 2.91m (9.5ft)	Radio: FuG5
Height: 2.44m (8ft)	

⊕ *Fall Blau*: the Eastern Front
28 June 1942

The summer offensive of 1942 saw the 13th Panzer Division at the heart of the main German advance of that year, towards the vital Caucasus oilfields.

ALONG WITH SS DIVISION *WIKING*, 13th Panzer captured Rostov-on-Don in July. The next objective was Armavir on the Kuban river. The Division advanced in several columns, through corn and sunflower fields that stretched to the horizon. Huge dust clouds, lack of water and extreme heat put a tremendous strain on both soldiers and equipment, and supply lines were stretched almost to breaking point. Nevertheless, by the end of September, the Division was at Elchetovo, known as the 'Gateway to the Caucasus'. However, the Stalingrad catastrophe threatened the survival of entire Army Group, and it had to retreat back to Rostov and beyond.

ORGANIZATION

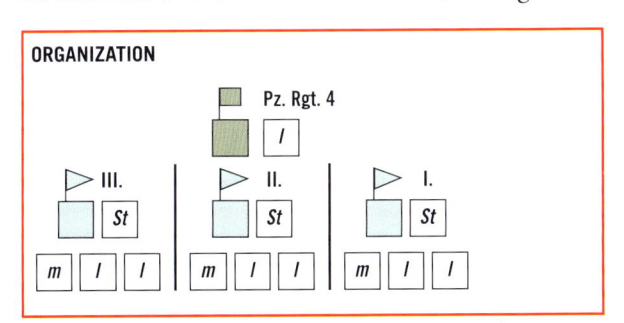

Pz. Rgt. 4 / I
- III. — St — m / I / I
- II. — St — m / I / I
- I. — St — m / I / I

Panzer Unit	Pz. II	Pz. III(5kz)	Pz. III(5lg)	Pz. IV(kz)	Pz. Bef.
4th Pz. Rgt.	15	41	30	12	5

119

13TH PANZER DIVISION

⊕ The last summer offensive
1 July 1943

While the offensive at Kursk was being planned, the German divisions that had fought their way to the Caucasus had to fight equally hard to get back to where they had started in 1942.

At the beginning of July, while German armies were launching their massive assault at Kursk, the tattered remnants of the 13th Panzer Division were being ferried across the Strait of Kerch to the Crimea. After refitting, in August the Division was moved to Stalino to support the weakened German divisions that were trying to hold the old Mius Line. These were gradually being pushed back toward the Dnieper by repeated Soviet attacks

The *Wehrmacht*'s panzer divisions were employed as 'Fire Brigades' during the long German retreat from the Russia. 13th Panzer units now operated in individual mobile *Kampfgruppen*, made up of tanks, *Panzerjägers*, mobile artillery and armoured infantry. Their task was to delay the Soviets by actively engaging them in sharp local counterattacks, which caused significant Red Army losses.

Fighting Retreat

As 13th Panzer reached Cherson, near the mouth of the Dnieper, it was instructed to safeguard

▼ **Panzerkampfwagen V Ausf D (Sd Kfz 171)**
Pz. Rgt 4 / I Battalion / 3rd Company / 3rd Zug / tank number 2
The 1st Battalion of the 4th Panzer Regiment was re-equipped with 76 Pz.Kpfw V Panthers in January 1944. As with most Panther-equipped divisions at the time, the 2nd Battalion of the regiment continued to operate with Pz.Kpfw IVs.

Panzer Unit	Pz. II	Pz. III(kz)	Pz. III(lg)	Pz. IV(lg)	Pz. Bef.
4th Pz. Rgt.	5	4	10	50	2

the passage of the 4th *Gebirgs* Division as it retreated back across the river. On 3 November 1943, more than 15,000 vehicles of the two divisions made it safely across before the bridge was blown in the face of the enemy.

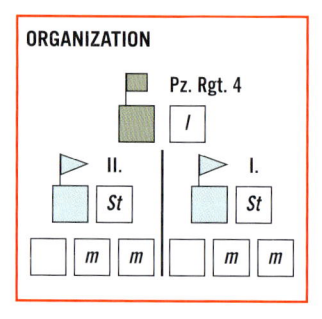

To help close the 150km (93-mile) gap torn by the Soviets in the German defences between Kremenchug and Dniepropetrovsk, the division was then ordered to the area of Krivoy Rog and Kirovograd, where it stemmed a number of potential Soviet breakthroughs in that sector of the front.

ORGANIZATION

Specifications
Crew: 5
Weight: 47.4 tonnes (43 tons)
Length: 8.86m (29ft)
Width: 3.4m (11.2ft)
Height: 2.95m (9.7ft)
Engine: Maybach HL230P30
Speed: 46km/hr (28.6mph)
Range: 200km (124.3 miles)
Radio: FuG5

13TH PANZER DIVISION

⊕ Last battles
1944/1945

The 1st Battalion of the 4th Panzer Regiment was detached and sent to Italy to be part of an independent Panzer unit, with orders to drive the Allies from their beachhead at Anzio.

MEANWHILE, THE REST of the Division had been coming to the relief of the large German force trapped in the Cherkassy Pocket. By May, the division had been forced back as far as Kishinev, on the Romanian border.

The overwhelming power of the Soviet summer offensives forced them back further, some of the fighting units making their way into Hungary through the Carpathians. Others were interned when Romania changed sides, and many were handed over to the Red Army.

In September, those units which had escaped, assembled at Oerkeny, to the southeast of Budapest. Over the next six months, 13th Panzer Division defended the city, ultimately being wiped out in March 1945.

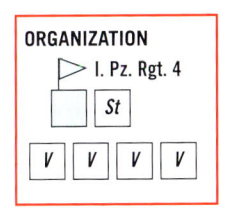

ORGANIZATION
I. Pz. Rgt. 4
St
V V V V

▶ Panzerkampfwagen V Ausf A (Sd Kfz 171)
Pz. Rgt 4 / I Battalion / Stabskompanie

The Allied landing at Anzio threatened Rome, but the Americans and British decided to dig in rather than break out, allowing the Germans to redeploy to attack the beachhead.

Specifications

Crew: 5	Height: 2.98m (9.8ft)
Weight: 49.4 tonnes (44.8 tons)	Engine: Maybach HL230P30
Length: 8.86m (29ft)	Speed: 46km/hr (28.6mph)
Width: 3.42m (11.2ft)	Range: 200km (124.3 miles)
	Radio: FuG5

▶ Panzerkampfwagen V Ausf A (Sd Kfz 171)
Pz. Rgt 4 / I Battalion / 1st Company / 2nd Zug / tank number 3

Under pressure by an eight-division German attack, the Allied VI Corps held firm. In spite of superior weapons, like the Panther, and greater combat experience gained in Russia, the *Wehrmacht* could not breach Allied defences at Anzio.

Weapon Specifications

Main: 7.5cm (3in) KwK42 L/70	Co-ax MG: 7.92mm (0.3in) MG 34
Ammunition: 79 rounds	Hull MG: 7.92mm (0.3in) MG 34
Traverse: 360° (hydraulic)	Ammunition: 5100 rounds
Elevation: -8° to +18°	MG Sight: KgZF2
Sight: TZF12a	

13TH PANZER DIVISION

▶ **15cm Schweres Infanteriegeschütz 33/1 auf Selbstfahrlafette 38(t) (Sf) Ausf M (Sd Kfz 138/1)**
93rd Panzergrenadier Battalion

282 SdKfz Ausf M were produced between April 1943 and September 1944. The self-propelled artillery piece was armed with one 15cm (6in) sIG33/2 cannon and carried 18 rounds of ammunition.

Specifications
Crew: 4
Weight: 13.2 tonnes (12 tons)
Length: 4.95m (16.2ft)
Width: 2.15m (7ft)
Height: 2.47m (8.1ft)
Engine: Praga AC
Speed: 35km/hr (21.7mph)
Range: 190km (118 miles)
Radio: FuG16

▼ **Panzer IV/70 (V) (Sd Kfz 162/1)**
Unknown formation

An improved version of the Jagdpanzer IV, the first series Panzer IV/70 tank hunter entered production in August 1944. It was armed with a long-barrelled 7.5cm (3in) PaK42 L/70 cannon and carried 55 rounds of ammunition. The long gun and extra front armour made the vehicle nose-heavy, so the first two road wheels were steel rather than rubber-rimmed.

Specifications
Crew: 4
Weight: 28.4 tonnes (25.8 tons)
Length: 8.5m (27.9ft)
Width: 3.17m (10.4ft)
Height: 1.85m (6ft)
Engine: Maybach HL120TRM
Speed: 35km/hr (21.7mph)
Range: 210km (130.5 miles)
Radio: FuG Spr 1

▼ **Panzer IV/70 (V) (Sd Kfz 162/1)**
Unknown formation

The vehicle depicted was from the second production series (September–November 1944), and was used at Budapest in January 1945. The 13th Panzer was sent to Hungary to take part in the futile defence of the city. The Division was destroyed early in 1945, and reformed as the *Panzer Division Feldherrnhalle 2*.

Weapons Specifications
Main: 7.5cm (3in) PaK42 L/70
Ammunition: 55 (estimated)
Traverse: 10° left and right (manual)
Elevation: -5° to +15°
Sights: SflZF
Secondary: 7.92mm (0.3in) MG42
Ammunition: 600 rounds
Sights: open

14th Panzer Division

The 14th Panzer Division actually predated the 12th and 13th Divisions, since it was first established at Koningsbruck/Milowitz in August of 1940.

THE 14TH PANZER DIVISION incorporated a mix of experienced and newly formed units. The 4th Infantry Division provided the basic structure and infantry strength, while the armoured component was provided by Panzer Regiment 36, from the 4th Panzer Division. By the time it went into action, 14th Panzer could deploy 45 Panzer IIs, 16 Panzer IIIs with 3.7cm (1.5in) guns, 35 Panzer IIIs with 5cm (2in) guns, 20 Panzer IVs, and eight command tanks.

Commanders

General der Infanterie E. Hansen
(15 Aug 1940 – 1 Oct 1940)

Generalleutnant H. von Prittwitz und Gaffron
(1 Oct 1940 – 22 Mar 1941)

General der Panzertruppen F. Kuhn
(22 Mar 1941 – 1 July 1942)

Generalleutnant F. Heim
(1 July 1942 – 1 Nov 1942)

Generalleutnant H. von Falkenstein
(1 Nov 1942 – 16 Nov 1942)

Generalleutnant J. BaBler
(16 Nov 1942 – 26 Nov 1942)

Generalmajor M. Lattmann
(26 Nov 1942 – 31 Jan 1943)

Generalleutnant F. Seiberg
(1 Apr 1943 – 29 Oct 1943)

Generalleutnant M. Unrein
(29 Oct 1943 – 5 Sept 1944)

Generalmajor O. Munzel
(5 Sept 1944 – 1 Dec 1944)

Generalleutnant M. Unrein
(1 Dec 1944 – 10 Feb 1945)

Oberst F. Jurgen
(10 Feb 1945 – 15 Mar 1945)

Oberst K. GraBel
(15 Mar 1945 – 12 Apr 1945)

▲ **War in Russia**
The Russian steppes offered almost perfect fighting terrain for tanks, and the Wehrmacht's panzers rampaged through the Soviet Union in the summer of 1941.

INSIGNIA

The standard tactical symbol carried by vehicles of the 14th Panzer Division. A similar, slightly elongated version was also used.

War in the Balkans
6 APRIL 1941

In March 1941, 14th Panzer Division, by now part of the 17th Army, was transferred from its home base in Germany to new bases in Hungary, ready for the invasion of Yugoslavia.

FOR THE ASSAULT ON YUGOSLAVIA, the division was controlled by General Maximilian von Weichs' 2nd Army. 14th Panzer was part of XLVI Corps which attacked into Croatia, being welcomed by the pro-German Croats. After taking Zagreb, the Division pressed on through mountainous terrain into Bosnia, heading for Sarajevo. Racing through Banja Luka, Trovnik and Jajce, 14th Panzer reached Sarajevo from the west on 15 April, at the same time as 8th Panzer Division of von Kleist's command entered from the east.

On the same day, the Yugoslav government began negotiations with General von Weichs. The armistice was concluded and signed on 17 April, coming into effect the next day.

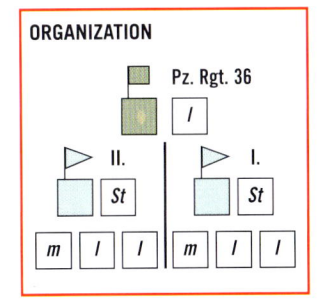

Panzer Unit	Pz. II	Pz. III(37)	Pz. III(50)	Pz. IV	Pz. Bef.
36th Pz. Rgt.	45	16	35	20	8

ORGANIZATION

Pz. Rgt. 36

14TH PANZER DIVISION

▶ **Panzerkampfwagen I Ausf B (Sd Kfz 101)**

Pz. Rgt 36 / Regiment Staff Company

Although no longer listed in the division inventory, a few Pz.Kpfw Is were retained for use as an 'armoured taxi' for the officers at Regimental level.

Specifications
Crew: 2
Weight: 6.4 tonnes (5.8 tons)
Length: 4.42m (14.5ft)
Width: 2.06m (6.8ft)
Height: 1.72m (5.6ft)
Engine: Maybach NL38TR
Speed: 40km/hr (24.9mph)
Range: 170km (105.6 miles)
Radio: FuG2

▶ **Panzerkampfwagen III Ausf H (Sd Kfz 141)**

Pz. Rgt 36 / II Battalion / 7th Company / 2nd Zug / tank number 2

This tank retains the yellow dot after the tactical number on the turret that was used as an identification mark when the 36th Panzer Regiment was still part of the 4th Panzer Division.

Specifications
Crew: 5
Weight: 24 tonnes (21.8 tons)
Length: 5.41m (17.7ft)
Width: 2.95m (9.7ft)
Height: 2.44m (8ft)
Engine: Maybach HL120TRM
Speed: 40km/hr (24.9mph)
Range: 165km (102.5 miles)
Radio: FuG5

Barbarossa: the attack on Russia
22 JUNE 1941

The campaign in Yugoslavia had been relatively easy for those units which had not gone on to fight in Greece, and most were rapidly deployed to take part in the invasion of Russia.

IN MAY 1941, soon after the end of the Balkans campaign, the 14th Panzer Division was returned to Germany. In June 1941, it was assigned to III *Panzerkorps* of von Kleist's 1st *Panzergruppe*, which was the main strike force for Field Marshal Gerd von Rundstedt's Army Group South in Operation *Barbarossa*. Following the invasion of the Soviet Union, the 14th Panzer Division was engaged in nearly continuous combat through the summer, autumn and winter of 1941. The Division took part in the major battles at Kiev, Rostov and in the Chernigovka Pocket.

When the German offensive ground to a halt as winter set in, 14th Panzer was part of the force that took part in the defensive engagements along the Mius River after the first Soviet winter counter-offensive pushed the 1st *Panzergruppe* out of Rostov and back through Taganrog.

ORGANIZATION

Pz. Rgt. 36
— I
— II. (St, m, l, l)
— I. (St, m, l, l)

Panzer Unit	Pz. II	Pz. III(37)	Pz. III(50)	Pz. IV	Pz. Bef.
36th Pz. Rgt.	45	15	56	20	11

14TH PANZER DIVISION

▶ Panzerkampfwagen III Ausf J (Sd Kfz 141)
Pz. Rgt 36

The tank depicted used a two-digit tactical number indicating that it was tank number four of the medium company's 1st Platoon. The white rhomboid painted onto the turret side and rear was non-standard, and may have been an indication of the company to which it belonged.

By 1941, the Panzer rhomboid beneath the tank's identification number was becoming a less common tank marking.

Specifications
Crew: 5
Weight: 24 tonnes (21.5 tons)
Length: 5.52m (18.1ft)
Width: 2.95m (9.7ft)
Height: 2.5m (8.2ft)
Engine: Maybach HL120TRM
Speed: 40km/hr (24.9mph)
Range: 155km (96.3 miles)
Radio: FuG5

▼ Mittlerer Gepanzerter Beobachtungskraftwagen (Sd Kfz 254)
4th Panzer Artillery Regiment

This vehicle was assigned to the 3rd Battery of a towed artillery battalion.

The front plate of the vehicle carried divisional and towed artillery tactical symbols.

Specifications
Crew: 7
Weight: 7 tonnes (6.4 tons)
Length: 4.56m (15ft)
Width: 2.02m (6.6ft)
Height: 1.88m (6.2ft)
Engine: Saurer CRDv diesel
Speed: 60km/hr (37.3mph)
Range: 500km (310.7 miles)
Radio: FuG8, FuG4, FuG Spr Ger 1

✠ *Fall Blau*: the Eastern Front
28 June 1942

14th Panzer raced through the Mius, Kharkov, Kupiansk and Don regions during the German Summer offensive of 1942.

In November 1942, 14th Panzer was transferred to the 6th Army at Stalingrad – just in time to be cut off when a Soviet offensive completely encircled the city. All German relief attempts having failed, the Division was completely destroyed by February 1943.

Panzer Unit	Pz. II	Pz. III(5kz)	Pz. III(5lg)	Pz. IV(kz)	Pz. Bef.
36th Pz. Rgt.	14	41	19	24	4

ORGANIZATION

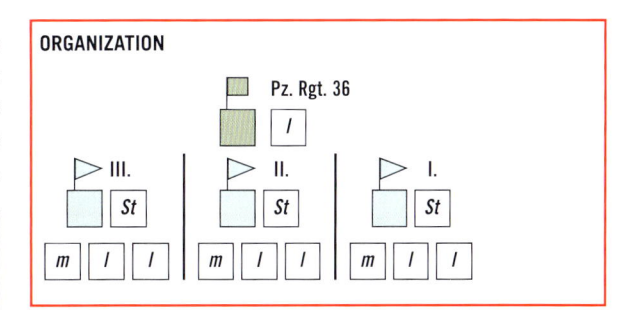

Pz. Rgt. 36 / I

III. St / m / l
II. St / m / l
I. St / m / l

14TH PANZER DIVISION

▶ Panzerkampfwagen IV Ausf F2 (Sd Kfz 161/2)
Pz. Rgt 36 / I Battalion / 4th Company / 3rd Zug / tank number 1

The Ausf F2 variant of the Panzer IV was armed with one 7.5cm (3in) KwK40 L/43 cannon, and it carried 87 rounds of ammunition. It was the first of the Panzer IVs to be equipped with the long-barrelled, high-velocity gun, and it went some way to redressing the balance with the heavier Soviet tanks.

Specifications
Crew: 5
Weight: 25.4 tonnes (23 tons)
Length: 5.62m (18.4ft)
Width: 2.84m (9.3ft)
Height: 2.68m (8.8ft)
Engine: Maybach HL120TRM
Speed: 40km/hr (24.9mph)
Range: 200km (124.3 miles)
Radio: FuG5

▶ Panzerkampfwagen III Ausf M (Sd Kfz 141/1)
Pz. Rgt 36

The number '10' indicates that this tank belonged to a company HQ section. The Ausf M variant was the last Panzer III in series production to be armed with a 5cm (2in) gun, and much of the production run was cancelled in favour of flamethrower tanks, assault guns, and the Ausf N with a short-barrelled 7.5cm (3in) gun.

Specifications
Crew: 5
Weight: 25 tonnes (22.7 tons)
Length: 6.41m (21ft)
Width: 2.95m (9.7ft)
Height: 2.5m (8.2ft)
Engine: Maybach HL120TRM
Speed: 40km/hr (24.9mph)
Range: 155km (96.3 miles)
Radio: FuG5

▶ Mittlerer Schützenpanzerwagen Ausf C (Sd Kfz 251/1)
14th Schützen Brigade

The 14th *Schützen* Brigade had in their Order of Battle the 1/, 2/103rd *Schützen* Regiment and the 1/, 2/108th *Schützen* Regiment. In June 1942, the motorized infantry components of the *Panzerwaffe* were renamed, becoming known as *Panzergrenadiers*. The 14th Panzer was destroyed at Stalingrad in February 1943.

Specifications
Crew: 2 plus 12 troops
Weight: 9.9 tonnes (9 tons)
Length: 5.98m (19.6ft)
Width: 2.1m (6.9ft)
Height: 2.16m (7ft) with MG shield
Engine: Maybach HL42TUKRM
Speed: 53km/hr (32.9mph)
Range: 300km (186.4 miles)
Radio: FuG Spr Ger f

14TH PANZER DIVISION

The year of retreat
NOVEMBER 1943

Ordered to be reformed in March 1943, following its complete destruction at Stalingrad, the 14th Panzer Division was reborn in Brittany, France in April of that year.

Now known as the 'Stalingrad Division', 4th Panzer remained in France until November 1943, when it was sent back to the East. During the division's reconstruction, plans were made to equip a third Panzer Battalion with Pz.Kpfw VI Tiger tanks in addition to the Pz.Kpfw IVs equipping the two regular battalions. However, the scheme was quickly changed and the Third Battalion was given StuG assault guns.

By June 1943, the 36th Panzer Regiment consisted of two four-company battalions of Panzer IVs, each company having 22 tanks, and a third Assault Gun battalion. This included two Panzer companies and two StuG assault gun companies, each fielding 22 Sturmgeschütz IIIs.

By November 1943, 14th Panzer was back with Army Group South, attached to LVII *Panzerkorps* of the 1st *Panzerarmee* at Krivoi Rog. In December, it had been moved to XI *Panzerkorps* of the 8th Army at Kirovograd. Early in 1944, it was transferred to the 8th Army Reserve at around the time of the Cherkassy battles.

Panzer Unit	Pz. IV	StuG	Pz. Bef	Flammpz
36th Pz. Rgt.	49	44	9	7

The last year on the Eastern Front
1944

The 14th Panzer Division remained in the Ukraine for the first six months of 1944. By August, the division's 1st Panzer Battalion had been refitted with 79 Pz.Kpfw V Panthers.

From January to June 1944, the 14th Panzer Division took part in actions in the Kirovograd, Zveningerodka, Kishinev and Jassy regions. The Division was pulled from the front in July 1944 for rest and refit at Ceterini, thus avoiding the massive series of offensives launched by nearly every Red Army Front or Army Group along more than 1000 km (621 miles) of battle lines.

In August 1944, the 14th Panzer Division was transported to the Army Group North sector of the Eastern Front, in order to take part in positional defensive actions in Courland ('Kurland' in German), an area that today includes the western parts of Latvia and Lithuania.

In January 1945, the Soviets launched a major offensive across four Fronts on the northern sector. After four days, the Red Army broke through the German defences on the borders of the Reich and started flooding into Germany, moving 30–40 km (18.6–24.8 miles) a day. In quick succession, Soviet forces overran the Baltic states, Danzig, East Prussia and Poznan. The advance came to a halt on a line just 60 km (37.3 miles) east of Berlin along the Oder River.

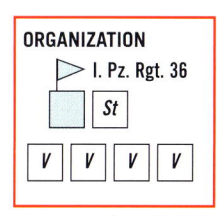

Much of Army Group North had been bypassed in the offensive: Hitler renamed the substantial forces trapped in the pocket as Army Group Courland. The 14th Panzer Division, located near Libau, (now Liepaja, Latvia) remained intact until the collapse of Germany in May 1945.

15TH PANZER DIVISION

15th Panzer Division

The 15th Panzer Division was formed from the 33rd Infantry Division. It was shipped to Libya as part of Rommel's original *Deutsches Afrika Korps* in 1941.

THE 15TH PANZER DIVISION was authorized in October 1940, and was fully formed at Darmstadt/Landau by the middle of March 1941. It was based on the 33rd Infantry Division, with the 8th Panzer Regiment, originally from the 3rd Panzer Division, providing the tank component.

INSIGNIA

The tactical insignia used by the 15th Panzer Divsion in North Africa from 1941 to 1943. It was also seen in black, and in white on a solid red circle.

Vehicles of the 15th Panzer Division were also seen carrying a variety of *Wolfsangel* (Wolf's Hook) or *Dopplehaken* (double hook) symbols.

The Wolf's Hook is an ancient runic symbol that was thought to protect against wolf attacks. Although used by several other army formations, it became infamous as part of the divisional insignia of a number of *Waffen-SS* units, including the 2nd SS Panzer Division *Das Reich*.

▲ **Advance towards Egypt**
15th Panzer arrived in Africa in time to play a part in Rommel's first offensive, which drove the British back through Libya to the Egyptian border.

Commanders

General der Panzertruppen F. Kuhn
(1 Nov 1940 – 22 Mar 1941)

Generalleutnant H. von Prittwitz und Gaffron
(22 Mar 1941 – 10 Apr 1941)

General der Panzertruppen H. von Esebeck
(13 Apr 1941 – 13 May 1941)

Generalleutnant W. Neumann-Silkow
(26 May 1941 – 6 Dec 1941)

Generalleutnant E. Menny
(6 Dec 1941 – 9 Dec 1941)

General der Panzertruppen G. von Varst
(9 Dec 1941 – 26 May 1942)

Generalleutnant E. Crasemann
(26 may 1942 – 15 July 1942)

Generalleutnant H. von Randow
(15 July 1942 – 25 Aug 1942)

General der Panzertruppen G. von Varst
(25 Aug 1942 – 10 Nov 1942)

Generalleutnant W. Borowitz
(10 Nov 1942 – 13 May 1943)

▲ Enter the Desert Fox
1941

The 15th Panzer Division spent its entire combat existence as a Panzer division in North Africa, originally as part of the *Afrika Korps* and then as part of *Panzerarmee Afrika*.

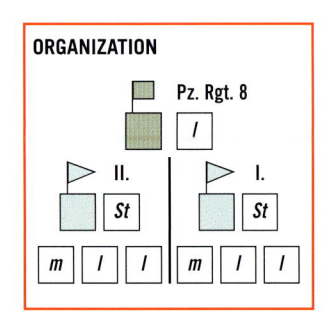

ORGANIZATION

Pz. Rgt. 8

ERWIN ROMMEL ARRIVED in North Africa in February 1941. 5th *Leichte* Division arrived in February, and 15th Panzer was in North Africa by May. Rommel's first offensive drove the British back as far as Halfaya Pass on the Egyptian border. But by the end of the year, the *Afrika Korps* had been pushed back beyond Benghazi. The back-and-forth pattern that dominated the war in the desert had been established.

Panzer Unit	Pz. II	Pz. III(50)	Pz. IV	Pz. Bef
8th Pz. Rgt.	45	71	20	10

128

15TH PANZER DIVISION

▶ **Panzerkampfwagen III Ausf J (Sd Kfz 141)**
Pz. Rgt 8 / I Battalion / 2nd Company

In 1941, an Italian Army of four corps had been annihilated by the British. 130,000 soldiers, 400 tanks and 1300 guns had been captured in North Africa, and Hitler was forced to come to aid of Germany's Fascist ally. He ordered two Panzer divisions, under the command of *Generalleutnant* Erwin Rommel, to be sent to Africa to stabilize the situation.

Specifications
Crew: 5
Weight: 24 tonnes (21.5 tons)
Length: 5.52m (18.1ft)
Width: 2.95m (9.7ft)
Height: 2.5m (8.2ft)
Engine: Maybach HL120TRM
Speed: 40km/hr (24.9mph)
Range: 155km (96.3 miles)
Radio: FuG5

▶ **Panzerkampfwagen II Ausf F (Sd Kfz 121)**
Pz. Rgt 8 / I Battalion / 2nd Company

Reconnaissance in the desert could be performed effectively only during the morning and evening. During the day, the dazzling sun would blur the outlines of tanks and other targets. Additionally, reconnaissance had to be pushed right up to the enemy's frontline, and the thinly armoured Pz.Kpfw II, while having the mobility required, proved to be too vulnerable to enemy fire.

Specifications
Crew: 5
Weight: 21.8 tonnes (19.8 tons)
Length: 5.38m (17.7ft)
Width: 2.91m (9.5ft)
Height: 2.44m (8ft)
Engine: Maybach HL120TR
Speed: 40km/hr (24.9mph)
Range: 165km (102.5 miles)
Radio: FuG5

▶ **Panzerkampfwagen III Ausf G (Sd Kfz 141)**
Pz. Rgt 8 / II Battalion / 8th Company

In June 1941, the British commander, General Wavell, initiated Operation *Battleaxe*, unaware that the 15th Panzer Division was now operational in North Africa. As British tanks were held up and channeled by minefields, they were engaged by 8.8cm (3.5in) Flak guns. Rommel then ordered the 8th Regiment to counterattack, catching the British off guard. After a six-hour battle, the British retreated, leaving 100 tanks destroyed or captured.

Specifications
Crew: 5
Weight: 20.6 tonnes (20.3 tons)
Length: 5.41m (17.7ft)
Width: 2.95m (9.7ft)
Height: 2.44m (8ft)
Engine: Maybach HL120TRM
Speed: 40km/hr (24.9mph)
Range: 165km (102.5 miles)
Radio: FuG5

15TH PANZER DIVISION

▶ Panzerkampfwagen IV Ausf F (Sd Kfz 161)
Pz. Rgt 8 / I Battalion / 4th Company

The tactical insignia depicted on this Panzer IV include the 15th Panzer Division symbol (a crossed triangle), the *Deutsches Afrika Korps* palm, the 4th *Kompanie* number and the *Wolfsangel*, or 'Wolf's Hook', of the 8th Regiment.

'Rommel' kit markings painted onto the back of the storage box added to the rear of the Panzer's turret.

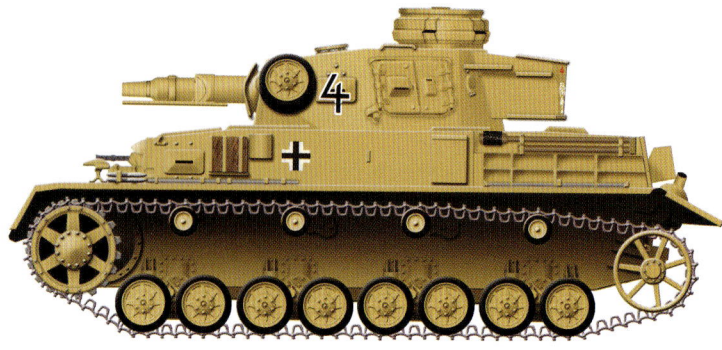

Specifications
Crew: 5
Weight: 24.6 tonnes (22.3 tons)
Length: 5.92m (19.4ft)
Width: 2.84m (9.3ft)
Height: 2.68m (8.8ft)
Engine: Maybach HL120TRM
Speed: 42km/hr (26mph)
Range: 200km (124.3 miles)
Radio: FuG5

▶ Panzerkampfwagen II Ausf C (Sd Kfz 121)
Pz. Rgt 8 / II Battalion / 8th Company

The Pz.Kpfw II could engage armoured targets beyond 600m (1968ft). The MG was used against soft targets at under 400m (1312ft) (200m (656ft) if on the move).

Specifications
Crew: 3
Weight: 9.8 tonnes (8.9 tons)
Length: 4.81m (15.8ft)
Width: 2.22m (7.3ft)
Height: 1.99m (6.5ft)
Engine: Maybach HL62TR
Speed: 40km/hr (24.9mph)
Range: 200km (124.3 miles)
Radio: FuG5

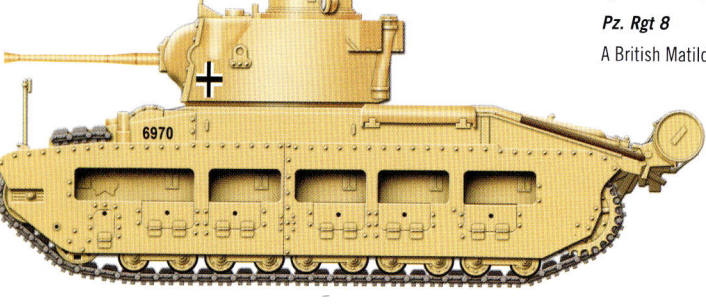

◀ Infanterie Panzerkampfwagen MkII 748(e)
Pz. Rgt 8

A British Matilda MkII infantry tank, captured during Operation *Battleaxe*.

Specifications
Crew: 4
Weight: 29.7 tonnes (26.9 tons)
Length: 5.613m (18.4ft)
Width: 2.59m (8.5ft)
Height: 2.515m (8.3ft)
Engine: Two AEC 6-cyl petrol
Speed: 24km/hr (15mph)
Range: 257km (159.7 miles)
Radio: British No.9 set

▶ Panzerkampfwagen IV Ausf E (Sd Kfz 161)
Pz. Rgt 8 / II Battalion / 8th Company

When General Auchinleck launched Operation *Crusader* in 1942, Rommel was forced to retreat, lifting the siege of Tobruk and returning to El Agheila.

Specifications
Crew: 5
Weight: 23.2 tonnes (21 tons)
Length: 5.92m (19.4ft)
Width: 2.84m (9.3ft)
Height: 2.68m (8.8ft)
Engine: Maybach HL120TRM
Speed: 42km/hr (26mph)
Range: 200km (124.3 miles)
Radio: FuG5

15TH PANZER DIVISION

▶ **Leichter Panzerspähwagen (2cm) (Sd Kfz 222)**
33rd Reconnaissance Battalion / Armoured Car Company

The Sd Kfz 222 was armed with one 2cm (0.8in) KwK30 or 38 L/55 cannon and carried 180 rounds of ammunition. All armoured reconnaissance units were equipped with an antitank detachment to protect themselves from enemy armour.

Specifications

Crew: 3	Engine: Horch 3.5l or 3.8l
Weight: 5.3 tonnes (4.8 tons)	Speed: 85km/hr (52.8mph)
Length: 4.8m (15.7ft)	Range: 200km (124.3 miles)
Width: 1.95m (6.4ft)	Radio: FuG Spr Ger 'a'
Height: 2m (6.6ft)	

War in the desert
25 MAY 1942

The 15th Panzer Division formed a key part of Erwin Rommel's armoury, as the German general proved himself a master of continually-moving desert warfare.

THE BRITISH CAPTURED BENGHAZI in January, but a counterattack by the Germans retook the city 10 days later. Rommel's offensive ran out of steam on 7 February at Gazala. Over the next three months, the British built up their forces at Gazala, but in May Rommel attacked before the British were ready to launch their own offensive. After fierce fighting at Gazala, the British were forced back towards the Egyptian frontier, leaving the key port of Tobruk under siege. Rommel captured Tobruk on 21 June, and continued to advance into Egypt. However, by the time he reached the strong British defensive positions at Alamein at the end of June, his troops were exhausted, and further advances were stopped after several weeks of fighting.

Panzer Unit	Pz. II	Pz. III(kz)	Pz. III(lg)	Pz. IV(kz)	Pz. Bef.
8th Pz. Rgt.	29	131	3	22	4

ORGANIZATION
- Pz. Rgt. 8
  - II. (St — m le le le)
  - I. (St — m le le le)

▶ **Panzerkampfwagen III Ausf H (Sd Kfz 141)**
Pz. Rgt 8 / I Battalion / Stabskompanie / Signal Platoon

With the *Luftwaffe* putting pressure on Malta, Rommel's supplies started to arrive safely, enabling him to quickly rebuild his forces – replacing Panzer IIs with more effective Panzer IIIs and IVs. Not prepared for a sudden offensive, the British lost Benghazi in January 1942 but held their defensive line at Gazala.

Specifications

Crew: 5	Engine: Maybach HL120TRM
Weight: 24 tonnes (21.8 tons)	Speed: 40km/hr (24.9mph)
Length: 5.41m (17.7ft)	Range: 165km (102.5 miles)
Width: 2.95m (9.7ft)	Radio: FuG5
Height: 2.44m (8ft)	

15TH PANZER DIVISION

▶ Panzerkampfwagen III Ausf J (Sd Kfz 141/1)
Pz. Rgt 8 / I Battalion / 1st Company

In May 1942 Rommel attacked the British at Gazala. The 15th Panzer Division attacked from the south.

Specifications
Crew: 5
Weight: 24 tonnes (21.5 tons)
Length: 5.52m (18.1ft)
Width: 2.95m (9.7ft)
Height: 2.5m (8.2ft)
Engine: Maybach HL120TRM
Speed: 40km/hr (24.9mph)
Range: 155km (96.3 miles)
Radio: FuG5

▶ Panzerkampfwagen III Ausf L (Sd Kfz 141/1)
Pz. Rgt 8 / I Battalion / 2nd Company

Recognizable by its long gun barrel, the Ausf L was known by the British as the 'Mark III Special'.

Specifications
Crew: 5
Weight: 24 tonnes (21.5 tons)
Length: 6.28m (20.6ft)
Width: 2.95m (9.7ft)
Height: 2.5m (8.2ft)
Engine: Maybach HL120TRM
Speed: 40km/hr (24.9mph)
Range: 155km (96.3 miles)
Radio: FuG5

▶ Panzerbefehlswagen III Ausf H
Pz. Rgt 8 / II Battalion / Stabskompanie / Signal Platoon

The standard crew of the command tank consisted of the commander, adjutant, driver and two radio operators. By June 1942, the British had evacuated Bir Hacheim, and Tobruk was once again under siege.

Specifications
Crew: 5
Weight: 24 tonnes (21.8 tons)
Length: 5.4m (17.7ft)
Width: 2.95m (9.7ft)
Height: 2.44m (8ft)
Engine: Maybach HL120TRM
Speed: 40km/hr (24.9mph)
Range: 165km (102.5 miles)
Radio: FuG6 plus FuG2 or FuG7 or FuG8

▶ Panzerkampfwagen III Ausf J (Sd Kfz 141)
Pz. Rgt 8 / II Battalion / 5th Company / 3rd Zug / tank number 1

Rommel pretended to bypass Tobruk for Bardia, then launched a sudden attack on 19 June. The British garrison of 30,000 soldiers along with large quantities of fuel and supplies were captured.

Weapons Specifications
Main: 5cm (2in) KwK39 L/60
Ammunition: 92 rounds
Traverse: 360° (manual)
Elevation: -10° to +20°
Sight: TZF5e
Co-axial: 7.92mm (0.3in) MG34
Hull: 7.92mm (0.3in) MG34
Ammunition: 4950 rounds
MG sight: KgZF2

132

15TH PANZER DIVISION

▶ **Panzerkampfwagen III Ausf J (Sd Kfz 141/1)**
Pz. Rgt 8 / II Battalion / 6th Company / 3rd Zug / tank number 2
1067 Ausf J 'Long' were produced between December 1941 and July 1942. The long 5cm (2in) KwK39 L/60 was very effective when engaging the American made 'Grant' and the British 'Valentine'.

Armour Specifications

Turret: 57mm (2.2in) front, 30mm (1.2in) side, 30mm (1.2in) rear, 10mm (0.4in) top
Superstructure: 5mm (0.2in) front, 30mm (1.2in) side, 50mm (2in) rear, 18mm (0.7in) top

Hull: 50mm (2in) front, 30mm (1.2in) side 50mm (2in) rear, 16mm (0.6in) bottom
Gun Mantlet: 50mm (2in) plus 20mm (0.8in) spaced armour

▶ **Panzerjäger 38(t) fur 7.62cm PaK36(r) (Sd Kfz 139)**
33rd Panzerjäger Battalion / Self-propelled Panzerjäger Company
Four Marder III were available in the Battalion inventory in August 1942. Based on the obsolete Panzer 38(t) chassis, it carried a long-barrelled Soviet gun, hundreds of which had been captured during Operation *Barbarossa*. In spite of its relatively high profile, the powerful gun made the Marder an effective tank-hunter.

National insignia used on armoured vehicles between 1940 and 1942. In the desert, the areas around the insignia were often not painted, leaving the original grey colour scheme showing through.

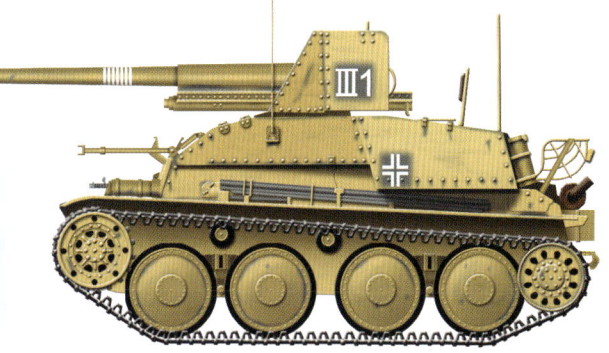

Specifications

Crew: 4
Weight: 11.76 tonnes (10.67 tons)
Length: 5.85m (19.2ft)
Width: 2.16m (7ft)
Height: 2.5m (8.2ft)

Engine: Praga EPA or EPA/2
Speed: 42km/hr (26mph)
Range: 185km (115 miles)
Radio: FuG Spr 'd'

▶ **15cm sIG33 auf Fahrgestell Panzerkampfwagen II (Sf)**
115th Panzergrenadier Regiment / 707th Schwere Infanteriegeschütz Abteilung (Attached)
Only 12 were produced between November and December of 1941 and all were shipped to North Africa. The Sturmpanzer II was a poor design, the engine tended to overheat and the chassis was overloaded. In its favour, it was armed with the well proven 150mm (6in) 3 L/12 heavy infantry gun.

Specifications

Crew: 4
Weight: 12.3 tonnes (11.2 tons)
Length: 5.41m (17.7ft)
Width: 2.6m (8.5ft)
Height: 1.9m (6.2ft)

Engine: Maybach HL62TRM
Speed: 40km/hr (24.9mph)
Range: 160km (99.4 miles)
Radio: FuG Spr 'f'

15TH PANZER DIVISION

▲ El Alamein: Egypt denied
23 October 1942

The British were given a new commander in August. General Bernard Law Montgomery was determined to use Allied material superiority to defeat Rommel in a battle of attrition.

IN NOVEMBER 1942, Montgomery launched his long-awaited offensive at El Alamein. The Germans were vastly outnumbered, resistance was futile, and Rommel's troops were soon reeling back. Not long afterwards, the Allies landed in Algeria, and the Germans in North Africa faced a two-front war.

Although fighting with their customary skill, *Panzerarmee Afrika* could not match the numbers of men, tanks, artillery pieces and aircraft available to the British and the Americans. Squeezed from east and west, the Axis forces were trapped in Tunisia, and eventually capitulated on 9 May 1943. The 15th Panzer Division was rebuilt, but as a *panzergrenadier* division.

Panzer Unit	Pz. II	Pz. III(kz)	Pz. III(lg)	Pz. IV	Pz. Bef.
8th Pz. Rgt.	14	43	44	18	2

ORGANIZATION

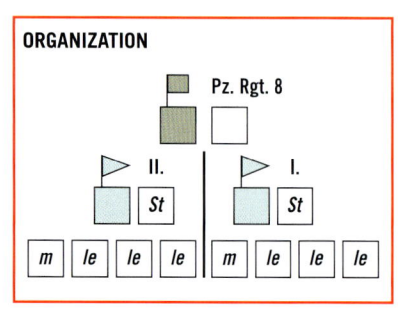

Pz. Rgt. 8

II. / I.
St / St
m le le le / m le le le

▶ Panzerkampfwagen IV Ausf F2 (Sd Kfz 161/1)
Pz. Rgt 8 / II Battalion / 8th Company

The Panzer IV 'Special' was capable of destroying any American or British tank up to a range of 1500m (4921ft). That superiority made it one of the primary targets of Allied aircraft, artillery and antitank guns.

Specifications
Crew: 5
Weight: 25.4 tonnes (23 tons)
Length: 5.62m (18.4ft)
Width: 2.84m (9.3ft)
Height: 2.68m (8.8ft)
Engine: Maybach HL120TRM
Speed: 40km/hr (24.9mph)
Range: 200km (124.3 miles)
Radio: FuG5

▶ Mittlerer Gepanzerter Beobachtungskraftwagen (Sd Kfz 254)
33rd Artillery Regiment

This vehicle was assigned to the 5th Battery of a towed artillery battalion. The frame aerial was for the FuG 8 radio set, intended for divisional use. It had a range of 40km (2.9-mile) transmitting by key, and a 10km (6.2-mile) voice telephony range. The unusual wheel-cum-track arrangement was complex, but it gave the SdKfz 254 good mobility both on roads and across country.

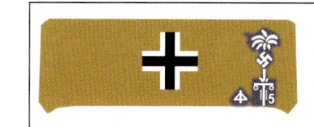

The vehicle front plate carried the artillery version of the *Afrika Korps* palm tree symbol. Licence plate WH-616664.

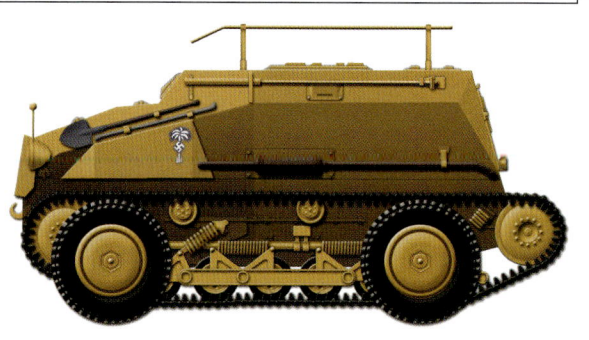

Specifications
Crew: 7
Weight: 7 tonnes (6.4 tons)
Length: 4.56m (15ft)
Width (on wheels): 2.2m (7.2ft)
Height: 1.88m (6.2ft)
Engine: Saurer CRDv
Speed: 60km/hr (37.3mph)
Range (on wheels): 500km (310.7 miles)
Radio: FuG4 plus FuG8 and FuG Spr Ger 'f'

134

15TH PANZER DIVISION

▶ 15cm sFH13/1 auf Geschützwagen Lorraine Schlepper (f) (Sd Kfz 135/1)
33rd Artillery Regiment / 4th Self-propelled Battalion

Initially 12 guns had been concentrated in a battery of three platoons, each with four guns and assigned to the 8th Panzer Regiment as artillery escorts. However, the captured French chassis lacked power: with a cross-country speed of only 8km/hr (5mph), it proved too slow to keep up with the panzers.

Specifications
Crew: 4
Weight: 9.4 tonnes (8.5 tons)
Length: 5.31m (17.4ft)
Width: 1.83m (6ft)
Height: 2.23m (7.3ft)
Engine: Delahaye 103TT
Speed (road): 34km/hr (21.1mph)
Range: 135km (83.9 miles)
Radio: FuG Spr 'f'

▶ Fiat-Ansaldo Carro Armato M 14-41
Kampfgruppe Nord / II. 133rd Italian Panzer Battalion (Littorio)

The Italian Army used a blue rectangle to identify units belonging to the 2nd Company of an armoured battalion. The M14-41 was identical to the M13-40 tank with the exception of a more powerful 145hp Fiat diesel engine. Armament consisted of one 4.7cm (1.9in) Ansaldo 47/32 gun with 104 rounds.

Specifications
Crew: 4
Weight: 15.8 tonnes (14.3 tons)
Length: 4.92m (16.1ft)
Width: 2.23m (7.3ft)
Height: 2.39m (7.8ft)
Engine: Fiat 8 t diesel
Speed: 32km/hr (19.9mph)
Range: 200km (124.3 miles)
Radio: RF 1 CA

▶ Fiat-Ansaldo Carro comando per semovente (M14-41 Chassis)
Kampfgruppe Sud / 554th Italian Assault Gun Battalion

The 15th Panzer Division had been broken up into three *kampfgruppe* (*Nord, Mitte, Sud*) just before the first battle of El Alamein. The attack started on 30 August. Soon afterwards, elements of 15th Panzer made contact with the British 8th Armoured Brigade. After a bitter fight, Rommel ordered a general withdrawal.

Specifications
Crew: 4
Weight: 14.7 tonnes (13.3 tons)
Length: 5.04m (16.5ft)
Width: 2.23m (7.3ft)
Height: 1.82m (6ft)
Engine: Fiat 15 TB V-8
Speed: 40km/hr (24.9mph)
Range: 200km (124.3 miles)
Radio: RF 1 CA plus RF 2 CA or RF 3M2

15TH PANZER DIVISION

▶ Fiat-Ansaldo Semovente da 75/18 (M13-40 Chassis)
Kampfgruppe Sud / 554th Italian Assault Gun Battalion

The British launched their own offensive at El Alamein on 23 October. The Germans had 489 tanks, half of them Italian. They were faced by 1029 British tanks. Under a massive artillery barrage, the British broke through and Rommel was forced to retreat, abandoning 200 irreplaceable tanks.

Specifications
Crew: 3
Weight: 16.5 tonnes (15 tons)
Length: 5.04m (16.5ft)
Width: 2.23m (7.3ft)
Height: 1.85m (6ft)
Engine: Fiat 15 TB V-8
Speed: 38km/hr (23.6mph)
Range: 230 km (142.9 miles)
Radio: RF 1 CA

▶ Panzerkampfwagen IV Ausf G (Sd Kfz 161/1 und 161/2)
Pz. Rgt 8 / II Battalion / 7th Company

Tunisia 1943: the 15th Panzer Division was forced to retreat to Tunisia and was maintained in reserve until committed in the battle for the Mareth Line. There it saw combat against the British, but by that time the overwhelming Allied superiority in material made the defence of North Africa hopeless.

Specifications
Crew: 5
Weight: 25.9 tonnes (23.5 tons)
Length: 6.62m (21.7ft)
Width: 2.88m (9.4ft)
Height: 2.68m (8.8ft)
Engine: Maybach HL120TRM
Speed: 40km/hr (24.9mph)
Range: 210km (130.5 miles)
Radio: FuG5

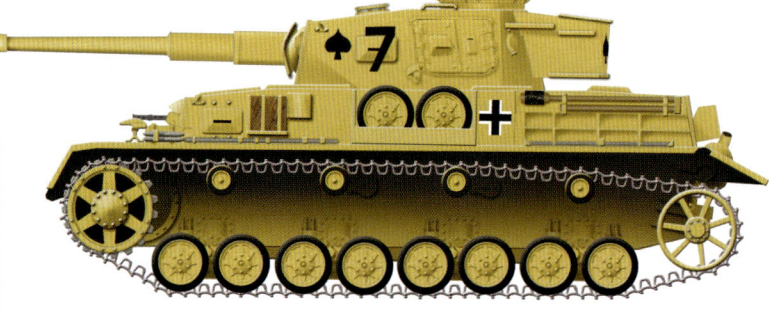

▶ Schwerer Panzerspähwagen I Ausf B (Sd Kfz 231)
33rd Reconnaissance Battalion / 1st Armoured Car Company

Tunisia 1943: the 15th Panzer Division surrendered along with other units of the *Panzerarmee Afrika* in May 1943. It was later reformed as the 15th Division.

Specifications
Crew: 4
Weight: 9.1 tonnes (8.3 tons)
Length: 5.85m (19.2ft)
Width: 2.2m (7.2ft)
Height: 2.35m (7.7ft)
Engine: Büssing-NAG L8V
Speed: 85km/hr (52.8mph)
Range: 300km (186.4 miles)
Radio: FuG Spr Ger 'a'

16th Panzer Division

The 16th Panzer Division was formed in 1940 at Munster. It was based on an already-existing infantry division, to which a Panzer regiment was added.

THE 16TH PANZER DIVISION was authorized in August 1940 and had formed at Munster by November. The Division was made up from elements of the 16th Infantry Division. The divisional Panzer strength was provided by the two veteran battalions of the 2nd Panzer Regiment, which had been detached from the 1st Panzer Division.

▶ **Attacking the Salerno Landings**
Assault guns pass through Naples on their way to Salerno. The 16th and 26th Panzer divisions almost defeated the Allied landings there in September 1943.

INSIGNIA

Divisional tactical insignia used between 1941 and 1942. A similar symbol was used in Italy in 1943, and in red was used in Russia in 1943 and 1944.

The divisional symbol enclosed within a yellow shield on a black field was a non-standard variant.

Commanders
Generaloberst H. Hube
(1 Nov 1940 – 15 Sept 1942)

Generalleutnant G. Angern
(15 Sept 1942 – 2 Feb 1943)

Generalmajor B. Muller-Hillebrand
(Mar 1943 – 5 May 1943)

Generalmajor R. Sieckenius
(5 May 1943 – 1 Nov 1943)

Generalmajor H. Back
(1 Nov 1943 – 14 Aug 1944)

Generalleutnant D. von Muller
(14 Aug 1944 – 19 Apr 1945)

Oberst K. Treuhaupt
(19 Apr 1945 – 8 May 1945)

Barbarossa: the attack on Russia
22 JUNE 1941

After being held in reserve in the Balkans, the 16th Panzer Division made its combat debut during Operation *Barbarossa*, the Axis invasion of the Soviet Union.

THE DIVISION WAS ASSIGNED to von Kleist's 1st *Panzergruppe*, part of Army Group South. The offensive was launched on 22 June, and made excellent progress. 16th Panzer fought with XIV *Panzerkorps* at Dubno in June, moving to LXVIII *Panzerkorps* at Zhitomir in July, and to XIV *Panzerkorps* at Uman and Nikolaev in August. In September, the Division fought in the battle of Kiev, when Army Groups Centre and South combined to encircle and capture over 650,000 Russian soldiers. However, the victory had diverted the *Wehrmacht* from its drive to the east, and when it resumed, winter was setting in. 16th Panzer ended the year on the Mius defensive line as the Soviets mounted their first winter attack.

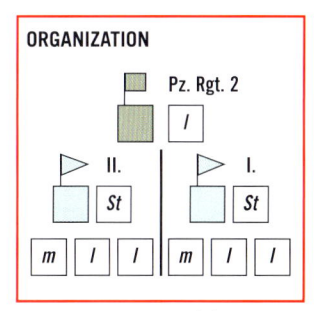

Panzer Unit	Pz. II	Pz. III(37)	Pz. III(50)	Pz. IV	Pz. Bef.
2nd Pz. Rgt.	45	23	48	20	10

ORGANIZATION
Pz. Rgt. 2

16TH PANZER DIVISION

⚐ *Fall Blau*: the Eastern Front
28 June 1942

Over the winter of 1941–42, the 16th Panzer Division was deployed in defensive positions along the Mius River, which reached the Sea of Azov at Taganrog.

SERVING WITH XIV *PANZERKORPS*, attached to 1st *Panzerarmee*, 16th Panzer was used in the fighting that took place after Kleist's Panzers had been forced out of Rostov on Don at the end of 1941. The Soviet Winter Offensive had forced the *Wehrmacht* back from Moscow far to the north. Here, in the south, Russian gains were much smaller, and by March Stalin had decided to call off the offensive.

In the spring, it was the Germans who began planning an offensive. In directive No. 41, dated 5 April, Hitler set out his objectives for the summer, an offensive codenamed *Fall Blau*. German forces were to concentrate in the south, annihilating Soviet forces on the Don before swinging north to take Stalingrad. This was to be followed by an assault on the vital oilfields in the Caucasus.

The offensive was launched on 28 June, with 16th Panzer being transferred from Kleist's *Panzerarmee* at

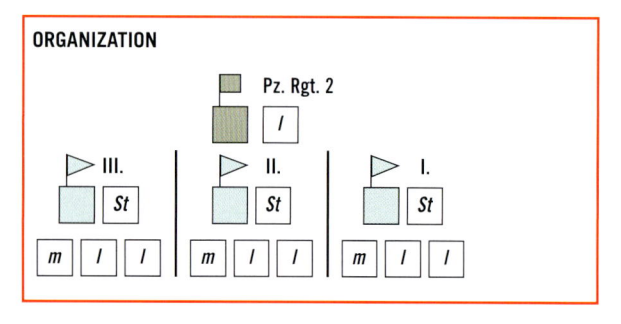

Panzer Unit	Pz. II	Pz. III(5kz)	Pz. III(5lg)	Pz. IV	Pz. Bef.
2nd Pz. Rgt.	13	39	18	27	3

Kharkov to 6th Army commanded by General Paulus, and then back to 1st *Panzerarmee*. The first attacks were successful, with the Russians being almost contemptuously swept aside. In July, Hitler became overambitious, splitting his forces to try to take Stalingrad and the Caucasus simultaneously, rather than in succession.

Advance to the Volga

From August 1942, 16th Panzer was attached to the XIV *Panzerkorps* of 6th Army. The Panzers led a headlong advance across the steppes towards the Volga, reaching the river on 23 August. All that was left was the assault on Stalingrad, and 6th Army began fighting through the outskirts of the sprawling city at the end of the month.

But the Soviets did not intend to give up the city. Over the next three months, 6th Army became bogged down in an increasingly bitter fight, in the kind of urban terrain in which tanks are most vulnerable. By November, Stalingrad appeared ready to fall to the Germans – until the Red Army unleashed a massive counteroffensive that trapped 6th Army in the city.

ORGANIZATION

▶ **Mittlerer Schützenpanzerwagen Ausf C (Sd Kfz 251/1)**
16th Schützen Brigade / 64th Schützen Regiment
In the summer of 1942, the 16th Panzer Division served with Army Group South before transferring to Army Group B for the drive on Stalingrad. The offensive started well, but was to end in catastrophe.

Specifications

Crew: 2 plus 12 troops
Weight: 9.9 tonnes (9 tons)
Length: 5.98m (19.6ft)
Width: 2.1m (6.9ft)
Height: 2.16m (7ft)
Engine: Maybach HL42TUKRM
Speed: 53km/hr (32.9mph)
Range: 300km (186.4 miles)
Radio: FuG Spr Ger f

16TH PANZER DIVISION

⅄ Destroyed at Stalingrad
FEBRUARY 1943

The massive Red Army envelopment of Stalingrad surrounded 6th Army in the city in just four days, and prevented Hoth's Panzers from breaking through to its relief from the south.

FROM BEING A GRINDING battle of attrition, the fighting in Stalingrad now became a struggle for survival for the Germans. Over the next two months, 16th Panzer lost most of its vehicles, and its tank crews were fighting as infantrymen. Supplies of food, winter clothing, fuel, weapons and ammunition were short or non-existent. As the temperatures sank and blizzards raged across the steppe, fighting rations were reduced to 200g (7 ounces) of bread and 200g (7 ounces) of horsemeat per day. Non-combatants received half that – and Soviet prisoners were given nothing.

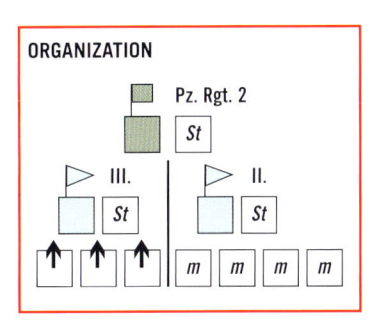

In January, Stalin ordered the pocket crushed. Only about a third of the 300,000 Germans who had been trapped were still alive. When another assault breached the perimeter west of the city, Stalingrad – and what was left of the 16th Panzer Division – was doomed. Paulus surrendered on 30 January.

Panzer Unit	Pz. IV	StuG	Pz. Bef
2nd Pz. Rgt.	98	42	12

⅄ The defence of Italy
1943/44

The 16th Panzer Division was ordered to be reformed on 17 February 1943, less than a fortnight after its destruction, and rebuilding began in Northern France soon afterwards.

IN JULY 1943, THE ALLIES LANDED in Sicily, and the Italian armistice forced the *Wehrmacht* to pull back to the Italian mainland. As British and American troops crossed to the toe of Italy, 16th Panzer was sent south to form part of XIV Corps. When the Allies tried to outflank the Germans by landing at Salerno near Naples, 16th Panzer along with 26th Panzer were close at hand, and were ordered into action against the Allies on the beachhead. For a week after 10 September, the two Panzer divisions and the Allied invasion force were engaged in a fierce battle. At one stage, the Allied commanders considered calling the landings off, so tough was the resistance. However, the British 8th Army was advancing northwards from the toe of Italy, and Allied naval gunfire was taking a fearsome toll of any German formations coming within 15 km (9.3 miles) of the coast. On 17 September, General von Vietinghoff, commander of German forces in southern Italy, requested permission to withdraw northwards to prepared defensive positions. 16th Panzer was sent to Termoli, then back towards the Sangro River and the defenses of the Gustav Line.

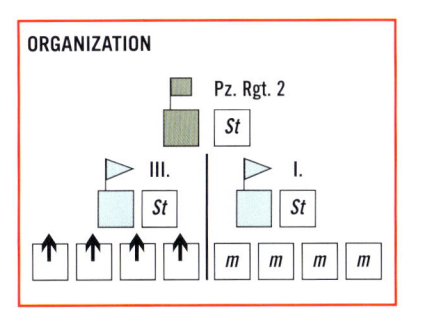

Panzer Unit	Pz. IV	Stug	Pz. Bef	Flammpz
2nd Pz. Rgt.	92	40	12	7

16TH PANZER DIVISION

▶ **Panzerkampfwagen IV Ausf G (Sd Kfz 161/1 und 161/2)**
Pz. Rgt 2 / I Batallion / 3rd Company / Company HQ tank
The 16th Panzer returned to the East at the end of 1943, fighting in the retreat from the Ukraine.

Specifications
Crew: 5
Weight: 25.9 tonnes (23.5 tons)
Length: 6.62m (21.7ft)
Width: 2.88m (9.4ft)
Height: 2.68m (8.8ft)
Engine: Maybach HL120TRM
Speed: 40km/hr (24.9mph)
Range: 210km (130.5 miles)
Radio: FuG5

▶ **7.5cm Sturmgeschütz 40 Ausf G (Sd Kfz 142/1)**
Pz. Rgt 2 / III Batallion / 10th Company / 2nd Zug / tank number 4
Some 7720 StuG 40 were produced from December 1942 to March 1945. A further 173 were converted from Pz.Kpfw III chassis in 1944. The Ausf G was armed with a 7.5cm (3in) StuG 40 L/48 cannon.

Specifications
Crew: 4
Weight: 26.3 tonnes (23.9 tons)
Length: 6.77m (22.2ft)
Width: 2.95m (9.7ft)
Height: 2.16m (7ft)
Engine: Maybach HL120TRM
Speed: 40km/hr (24.9mph)
Range: 155km (96.3 miles)
Radio: FuG15 and FuG16

Panzer-Sturmgeschütz-Kompanie

During the rebuilding of the 16th Panzer Division in February 1943, it was intended that the 2nd Panzer Regiment should have three battalions – of Panthers, Panzer IVs and Tigers. However, by March it was decided to equip the third battalion with assault guns in place of the heavy Tigers, which were not yet available in any numbers, and the first battalion was to be equipped with Panzer IVs. Initial plans for the Sturmgeschütz companies to be equipped with four five-vehicle *Zugen* were modified over the course of the next few months, and in an order dated 18 November 1943 the High Command directed that the third battalion should consist of three companies of 14 assault guns, as depicted here, giving the battalion a total strength of 42 StuGs.

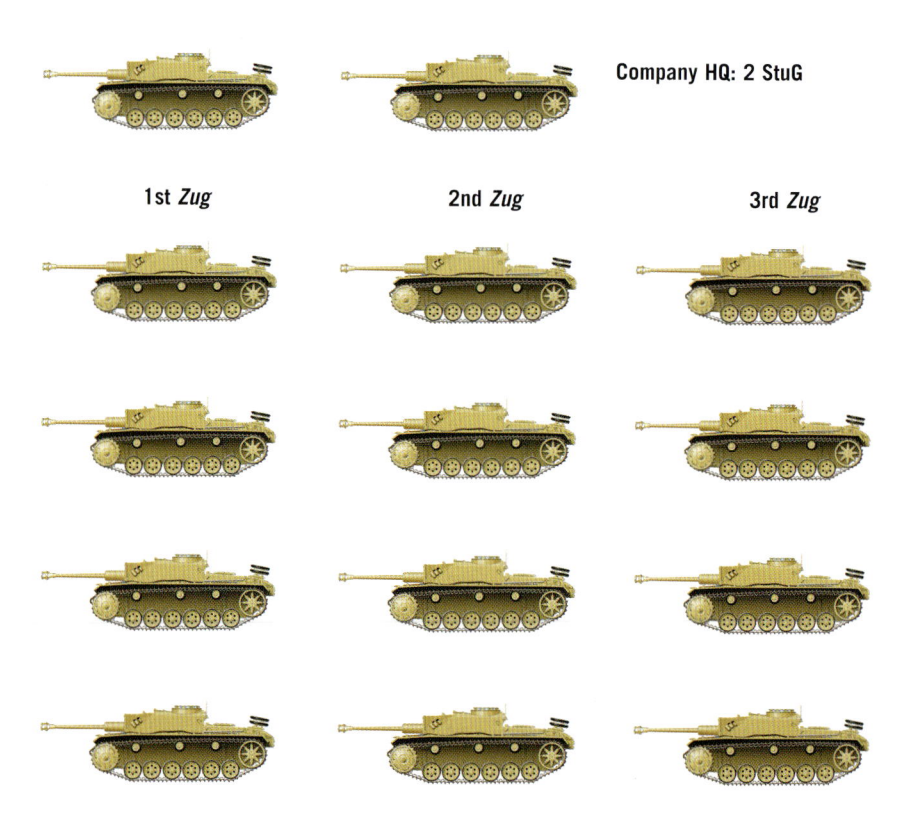

Company HQ: 2 StuG

1st *Zug* 2nd *Zug* 3rd *Zug*

16TH PANZER DIVISION

▶ Panzerkampfwagen III (Fl) (Sd Kfz 141/3)
Pz. Rgt 2

This vehicle was used against the Allied landings at Salerno in 1943. The Italian campaign was a hard-fought battle of attrition, as the Germans retreated up the Italian peninsula.

Specifications

Crew: 5
Weight: 25.4 tonnes (23 tons)
Length: 6.41m (21ft)
Width: 2.95m (9.7ft)
Height: 2.5m (8.2ft)
Engine: Maybach HL120TR
Speed: 40km/hr (24.9mph)
Range: 155km (96.3 miles)
Radio: FuG5, plus FuG2 in commanders' tanks

⚔ Retreat from the Ukraine
NOVEMBER 1943–1945

At the end of 1943, 16th Panzer was withdrawn from Italy and sent back to Russia. Italy was essentially an infantryman's war, and tanks were more valuable on the Eastern Front.

THE 16TH PANZER DIVISION was shipped back to the Eastern Front through November and December 1943, arriving in Bobruisk in Army Group Centre's sector on 13 December. There it fought in a series of defensive actions, before moving south to the Ukraine, where it was used in support of the attempt to relieve the Cherkassy Pocket. It also saw action as the *Wehrmacht* was pushed back from Kiev. By the summer, the remnants of the 16th Panzer Division had withdrawn to the the Baranov area on the Vistula River.

During the summer of 1944, 16th Panzer was pulled back through Cholm and Lublin into Poland, where it was refitted. It was transferred to the Baranov region, where it remained in action until January 1945. As the Soviets advanced, the 16th Panzer Division was pushed back, and was located around Lauban and Brno in April 1945. The division was scattered. Some units surrendered to the Soviets, while others were taken by the US Army.

▲ Leichter Schützenpanzerwagen (Sd Kfz 250/1)
Unknown formation

After fighting the Americans at Salerno, the Division was sent to the southern sector of the Russian front. The 16th Panzer ended the war in Czechoslovakia, where some surrendered to the Soviets and others to the Americans.

Specifications

Crew: 2 plus 4 grenadiers
Weight: 5.9 tonnes (5.38 tons)
Length: 4.61m (15.1ft)
Width: 1.95m (6.4ft)
Height: 1.66m (5.4ft) without gun shield
Engine: Maybach HL42TUKRM
Speed: 60km/hr (37.3mph)
Range: 300km (186.4 miles)
Radio: FuG Spr Ger 'f'

ORGANIZATIONS

Pz. Rgt. 2 — St
- III. — St — IV, III, III, III
- I. — St — IV, V, V, V

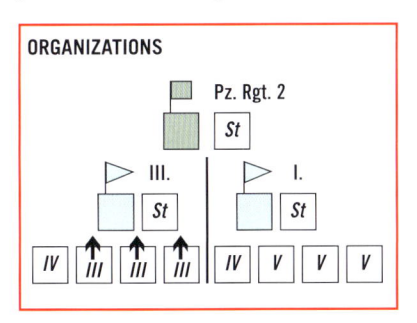

Panzer Unit	Pz. IV	StuG	Pz. V	Pz. IV70V
2nd Pz. Rgt.	7	37	10	10

17th Panzer Division

The expansion of the *Panzerwaffe* continued in the autumn of 1940. In November of that year, four new divisions were formed. Among that number was the 17th Panzer Division.

Formed at Augsberg, the 17th Panzer Division, like its contemporaries, was created around a nucleus of already-existing units. Much of the troop stength came from the 27th Infantry Division, while the division's Panzer component was provided by the replacement battalions of the 4th and 33rd Regiments. The division was assigned to the 2nd Army while it worked up to operational levels, and it was assigned to Guderian's 2nd *Panzergruppe* in May 1941.

Commanders

Generalmajor K. von Weber
(1 Nov 1940 – 17 July 1941)

General der Panzertruppen W. von Thoma
(17 July 1941 – 15 Sept 1941)

Generaloberst H. von Arnim
(15 Sept 1941 – 11 Nov 1941)

Generalleutnant R. Licht
(11 Nov 1941 – 10 Oct 1942)

General der Panzertruppen F. von Senger und Etterlin
(10 Oct 1942 – 16 June 1943)

Generalleutnant W. Schilling
(16 June 1943 – 21 July 1943)

Generalleutnant K. von der Meden
(21 July 1943 – 20 Sept 1944)

Generalmajor R. Demme
(20 Sept 1944 – 2 Dec 1944)

Oberst A. Brux
(2 Dec 1944 – 19 Jan 1945)

Generalmajor T. Kretschmer
(1 feb 1945 – 8 May 1945)

▲ **Fighting in Russia**
Although the steppe offered tanks almost perfect fighting terrain, the vast distances involved in the USSR was hard on both men and machinery.

INSIGNIA

The tactical insignia used on vehicles of the 17th Panzer Division remained the same through the four and a half years of the formation's existence.

Barbarossa: the attack on Russia
22 June 1941

As part of Guderian's 2nd *Panzergruppe*, the 17th Panzer Division formed part of the armoured spearhead of Army Group Centre during the attack on Russia in 1941.

As part of Guderian's command, 17th Panzer fought through the battles for Smolensk and Kiev. However, it was unusual in that it was equipped with *Tauschpanzer*, or 'diving tanks'. These submersible, snorkel-equipped Panzer IIIs and IVs had been designed for the cancelled invasion of Britain. They instead saw their combat debut at the opening of Operation *Barbarossa*, crossing the River Bug.

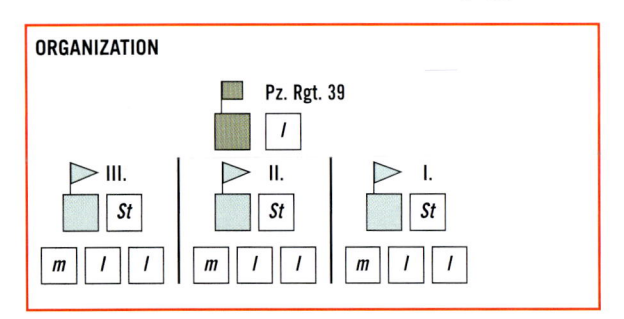

After the Kiev encirclement, 17th Panzer returned to the assault on Moscow. Fighting in the Tula area before pulling back to Orel, it suffered like all German units from the unforgiving Russian winter.

Panzer Unit	Pz. I	Pz. II	Pz. III(50)	Pz. IV	Pz. Bef
39th Pz. Rgt.	12	44	106	40	10

17TH PANZER DIVISION

Leichte PanzerKompanie K.St.N.1171

By the time of the invasion of the Soviet Union, the light panzer companies of Germany's panzer divisions had traded in their obsolete Panzer Is for much more powerful Panzer IIIs. However, the standard table of organization retained a platoon of lightweight Panzer IIs, which were primarily used for local reconnaissance when the unit was on the move, and to mount security patrols when it was stationary for any length of time. Security patrols became even more important as the war in Russia progressed, since partisan activity behind the lines was to become a major threat.

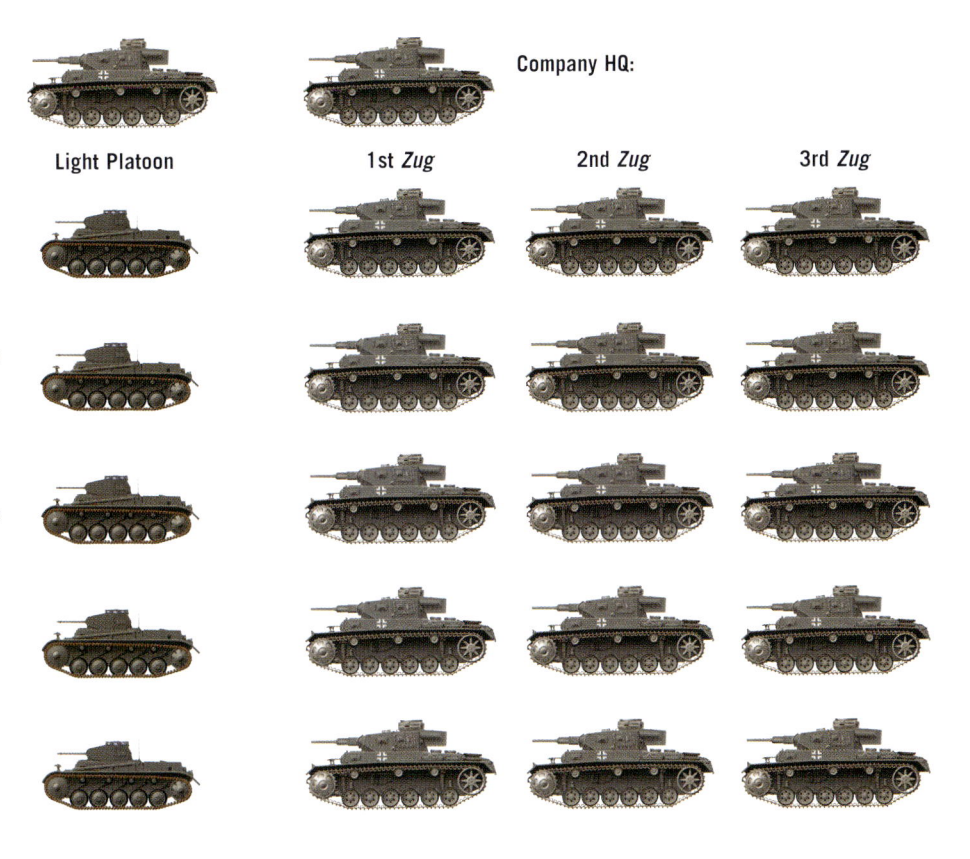

Light Platoon | **1st** *Zug* | **2nd** *Zug* | **3rd** *Zug*

Company HQ:

¥ *Fall Blau*: the Eastern Front
28 JUNE 1942

The 17th Panzer Division played little part in the initial stages of the German summer offensive in 1942, though it would have an important role later in the campaign.

MOST WEHRMACHT REINFORCEMENT had gone south when *Fall Blau* got under way in June 1942. The 17th Panzer Division remained with Army Group Centre in the Orel Sector for much of the year. The primary mission was to hold the line, and to prevent any Soviet breakthrough while the German Army conquered the south of the USSR.

Initial stages of *Fall Blau* had gone very well for the Germans, but the ill-advised attempt to take both major objectives of Stalingrad and the Caucasus simultaneously ran into serious trouble when the Soviets, who had learned to trade space for time, avoided any major action until they were ready. Stalin, unlike Hitler, allowed his generals to fall back when necessary – just as long as they had plans to mount a counterattack as quickly as possible. The attack came at Stalingrad.

Panzer Unit	Pz. II	Pz. III(50)	Pz. IV	Pz. Bef
39th Pz. Rgt.	17	36	16	2

ORGANIZATION

Pz. Rgt. 39

II.
St
m le le

143

17TH PANZER DIVISION

Stalingrad and Kursk
DECEMBER 1942 – 1 JULY 1943

At the end of 1942, 17th Panzer Division was transferred to von Manstein's Army Group Don to take part in the attempt to relieve the beleaguered German 6th Army in Stalingrad.

MANSTEIN'S PLAN WAS SIMPLE. Hoth's 4th *Panzerarmee* would strike northwards from Kotelnikova, while the XLVIII *Panzerkorps* would attack eastwards from the Chir front, 65 km (40.4 miles) west of the city. Once the attackers got within range of Stalingrad, 6th Army would break out of the encirclement. However, the Soviets had been attacking all along the Chir River since 10 December, and the rescue would have to be performed by 4th *Panzerarmee* alone.

17th Panzer had been transferred down from Orel to take part in the operation, but on Hitler's direct orders, and over Manstein's objections, it was to be held in reserve. In the event, the 17th was available to cover the flanks of Hoth's Panzers as they became bogged down fighting towards Stalingrad in an attempt to relieve the beleaguered city. The entire *Panzerarmee* could have been destroyed had not 17th Panzer been there to protect the column's flanks when heavy Soviet attacks on the crumbling Romanian army threatened Hoth's advance. Even so, the relief effort had to be cancelled.

Kharkov, Kursk and after

The Soviet offensive after Stalingrad fell was countered in the south by Manstein's brilliant counterattack at Kharkov. 17th Panzer was part of 4th *Panzerarmee* for that operation. During the battle

Panzer Unit	Pz. II	Pz. III	Pz. III(75)	Pz. IV	Pz. Bef
39th Pz. Rgt.	4	20	9	32	2

of Kursk, 17th Panzer was with 1st *Panzerarmee*, operating in the Donetz basin to the south of the main action. After the failure of the Kursk offensive, the Division remained with Army Group South for the long retreat through the Ukraine, from the Donetz back across the Dnieper River.

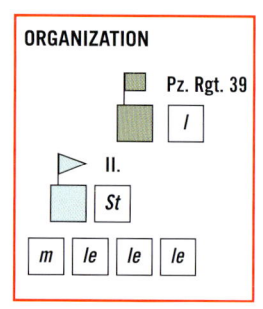

In January 1944, 17th Panzer was with 4th *Panzerarmee* at Vinnitsa. It took part in operations around the Cherkassy Pocket, supporting III *Panzerkorps* as it broke through to relieve a force of 50,000 trapped German soldiers.

The Division remained with the 1st *Panzerarmee* until July, when it moved to 4th *Panzerarmee*. From Kamanetz-Pudolsk in March, the division retreated through Stanislav, Lemberg and Tarnow, and in September 1944 it had been driven back to Baranov, by which time it formed part of LXII *Panzerkorps*.

In November 1944, the Division was moved back into reserve for refitting.

ORGANIZATION

Pz. Rgt. 39
I
II.
St
m le le le

▶ **Leichte Feldhaubitze 18/2 auf Fahrgestell Panzerkampfwagen II (Sf)**

27th Panzer Artillery Regiment / 1st (Self-propelled) Battalion

1st Battalion was equipped with two 'Wespe' batteries, each with six guns, together with a Heavy 'Hummel' battery with six guns.

Specifications

Crew: 4
Weight: 12.1 tonnes (11 tons)
Length: 4.81m (15.8ft)
Width: 2.28m (7.5ft)
Height: 2.3m (7.5ft)
Engine: Maybach HL62TR
Speed: 40km/hr (24.9mph)
Range: 220km (136.7 miles)
Radio: FuG Spr 'f'

17TH PANZER DIVISION

In defence of the Fatherland
1945

The Division was organized in January 1945 as a *Kampfgruppe* with a mixed battalion armed with a Pz.Kpfw IV company of 16 tanks and two Pz.Kpfw IV/70(V) companies of 28 *panzerjägers*.

AT THE BEGINNING OF 1945, Germany's once victorious Panzer divisions had been driven right back to the borders of the Reich itself. As the Soviet armies began massing for a new offensive in January, the *Panzerwaffe* was no longer fighting to win, but for survival.

In February 1945, the 17th Panzer Division, by now reduced in size to a *Kampfgruppe,* was attached to Army Group Centre on the Oder River. By March 1945, it had been pushed back as far as Jägerndorf by the overwhelming might of the Red Army. Early in April, it had retreated southwest into Moravia, where in quick succession it came under the orders of 17th Army and 1st Army. The division finally surrendered to the Soviet army near Görlitz at the end of April 1945.

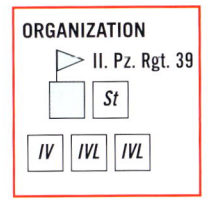

ORGANIZATION
- II. Pz. Rgt. 39
- St
- IV | IV/L | IV/L

▲ Panzer IV/70 (V) (Sd Kfz 162/1)
17 Panzer Division Kampfgruppe / Pz. Rgt 39 / II Battalion

930 Pz.Kpfw IV/70 (V) were produced between August 1944 and March 1945. The powerful high-velocity 7.5cm (3in) L/70 cannon was capable of penetrating 194mm (7.6in) of armour at 100m (328ft) or 106mm (4.2in) at 2000m (6562ft).

Specifications
- Crew: 4
- Weight: 28.4 tonnes (25.8 tons)
- Length: 8.5m (27.9ft)
- Width: 3.17m (10.4ft)
- Height: 1.85m (6ft)
- Engine: Maybach HL120TRM
- Speed: 35km/hr (21.7mph)
- Range: 210km (130.5 miles)
- Radio: FuG Spr 1

▶ Mittlerer Schützenpanzerwagen Ausf D (Sd Kfz 251/22)
17 Panzer Division Kampfgruppe / Panzerjäger Battalion / 4th Half-track Company

This vehicle was used on the Vistula in January 1945. It was armed with a 7.5cm (3in) PaK40 L/46 cannon and carried 22 rounds of ammunition. The Division was overrun in Eastern Germany by the Soviets.

Specifications
- Crew: 4
- Weight: 9.9 tonnes (9 tons)
- Length: 5.98m (19.6ft)
- Width: 2.1m (6.9ft)
- Height: 2.16m (7ft)
- Engine: Maybach HL42TUKRM
- Speed: 53km/hr (32.9mph)
- Range: 300km (186.4 miles)
- Radio: FuG Spr Ger 'f'

18th Panzer Division

The 18th Panzer Division was formed at Chemnitz on 26 October 1940, with manpower being provided by parts of the 4th and 14th Infantry Divisions.

The Panzer strength of the Division was drawn from the four battalions of 'diving' or submersible tanks created for Operation *Seelöwe* (Sea Lion), the planned invasion of England in the summer of 1940. Originally known as A, B, C and D battalions before the invasion was called off by Hitler, they were renamed as the 1st and 2nd Battalions, 18th Panzer Regiment and the 1st and 2nd Battalions, 28th Panzer Regiment, 18th Panzer Division.

In March 1941, as Panzer organizations were revised, the 28th Regiment was disbanded. The 1st Battalion became the 3rd Battalion, 18th Panzer Regiment, and the 2nd Battalion was transferred to the 3rd Panzer Division to become the 3rd Battalion, 6th Panzer Regiment.

Commanders

General der Panzertruppen W. Nehring
(26 Oct 1940 – 26 Jan 1942)

Generalleutnant K. von Thungen
(26 Jan 1942 – July 1942)

General der Nachrichtentruppen A. Praun
(July 1942 – 24 Aug 1942)

Generalleutnant K. von Thungen
(24 Aug 1942 – 15 Sept 1942)

Generalleutnant E. Menny
(15 Sept 1942 – Feb 1943)

Generalleutnant K. von Thungen
(Feb 1943 – 1 Apr 1943)

Generalleutnant K. von Schlieben
(1 Apr 1943 – 7 Sept 1943)

INSIGNIA

The standard tactical symbol for the 18th Panzer Division was related to those of the 16th and 17th Divisions, the number of crossbars on the 'Y' being the key recognition point.

The *Zusatzsymbols*, or additional marks, carried by panzers of the 18th were often much larger than the official tactical symbol. They showed a Panzer *Totenkopf*, or Death's Head, emerging from a stylized representation of the sea, recalling the division's origins as an amphibious assault unit.

Barbarossa: the attack on Russia
22 June 1941

In May 1941, the 18th Panzer Division was assigned to the 2nd *Panzergruppe* then assembling in the *Reichsprotectorate* of Bohemia and Moravia.

The 2nd *Panzergruppe* was commanded by Heinz Guderian. Guderian's *Gruppe* formed the southern prong of Army Group Centre's advance into Russia in June 1941, and 18th Panzer used its diving tanks alongside those of the 17th Panzer in the crossing of the River Bug early in the campaign.

As part of the LXVII *Panzerkorps* of Guderian's Gruppe, 18th Panzer was in the central offensive drive through Russia, and over the next six months was involved in seizing the key Soviet cities of Smolensk, Bryansk and Tula. However, like much of Army Group Centre, the division was unprepared for the Soviet winter, and was driven back from Moscow to the Orel sector in January 1942.

Panzer Unit	Pz. I	Pz. II	Pz. III	Pz. IV	Pz. Bef
18th Pz. Rgt.	6	50	114	36	12

18TH PANZER DIVISION

▶ Panzerbefehlswagen III als Tauchpanzer
Pz. Rgt 18 / Submersible battle tank

After the cancellation of the invasion of Britain, the *Tauchpanzer* of the 18th Panzer Division had their hose snorkel replaced by a steel one. Gyroscopes and radios were used to navigate under water.

Specifications
Crew: 5	Engine: Maybach HL120TR
Weight: 21.5 tonnes (19.5 tons)	Speed: 40km/hr (24.9mph)
Length: 5.38m (17.7ft)	Range: 165km (102.5 miles)
Width: 2.91m (9.5ft)	Radio: FuG6 plus FuG2 or FuG7 or
Height: 2.44m (8ft)	FuG8

▶ Panzerkampfwagen II Ausf C (SdKfz 121)
Pz. Rgt 18 / Regimental Staff Company

In March 1941, the division included six Panzer Is and 50 Panzer IIs in addition to the 'Diving' Panzer IIIs and Panzer IVs from which it had been formed.

Specifications
Crew: 3	Engine: Maybach HL62TR
Weight: 9.8 tonnes (8.9 tons)	Speed: 40km/hr (24.9mph)
Length: 4.81m (15.8ft)	Range: 200km (124.3 miles)
Width: 2.22m (7.3ft)	Radio: FuG5
Height: 1.99m (6.5ft)	

▶ Panzerkampfwagen III Ausf H (Sd Kfz 141)
Pz. Rgt 18 / II Battalion / 8th Company / 3rd Zug / tank number 2

The 18th Panzer was part of Guderian's 2nd *Panzergruppe* during Operation *Barbarossa*. Only 15 of the Pz.Kpfw IIIs listed on the Division's inventory at that time were armed with the 5cm (2in) cannon.

Specifications
Crew: 5	Engine: Maybach HL120TRM
Weight: 24 tonnes (21.8 tons)	Speed: 40km/hr (24.9mph)
Length: 5.41m (17.7ft)	Range: 165km (102.5 miles)
Width: 2.95m (9.7ft)	Radio: FuG5
Height: 2.44m (8ft)	

▶ Panzerkampfwagen IV Ausf E (Sd Kfz 161)
Pz. Rgt 18 / III Battalion / 9th Company / 3rd Zug / tank number 3

A tank with these markings was captured intact by Soviet troops in 1941 during the early stages of the war in Russia.

Specifications
Crew: 5	Engine: Maybach HL120TRM
Weight: 23.2 tonnes (21 tons)	Speed: 42km/hr (26mph)
Length: 5.92m (19.4ft)	Range: 200km (124.3 miles)
Width: 2.84m (9.3ft)	Radio: FuG5
Height: 2.68m (8.8ft)	

18TH PANZER DIVISION

Fall Blau: the Eastern Front
28 JUNE 1942

In May 1942, the 18th Panzer Regiment became the 18th Panzer Battalion. Its staff and surplus combat units were allocated to other formations.

THE DIVISION REMAINED WITH Army Group Centre through 1942, mostly in the area around Orel. The Division's single tank battalion was commanded by the aristocratic Hyazinth Graf von Strachwitz, one of Germany's finest Panzer commanders, whose daring tactics and inspiring leadership led to his acquiring the nickname 'The Panzer Count'. In the summer of 1942, he was promoted to command a regiment of the 16th Panzer Division.

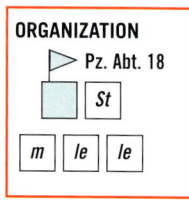

ORGANIZATION
Pz. Abt. 18
St
m le le

Panzer Unit	Pz. II	Pz. III(50)	Pz. IV	Pz. Bef
18th Pz. Rgt.	11	26	8	2

The last summer offensive
1 JULY 1943

As 1943 progressed, 18th Panzer remained with Army Group Centre, where defensive fighting against the Soviet winter offensive was followed by planning for Operation *Zitadelle*.

THE 18TH PANZER DIVISION remained with 2nd *Panzerarmee* in the run up to the Battle of Kursk. 2nd *Panzerarmee* had a subsidiary role during the battle, providing flank protection to Model's 9th Army. However, just before the offensive began, 18th Panzer transferred to LXI *Panzerkorps* of 9th Army.

As part of the northern prong of the German pincer movement designed to destroy the Kursk Salient, 18th Panzer suffered heavy losses for very little gain. After Kursk, the 18th Panzer Division was disbanded. The 18th Panzer Battalion was to become the 504th Panzer Battalion, and the rest of the Division was used to build the 18th Artillery Division.

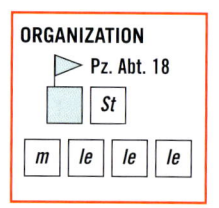

ORGANIZATION
Pz. Abt. 18
St
m le le le

Panzer Unit	Pz. II	Pz. III	Pz. III(75)	Pz. IV	Pz. Bef
18th Pz. Rgt.	5	10	20	24	3

▶ **Panzerkampfwagen III Ausf M (Sd Kfz 141/1)**
Pz. Abt 18 / 2nd Company / HQ tank

The Ausf M was the last new production model of the PzKpfw III. Only 250 tanks out of an order of 1000 were completed: the production capacity released was to be used for assault guns.

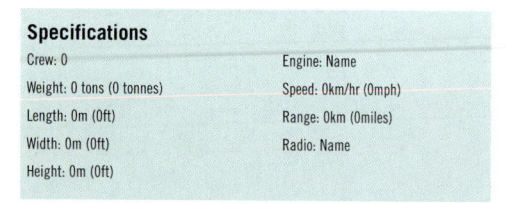

Specifications
Crew: 0
Weight: 0 tons (0 tonnes)
Length: 0m (0ft)
Width: 0m (0ft)
Height: 0m (0ft)
Engine: Name
Speed: 0km/hr (0mph)
Range: 0km (0miles)
Radio: Name

19th Panzer Division

Formed at Hanover in November 1940, the 19th Panzer Division was one of four new Panzer divisions created by the German Army in that month

CREATED AROUND A NUCLEUS provided by the combat-tested 19th Infantry Division, the divisional Panzer force was provided by the 10th, 11th and 25th *Ersatz* (Replacement) Panzer Battalions. As with four other Panzer divisions formed after the fall of France, the bulk of the 19th Division's tank inventory in June 1941 was provided by 110 Panzer 38(t)s. The Division also operated 42 Panzer Is, 35 Panzer IIs and 30 Panzer IVs.

Commanders

General der Panzertruppen O. von Knobelsdorff
(1 Nov 1940 – 5 Jan 1942)

Generalleutnant G. Schmidt
(5 Jan 1942 – 7 Aug 1943)

Generalleutnant H. Kallner
(7 Aug 1943 – 28 Mar 1944)

Generalleutnant W. Denkert
(28 Mar 1944 – May 1944)

Generalleutnant H. Kallner
(May 1944 – 22 Mar 1945)

Generalmajor H. Deckert
(22 Mar 1945 – 8 May 1945)

▲ Combat in the Ukraine
The winter of 1943–44 saw the 19th Panzer Division taking part in some of the toughest and most bitter fighting of the whole war.

INSIGNIA

The original tactical symbol of the 19th Panzer Division was a variant of the ancient runic *Wolfsangel*, or Wolf's Hook.

Units involved at Kursk were given new tactical insignia, which during the battle itself were in black on white panels.

Barbarossa: the attack on Russia
22 JUNE 1941

After being assigned to LXVII Corps in Germany while working up to operational readiness, 19th Panzer was transferred to the 3rd Panzer *Gruppe* for the invasion of the Soviet Union.

UNDER THE COMMAND OF General Hermann Hoth, the 3rd *Panzergruppe* operated with Guderian's 2nd *Panzergruppe* to surround the Soviet border armies, forming a pincer that met at Minsk on 27 June. Hoth's panzers had covered 350 km (217.5 miles) in just five days. The two *Panzergruppe* moved on towards Smolensk. Progress was delayed when Guderian was diverted south to Kiev. Some of Hoth's Panzers were sent to Army Group North, while the others, including 19th Panzer, were attached to 9th Army. 19th Panzer resumed the advance towards Moscow in November.

Panzer Unit	Pz. I	Pz. II	Pz. 38(t)	Pz. IV	Pz.Bef38(t)
27th Pz. Rgt.	42	35	110	30	11

19TH PANZER DIVISION

⚡ *Fall Blau*: the Eastern Front
28 JUNE 1942

In August 1941, the 3rd Battalion was disbanded. The next year, the 1st Battalion was also disbanded, leaving only the 2nd Battalion listed in the order of battle of the Division.

THE 19TH PANZER DIVISION'S strength was greatly reduced in 1941 and 1942. In August 1941, the 3rd Battalion was disbanded, while the 1st Battalion was disbanded in March 1942, leaving only the 2nd Battalion listed in the divisional order of battle.

Until August 1942, 19th Panzer served with 4th Army, which was trying to hold and expand a large German salient around Vyazma, which had been created after the Soviet winter offensive. Based initially at Juhno southeast of Vyazma, the Division was moved back to Jelnja near Smolensk in May, going into reserve in July. In addition to fighting off regular Soviet attacks, the Division's troops had to be wary of intense partisan activity in the area between Smolensk and Vyazma.

In August 1942, the 19th Panzer Division was moved over 350 km (217.5 miles) south to the southern end of Army Group Centre's front. It was attached to the 2nd *Panzerarmee* at Orel, again going into reserve to refit in November of 1942.

Panzer Unit	Pz. II	Pz. III(50)	Pz. 38(t)	Pz. IV(kz)
27th Pz. Rgt.	6	12	35	4

ORGANIZATION

Pz. Rgt. 27
 I
 II.
 St
 le m le le

▶ **Panzerkampfwagen II Flamm Ausf A und B (Sd Kfz 122)**
27 Pz. Rgt (Attached)
155 flamethrower Panzer IIs were built or converted from Ausf D variants.

Specifications
Crew: 3
Weight: 13.2 tonnes (12 tons)
Length: 4.9m (16ft)
Width: 2.4m (7.9ft)
Height: 1.85m (6ft)
Engine: Maybach HL62TRM
Speed: 55km/hr (34.2mph)
Range: 250km (155.3 miles)
Radio: FuG2

When Germany went to war in the Soviet Union in 1941 all AFVs carried the same national insignia. However, by 1942, the Werhmacht was using low-visibility symbols in summer.

▼ **Panzerbefehlswagen mit 5cm KwK39 L/60**
27 Pz. Rgt
In 1943, the 18th Panzer Division had three command tanks in its inventory.

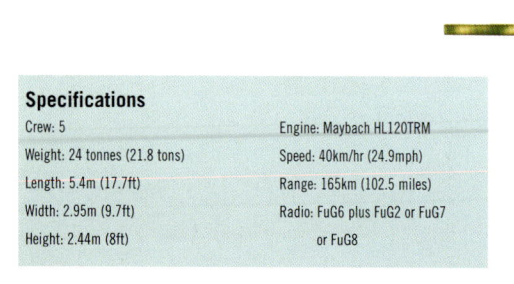

Specifications
Crew: 5
Weight: 24 tonnes (21.8 tons)
Length: 5.4m (17.7ft)
Width: 2.95m (9.7ft)
Height: 2.44m (8ft)
Engine: Maybach HL120TRM
Speed: 40km/hr (24.9mph)
Range: 165km (102.5 miles)
Radio: FuG6 plus FuG2 or FuG7 or FuG8

19TH PANZER DIVISION

⚡ The last summer offensive
1 July 1943

The 19th Panzer Division moved south to stiffen the 8th Italian Army after Stalingrad. In February 1943, it was attached to III *Panzerkorps* of the 1st *Panzerarmee* on the Donetz.

THE DIVISION FORMED PART OF Army Detachment *Kempf* during the Battle of Kursk. Fighting alongside Hoth's 4th *Panzerarmee* on the southern flank of the Kursk Salient, 19th Panzer bridged the Donetz on the night of 5–6 July, taking its Panzers (which included a detachment of new Tiger heavy tanks) to the east bank. Kempf's Panzers were to support the flank of II SS *Panzerkorps*, but were unable to do so because of heavy Soviet resistance. As a consequence, the SS Panzers were halted themselves in the large tank battle at Prokorovka. 19th Panzer had advanced only a short distance from the River when Hitler called off the offensive.

Back to the Dniepr

As German forces were forced back through the Ukraine, 19th Panzer fought a delaying battle in September, with two Soviet brigades seeking to expand a bridgehead over the Dniepr south of Kiev. The Division continued fighting in the area around Kiev for the next two months before falling back towards Zhitomir.

Panzer Unit	Pz. II	Pz. III	Pz. III(75)	Pz. IV	Pz. Bef
27th Pz. Rgt.	2	27	11	38	14

▶ **Leichter Schützenpanzerwagen (Sd Kfz 250/9)**
19th Reconnaissance Battalion / 2nd Armoured Car (half-track) Company
The 'Caesar' is armed with one 2cm (0.8in) KwK38 L/55 cannon and carries 100 rounds of ammunition fed in ten 10-round box magazines.

Specifications
Crew: 3
Weight: 6.9 tonnes (6.3 tons)
Length: 4.56m (15ft)
Width: 1.95m (6.4ft)
Height: 2.16m (7ft)
Engine: Maybach HL42TRKM
Speed: 60km/hr (37.3mph)
Range: 32km (19.9 miles)
Radio: FuG Spr Ger 'f'

▶ **Mittlerer Schützenpanzerwagen I Ausf C (Sd Kfz 251/9)**
Unknown formation
The SdKfz 251 was built in a wide variety of variants. The SdKfz 251/9 was armed with a 7.5cm (3in) KwK37 L/24, and carried 52 rounds of ammunition.

Specifications
Crew: 3
Weight: 9.4 tonnes (8.53 tons)
Length: 5.98m (19.6ft)
Width: 2.83m (9.3ft)
Height: 2.07m (6.8ft)
Engine: Maybach HL42TUKRM
Speed: 53km/hr (32.9mph)
Range: 300km (186.4 miles)
Radio: FuG Spr Ger 'f'

19TH PANZER DIVISION

Last year on the Eastern Front
1944

The 19th Panzer Division took part in some of the most bitter fighting of the war in 1944, suffering heavy losses in the process.

THE ASSAULT ON ZHITOMIR at the end of 1943 was one of the *Wehrmacht*'s last major successes on the Eastern Front. An armoured force comprising six Panzer and one infantry division under the command of General Herman Balck trapped a large Soviet force in a pocket at Zhitomir. 19th Panzer, part of Balck's XLVIII *Panzerkorps*, played a major part in the battle, which destroyed two Russian armies and badly mauled a third.

Over the next six months, 19th Panzer continued to fight with Army Group North Ukraine. After heavy losses, it was pulled out of the line in May 1944. In June, it was sent to the Netherlands, where it was to be rebuilt as a 'Type 44' Panzer Division, equipped with 81 long-barrelled Pz.Kpfw IVs, 79 Pz.Kpfw V Panthers, and eight 3.7cm (1.5in) Flakpanzer IVs.

Warsaw Uprising

No sooner had the Division re-equipped than it was sent back east, this time to Army Group Centre. It arrived outside Warsaw in August 1944, where its primary mission was to stabilize the defensive line on the Vistula, and its secondary mission to assist in putting down the Polish Home Army, which was then leading an uprising in the Polish capital

Panzer Unit	Pz. IV	Pz. V	Flk.Pz
27th Pz. Rgt.	81	79	8

Along with the 3rd and 5th SS Panzer Divisions and the *Luftwaffe* Hermann Göring Division, the 19th beat off an attack by a Soviet tank corps. The Soviets held off from attacking Warsaw itself for several months, giving the Germans time to deal with the rising. 19th Panzer dealt with the last Polish resistance in the suburbs of Sadyba and Sielce in the southern part of the city, followed by a powerful attack at Zoliborz on 29 September.

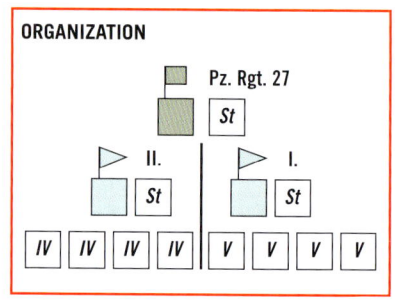

The division moved back though Poland in December 1944, ending the war in Czechoslovakia where it surrendered in May 1945.

Specifications
Crew: 6
Weight: 26.5 tonnes (24 tons)
Length: 7.17m (23.5ft)
Width: 2.97m (9.7ft)
Height: 2.81m (9.2ft)
Engine: HL120TRM
Speed: 42km/hr (26mph)
Range: 215km (133.6 miles)
Radio: FuG Spr 1

▲ **15cm Schwere Panzerhaubitze auf Fahrgestell Panzerkampfwagen III/IV (Sf) (Sd Kfz 165)**
19th Panzer Artillery Regiment / Self-propelled Battalion / 3rd Self-propelled Battery

Also known as the 'Hummel', this powerful self-propelled artillery piece was issued to the armoured artillery detachments in several Panzer divisions, initially at a rate of one six-gun battery per division. The Hummel made its combat debut at Kursk in 1943.

20th Panzer Division

Last (numerically) of the divisions formed in the second phase of the *Panzerwaffe*'s expansion, the 20th Panzer Division began assembling at Erfurt in October 1940.

Formed from elements of the 19th Infantry Division not used in the creation of the 19th Panzer Division, the 20th Panzer Division incorporated the three battalions of the 21st Panzer Regiment, which had been supplied by the 7th and 35th Panzer Replacement Battalions. As with the 19th Division, the most numerous tank in 20th Panzer's inventory in its early days was the Panzer 38(t), providing 123 out of a total tank strength of 229 vehicles. Nearly all were destroyed or had been replaced by Panzer IIIs in the first few months of the war in Russia, but more of the Czech-built tanks were delivered in 1942. About nine Panzer 38(t)s were still in service with the 20th Panzer Division in July 1943 at the time of the Battle of Kursk.

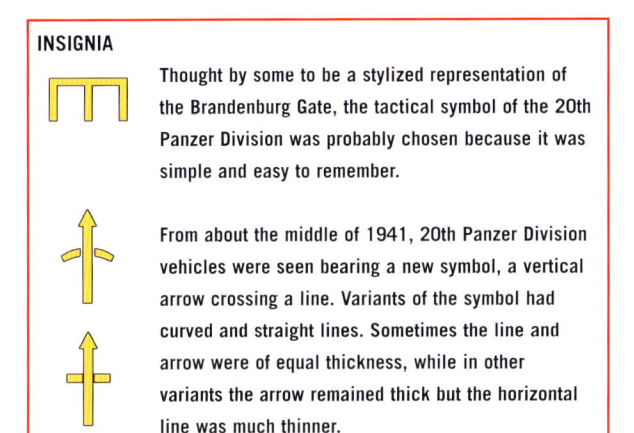

INSIGNIA

Thought by some to be a stylized representation of the Brandenburg Gate, the tactical symbol of the 20th Panzer Division was probably chosen because it was simple and easy to remember.

From about the middle of 1941, 20th Panzer Division vehicles were seen bearing a new symbol, a vertical arrow crossing a line. Variants of the symbol had curved and straight lines. Sometimes the line and arrow were of equal thickness, while in other variants the arrow remained thick but the horizontal line was much thinner.

Commanders

General der Panzertruppen H. Stumpff
(13 Nov 1940 – 10 Sept 1941)

Generalleutnant G. von Bismarck
(10 Sept 1941 – 14 Oct 1941)

General der Panzertruppen W. von Thoma
(14 Oct 1941 – 1 July 1942)

Generalleutnant W. Duvert
(1 July 1942 – 1 Oct 1942)

General der Panzertruppen H. von Luttwitz
(1 Oct 1942 – 5 May 1943)

General der Panzertruppen M. von Kessel
(5 May 1943 – 1 Jan 1944)

Generalleutnant W. Marcks
(1 Jan 1944 – 7 Feb 1944)

General der Panzertruppen M. von Kessel
(7 Feb 1944 – 6 Nov 1944)

Generalmajor H. von Oppeln-Bronikowski
(6 Nov 1944 – 8 May 1944)

Barbarossa: the attack on Russia
22 June 1941

The 20th Panzer Division fought with the 3rd *Panzergruppe* during the opening stages of Operation *Barbarossa* in June 1941.

Like the 19th Panzer Division, 20th Panzer took part in the initial battles of encirclement at Minsk and Smolensk, during which tens of thousands of Soviet prisoners were captured. Remaining near Smolensk after part of the 3rd *Panzergruppe* had been diverted to assist Army Group North at Leningrad, it transferred to the 4th *Panzergruppe* at Vyasma for the delayed German push towards Moscow. The delay allowed the Soviets to improve Moscow's defences. It also meant that the *Wehrmacht* would have to contend with the Russian winter, for which it was far from well prepared.

ORGANIZATION

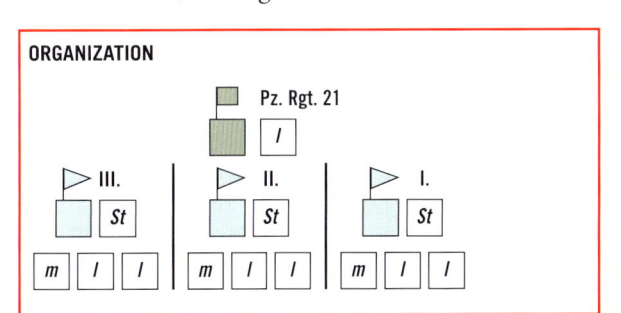

Pz. Rgt. 21
- III. St / m / l / l
- II. St / m / l / l
- I. St / m / l / l

Panzer Unit	Pz. I	Pz. II	Pz. 38(t)	Pz. IV	Pz.Bef38(t)
21th Pz. Rgt.	44	31	121	31	2

20TH PANZER DIVISION

▶ Panzerkampfwagen 38(t) Ausf E/F
Pz. Rgt 21

Some 525 Ausf E/F variants of the Pz.Kpfw 38(t) were produced for the *Wehrmacht* by Czech factories between November 1940 and October 1941. During Operation *Barbarossa*, the 20th Panzer Division used these tanks with Army Group Centre, seeing combat with *Panzergruppe 3*.

Specifications

Crew: 4
Weight: 10.9 tonnes (9.85 tons)
Length: 4.61m (15.1ft)
Width: 2.14m (7ft)
Height: 2.4m (7.9ft)
Engine: Praga EPA
Speed: 42km/hr (26mph)
Range: 250km (155.3 miles)
Radio: FuG37(t)

▶ Panzerkampfwagen 38(t) Ausf E/F
Pz. Rgt 21

Manufactured by the BMM concern, the 525 examples of the Ausf E/F variant were used in Russia by the 7th, 8th, 12th and 19th Panzer Divisions in addition to the 20th. This model had more armour protection on the turret and hull front than the first Panzer 38(t)s, which had seen combat in Poland and France.

Weapons Specifications

Main: 3.7cm (1.5in) KwK38(t) L/47.8
Ammunition: 42 rounds
Traverse: 360° manual
Elevation: −10° to +25°
Sight: 0m TZF (t)
Turret MG: 7.92mm (0.3in) MG37(t)
Hull MG: 7.92mm (0.3in) MG37(t)
Ammunition: 2400 rounds
MG Sight: MGZF(t)

▶ Panzerkampfwagen 38(t) Ausf G
Pz. Rgt 25 / II Battalion / 6th Company

90 Ausf G were produced between May and December 1941. The Ausf G was the final production model for the turreted version on the Pz.Kpfw 38(t). After 1941, the tank was considered obsolete and the Czech production lines were used to produce self-propelled antitank vehicles.

Specifications

Crew: 4
Weight: 10.9 tonnes (9.85 tons)
Length: 4.61m (15.1ft)
Width: 2.14m (7ft)
Height: 2.4m (7.9ft)
Engine: Praga EPA
Speed: 42km/hr (26mph)
Range: 250km (155.3 miles)
Radio: FuG5

20TH PANZER DIVISION

▶ **Panzerkampfwagen IV Ausf E (Sd Kfz 161)**
Pz. Rgt 21 / II Battalion

Built by Krupp-Gruson, the Ausf E variant of the Panzer IV had a new commander's cupola and increased armour protection. By the time Operation *Barbarossa* was launched, 438 Panzer IVs equipped the medium tank companies of the 17 Panzer divisions involved in the invasion of the USSR.

Specifications
Crew: 5
Weight: 23.2 tonnes (21 tons)
Length: 5.92m (19.4ft)
Width: 2.84m (9.3ft)
Height: 2.68m (8.8ft)
Engine: Maybach HL120TRM
Speed: 42km/hr (26mph)
Range: 200km (124.3 miles)
Radio: FuG5

⚔ *Fall Blau*: the Eastern Front
28 JUNE 1942

After the Battle of Moscow, the two battalions of the 21st Panzer Regiment, one battalion of the 112th *Schützen* Regiment and the 92nd Reconnaissance Battalion were disbanded.

EARLY IN 1942, AFTER THE FAILURE of the German assault on Moscow, the 20th Panzer Division's Panzer strength was reduced to a single battalion when the 1st and 2nd Battalions of the 21st Panzer Regiment were disbanded. Additionally, the 20th Panzer lost the 2nd Battalion of the 112th *Schützen* Regiment and the 92nd Reconnaissance Battalion.

20th Panzer served with Army Group Centre for most of its existence. In 1942, it was attached successively to 4th Panzer, 3rd Panzer and 9th Armies around Gshatsk (renamed Gagarin in the 1960s, after the first man in space). In August 1942, the Division was moved from the salient around Vyasma further south to the Orel sector, where it was attached to the 2nd *Panzerarmee*.

In November 1942, the Division was moved north again, and was dispersed around the small towns of Byelo and Toropets. In February 1943, it was placed in 9th Army reserve at Orel, before going back into the line with the 2nd *Panzerarmee*, where it would remain until just before the Battle of Kursk.

In spring 1943, the single battalion of the 21st Panzer Regiment was made up of a Regimental Staff Company equipped with a few flame-throwing tanks, and three medium Panzer companies, which were about to trade in their 3.7cm (1.5in) and 5cm (2in) armed Panzer IIIs for long-barrelled Panzer IVs and a single company of short-barrelled Panzer IVs. The battalion still had nine Panzer 38(t)s listed as operational.

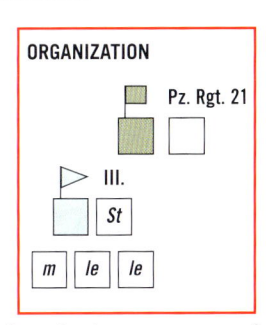

Divisional artillery was still towed equipment. Two battalions of the 92nd Panzer Artillery Regiment were equipped with 10.5cm (4.1in) leFH light field howitzers. Each battalion had three batteries: each battery had three guns. A third battalion was equipped with two batteries of three heavy 15cm (6in) sFH howitzers, and a single battery equipped with three long-range 10cm (4in) K18 cannon.

The reconnaissance battalion had one armoured car company and three motorcycle companies. The battalion's heavy company, designed to provide fire support, was equipped with four 7.5cm (3in) infantry guns, three 7.5cm (3in) antitank guns and three sPzBu 41 high velocity taper-bore guns.

ORGANIZATION

Pz. Rgt. 21
III.
St
m le le

Panzer Unit	Pz. II	Pz. 38(t)	Pz. III	Pz. IV	Pz. Bef
21st Pz. Rgt.	8	39	20	13	7

20TH PANZER DIVISION

The last summer offensive
1 July 1943

In June 1943, the 3rd Battalion, 21st Panzer Regiment was renamed the 21st Panzer Battalion. Soon it was to be embroiled in the biggest tank battle of the war.

ATTACHED TO THE LXVIII Corps of Model's 9th Army, 20th Panzer saw intensive action in the northern assault on the Kursk Salient. Heavy losses meant that the Division went into reserve to refit after the battle.

Over the next year, 20th Panzer was forced back with the rest of Army Group Centre, retreating through cities which had been captured in the heady days of victory in 1941. By the summer of 1944, 20th Panzer was at Cholm when the largest offensive in history burst over Army Group Centre. During Operation Bagration, 20th Panzer was encircled with the rest of 9th Army near Bobruisk, and few of the 40,000 German soldiers in the pocket escaped being killed or captured.

What was left of the 20th Panzer Division had been reduced to a *Kampfgruppe* and was withdrawn to Romania for refitting. It returned to fight in East Prussia and later Hungary before being overrun by the Soviets in May 1945.

ORGANIZATION
- Pz. Abt. 21
  - St
  - m | le | le | le

Panzer Unit	Pz. 38(t)	Pz. III	Pz. III(75)	Pz. IV	Pz. Bef
21st Pz. Rgt.	9	12	5	49	7

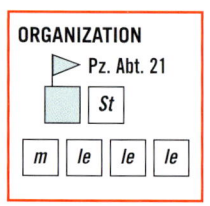

▶ Leichter Panzerspähwagen (2cm) (Sd Kfz 222)
20th Reconnaissance Battalion

The SdKfz 222 was a modified version of the earlier SdKfz 221, with a larger turret designed to carry a 2cm (0.8in) automatic cannon. It was designed to act as an escort for larger armoured cars, which were equipped with longer-ranged radios. 989 Sd Kfz 222 were produced between 1936 and June 1943.

Specifications
Crew: 3
Weight: 5.3 tonnes (4.8 tons)
Length: 4.8m (15.7ft)
Width: 1.95m (6.4ft)
Height: 2m (6.6ft)
Engine: Horch 3.5 or 3.8
Speed: 85km/hr (52.8mph)
Range: 300km (186.4 miles)
Radio: FuG Spr Ger 'a'

The toned-down tactical insignia carried by this SdKfz 222 include a stylized representation of the divisional markings, together with a standard German map symbol for armoured reconnaissance units.

▶ Mittlerer Schützenpanzerwagen Ausf D (Sd Kfz 251/9)
20th Reconnaissance Battalion / Half-track Gun Section

The SdKfz 251 was designed by Hanomag and built by eight other companies, and over 4600 examples were produced between 1939 and 1943. Built in dozens of variants, it was the principal carrier of *Panzergrenadiers* and their weapons.

Specifications
Crew: 3
Weight: 9.4 tonnes (8.53 tons)
Length: 5.98m (19.6ft)
Width: 2.1m (6.9ft)
Height: 2.07m (6.8ft)
Engine: Maybach HL42TUKRM
Speed: 53km/hr (32.9mph)
Range: 300km (186.4 miles)
Radio: FuG Spr Ger 'f'

21st Panzer Division

The creation of the 21st Panzer Division was authorized on 1 August 1941. It had already been in action in North Africa for several months as the 5th Light Division.

THE 5TH LIGHT DIVISION was formed on 18 February 1941 from German troops sent to Africa to help the Italians. The division staff came from the 3rd Panzer Brigade, the Panzers and artillery were drawn from the 3rd Panzer Division, and Infantry Regiment zbV 200 was created to control the infantry (zbV standing for *zur besonderen Verwendung*, 'For Special Duties'). 5th Light was in action as soon as it arrived in Africa. It first went into action as 21st Panzer during Operation *Crusader*, the British offensive launched at the end of 1941.

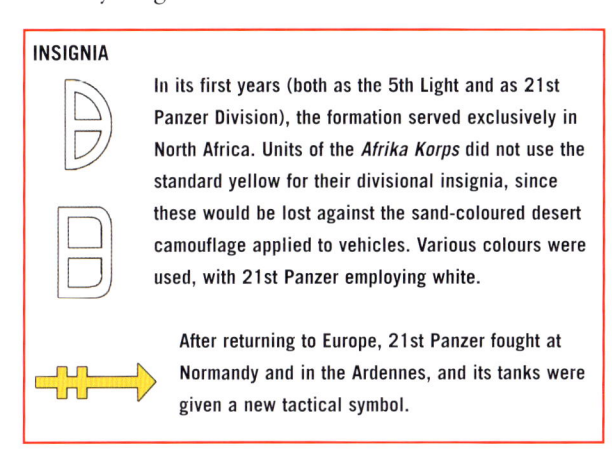

INSIGNIA

In its first years (both as the 5th Light and as 21st Panzer Division), the formation served exclusively in North Africa. Units of the *Afrika Korps* did not use the standard yellow for their divisional insignia, since these would be lost against the sand-coloured desert camouflage applied to vehicles. Various colours were used, with 21st Panzer employing white.

After returning to Europe, 21st Panzer fought at Normandy and in the Ardennes, and its tanks were given a new tactical symbol.

Commanders

Generalleutnant K. Bottcher (1 Aug 1941 – 20 May 1941)
Generalleutnant J. von Ravenstein (20 May 1941 – 29 Nov 1941)
Generalleutnant G. Knabe (29 Nov 1941 – 1 Dec 1941)
Generalleutnant K. Bottcher (1 Dec 1941 – 11 Feb 1942)
Generalleutnant G. von Bismarck (11 Feb 1942 – 21 July 1942)
Oberst A. Bruer (21 July 1942 – Aug 1942)
Generalleutnant G. von Bismarck (Aug 1942 – 1 Sept 1942)
Generalleutnant C. Lungershausen (1 Sept 1942 – 18 Sept 1942)

Generalleutnant H. von Randow (18 Sept 1942 – 21 Dec 1942)
Generalleutnant H. Hiidebrandt (1 Jan 1943 – 15 Mar 1943)
Generalmajor H. von Hulsen (15 Mar 1943 – 15 May 1943)
Generalleutnant E. Feuchtinger (15 May 1943 – 15 Jan 1944)
Generalmajor O. Grolig (15 Jan 1944 – 8 May 1944)
Generalleutnant E. Feuchtinger (8 May 1944 – 25 Jan 1945)
Oberst H. Zollenkopt (25 Jan 1945 – 12 Feb 1945)
Generalleutnant W. Marcks (12 Feb 1945 – Apr 1945)

Enter the Desert Fox
1941

The 5th Light Panzer Division had been formed from troops sent to Africa together with the 5th Panzer Regiment, which had been detached from the 3rd Panzer Division.

ROMMEL LAUNCHED HIS FIRST attack against El Agheila in March 1941, only days after 5th Light's Panzers had arrived in the desert. The British, believing the Germans to be much stronger than they were, retreated. Rommel seized the initiative and chased the British through Mersa Braga, Mechili, Bardia, and reached the Halfaya Pass.

The British Operation *Battleaxe*, intended to push the Germans back, was a failure. But Rommel was at the end of a very long supply chain and could advance no further. On September 14 1941, units of the new 21st Panzer Division took part in Operation *Sommernachtstraum*, a reconnaissance in force eastwards across the Egyptian border. In November, the British Operation *Crusader* forced the Germans all the way back to Gazala, and then even further back to prepared positions at El Agheila.

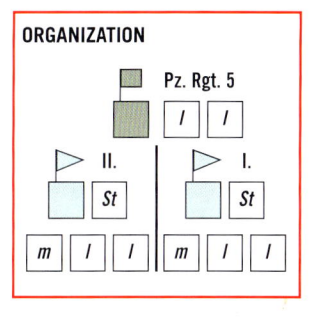

ORGANIZATION

Pz. Rgt. 5 — I, II. St, I. St, m/l/l, m/l/l

Panzer Unit	Pz. I	Pz. II	Pz. III(50)	Pz. IV	Pz. Bef
5th Pz. Rgt.	25	45	71	20	7

21ST PANZER DIVISION

▶ **Kleiner Panzerbefehlswagen (Sd Kfz 265)**
5 Leichte Division / Pz. Rgt 5 / I Battalion / Stabskompanie / Signal Platoon
'I04' is one of the three kl.Pz.Bef.Wg that landed in Tripoli in March 1941. It still carries its original 3rd Panzer Division insignia.

Specifications
Crew: 3	Engine: Maybach NL38TR
Weight: 6.5 tonnes (5.9 tons)	Speed: 40km/hr (24.9mph)
Length: 4.42m (14.5ft)	Range: 170km (105.6 miles)
Width: 2.06m (6.8ft)	Radio: FuG2 and FuG6
Height: 1.99m (6.5ft)	

▶ **Panzerkampfwagen I Ausf A (Sd Kfz 101)**
5 Leichte Division / Pz. Rgt 5 / I Battalion / Stabskompanie / Light Platoon
It was far from being a front-line weapon, but the mobility of the machine gun-armed Panzer I made it a useful weapon in the fluid, back-and-forth combat that was typical in North Africa.

Specifications
Crew: 2	Engine: Krupp M305
Weight: 6 tonnes (5.4 tons)	Speed: 37km/hr (23mph)
Length: 4.02m (13.2ft)	Range: 145km (90 miles)
Width: 2.06m (6.8ft)	Radio: FuG2
Height: 1.72m (5.6ft)	

▶ **Panzerkampfwagen II Ausf C (Sd Kfz 121)**
5 Leichte Division / Pz. Rgt 5 / I Battalion / 2nd Company / 4th Zug / tank number 1
The Panzer II's 2cm (0.8in) cannon made it much more useful than the Panzer I.

Specifications
Crew: 3	Engine: Maybach HL62TR
Weight: 9.8 tonnes (8.9 tons)	Speed: 40km/hr (24.9mph)
Length: 4.81m (15.8ft)	Range: 200km (124.3 miles)
Width: 2.22m (7.3ft)	Radio: FuG5
Height: 1.99m (6.5ft)	

▶ **Panzerkampfwagen IV Ausf D (Sd Kfz 161)**
5 Leichte Division / Pz. Rgt 5 / II Battalion / 8th Company / HQ tank
When it arrived in North Africa, the Panzer IV was the most powerfully armed tank in that theatre of combat, its 7.5cm (3in) armament being much more potent than the 2pdr (40mm) guns carried by most British tanks.

Specifications
Crew: 5	Engine: Maybach HL120TRM
Weight: 22 tonnes (20 tons)	Speed: 40km/hr (24.9mph)
Length: 5.92m (19.4ft)	Range: 200km (124.3 miles)
Width: 2.84m (9.3ft)	Radio: FuG5
Height: 2.68m (8.8ft)	

21ST PANZER DIVISION

▶ 4.7cm PaK (t) (Sf) auf Panzerkampfwagen I Ausf B
5 Leichte Division / 605th Panzerjäger Battalion

202 *Panzerjäger* I were converted from Pz.Kpfw I Ausf B between March 1940 and February 1941 by the addition of a Czech 4.7cm (1.9in) antitank gun.

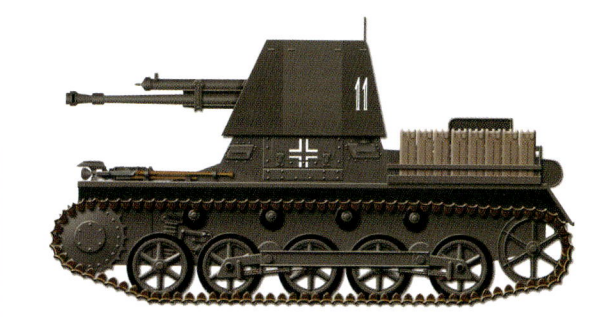

Specifications

Crew: 3	Engine: Maybach NL38TR
Weight: 7 tonnes (6.4 tons)	Speed: 40km/hr (24.9mph)
Length: 4.42m (14.5ft)	Range: 140km (87 miles)
Width: 2.06m (6.8ft)	Radio: FuG2
Height: 2.25m (7.4ft)	

▶ Panzerkampfwagen I Ausf A (Sd Kfz 101)
5 Leichte Division / Pz. Rgt 5 / Regiment Staff

Some Pz.Kpfw I Ausf A were field modified to mount a *Kleine Flammwerfer* 42 (portable flamethrower) in place of the right-hand turret machine gun.

Specifications

Crew: 2	Engine: Krupp M305
Weight: 6 tonnes (5.4 tons)	Speed: 37km/hr (23mph)
Length: 4.02m (13.2ft)	Range: 145km (90 miles)
Width: 2.06m (6.8ft)	Radio: FuG2
Height: 1.72m (5.6ft)	

▶ Panzerkampfwagen III Ausf G (Sd Kfz 141)
5 Leichte Division / Pz. Rgt 5 / Regiment Staff / Signal Platoon / signal officer's tank

This vehicle was used during Operation *Battleaxe*, the British and Commonwealth offensive intended to relieve the siege of Tobruk.

Specifications

Crew: 5	Engine: Maybach HL120TRM
Weight: 22.4 tonnes (20.3 tons)	Speed: 40km/hr (24.9mph)
Length: 5.41m (17.7ft)	Range: 165km (102.5 miles)
Width: 2.95m (9.7ft)	Radio: FuG5
Height: 2.44m (8ft)	

▶ Panzerbefehlswagen III Ausf E (Sd Kfz 266-267-268)
5 Leichte Division / Pz. Rgt 5 / I Battalion / Stabskompanie

The 5th Light Division attempted to outflank the British during *Battleaxe*, a move typical of Rommel's tactics, which made great use of the wide expanses of desert and enabled his troops to move with lightning speed.

Specifications

Crew: 5	Engine: Maybach HL120TR
Weight: 21.5 tonnes (19.5 tons)	Speed: 40km/hr (24.9mph)
Length: 5.38m (17.7ft)	Range: 165km (102.5 miles)
Width: 2.91m (9.5ft)	Radio: FuG6 plus FuG2 or FuG7 or FuG8
Height: 2.44m (8ft)	

21ST PANZER DIVISION

▶ Panzerkampfwagen I Ausf A (Sd Kfz 101)
5 Leichte Division / Pz. Rgt 5 / I Battalion / 1st Company / 2nd Zug / tank number 5

5th Light still had a number of early Panzer I Ausf As on strength. Long out of date, it had been the first German tank to go into mass production.

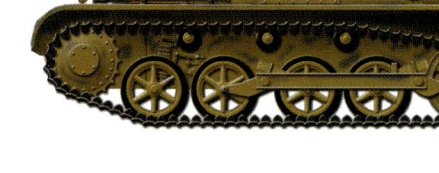

Specifications
Crew: 2	Engine: Krupp M305
Weight: 6 tonnes (5.4 tons)	Speed: 37km/hr (23mph)
Length: 4.02m (13.2ft)	Range: 145km (90 miles)
Width: 2.06m (6.8ft)	Radio: FuG2
Height: 1.72m (5.6ft)	

▶ Panzerkampfwagen III Ausf G (Sd Kfz 141)
5 Leichte Division / Pz. Rgt 5 / I Battalion / 1st Coy. / 3rd Zug / tank number 1

Although the DAK (*Deutsches Afrika Korps*) had a number of battleworthy tanks in the shapes of the Panzer III and IV, its armoured vehicle laagers in 1941 still contained obsolete Pz.Kfw Is and IIs

Specifications
Crew: 5	Engine: Maybach HL120TRM
Weight: 22.4 tonnes (20.3 tons)	Speed: 40km/hr (24.9mph)
Length: 5.41m (17.7ft)	Range: 165km (102.5 miles)
Width: 2.95m (9.7ft)	Radio: FuG5
Height: 2.44m (8ft)	

▶ Panzerkampfwagen I Ausf B (Sd Kfz 101)
5 Leichte Division / Pz. Rgt 5 / II Battalion / 8th Company / 3d Zug / tank number 3

The 5th Light Panzer Division was renamed 21st Panzer Division on August 1941.

Specifications
Crew: 2	Engine: Maybach NL38TR
Weight: 6.4 tonnes (5.8 tons)	Speed: 40km/hr (24.9mph)
Length: 4.42m (14.5ft)	Range: 170km (105.6 miles)
Width: 2.06m (6.8ft)	Radio: FuG2
Height: 1.72m (5.6ft)	

▶ Kleiner Panzerbefehlswagen (Sd Kfz 265)
Pz. Rgt 5 / I Battalion / Stabskompanie / Signal Platoon / signal officer's tank

The 21st's first operation was a reconnaissance in force aimed at a British supply dump near the Egypt frontier. The Division took heavy casualties from air attacks.

Specifications
Crew: 3	Engine: Maybach NL38TR
Weight: 6.5 tonnes (5.9 tons)	Speed: 40km/hr (24.9mph)
Length: 4.42m (14.5ft)	Range: 170km (105.6 miles)
Width: 2.06m (6.8ft)	Radio: FuG2 and FuG6
Height: 1.99m (6.5ft)	

21ST PANZER DIVISION

▶ Panzerkampfwagen III Ausf G (Sd Kfz 141)
Pz. Rgt 5 / I Battalion / 3rd Company / 2nd Zug / tank number 1

The Germans in Africa had a technological edge over the British, in that tanks like the Panzer III were combat-tested and reliable. British tanks built before 1943 were notoriously unreliable, and the situation did not change until large numbers of American M3s and M4s reached Commonwealth forces in the desert.

Weapons Specifications

Main: 5cm (2in) KwK L/42
Ammunition: 99 rounds
Traverse: 360° manual
Elevation: -10° to +20°
Sights: TZF5d

Turret MG: 7.92mm (0.3in) MG34
Hull MG: /.92mm (0.3in) MG34
Ammunition: 2700 rounds
MG sights: KgZF2

▶ Mittlerer Schützenpanzerwagen I Ausf B (Sd Kfz 251)
Unknown formation

The medium armoured troop carrier, the forerunner of the modern armoured personnel carrier, was proposed at the time the first armoured divisions were formed in 1935. However, the first production models of the SdKfz 251 did not enter service until 1939.

Specifications

Crew: 2 plus 10 troops
Weight: 8.8 tonnes (8 tons)
Length: 5.98m (19.6ft)
Width: 2.1m (6.9ft)
Height: 1.75m (5.7ft)

Engine: Maybach HL42TUKRM
Speed: 53km/hr (32.9mph)
Range: 300km (186.4 miles)
Radio: FuG Spr Ger 1

▶ Panzerkampfwagen IV Ausf D (Sd Kfz 161)
Pz. Rgt 5 / II Battalion / 8th Company / HQ tank

Headquarters Company tactical numbers indicated to whom a tank was assigned. The company commander's vehicle was 01; 02 was the adjutant's tank, while numbers from 03 onwards were used by other HQ vehicles.

Specifications

Crew: 5
Weight: 22 tonnes (20 tons)
Length: 5.92m (19.4ft)
Width: 2.84m (9.3ft)
Height: 2.68m (8.8ft)

Engine: Maybach HL120TRM
Speed: 40km/hr (24.9mph)
Range: 200km (124.3 miles)
Radio: FuG5

21ST PANZER DIVISION

War in the desert
25 May 1942

After Rommel secured his supply lines, he decided to take the offensive against the British and Commonwealth forces in North Africa. He also wanted to capture the port of Tobruk.

THE GERMAN SUPPLY SITUATION started to change early in 1942. Air attacks on Malta prevented British aircraft and submarines from interfering with convoys, and for the first time, the *Afrika Korps* was receiving adequate support.

In May 1942, Rommel launched an assault on the British. 21st Panzer Division led a flanking manoeuvre around Gazala, where the British were dug in.

British tank losses in the Gazala fighting were huge. As the British withdrew, 21st Panzer was ready to lead the attack that finally took the port of Tobruk.

Pushing on towards Egypt, Rommel tried to outflank the heavily fortified position at El Alamein, but failed. Flanked by the sea on one side and the impassable Qattara Depression on the other, Alamein was just too tough. Rommel had more problems, however. At the end of a supply line stretching all the way to Benghazi and exposed to RAF air attack, the German troops were beginning to feel the pinch.

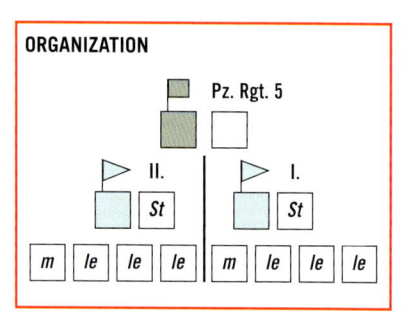

Panzer Unit	Pz. II	Pz. III(kz)	Pz. III(lg)	Pz. IV(kz)	Pz. Bef
5th Pz. Rgt.	29	131	3	22	4

▶ Panzerkampfwagen II Ausf C (Sd Kfz 121)
Pz. Rgt 5 / Regiment Staff

This Pz.Kpfw II was assigned to the Regimental Medical Officer. Note the caduceus painted by the tactical marking 'RA' (which stands for Regiment Arzt, or 'Doctor').

Specifications
Crew: 3
Weight: 9.8 tonnes (8.9 tons)
Length: 4.81m (15.8ft)
Width: 2.22m (7.3ft)
Height: 1.99m (6.5ft)
Engine: Maybach HL62TR
Speed: 40km/hr (24.9mph)
Range: 200km (124.3 miles)
Radio: FuG5

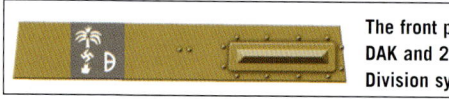

The front plate has both DAK and 21st Panzer Division symbols.

▶ Panzerkampfwagen I Ausf A (Sd Kfz 101)
Pz. Rgt 5 / Regiment Staff

With regular supply convoys arriving in North Africa thanks to the aerial blockade of Malta by the *Luftwaffe* and the *Regia Aeronautica*, the *Deutsches Afrika Korps* could look forward to replacing old equipment like this early model Panzer I.

Specifications
Crew: 2
Weight: 6 tonnes (5.4 tons)
Length: 4.02m (13.2ft)
Width: 2.06m (6.8ft)
Height: 1.72m (5.6ft)
Engine: Krupp M305
Speed: 37km/hr (23mph)
Range: 145km (90 miles)
Radio: FuG2

21ST PANZER DIVISION

▶ **Panzerkampfwagen IV Ausf F2 (Sd Kfz 161/1)**
Pz. Rgt 5 / I Battalion / 4th Company / 1st Zug / tank number 2

Known to the British as the 'Mark IV Special', the long-barrelled 7.5cm (3in) variant of the Panzer IV was more than a match for any British or American tank in Africa.

Specifications
Crew: 5
Weight: 25.4 tonnes (23 tons)
Length: 5.62m (18.4ft)
Width: 2.84m (9.3ft)
Height: 2.68m (8.8ft)
Engine: Maybach HL120TRM
Speed: 40km/hr (24.9mph)
Range: 200km (124.3 miles)
Radio: FuG5

▶ **Panzerfunkwagen (Sd Kfz 263) 8-Rad**
3rd Nachtrichten Abteilung (Signal Battalion)

Specialist communications vehicles were equipped with Enigma code machines. The Germans thought that their signals were secure, little realizing that Allied code-breakers could read much of what they sent.

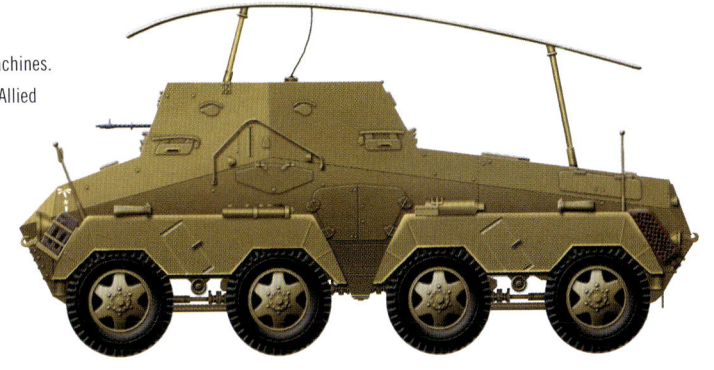

Specifications
Crew: 5
Weight: 8.9 tonnes (8.1 tons)
Length: 5.85m (19.2ft)
Width: 2.2m (7.2ft)
Height: 2.9m (9.5ft)
Engine: Büssing-NAG L8V
Speed: 100km/hr (62.1mph)
Range: 300km (186.4 miles)
Radio: 1 Satz Funkgerat fur (m) Pz.Funktrupp b

El Alamein: Egypt denied
23 October 1942

General Bernard Law Montgomery, the new commander of the British 8th Army, intended to use the sheer weight of Allied materiel to force the exhausted Axis troops into retreat.

OPENING THE ASSAULT on 23 October 1942 with an artillery barrage of World War I proportions, Montgomery launched a grinding attack that wore the German and Italian forces down. Progress was slow, but sheer Allied weight began to be felt. Rommel, who had been home on sick leave, arrived from Germany on the third day of the attack, and realized that the situation was hopeless. Disobeying orders, he withdrew the *Afrika Korps*, using the 21st Panzer Division to fight a series of Rearguard actions.

El Alamein was the start of a long retreat for German troops in North Africa. By the time the Axis forces surrendered to the Allies in Tunisia in 1943, they had lost almost as heavily as they had done at Stalingrad. Among the German losses was the 21st Panzer Division.

ORGANIZATION

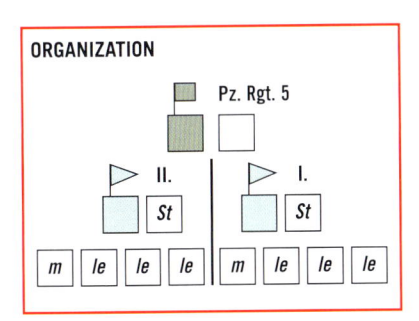

Pz. Rgt. 5
— II. — I.
St — St
m le le le — m le le le

Panzer Unit	Pz. II	Pz. III(kz)	Pz. III(lg)	Pz. IV	Pz. Bef
5th Pz. Rgt.	14	43	44	18	2

163

21ST PANZER DIVISION

▶ **Panzerkampfwagen IV Ausf F2 (Sd Kfz 161/1)**
Pz. Rgt 5 / I Battalion / 2nd Company / 1st Zug / tank number 5
Water is precious in the desert. Any of the ubiquitous 'Jerry Cans' intended for fresh water were marked with a white cross, indicating that they should be used for no other liquids.

Specifications
Crew: 5	Engine: Maybach HL120TRM
Weight: 25.4 tonnes (23 tons)	Speed: 40km/hr (24.9mph)
Length: 5.62m (18.4ft)	Range: 200km (124.3 miles)
Width: 2.84m (9.3ft)	Radio: FuG5
Height: 2.68m (8.8ft)	

▶ **Panzerkampfwagen II Ausf F (Sd Kfz 121)**
Pz. Rgt 5 / II Battalion / Stabskompanie / Light Platoon
In October 1942, as the second battle of Alamein got under way, 21st Panzer still had 19 Panzer IIs in its vehicle inventory.

Specifications
Crew: 3	Engine: Maybach HL62TR
Weight: 10.5 tonnes (9.5 tons)	Speed: 40km/hr (24.9mph)
Length: 4.81m (15.8ft)	Range: 200km (124.3 miles)
Width: 2.28m (7.5ft)	Radio: FuG5
Height: 2.15m (7ft)	

▶ **Panzerkampfwagen III Ausf J (Sd Kfz 141)**
Pz. Rgt 5 / I Battalion / 3rd Company / 3rd Zug / tank number 3
This Ausf J has been up-armoured, with a 20mm (0.8in) spaced armour plate added to the front of the hull and turret.

Specifications
Crew: 5	Engine: Maybach HL120TRM
Weight: 24 tonnes (21.5 tons)	Speed: 40km/hr (24.9mph)
Length: 5.52m (18.1ft)	Range: 155km (96.3 miles)
Width: 2.95m (9.7ft)	Radio: FuG5
Height: 2.5m (8.2ft)	

▶ **Panzerkampfwagen IV Ausf D (Sd Kfz 161)**
Pz. Rgt 5 / I Battalion / 4th Company / 1st Zug / tank number 9
Captured by the British, this Ausf D has been upgunned with a 7.5cm (3in) KwK40 L/48 and has extra turret armour. These vehicles were issued to training and replacement units.

Specifications
Crew: 5	Engine: Maybach HL120TRM
Weight: 22 tonnes (20 tons)	Speed: 40km/hr (24.9mph)
Length: 5.92m (19.4ft)	Range: 200km (124.3 miles)
Width: 2.84m (9.3ft)	Radio: FuG5
Height: 2.68m (8.8ft)	

21ST PANZER DIVISION

▶ **Leichter Gepanzerter Beobachtungskraftwagen (Sd Kfz 253)**
115th Artillery Regiment
This light armoured observation post was based on the DEMAG 1 tonne tractor.

Specifications
Crew: 4
Weight: 6.3 tonnes (5.73 tons)
Length: 4.7m (15.4ft)
Width: 1.95m (6.4ft)
Height: 1.8m (5.9ft)
Engine: Maybach HL42TRKM
Speed: 65km/hr (40.4mph)
Range: 320km (198.8 miles)
Radio: FuG15 plus FuG16

▶ **15cm sFH13/1 (Sf) auf Geschützwagen Lorraine Schlepper (f) (Sd Kfz 135/1)**
115th Artillery Regiment / 3rd Battalion
The German vehicle park was a quartermaster's nightmare, containing vehicles from all over Europe. This howitzer is mounted on a French Lorraine chassis.

Specifications
Crew: 4
Weight: 9.4 tonnes (8.5 tons)
Length: 5.31m (17.4ft)
Width: 1.83m (6ft)
Height: 2.23m (7.3ft)
Engine: Delahaye 103TT
Speed: (road): 34km/hr (21.1mph)
Range: 135km (83.9 miles)
Radio: FuG Spr 'f'

▶ **Panzerkampfwagen IV Ausf F2 (Sd Kfz 161/1)**
Pz. Rgt 5
The first of the long-gunned Panzer IVs, the Ausf F2 was more than a match for tanks like the Sherman. But the few available could not match the sheer numbers of Allied tanks.

Weapons Specifications
Main: 7.5cm (3in) Kw40 L/43
Ammunition: 87 rounds
Traverse: 360° electric
Elevation: -8° to +20°
Sights: TZF5f
Turret MG: 7.92mm (0.3in) MG34
Hull MG: 7.92mm (0.3in) MG34
Ammunition: 3000 rounds
MG sights: KgZF2

▶ **Panzerkampfwagen IV Ausf G (Sd Kfz 161/1 und 161/2)**
Pz. Rgt 5 / II Battalion / 8th Company / 5th Zug / tank number 2
Kasserine Pass was the last operation in divisional strength for 21st Panzer in North Africa. After that, it was split into *Kampfgruppen* until surrendering in May 1943.

Specifications
Crew: 5
Weight: 25.9 tonnes (23.5 tons)
Length: 6.62m (21.7ft)
Width: 2.88m (9.4ft)
Height: 2.68m (8.8ft)
Engine: Maybach HL120TRM
Speed: 40km/hr (24.9mph)
Range: 210km (130.5 miles)
Radio: FuG5

21ST PANZER DIVISION

The Western Front
June 1944

Ordered to be rebuilt around a small nucleus of ex-African veterans, the 21st Panzer Division was reformed at Rennes in France on 15 July 1943.

INITIALLY EQUIPPED WITH captured French tanks, the recreated 21st was rapidly re-equipped with Panzer IIIs and Panzer IVs. On June 6 1944, the 21st Panzer Division was the only armoured formation close enough to the Normandy landings to have a chance to interfere with Allied consolidation of the beachhead. It was the only Panzer unit to attack on the day of the invasion, 6 June.

The slow German response to the Allied landings reflected a disagreement in the German High Command. Rommel wanted the Panzers deployed immediately to stop the Allies on the beach. Rundstedt, Guderian and others wanted to hold the Panzers inland, ready for a mobile campaign.

ORGANIZATION

Pz. Rgt. 22 / St
II. St / I. St
Pz.Kp. (Fkl) 315
Fkl | IV IV IV IV | IV IV IV IV

Panzer Unit	Pz. III(75)	Pz. IV	FlkPz	StuG	Pz. Bef
22nd Pz. Rgt.	4	117	12	10	2

▶ **Panzerkampfwagen IV Ausf H (Sd Kfz 161/2)**
Pz. Rgt 22 / II Battalion / 6th Company / 1st Zug / tank number 1

On 6 June, the 21st Panzer Division was the only armour formation in a position to influence the landings at Normandy. However, even veterans of the Eastern Front had not anticipated the devastating effects of Allied naval gunfire and air power.

Specifications
Crew: 5
Weight: 27.6 tonnes (25 tons)
Length: 7.02m (23ft)
Width: 2.88m (9.4ft)
Height: 2.68m (8.8ft)
Engine: Maybach HL120TRM
Speed: 38km/hr (23.6mph)
Range: 210km (130.5 miles)
Radio: FuG5

▶ **7.5cm PaK40 (Sf) auf Geschützwagen 39H (f)**
200th Sturmgeschütz Battalion

The 200th *Sturmgeschütz* Battalion engaged British tanks during Operation *Goodwood*. After early progress, the British were hit hard by fire from 88mm (3.2in) antitank guns and heavy tanks.

Specifications
Crew: 4
Weight: 13.8 tonnes (12.5 tons)
Length: 4.7m (15.4ft)
Width: 2.14m (7ft)
Height: 2.22m (7.3ft)
Engine: Hotchkiss 6-cylinder
Speed: 36 km/hr (22.3mph)
Range: 150 km (93 miles)
Radio: FuG Spr 'd'

21ST PANZER DIVISION

▶ 10.5cm leFH18(Sf) auf Geschützwagen 39H (f)
200th Sturmgeschütz Battalion
The Germans converted 48 French Hotchkiss tanks into a light self-propelled gun armed with a 10.5cm (4.1in) leFH18 cannon.

Specifications
Crew: 4
Weight: 13.8 tonnes (12.5 tons)
Length: 4.22m (13.8ft)
Width: 2.14m (7ft)
Height: 2.22m (7.3ft)
Engine: Hotchkiss 6-cylinder
Speed: 3 km/hr (22.4mph)
Range: 150km (93.2 miles)
Radio: FuG Spr 'd'

▶ 7.5cm Sturmgeschütz 40 Ausf G (Sd Kfz 142/1)
Panzer-Kompanie (Fkl) 315 (Attached)
The *Panzer-Kompanie* (Fkl) 315 was attached to the 21st Panzer Division in January 1944. It was to use its force of assault guns in combat against the British and Canadians north of Caen.

Specifications
Crew: 4
Weight: 26.3 tonnes (23.9 tons)
Length: 6.77m (22.2ft)
Width: 2.95m (9.7ft)
Height: 2.16m (7ft)
Engine: Maybach HL120TRM
Speed: 40km/hr (24.9mph)
Range: 155km (96.3 miles)
Radio: FuG15 and FuG16

Specifications
Crew: 1 (or 0 when remote-controlled)
Weight: 4 tonnes (3.6 tons)
Length: 3.65m (12ft)
Width: 1.8m (6.2ft)
Height: 1.19m (3.9ft)
Engine: Borgward 6M RTBV
Speed: 38km/hr (23.6mph)
Range: 212km (131.7 miles)
Radio: EP3 mit UKE6

▲ **Schwerer Ladungstrager Ausf A (Sd Kfz 301)**
Panzer-Kompanie (Fkl) 315 (Attached)
Remote-controlled tracked demolition charge layer.

The Last Battles
14 December 1944

After refitting, 21st Panzer was sent to the southern sector of the Western Front, where Germany and France shared a border.

ROMMEL'S FEARS OF ALLIED air power and of the devastating effect of naval gunfire were justified: in addition to normal combat losses and mechanical breakdowns, the constant fighter-bomber attacks and the hail of high explosive from battleships, cruisers and destroyers off the Normandy coast meant that most of the 21st's Panzers were destroyed in the first few days. However, the Division's grenadiers fought in and around Caen for many weeks.

Infantry losses could be made good by drafting in stragglers and remnants of other units: at the beginning of August, 21st Panzer received an influx

21ST PANZER DIVISION

of manpower when it absorbed surviving units of the 16th *Luftwaffe* Field Division. Many of these were killed or taken prisoner after the Allies broke out of the Beachhead in August, creating the Falaise pocket in which much of the German army lost its equipment. The battered remnants of 21st Panzer were withdrawn to Germany for rebuilding.

The 21st Panzer Division was rushed back to the Western Front after refitting with new tanks and drafting infantry from the 112th *Panzergrenadier* Regiment. It fought during the general withdrawal through France, mainly in the Saar and Alsace regions. In November, it was attached to LXIV Corps of the 19th Army near Lothringen.

Panzer Unit	Pz. IV	Pz. V	FlkPz(20)	FlkPz(37)
22nd Pz. Rgt.	34	38	5	3

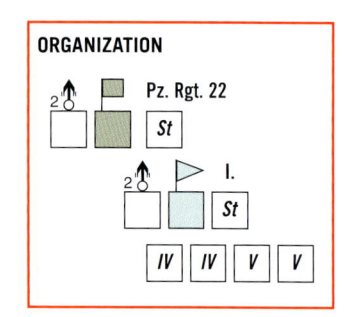

➔ In defence of the Fatherland
1945

The Battle of the Bulge is well known as Germany's last offensive in the West – except that it was not. 21st Panzer took part in Operation *Nordwind*, launched two weeks later.

With the slowing of the Ardennes offensive on 22 December 1944, Hitler ordered Army Group G to begin planning an attack on Alsace. Three days later, Hitler and von Rundstedt reviewed the plans and approved the attack, codenamed Operation *Nordwind*, for New Year's Eve. The primary target was Strasbourg. It had been annexed by the Germans in 1871, returned to France in 1918, retaken by the Germans in 1940 and was now again French. The offensive sparked off a three-week battle, but by 16 January Hitler's last reserves had been committed. The battle was over by 25 January.

In February 1945, the 21st Panzer Division was transported to the Oder front in Eastern Germany. There it fought in a series of hopeless defensive actions until surrendering to the Soviets at the end of April 1945.

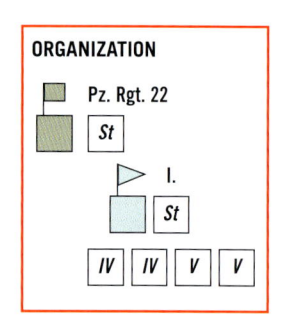

Panzer Unit	StuG	Pz. IV	Pz. IV(70)	Pz. V	FlkPz
22nd Pz. Rgt.	1	31	16	33	4

▶ **Panzerbeobachtungswagen IV (7.5cm) Ausf J**
155th Panzer Artillery Regiment
This armoured observation post is armed with a 7.5cm (3in) KwK40 L/48 cannon, and has been fitted with the cupola from a StuG assault gun. The 21st Panzer Division was overrun by the Soviets in April 1945.

Specifications
Crew: 5
Weight: 27.6 tonnes (25 tons)
Length: 7.02m (23ft)
Width: 2.88m (9.4ft)
Height: 2.68m (8.8ft)
Engine: Maybach HL120TRM112
Speed: 38km/hr (23.6mph)
Range: 320km (198.8 miles)
Radio: FuG5

22nd Panzer Division

Two new armoured formations were created in France in September 1941, the 22nd and 23rd Panzer Divisions. Both were to serve exclusively on the Eastern Front.

THE 22ND PANZER DIVISION was formed in Northern France by the upgrading of the 204th Panzer Regiment and by the addition of two newly formed *Schützen* Regiments making up the 22nd *Schützen* Brigade. 22nd Panzer was sent to southern Russia as part of Army Group South's reserve. In April 1942, it was attached to Manstein's 11th Army in Southern Russia.

On 8 May, Manstein launched an attack along the Kamenskoye Isthmus against Kerch. Although outnumbered, Manstein's Panzers attacked the weakest point of the Soviet defences. By 20 May, the Soviets had imploded and been driven back into the Black Sea.

As Manstein went on to invest Sevastopol, 2nd Panzer was transferred north to 6th Army.

Commanders
Generalleutnant W. von Apell
(25 Sept 1941 – 7 Oct 1942)
Generalleutnant H. von der Chevallerie
(7 Oct 1942 – 1 Nov 1942)
Generalleutnant E. Rodt
(1 Nov 1942 – 4 Mar 1943)

▶ **Graveyard for tanks**
The fighting in and around Stalingrad saw German panzers fighting through built-up terrain, where armoured vehicles are at their most vulnerable.

INSIGNIA

22nd Panzer's tactical sign was related to the symbol used by the 21st Panzer Division after its return from Africa, simply rotated clockwise through 45°.

Fall Blau: the Eastern Front
28 JUNE 1942

After the victory at Kerch, 22nd Panzer now took part in the German drive towards the Volga. Its primary target was the city of Stalingrad.

JOINING 6TH ARMY AT CHERSON, the 22nd Panzer Division operated with the 1st *Panzerarmee* against Rostov in July 1942. In August 1942, it was on the Chir River about 60km (37 miles) west of Stalingrad. The city was cut off after the launch of the Soviet Operation *Uranus* in November 1942, and 22nd Panzer was attached to Army Detachment *Hollidt*. This also included one Romanian tank division, three German and four Romanian infantry divisions. Although intended to relieve Stalingrad, strong Soviet forces prevented Hollidt from advancing beyond the Chir. In the fighting that followed, 22nd Panzer was almost destroyed. The remnants of the division were redesignated as *Kampfgruppe Brugsthaler* in March 1943, and the unit was disbanded and absorbed into the 23rd Panzer Division in April 1943.

Panzer Unit	Pz. II	38(t)	Pz. III	Pz. IV(kz)	Pz. IV(lg)
204th Pz. Rgt.	28	114	12	11	11

ORGANIZATIONS

Pz. Rgt. 204

22ND PANZER DIVISION

▶ **Panzerkampfwagen 38(t) Ausf C**

Pz. Rgt 204 / II Battalion / 5th Company / 2nd Zug / tank number 2

The 204th was the last unit to be issued with the Pz.Kpfw 38(t).

Specifications
Crew: 4
Weight: 10.5 tonnes (9.5 tons)
Length: 4.61m (15.1ft)
Width: 2.14m (7ft)
Height: 2.4m (7.9ft)
Engine: Praga EPA
Speed: 42km/hr (26mph)
Range: 250km (155.3 miles)
Radio: FuG37(t)

▼ **Panzerkampfwagen KV Ia 753(r)**

Pz. Rgt 204

The 76mm (3in) gun on this captured Russian KV-1 tank has been replaced by a German 7.5cm (3in) KwK40 L/48 cannon.

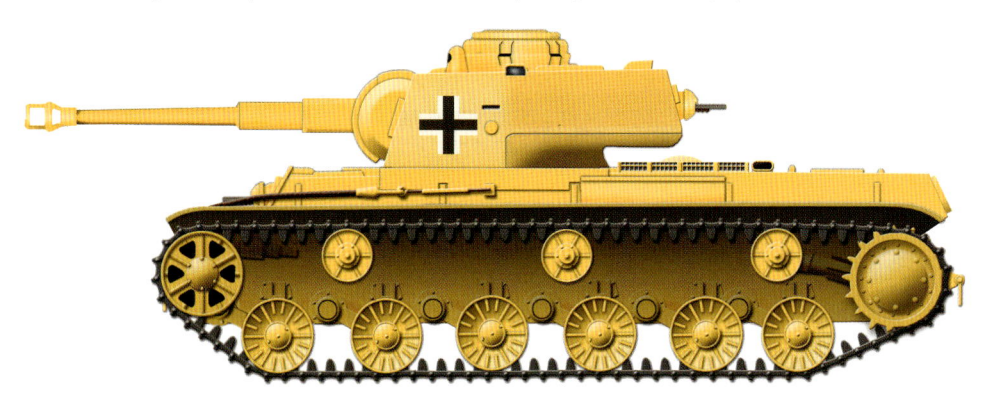

Specifications
Crew: 5
Weight: 46.6 tonnes (42.3 tons)
Length: 6.68m (21.9ft)
Width: 3.32m (10.9ft)
Height: 2.71m (8.9ft)
Engine: V-2K
Speed: 35km/hr (21.7mph)
Range: 180km (111.8 miles)
Radio: 10R

▶ **Leichter Panzerspähwagen (Fu) (Sd Kfz 223)**

140th Reconnaissance Battalion

The Sd Kfz 223 was designed to provide long-range radio communication for the far-ranging reconnaissance units equipped with light armoured cars.

Specifications
Crew: 3
Weight: 4.9 tonnes (4.4 tons)
Length: 4.8m (15.7ft)
Width: 1.95m (6.4ft)
Height: 1.75m (5.7ft)
Engine: Maybach Horch 3.5 or 3.8
Speed: 85km/hr (52.8mph)
Range: 300km (186.4 miles)
Radio: FuG10 + Spr Ger 'a'

▶ **Panzerkampfwagen 38(t) Ausf E/F**

Pz. Rgt 204 / II Battalion / 7th Company / 1st Zug / tank number 1

22nd Panzer still used the Panzer 38(t) when it was shattered north of Stalingrad.

Specifications
Crew: 4
Weight: 10.9 tonnes (9.85 tons)
Length: 4.61m (15.1ft)
Width: 2.14m (7ft)
Height: 2.4m (7.9ft)
Engine: Praga EPA
Speed: 42km/hr (26mph)
Range: 250km (155.3 miles)
Radio: FuG37(t)

23rd Panzer Division

The 23rd Panzer Division was formed in the Paris area in September 1941. Like the 22nd Division formed at the same time, it was sent to fight in the Soviet Union.

THE 23RD PANZER DIVISION incorporated the 101st Panzer Brigade, an occupation formation equipped with captured French armour. The French vehicles were only a temporary measure, however. By March 1942, when the division became fully operational, it had been re-equipped with 34 Panzer IIs, 112 Panzer IIIs, 32 short-barrel Panzer IVs and three command tanks.

In April 1942, the Division began the transfer to Army Group South on the Don River at Kharkov. In June 1942, the division was moved from the corps reserve and was assigned to LX *Panzerkorps* of Army Group A.

Attached to Kleist's 1st *Panzerarmee*, the Division fought through the searing heat towards the Caucasus. The Soviet attack at Stalingrad threatened to cut off the entire Army Group, and the Panzers made fighting retreat to the Don.

Commanders

Generalleutnant H. von Boineburg-Legsfeld
(25 Sept 1941 – 16 Nov 1941)

Generalmajor H. Werner-Ehrenfeucht
(16 Nov 1941 – 22 Nov 1941)

Generalleutnant H. von Boineburg-Legsfeld
(22 Nov 1941 – 20 July 1942)

Generalmajor E. Mack
(20 July 1942 – 26 Aug 1942)

Generalleutnant H. von Boineburg-Legsfeld
(26 Aug 1942 – 26 Dec 1942)

General der Panzertruppen N. von Vormann
(26 Dec 1942 – 25 Oct 1943)

Generalmajor E. Kraber
(25 Oct 1943 – 1 Nov 1943)

Generalmajor H. Werner-Ehrenfeucht
(1 Nov 1943 – 18 Nov 1943)

Generalmajor E. Kraber
(18 Nov 1943 – 9 June 1944)

Generalleutnant J. von Rodowitz
(9 June 1944 – 8 May 1945)

INSIGNIA

Following on from the 21st and 22nd Panzer Divisions, the 23rd Panzer Division used a similar tactical symbol but with a single cross bar.

The 'Eiffel Tower' *Zusatzsymbol* reflects the division's origins in occupied France.

From the Caucasus to Stalingrad
1942–43

Following the withdrawal from the Caucasus, 23rd Panzer was transferred to Hoth's 4th *Panzerarmee* in the failed attempt to relieve the besieged 6th Army at Stalingrad.

THE 23RD PANZER DIVISION had been battered by the hard fighting of the previous months, and more was to come as the Division's Panzer strength had been reduced to only 30 badly worn tanks.

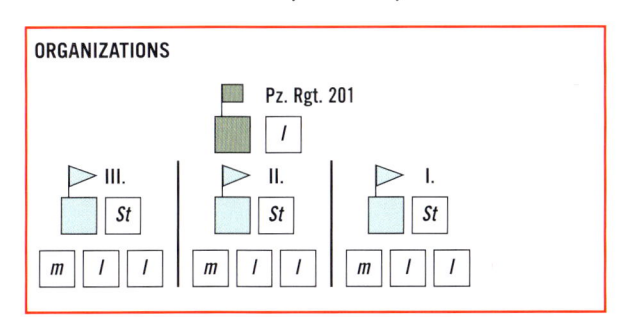

After the relief force failed to get through to Paulus' trapped 6th Army at Stalingrad, 23rd Panzer was brought up to strength by absorbing what remained of the 22nd Panzer Division, which had been badly mauled in the fighting on the Chir.

By the spring of 1943, the Division's Panzer strength was in the process of being increased, with the 201st Panzer Regiment refitting to deploy one battalion with Panzer IVs and one battalion with Panzer V Panthers.

Panzer Unit	Pz. II	Pz. III(5kz)	Pz. III(5lg)	Pz. IV	Pz. Bef
201st Pz. Rgt.	27	50	34	17	10

23RD PANZER DIVISION

The last summer offensive
1 July 1943

After being attached to Army Detachment *Hollidt* during the withdrawal from Stalingrad, 23rd Panzer Division was reconstructed between April and June 1943.

THE DIVISION WAS BACK in action in July, as part of 1st *Panzerarmee*'s reserve on the Mius River. Following the cancellation of the Kursk offensive by Hitler, the Soviets launched a series of offensives along the length of the front. It is believed that these were designed to force the Germans to disperse the powerful Panzer force, which was still a threat to the Red Army even after the losses in the battles in July.

23rd Panzer met the Soviet offensive on the Mius, where it was joined by the 3rd Panzer Division, the 2nd SS Panzer Division *Das Reich* and the 3rd SS Panzer Division *Totenkopf*. In August, 23rd Panzer was moved to Izium, where further reinforcements arrived in the shape of the 5th SS Panzer Division *Wiking* and the 17th Panzer Division.

Long retreat

The 23rd Panzer Division now began the long retreat through the Ukraine and Poland. In September 1943, it was involved in the heavy fighting on the Dnieper. At the end of the year, it was attached to LVII *Panzerkorps* at Dniepropetrovsk, initially with 1st *Panzerarmee* and then with the rebuilt 6th Army. In March 1944, it was fighting at Nikolaev, before being withdrawn to Jassy for rest and recuperation at the end of April.

From August 1944, the 23rd Panzer Division fought as part of XLVIII *Panzerkorps* as the *Wehrmacht* tried to stabilize the front in the face of repeated Soviet offensives being launched from the Arctic to the Black Sea.

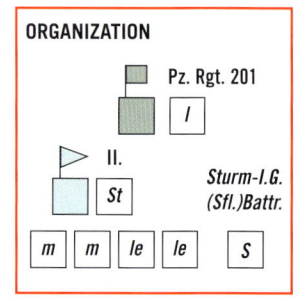

In October 1944, the Division was sent to Hungary after further Soviet advances threatened Budapest. The division continued to fight in Hungary and Slovakia before being destroyed by the Red Army in Austria in May 1945.

Panzer Unit	Pz. III	Pz. III(75)	Pz. IV	Sturm-I.G	Pz. Bef
201st Pz. Rgt.	24	17	30	7	1

ORGANIZATION
Pz. Rgt. 201
I
II.
St
Sturm-I.G. (Sfl.)Battr.
m | m | le | le | S

▲ **Sturminfanteriegschütz 33B**
Pz. Rgt 201 / 9th Company

A vast improvement over the sIG33(SF), 24 of these infantry assault guns were produced between December 1941 and October 1942. The StuG33b is armed with one 15cm (6in) StuIG L/11 and has a fully enclosed fighting compartment.

Specifications
Crew: 5
Weight: 23.2 tonnes (21 tons)
Length: 5.4m (17.7ft)
Width: 2.9m (9.5ft)
Height: 2.3m (7.5ft)
Engine: Maybach HL120TRM
Speed: 40km/hr (24.9mph)
Range: 155km (96.3 miles)
Radio: FuG Spr 'd'

23RD PANZER DIVISION

Staff Platoon, Medium Panzer Company, Type 44 Panzer Division

By the end of the war, Panzer Divisions were equipped with just two types of tank, the Pz.Kpfw IV and the Pz.Kpfw V Panther. One of the platoons in the HQ company was tasked with reconnaissance.

Company HQ: 3 Pz.Bef V

Reconnaissance *Zug*: 5 Pz.Kpfw V

▶ 7.5cm PaK40/3 auf Panzerkampfwagen 38(t) Ausf H (Sd Kfz 138)

128th Panzerjäger Battalion / Self-propelled Panzerjäger Company

Armed with a 7.5cm (3in) PaK40/3 L/46 cannon, it carried 38 rounds of ammunition.

Specifications

Crew: 4
Weight: 11.9 tonnes (10.8 tons)
Length: 5.77m (18.9ft)
Width: 2.16m (7ft)
Height: 2.51m (8.2ft)
Engine: Praga EPA/2
Speed: 35km/hr (21.7mph)
Range: 240km (149.1 miles)
Radio: FuG5

▲ Panzer IV/70 (V) (Sd Kfz 162/1)

Unknown formation

The vehicle shown, from the second series built between September and November 1944, was in action in Hungary, mid-March 1945. The 23rd Panzer Division made a fighting retreat to Austria before it was overrun by the Soviets in May 1945.

Specifications

Crew: 4
Weight: 28.4 tonnes (25.8 tons)
Length: 8.5m (27.9ft)
Width: 3.17m (10.4ft)
Height: 1.85m (6ft)
Engine: Maybach HL120TRM
Speed: 35km/hr (21.7mph)
Range: 210km (130.5 miles)
Radio: FuG Spr 1

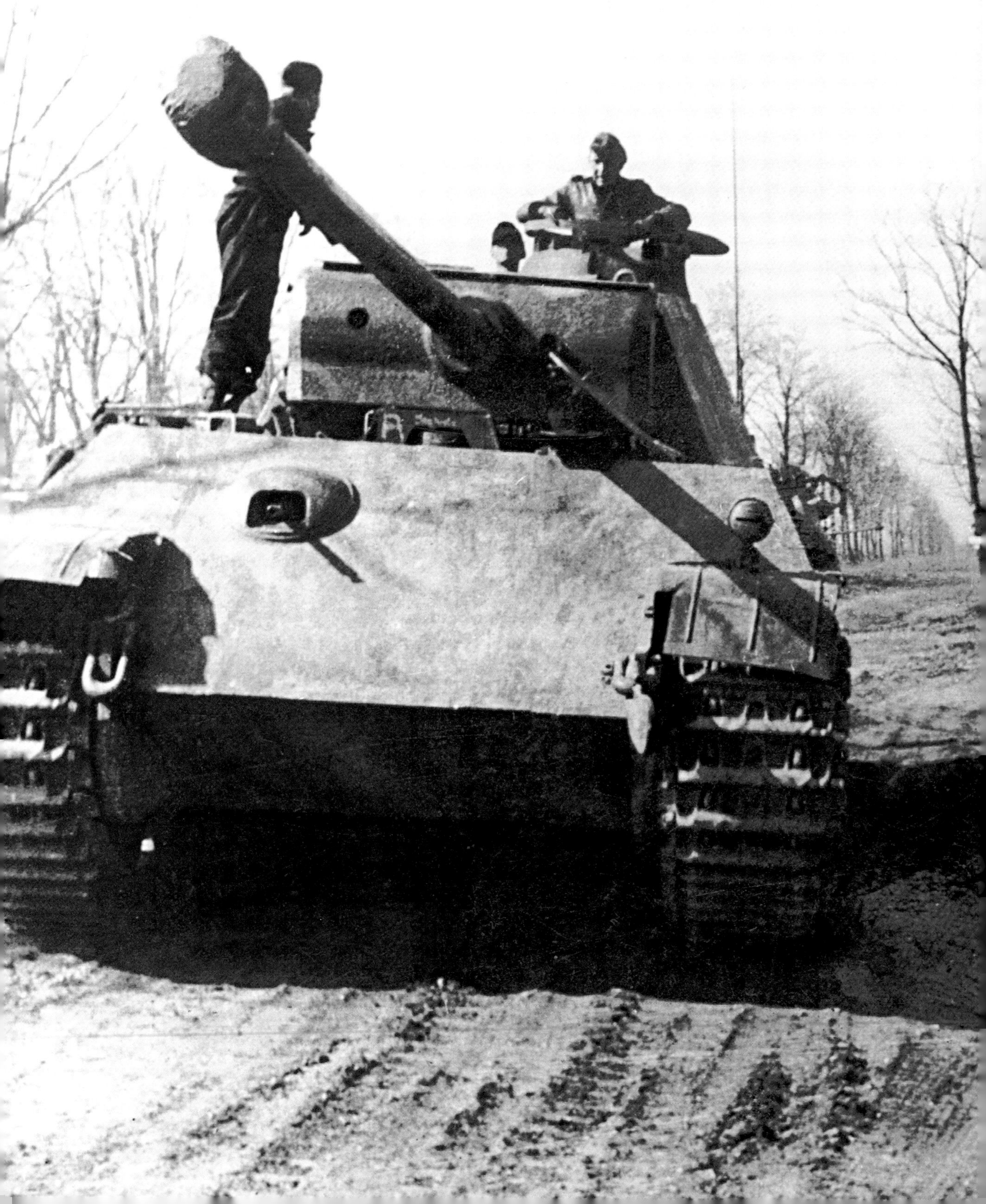

Chapter 4

Later Wartime Panzer Divisions

The rapid expansion of the *Panzerwaffe* in the first three years of the war tailed off dramatically from 1943. The numerical sequence of panzer divisions ended after the establishment of the 27th Panzer Division in October 1942. Thereafter, only a few numbered divisions were formed. At the end of the war, with Germany assailed by enemies on all sides, several nominal Panzer divisions were created from remnants of other units destroyed in battle. They were usually given regional or historical names, but in the chaos into which the Reich had fallen, few were anything like true divisions in strength.

◀ **Panthers to the Fore**
Although the late war Panzer division had a third as many tanks as had those of 1939, its fighting power was much greater — because more than half of its panzers were the superb Panzerkampfwagen V Panther.

24th Panzer Division

The 24th Panzer Division began forming at Stablack in East Prussia in November 1941, working up to operational capacity at the *Truppenübungsplatz*, Ohrdruf, in February 1942.

THE CORE OF THE NEW DIVISION was provided by the 1st Cavalry Division. Cavalry had little place on the modern battlefield, but for political and sentimental reasons the German Army had retained a cavalry brigade when it expanded in the 1930s. The Brigade had been expanded to divisional size in February 1940, but its performance in the French campaign had been modest, especially in contrast to the astonishing success of the *Panzerwaffe*.

In April 1942, the 24th Panzer Division was sent to France to complete its training while acting as a reserve for 7th Army in Army Group D. Its primary equipment as a Panzer division included 32 Panzer IIs, 54 short-barrelled Panzer IIIs, 56 long-barrelled Panzer IIIs, 20 short-barrelled Panzer IVs and 12 long-barrelled Panzer IVs. Divisional units included the 24th *Schützen* Brigade, the 24th Panzer Regiment and the 89th Artillery Regiment.

Commanders

General der Kavallerie K. Feldt
(28 Nov 1941 – 15 Apr 1942)

General der Panzertruppen B. Ritter von Hauenschild
(15 Apr 1942 – 12 Sep 1942)

Generalleutnant A. von Lenski
(12 Sep 1942 – 31 Jan 1943)

General der Panzertruppen M. Freiherr von Edelsheim
(1 Mar 1943 – 1 Aug 1944)

Generalmajor G-A. von Nostitz-Wallwitz
(1 Aug 1944 – 25 Mar 1945)

Major R. von Knebel-Döberitz
(25 Mar 1945 – 8 May 1945)

INSIGNIA

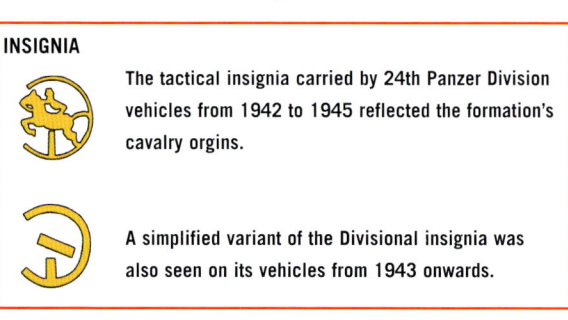

The tactical insignia carried by 24th Panzer Division vehicles from 1942 to 1945 reflected the formation's cavalry orgins.

A simplified variant of the Divisional insignia was also seen on its vehicles from 1943 onwards.

Fall Blau: the Eastern Front
28 JUNE 1942

In preparing for the 1942 summer campaign in Russia, the *Wehrmacht* deployed as many Panzer units to Army Group South as it could gather.

ARRIVING ON THE EASTERN FRONT in June 1942, 24th Panzer made its combat debut with LXVIII *Panzerkorps* in the fighting around Voronezh, before being transferred to the 6th Army in August. After participating in the drive on the Volga, it transferred back to 4th *Panzerarmee* for the assault on Stalingrad. In October, it was returned to 6th Army control, and was tasked with leading the final assault on the city. The Division was trapped when the Soviets completed their encircling attack in November. By January, the remains of 24th Panzer had been combined with those of 16th Panzer and 94th Infantry Divisions to form a single *kampfgruppe*. The survivors surrendered on 2 February.

ORGANIZATION

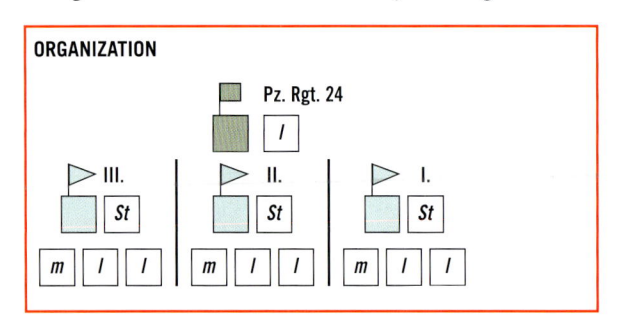

Pz. Rgt. 24 — I

III. — St — m / l / l
II. — St — m / l / l
I. — St — m / l / l

Panzer Unit	Pz. II	Pz. III(5kz)	Pz. III(5lg)	Pz. IV	Pz. Bef.
24th Pz. Rgt.	32	54	36	32	7

24TH PANZER DIVISION

▲ Panzerkampfwagen III Ausf J (Sd Kfz 141/1)
Pz. Rgt 24 / II Battalion / 5th Company / 2nd Zug / tank number 5

During the summer of 1942, before it was trapped in the Stalingrad pocket, the 24th Panzer Division numbered 56 Panzer IIIs with long-barrelled 5cm (2in) guns, out of a total strength of around 180 tanks.

Specifications
Crew: 5
Weight: 24 tonnes (21.5 tons)
Length: 6.28m (20.6ft)
Width: 2.95m (9.7ft)
Height: 2.5m (8.2ft)
Engine: Maybach HL120TRM
Speed: 40km/hr (24.9mph)
Range: 155km (96.3 miles)
Radio: FuG5

◀ Leichter Schützenpanzerwagen (Sd Kfz 250/1)
Unknown formation

Designed to carry an *Halbgruppe*, or half-section, of four grenadiers, the crew of the Sd Kfz 251/1 consisted of a commander/gunner and driver.

Specifications
Crew: 2 plus 4 troops
Weight: 6.5 tonnes (5.89 tons)
Length: 4.7m (15.4ft)
Width: 1.94m (6.4ft)
Height: 1.52m (5ft)
Engine: Maybach HL42 TRKM
Speed: 59.5km/hr (37mph)
Range: 198km (123 miles)
Radio: FuSpr Ger 5

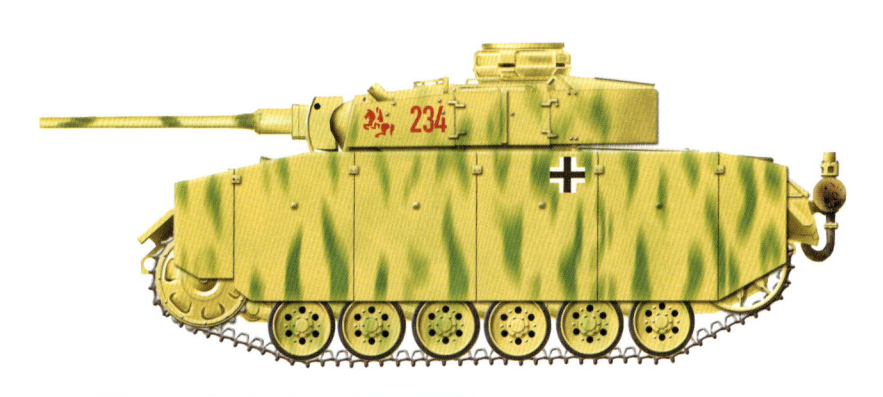

▲ Panzerkampfwagen III Ausf M (Sd Kfz 141/1)
Pz. Rgt 24 / I Battalion / 2nd Company / 3rd Zug / tank number 4

A vehicle with these markings was captured by the Russians in the autumn of 1943. The *Schürzen*, or side skirts, offered extra protection against both armour-piercing and shaped charge high-explosive warheads.

Specifications
Crew: 5
Weight: 25 tonnes (22.7 tons)
Length: 6.41m (21ft)
Width: 2.95m (9.7ft)
Height: 2.5m (8.2ft)
Engine: Maybach HL120TRM
Speed: 40km/hr (24.9mph)
Range: 155km (96.3 miles)
Radio: FuG5

24TH PANZER DIVISION

Defence of Italy
1944

After the 24th Panzer Division was wiped out at Stalingrad in February 1943, the decision was taken to recreate it from scratch, based on the 891st *Panzergrenadier* Regiment.

Between April and August of 1943, the component parts of the new 24th Panzer Division were assembled in Northern France. The 1st, 2nd and 3rd Panzer Battalions received Pz.Kpfw IVs, Panthers and assault guns respectively.

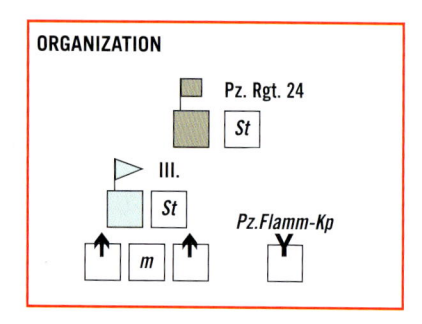

In August 1943, the Division was ordered to join the II SS *Panzerkorps* in Italy as German forces occupied their former ally following Mussolini's downfall. Their first task was to disarm the Italian army. The Division remained in Northern Italy, fighting partisans and helping to man the series of defensive lines that Army Group B was preparing for the Allied armies advancing up the Italian peninsula.

Too far away to influence the Salerno landings, 24th Panzer was transferred to LI *Panzerkorps* in October, before being ordered back to the Eastern Front in November.

Panzer Unit	Pz. IV	StuG	Pz. Bef	Flammpz
24th Pz. Rgt.	49	42	9	14

▶ Panzerkampfwagen IV Ausf H (Sd Kfz 161/2)
Pz. Rgt 24 / III Battalion / 12th Company / 4th Zug / tank number 1

As the war progressed, the shortage of resources was so critical that vehicles left for the front in the basic factory colour and rarely received any other treatment.

Specifications
Crew: 5
Weight: 27.6 tonnes (25 tons)
Length: 7.02m (23ft)
Width: 2.88m (9.4ft)
Height: 2.68m (8.8ft)
Engine: Maybach HL120TRM
Speed: 38km/hr (23.6mph)
Range: 210km (130.5 miles)
Radio: FuG5

▶ Sturmpanzer IV (Sd Kfz 166)
89th Panzer Artillery Regiment

Seen here in Russia in September 1944, the Sturmpanzer IV was also known as *Brummbar*, or 'grizzly bear'. It was armed with a 15cm (6in) StuH43 L/12 demolition gun. Some 298 Sd Kfz 166 were produced from April 1943.

Specifications
Crew: 5
Weight: 31 tonnes (28.2 tons)
Length: 5.93m (19.5ft)
Width: 2.88m (9.4ft)
Height: 2.52m (8.3ft)
Engine: Maybach HL120TRM plus TRM112
Speed: 40km/hr (24.9mph)
Range: 210km (130.5 miles)
Radio: FuG5 plus FuG2

Defence of the Fatherland
1944/45

The 24th Panzer Division had been outfitted with Panthers in addition to its Pz.Kpfw IVs. It was ordered to the Eastern Front in October 1943, where it remained to the end of the war.

THE DIVISION ARRIVED in Army Group South's area of operations in November 1943, and was attached to XL *Panzerkorps* of the 1st *Panzerarmee* at Nikopol. In December, 24th Panzer transferred to IV *Panzerkorps* at Krivoi Rog. The city had been under attack by the Soviet 46th Army since October, as Malinovsky's 3rd Ukrainian Front and Konev's 2nd Belorussian Front launched an autumn offensive from its bridgeheads on the Dnieper River.

The battle for Krivoi Rog lasted until February as the Soviets maintained the pressure all along the Front. Threatened with encirclement like their comrades at Cherkassy, the Germans retreated before being cut off. In March, 24th Panzer fought to relieve German forces in Nikolaev, before retreating to Jassy and across the San and Weichsel rivers into Poland.

Soviet Summer Offensive

The massive Soviet offensives in the summer of 1944 continued to force the *Wehrmacht* westward. In October 1944, 24th Panzer retreated into Hungary with Army Group South. As the Red Army juggernaut continued to attack, the Division fought defensive actions in Hungary until the end of November, being driven back into Slovakia in December. After operating with the 8th Army until January, 24th Panzer was transferred to East Prussia, where further Soviet attacks threatened to pour across the German border. In February, it joined the *Luftwaffe*'s *Hermann Göring* Parachute-Panzer Corps.

By now, the Division had been reduced to a *kampfgruppe* consisting of two Panther companies, the 21st *Panzergrenadier* Regiment and a single antitank battalion. As the Soviets pressed forward into Germany, 24th Panzer withdrew westward, eventually surrendering to the British Army in Schleswig-Holstein on 4 May 1945.

ORGANIZATION
I. Pz. Rgt. 24

▲ Panzerkampfwagen V Ausf G (Sd Kfz 171)
Kampfgruppe / Pz. Rgt 24 / I Battalion / 3rd Company / 3rd Zug / tank no. 2

The Pz.Kpfw Ausf G was the final production version of the Panther, incorporating extra armour and a redesigned hull. By the end of the war, it made up more than half the tank strength of the *Wehrmacht's* panzer divisions.

Specifications

Crew: 5
Weight: 50.2 tonnes (45.5 tons)
Length: 8.86m (29ft)
Width: 3.4m (11.2ft)
Height: 2.98m (9.8ft)

Engine: Maybach HL230P30
Speed: 46km/hr (28.6mph)
Range: 200km (124.3 miles)
Radio: FuG5

25th Panzer Division

The 25th Panzer Division was formed in February 1942 in Eberswalde and was to remain in Norway until August 1943. It was equipped with 108 Panzer IV tanks.

PANZERS HAD NOT PLAYED a major part in the Norwegian campaign, but from 1940 to 1942 the *Panzer Abteilung zur besonderer Vervendung 40* provided what little armoured support was needed in the country. In February 1942, it became one of the constituent parts of the newly formed 25th Panzer Division. In September 1943, the Division was transferred to France, before being moved to the Eastern Front. The Division fought at Zhitomir and at Kamanets-Podolsk, suffering heavy losses.

Commanders

Generalleutnant J. Haarde
(25 Feb 1942 – 31 Dec 1942)

Generalleutnant A. von Schell
(1 Jan 1943 – 15 Nov 1943)

General der Panzertruppen G. Jauer
(15 Nov 1943 – 20 Nov 1943)

Generalleutnant H. Tröger
(20 Nov 1943 – 10 May 1944)

Generalmajor O. Grolig
(1 June 1944 – 18 Aug 1944)

Generalmajor O. Audörsch
(18 Aug 1944 – 8 May 1945)

INSIGNIA

As a panzer division with non-standard origins, it is not surprising that 25th Panzer should also make use of non-standard tactical insignia.

After moving from Norway to the Eastern Front, the division adopted a simplified version of its symbol. It was also seen in yellow.

Retreat and defence of the Fatherland
NOVEMBER 1943 – 1945

In June 1944, the Division was sent to be reformed in Denmark, being redeployed as a *kampfgruppe* to the Polish sector of the Eastern Front in August and September 1944.

ALTHOUGH THE MAIN CHARGES for the violent and brutal suppression of the Warsaw Rising can be laid against SS units, *Obergruppenführer* Erich von dem Bach Zalewski also made use of detachments from the 25th, 19th and *Hermann Göring* Panzer Divisions to crush the Polish Home Army, which had risen in revolt in August 1944. The Poles were forced to surrender to the Germans at the beginning of October.

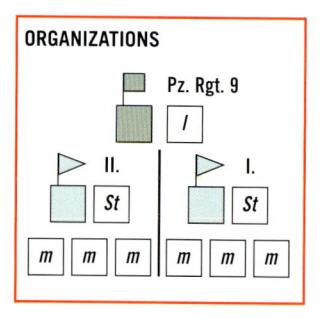

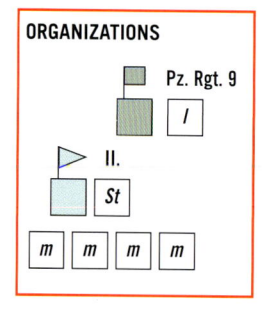

Soviet inactivity on the other side of the Vistula allowed the Germans to deal with Warsaw without any distractions. But once the Soviet Armies resumed their advance, 25th Panzer was forced to retreat through Poland, eventually fighting on the Oder River in February 1945. Heavy losses meant that the Division had to be reorganized as a *kampfgruppe*, featuring a mixed battalion equipped with two Pz.Kpfw IV companies that had 21 tanks and a company of Pz.Kpfw IV/70(V) with 10 powerfully armed tank destroyers.

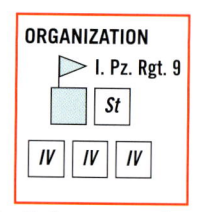

Through February and into March 1945, the division continued to fight on the Oder Front, before being transferred south to Austria to fight with the 8th Army on the Lower Danube. The 25th Panzer Division had fewer than 30 armoured vehicles left when it was overrun by the Soviets in May 1945.

26th Panzer Division

The 26th Panzer Division was formed in September 1942 in France and Belgium from elements of the 23rd Infantry Division, with Panzers provided by the 202nd Panzer Regiment.

IN OCTOBER 1942, THE DIVISION was moved to Amiens. There it remained, continuing to train and to act as a coastal defence force, until July 1943. The Allied invasion of Sicily and the Italian Armistice forced Germany to take control of Italy. 26th Panzer was one of a number of units sent south to reinforce Army Group South (later Army Group C).

Commanders

General der Panzertruppen S. Frh von Lüttwitz
(Sep 1942 – Jan 1944/ Feb 1944 – July 1944)

Generalmajor H. Hecker
(22 Jan 1944 – 20 Feb 1944)

Generalleutnant E. Crasemann
(6 July 1944 – 29 Jan 1945)

Generalmajor A. Kuhnert
(29 Jan 1945 – 19 Apr 1945)

Generalleutnant V. Linnarz
(19 Apr 1945 – 8 May 1945)

INSIGNIA

The tactical symbol of the 26th Panzer Division was a representation of a Grenadier from the time of Frederick the Great.

Defence of Italy and the Eastern Front
1944

While the Division was fighting in Italy, the 1st Battalion had been detached and sent to the Eastern Front. It was equipped with 76 Panthers.

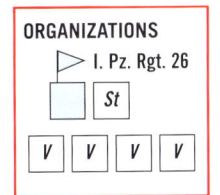

SENT TO CALABRIA in Southern Italy, 26th Panzer saw action against the Allied landings at Salerno and on the Volturno. At the beginning of 1944, the Division was thrown into the fight against the Allied landings at Anzio and Nettuno. It remained at Anzio until the Germans were forced to retreat by the Allied success in outflanking Monte Cassino. Retreating through Tuscany and Rimini, it surrendered in Northern Italy in 1945.

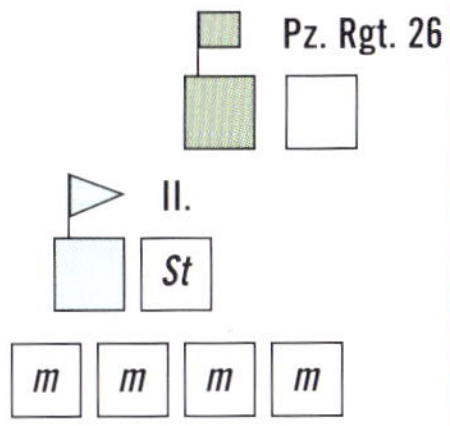

Panzer Unit	Pz. III(75)	Pz. IV(kz)	Pz. IV(lg)	Pz. Bef	Flammpz
26th Pz. Rgt.	16	17	36	9	14

▶ **Panzerkampfwagen V Ausf G (Sd Kfz 171)**
Pz. Rgt 26 / I Battalion / 2nd Company / 1st Zug / tank number 1
Some 3126 Ausf G were produced between March 1944 and April 1945.

Specifications

Crew: 5
Weight: 50.2 tonnes (45.5 tons)
Length: 8.86m (29ft)
Width: 3.4m (11.2ft)
Height: 2.98m (9.8ft)
Engine: Maybach HL230P30
Speed: 46km/hr (28.6mph)
Range: 200km (124.3 miles)
Radio: FuG5

116th Panzer Division

The 116th Panzer Division was formed at the end of March 1944 from the remnants of the 16th *Panzergrenadier* Division, absorbing the 179th Reserve Panzer Division in the process.

APART FROM THE SHORT-LIVED 27th Panzer Division (which had been formed in October 1942 in southern Russia from *Kampfgruppe* Michalik and had been disbanded on 15 February 1943), the 26th Panzer Division was the last of the sequentially numbered Panzer formations to be formed. The next division to be created was the 116th, which began assembling in the Rhineland and Westphalia in February 1944. It included troops from the 16th *Panzergrenadier* Division, which had been badly mauled in Southern Russia, and from the second-line 179th Reserve Panzer Division, which had been on occupation duty in France since 1943.

INSIGNIA

The 116th Panzer Division was known as 'The Greyhound Division', and the formation's tactical symbol was chosen accordingly.

Commanders

Generalmajor G. Müller
(28 Mar 1944 – 1 May 1944)

General der Panzertruppen G. Graf von Schwerin
(1 May 1944 – 1 Sep 1944)

Generalmajor H. Voigtsberger
(1 Sep 1944 – 14 Sep 1944)

Generalmajor S. von Waldenburg
(14 Sep 1944 – ? Apr 1945)

▲ **Through the Ardennes**
The 116th Panzer Division penetrated deep into Allied lines during the Battle of the Bulge, but Germany's last panzer offensive was ultimately a failure.

The Western Front

JUNE 1944

The 116th Panzer Division was sent to the Pas-de-Calais in France immediately after its formation. Calais was where the German High Command expected the imminent Allied landings.

STILL NORTH OF THE SEINE when the Allies landed in Normandy, the Division was not sent to the front until July. It was thrown into action during Operation *Luttich*, the German offensive at Mortain, which resulted in the largest tank battle of the Normandy campaign.

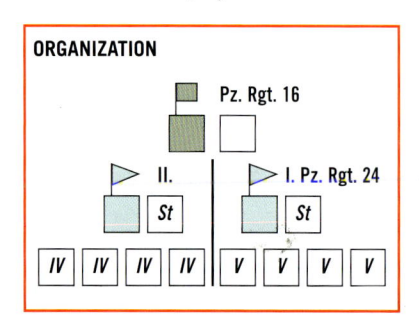

Unable to block the US 3rd Army from breaking out of the beachhead, the Division was caught in the Falaise Pocket. It broke out with tremendous losses when Hitler finally allowed a general withdrawal on 16 August 1944. By 21 August 1944, the division numbered just 600 men, 12 tanks and no artillery.

Retreating to Aachen, it was the only German unit defending the city when the US 1st Army began its assault on the *Westwall* in September 1944.

ORGANIZATION

Pz. Rgt. 16
II.
I. Pz. Rgt. 24
St St
IV IV IV V V V

Panzer Unit	Pz. III	Pz. IV	Pz. V	FlkPz(37)
116th Pz. Div.	6	73	79	8

182

116TH PANZER DIVISION

▶ **Sturmgeschütz neuer Art mit 7.5cm PaK I/48 auf Fahrgestell Panzerkampfwagen IV (Sd Kfz 162)**

228th Panzerjäger Battalion

An early Jagdpanzer IV. The gun on later production vehicles had a muzzle brake.

Specifications
Crew: 4
Weight: 26.5 tonnes (24 tons)
Length: 6.85m (22.5ft)
Width: 3.17m (10.4ft)
Height: 1.85m (6ft)
Engine: Maybach HL120TRM
Speed: 40km/hr (24.9mph)
Range: 210km (130.5 miles)
Radio: FuG Spr 'f'

▶ **3.7cm FlaK auf Fahrgestell Panzerkampfwagen IV (Sf) (Sd Kfz 161/3)**

Pz. Rgt 16

Known as the *Möbelwagen,* or 'moving van', the four-sided superstructure folded down to provide a firing platform.

Specifications
Crew: 6
Weight: 26.5 tonnes (24 tons)
Length: 5.92m (19.4ft)
Width: 2.95m (9.7ft)
Height: 2.73m (9ft)
Engine: Maybach HL120TRM
Speed: 38km/hr (23.6mph)
Range: 200km (124.3 miles)
Radio: FuG5 + FuG2

The Battle of the Bulge
14 December 1944

After refitting at Düsseldorf, the division returned to defend Aachen, and was then involved in the bloody battle of the Hürtgen Forest early in November.

ASSIGNED TO THE 5TH *PANZERARMEE* in December 1944, 116th Panzer was one of the spearhead formations that ripped through the Allied lines in the Ardennes during the Battle of the Bulge. 5th Panzerarmee almost reached the Meuse at Dinant, where Rommel's 7th Panzer had crossed only four years previously. However, lack of fuel, Allied air power along with the arrival of American reinforcements brought the offensive to an end. After again suffering heavy casualties, 116th Panzer was withdrawn to Cleves, on the Dutch-German border.

Defending the Roer River dams against an Anglo-Canadian Offensive, 116th Panzer was trapped in the Wesel Pocket in February 1945. In March 1945, the division withdrew across the Rhine. Fighting in the Ruhr Pocket, it surrendered to the US 9th Army on 18 April 1945.

Panzer Unit	Pz. IV	Pz. V	StuG	FlkPz(37)
116th Pz. Div.	21	41	14	3

ORGANIZATION

116TH PANZER DIVISION

▲ **Panzerkampfwagen V Ausf G (Sd Kfz 171)**
Pz. Rgt 16 / I Battalion / 3rd Company / 2nd Zug / tank number 1

The Pz.Kpfw V Panther equipped the four medium companies of the 1st Battalion, 16th Panzer Regiment, which had been formed around the remnants of the 16th *Panzergrenadier* Divisions 116th Panzer Regiment.

Weapons Specifications

Main: 7.5cm (3in) KwK42 L/70	Turret MG: 7.92mm (0.3in) MG 34
Ammunition: 81 rounds	Hull MG: 7.92mm (0.3in) MG 34
Traverse: 360° (hydraulic)	Ammunition: 4800 rounds
Elevation: -8° to +18°	MG Sight: KgZF2
Sight: TZF12a	

▲ **38cm RW61 auf Sturmmörser Tiger**
Kampfgruppe / Pz. Rgt 16

Assault mortar-firing rocket-assisted projectiles mounted on a Tiger chassis. It was designed to destroy strongpoints and fortifications at close quarters. In April 1945, the remnants of 116th Panzer were formed into a *Kampfgruppe*. It had a single Panzer company with 14 PzKpfw V Panthers and a platoon of 4 Sturmtigers.

Specifications

Crew: 5	Engine: Maybach HL230P45
Weight: 71.7 tonnes (65 tons)	Speed: 40km/hr (24.9mph)
Length: 6.28m (20.6ft)	Range: 120km (74.6 miles)
Width: 3.57m (11.7ft)	Radio: FuG5
Height: 2.85m (9.4ft)	

(130th) Panzer *Lehr* Division

Although it existed for only a year from its formation early in 1944, the Panzer *Lehr* Division proved itself to be one of the crack armoured units in the German Army.

Commanders
Generalleutnant F. Bayerlein
(10 Jan 1944 – 20 Jan 1944)
Generalmajor H. Niemack
(20 Jan 1944 – Apr 1945)

The Panzer Lehr Division was formed in the area around Nancy and Verdun in January 1941. The word *Lehr* means 'teaching' or 'demonstration', and the Division's cadre was provided by German Army training and demonstration units. Led by instructors and combat veterans, the Division was considered an elite unit from its foundation. In March 1944, the Division was sent to Hungary, but returned to the West in May. It was part of the High Command's reserve Panzer force, which they intended using to throw the expected Allied invasion back into the sea.

▲ **Destroyed in Normandy**
Panzer Lehr Division fought hard against Allied armies in Normandy, but in the process it lost most of its vehicles in bloody battles of attrition.

INSIGNIA

The tactical symbol used by the 130th Panzer Division included the letter 'L' for *Lehr*, or demonstration, carried within the rhomboidal military map symbol for armour.

Variants of the insignia usually did away with the rhomboid.

The Western Front
JUNE 1944

The *Lehr*, or demonstration, units were led by the most expert troops in the German Army, and the Panzer-Lehr Division was one of the largest and best equipped Panzer formations.

When the full fury of the Allied landings in Normandy finally hit in June 1944, Panzer Lehr, officially known as the 130th Panzer Division, was one of the strongest units in the West. Ordered north on 6 June, it suffered heavily from Allied air attacks. After entering the battle at Bayeux on 9 June, Panzer-Lehr continued to fight the British in bloody battles of attrition around Caen before being switched to fight the Americans at St Lo. Weeks of fighting against the odds left Panzer-Lehr so depleted that it had only a fraction of the armour it had started with. The shattered division withdrew across France, reaching Luxembourg as an understrength *kampfgruppe*. It was pulled out of the lines and reformed and re-equipped at Sennelager.

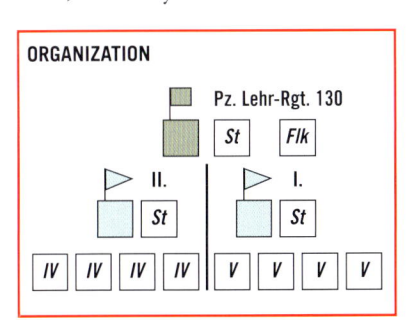

ORGANIZATION

Pz. Lehr-Rgt. 130
St Flk
II. I.
St St
IV IV IV IV V V V V

Panzer Unit	StuG	Pz. IV	Pz. V	Pz. VI	FlkPz38
130th Pz. Rgt.	9	101	89	8	12

185

130TH PANZER DIVISION

▶ **Panzerkampfwagen IV Ausf H (Sd Kfz 161/2)**

Pz.Lehr Rgt 130 / II Battalion / 6th Company / 3rd Zug / tank number 4

The original Panzer-Lehr Battalion was renamed the 2nd Battalion, Panzer-Lehr Regiment early in 1944. It was composed of four companies, each with 22 Pz.Kpfw IV.

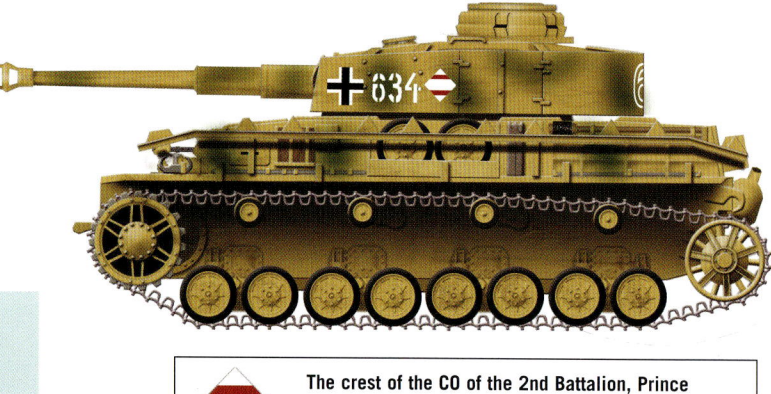

Specifications
Crew: 5
Weight: 27.6 tonnes (25 tons)
Length: 7.02m (23ft)
Width: 2.88m (9.4ft)
Height: 2.68m (8.8ft)
Engine: Maybach HL120TRM
Speed: 38km/hr (23.6mph)
Range: 210km (130.5 miles)
Radio: FuG5

The crest of the CO of the 2nd Battalion, Prince Schoenburg-Waldenburg (KIA June 1944) was used as a memorial by tanks of his unit.

The Gothic letter 'L' carried as an identification sign by the vehicles of the Panzer-Lehr Division.

Specifications
Crew: 5
Weight: 49.4 tonnes (44.8 tons)
Length: 8.86m (29ft)
Width: 3.42m (11.2ft)
Height: 2.98m (9.8ft)
Engine: Maybach HL230P30
Speed: 46km/hr (28.6mph)
Range: 200km (124.3 miles)
Radio: FuG5

▲ **Panzerkampfwagen V Ausf A (Sd Kfz 171)**

1st Battalion 6th Pz. Rgt

As with most frontline Panzer formations in 1944, the Panzer-Lehr Division operated a mixed tank force with one battalion of Panzer IVs and one of Panzer V Panthers.

▶ **Flakpanzer 38(t) auf Selbstfahrlafette 38(t) Ausf M (Sd Kfz 140)**

Pz.Lehr Rgt 130

The Flakpanzer 38(t) was armed with one 2cm (0.8in) FlakK38 L/112.5 AA gun.

Specifications
Crew: 4
Weight: 10 tonnes (9.8 tons)
Length: 4.61m (15.1ft)
Width: 2.15m (7ft)
Height: 2.25m (7.4ft)
Engine: Name
Speed: 42km/hr (26mph)
Range: 210km (130.5 miles)
Radio: FuG5 or FuG2

130TH PANZER DIVISION

The Battle of the Bulge
14 December 1944

Destroyed in Normandy, Panzer *Lehr* was reorganized in October 1944. Even after rebuilding, the once elite unit was not as powerful as it had been before the Allied invasion.

In November 1944, Panzer *Lehr* returned to defend the Saar, which was threatened by the advancing Americans. However, in December the division became part of LXVII *Panzerkorps* in Hasso von Manteuffel's 5th *Panzerarmee*. This was the southern prong of *Wacht am Rhein*, Hitler's last throw of the dice in the west. Along with Sepp Dietrich's 6th *Panzerarmee*, 5th Panzer was to smash through the Ardennes, aiming for Antwerp.

Battle of the Bulge

The German attack came as a complete surprise to the Allies, and Manteuffel's Panzers penetrated deep into the Allied rear. However, Panzer-Lehr was held up by the stubborn resistance of the American defenders of Bastogne. As fuel supplies became critically low, the weather cleared, allowing Allied fighter bombers to wreak havoc on the advancing panzers. Once the Allies regrouped and started bringing numbers to bear on the battle, there was nowhere for the Germans to go but backwards.

When the Ardennes offensive failed, Panzer-Lehr saw further defensive action in the battles for the Maas Line in the Netherlands. Early in March, it was used in an attempt to smash the American Rhine bridgehead at Remagen, which also failed.

Short of men and ammunition and with few tanks left, Panzer-Lehr was trapped in the Ruhr Pocket at the end of March. Unable to put up more than a token resistance, the division surrendered to the US Army when the Ruhr Pocket finally fell at the end of April 1945.

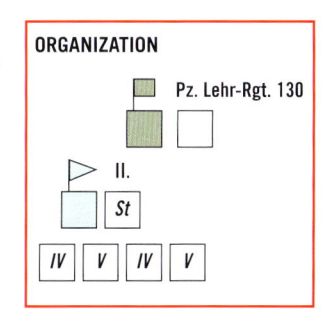

ORGANIZATION

Pz. Lehr-Rgt. 130

II.
St

IV V IV V

Panzer Unit	Pz. IV	Pz. V	FlkPz(20)	FlkPz(37)
130th Pz. Rgt.	27	30	3	4

▲ **Jagdpanther (Sd Kfz 173)**
559th Schwere Panzerjäger Abteilung (Attached from Army Reserve)
This was one of the most powerful and effective tank destroyers of the war, and 392 SdKfz 173 Jagdpanthers were produced between January 1944 and March 1945. This is a late production model, with a two-piece barrel.

Specifications
Crew: 5
Weight: 50.7 tonnes (46 tons)
Length: 9.9m (32.5ft)
Width: 3.42m (11.2ft)
Height: 2.72m (8.9ft)
Engine: Maybach HL230P30
Speed: 46km/hr (28.6mph)
Range: 160km (99.4 miles)
Radio: FuG5 plus FuG2

Index

Page numbers in *italics* refer to illustrations.

1st Panzer Division 23, 137
  formed 12, 36
  France 14–15, 19, 21, 25, 98
  insignia *12, 14*
  organization 12–13, *14, 16,* 19, *21*
  Poland 13–14, 43, 63
  Russia 16–18, 16–21
  surrender 21, 22
2nd Panzer Division 118
  Austria 13, 23, 25, 30
  formed 23, 36
  France 25, 27, 31, 34, 35, 98
  Greece 26, 27
  insignia 23, 24, *27*
  organization 23, *24, 25, 27,* 29, *31, 35*
  Poland 24, 26, 27
  Russia 27, 29–30
3rd *Kavallerie-Division* 12
3rd Panzer Division 23, 36, 128, 146, 157
  Czechoslovakia *10,* 13, 36
  France 37, 38, 44
  insignia 36, 39, *39,* 41, 158
  organization *37, 39*
  Poland 36–7, 41
  Russia 39–41, 172
  surrendered 41
4th Panzer Division 54, 123
  formed 43, 52
  France 44–5, 46
  insignia 43, *44,* 51
  organization 43, *45, 46, 47, 48*
  Poland 43–4, 51
  Russia 46–9, 50–1
  surrendered 48, 51
5th Panzer Division 108
  Balkans 54–5, 108
  insignia 52, 53, 59
  organization 52, *53,* 54, *57*
  Poland 52–3, 58
  Russia 56, 57–8
  surrendered 58, 59
6th Panzer Division
  formed 62–3
  France 64–5, 66, 68, 69
  insignia 64, *68*
  organization 64, *66, 72*
  Russia 66–9
  Schwere Panzergruppe Bake 72
  surrendered 69
7th Panzer Division 53
  formed 73, 74
  France 74–5, 77, 79, 183
  insignia 73, 75, 78
  organization *74, 77, 79, 80*
  Russia 77–80, 154
  surrendered 80
8th Panzer Division
  formed 81, 82
  organization *82, 83, 84, 86,* 87
  Poland 82, 87
  Russia 84–7, 154
  surrendered 87

Yugoslavia 84, 123
9th Panzer Division 27
  Balkans *88,* 90
  formed 88–9
  France 89, 94, 95
  insignia 88, 91
  organization *89, 90, 91, 94, 95*
  Poland 88, 89
  Russia 90–2
  surrendered 96
10th Panzer Division 25
  Czechoslovakia 97
  insignia 97, 100, 104
  North Africa *97,* 102, 104, 105
  organization *98, 102*
  Russia 100–1
  surrendered 102, 105
11th Panzer Division 47
  France 113, 114
  insignia 108, 109, *110, 111*
  organization 108, *110, 112, 113*
  Russia 110–13
  surrendered 114
12th Panzer Division 123
  insignia 115, *118*
  organization 115, *115, 117*
  Russia 115–17, 154
  surrendered 117
13th Panzer Division 72, 117, 123
  formed 26, 118
  Hungary 121, 122
  organization *118, 119, 120, 121*
  Russia 118–21
14th Panzer Division
  Balkans 123, 124
  destroyed 125, 126
  formed 46, 123
  insignia 123, 124, *125*
  organization *123, 125, 127*
  Russia 124–7
15th Panzer Division
  insignia 128, 130, 133, *134*
  North Africa 100, 102, 128–9, 130–6
  organization 128, *131, 134*
  surrendered 102, 134, 136
16th Panzer Division 148
  formed 86, 137
  insignia 137, 146
  Italy 139, 141
  organization *137,* 138, 139, *141*
  Russia 137–9, 140, 141, 176
  surrendered 139, 141
17th Panzer Division
  insignia 142, 146
  organization *142, 143, 144,* 145
  Russia 142–4, 146, 172
18th Panzer Division 146–8
19th Panzer Division
  formed 149, 153
  insignia 149, 150
  organization 148, *149, 150, 151,* 152
  Poland 152, 180

Russia 149–52, 153, 154
  surrendered 152
20th Panzer Division 153–6
21st Panzer Division
  formed 157, 160
  France 166–8
  Germany 168
  insignia 157, 161, 162
  North Africa 102, 157–65
  organization 157, *162, 163, 166, 168*
  surrendered 102, 163, 165, 168
22nd Panzer Division 169, 171
23rd Panzer Division
  destroyed 172, 173
  formed 169, 171
  organization 171, *172*
24th Panzer Division 29, 176–9
25th Panzer Division 180
26th Panzer Division 139, 181, 182
27th Panzer Division 175, 182
37th Communications Company 12
77th Panzer Signal Battalion 58
116th Panzer Division 182–3
130th Panzer Division 185–7
273rd Army Flak Battalion 29
700th *Panzer Verband* 48

Afrika Korps
  39, 56, 104, 105, 128, 160, 162, 163
  see also North Africa
Algeria 102, 134
Alsace 113, 114, 168
antitank guns 18
  Czech 4.7cm 67, 159
  FK296 76.2mm 19
  PaK 36 81
  PaK 40 22, 80, 92, 145, 173
  Panzerbuchse 41 2.8cm 40, 155
  PTRD-41 40
Anzio 121, 181
Ardennes 1944
  1940 14, 25, 45, 53, 64, 65, 74, 83, 98
  1944 35, 95, 114, 168, *182*
armies
  2nd 84, 123, 142
  6th 40, 44, 69, 92, 112, 125, 138, 139, 144, 169, 172, 176
  7th 114, 176
  8th 127, 179, 180
  9th 29, 48, 57, 58, 66, 87, 92, 148, 149, 155, 156
  10th 13, 43, 63, 74, 82
  11th 169
  12th 26, 90, 108
  14th 24, 52, 88
  15th 86, 114
  17th 87, 145
  18th 16
  19th 168
army corps
  XXXIX 86, 115
  XXXX 27, 90

188

INDEX

XLVI 115, 123
LXVII 149
Burdach 92
Scheele 92
Army Detachments
  Hollidt 169, 172
  Kempf 69, 79, 151
Army Group A 25, 40, 74, 83, 98, 171
Army Group B 37, 44, 46, 82, 89, 138, 178
Army Group C 115, 181
Army Group Centre 27, 66, 100, 141, 150
  1st Panzer Division 16, 21
  3rd Panzer Division 40, 41
  4th Panzer Division 46, 48, 49
  5th Panzer Division 57, 58
  7th Panzer Division 77, 80
  8th Panzer Division 84, 86, 87
  9th Panzer Division 91, 92
  11th Panzer Division 110, 112
  12th Panzer Division 115, 116
  17th Panzer Division 142, 143, 145
  18th Panzer Division 146, 148
  20th Panzer Division 152, 154, 155, 156
Army Group Courland 127
Army Group D 100, 176
Army Group Don 40, 79, 112, 144
Army Group G 114
Army Group North 16, 48, 66, 84, 86, 87, 91, 97, 115, 117, 127, 149, 152
Army Group South 24, 41, 46, 52, 144, 169, 171, 179
  6th Panzer Division 63, 69
  7th Panzer Division 74, 79
  8th Panzer Division 82, 86, 87
  9th Panzer Division 88, 90, 91, 92
  11th Panzer Division 110, 112
  13th Panzer Division 118, 119
  14th Panzer Division 124, 127
  16th Panzer Division 137, 138
Arnim, General Hans-Jürgen von 102, 142
artillery divisions 72, 148
artillery regiments 12, 18, 81, 134
  see also panzer artillery regiments
Aufklärungs-Abteilung 5 29
Aufklärungspanzerwagen 38 (2cm) (Sd Kfz 140/1) 42, 186
Austria 13, *21*, *23*, *25*, 30, 41, 68, 69, 88, 110, 172, 173, 180

Balck, General der Panzertruppen Hermann 79, 80, 108, 112, 152
Baranov 141, 144
Barbarossa 16–18, 27, 39, 46–7, 66–8, 77–8, 84, 90, 100–1, *106*, 110–11, 115, 124, 137, 142–3, 146–7, 149, 153–5
Bardia 132, 157
Bayerlein, Generalleutnant Fritz 36, 41, 185
Belfort Gap 113, 114
Belgium 14, 37, 44–5, 65, 89, 99, 181, 187
Belgrade 54, 84, 108
Benghazi 128, 131, 162
Blitzkrieg 23, 107
Bobruisk 141, 156
Brest-Litovsk 37, 52, 97
Brno 87, 141
Bryansk 58, 87, 90, 117, 146
Budapest 22, 69, 87, 121, 122
Bug, River 41, 118, 142, 146

Bulgaria 54, 108
Bulge, Battle of the 35, 95, 114, 168, *182*, 183, 187
Bzura, Battle of 13, 14, 44, 63, 74, 82

Caen 94, 167, 185
Caucasus 40, 47, 86, *118*, 119, 120, 138, 143, 171
Cherkassy Pocket 121, 127, 141, 144, 179
Cherson, Russia 120, 169
Chir River 112, 144, 169, 171
Cholm, Russia 86, 141, 156
Courland pocket 48, 50, 58, 117
Croatia 26, 123
Czechoslovakia *10,* 13, 36, 88, 97, 152

Danzig 58, 59, 80, 127
Demjansk 58, 86
Dinant 53, 74, 183
divisions
  2nd (mot) 115
  4th 108, 123, 146
  7th 14
  10th 14
  13th (mot) 118
  14th 146
  16th 137
  19th 149, 153
  23rd 181
  27th 142
  33rd 128
  44th 118
  94th 176
  209th 108
  311th 108
  352nd 35
Dnieper, River 69, 90, 92, 115, 117, 118, 120, 144, 151, 172, 179
Don River *118*, 125, 138, 171
Donetz, River 144, 151
Dunkirk 14, 25, 45, 53, 89

East Prussia 16, 24, 46, 58, 127, 156, 176, 179
Egypt 131, 160, 162
El Agheila 130, 157
El Alamein 102, 131, 134, 135, 136, 162, 163, 164
Enigma cryptographic machine 50, 163

Falaise Pocket 31, 32, 35, 94, 95, 168, 183
Fall Blau 19–21, 27, 40, 47, 57, 86, 91, 112–13, *118,* 119, 125, 138, 143, 148, 150, 155, 169, 176
Fall Gelb 14–15, 25, 37, 44, 53, 64, 74–5, 83, 89, 98–100
Fall Weiss 13–14, 24, 36–7, 43–4, 52–3, 63, 74, 82, 88, 97
Feldherrnhalle 2 Panzer Dovosion 122
Fiat-Ansaldo Carro Armato comando per semovente 135
  L 6/40 59
  M 14-41 135
Fiat-Ansaldo Semovente da 75/18 (M13-40 Chassis) 136
'Fire Brigade' 72, 120
FlaK 18 (Sf) 8.8cm auf Zugkraftwagen 12t (Sd Kfz 8) 78
Flakpanzer IV

2cm Vierling *Wirbelwind* 35, 113
3.7cm *Möbelwagen* 113, 152, 183
Flammpanzer II (Sd Kfz 122) 85
Flammpanzer III Ausf M (F1) (Sd Kfz 141/3) 70, 71, 141
France 19, 21, 27, 46, 79, 95, 107, 113, 169, 181
  invasion of 14–15, 25, 37, 38, 44, 53, 64–5, 74–5, 83, 89, 98–9
  Normandy landings 31, 32, 34, 94, 166–8, 182, 185

Gazala 131, 132, 157, 162
Gebirgs Divisions 26, 120
Gepanzerter Selbsfahrlafette für Sturmgeschütz 7.5cm Kanone Ausf B (Sd Kfz 142) 68
Gomel 29, 46, 48, 58, 117
Greece 21, 26, 27, 54–5, 124
Grossdeutschland Division 41, 98, 112
Gshatsk, Russia 57, 155
Guderian, General Heinz 23
  2nd *Panzergruppe* 149
  France 14, 25, 64, 83, 98
  Poland 24, 36, 97
  Russia 46, 90, 142, 146
  T-34 tank 101

Halfaya Pass 128, 157
Hitler, Adolf 62, 87, 129, 146
  accession to power 11, 12
  Ardennes Offensive 95, 168, 182, 187
  Balkans 26, 84
  Russia 58, 86, 91, 112, 138, 143, 144, 151, 172
Hoeppner, General Erich 13, 16, 43, 44, 84
Holland 37, 44–5, 89, 152, 187
Horneck, Silesia 74, 82
Hoth, General Hermann 16, 53, 64, 69, 74, 77, 83, 100, 139, 144, 149, 151, 171
Hubicki, General der Panzertruppen Dr. Alfred Ritter von 88
Hummel 15cm self-propelled guns 29, 50, 58, 72, 144, 152
Hungary 21, 22, 41, 84, 87, 121, 172, 179, 185

Infanterie Panzerkampfwagen
  Mk II 748(e) 130
  Mk III 749(e) 104
Infanterie Sturmsteg auf Fahrgestell Panzerkampfwagen IV 38
Italy 26, 59, 121, *137*, 139, 141, 178, 181
  3rd Armoured Battalion 59
  8th Italian Army 151
  North Africa 129, 135, 136, 157, 163

Jagdpanther (Sd Kfz 173) 187
Jagdpanzer 38(t) Hetzer (Panzerjäger 38(t)) fur 7.5cm PaK39 94
Jagdpanzer IV (Sd Kfz 162) 35, 122, 145, 173, 183
Jägerndorf (Krnov), Czechoslovakia 145
Jassy, Russia 127, 172, 179
JS-122 42

Kamenez-Podolsk, Russia 80, 87, 144, 180
Kasserine Pass 102, 104, 165
Kavallerieschützen 62, 73, 81, 176

189

INDEX

Kharkhov 40, 69, 112, 125, 144, 171
Kielce, Poland 74, 82
Kiev 21, 29, 46, 79, 87, 90, 110, 112, 124, 137, 141, 142, 149, 151
Kirchner, General der Panzertruppen Friedrich 13, 14
Kirovograd 41, 120, 127
Kishinev 121, 127
Kleiner Panzerbefehlswagen (Sd Kfz 265) 26, 28, 46, 109, 158, 160
Kleist, General Ewald von 40, 108, 118, 123, 137, 138, 171
Kradschützen-Abteilung 24 29
Krivoi Rog 92, 112, 120, 127, 179
Kuhn, General der Panzertruppen F. 36, 123, 128
Kurland *see* Courland pocket
Kursk, Battle of 29, 41, 48, 49, 50, 58, 69, 79, 87, 91, 92, 112–13, 117, 120, 144, 148, 151, 153, 155, 156
KV 1a 20, 119

Ladungsleger auf Panzerkampfwagen I Ausf B 18, 76
Latvia 48, 58, 127
leFH18(Sf) 10.5cm auf Geschützwagen 39H (f) 167
Leibstandarte Adolf Hitler Regiment 23
Leichte Divisions 61
  1st 61, 62–3
  2nd 63, 73–4, 82
  3rd 63, 74, 81–2
  4th 88
  5th 128, 157, 158–60
Leichte Feldhaubitze 18/2 auf Fahrgestell Panzerkampfwagen II (Sf) 29, 95, 144
Leichte Panzerkompanie 111
  'Gliederung' 109, 113
  K.St.N.1171 37, 143
Leichter Gepanzerter Beobachtungswagen (Sd Kfz 253) 18, 165
Leichter Panzerspähwagen
  (Sd Kfz 222) (2cm) 51, 131, 156
  (Sd Kfz 223) (Fu) 170
  (Sd Kfz 261) 58
Leichter Schützenpanzerwagen
  (Sd Kfz 250/1) 141, 177
  (Sd Kfz 250/9) 33, 151
  (Sd Kfz 250/10) (3.7cm PaK) 49
Leningrad 16, 57, 66, 68, 84, 86, 115, 117, 153
Libya 102, *128*
List, Field Marshal Sigmund 24, 26, 52, 54, 88
Lithuania 48, 77, 80, 127
Luftwaffe 75, 162
  16th Field Division 168
  Hermann Göring Division 152, 179, 180
Lüttwitz, General der Panzertruppen H. 23, 153, 181

M4 Sherman 59, 161, 165
Macedonia 26, 90
Manstein, Field Marshal Erich von 40, 112, 144, 169
Manteuffel, General der Panzertruppen Hasso von 35, 73, 95, 187
Marcks, Generalleutnant W. 13, 62, 153, 157

Marder III 22, 92, 96, 101, 133, 173
Matilda MkII infantry tank 130
Meuse, River 53, 64, 74, 98, 99, 183
Minsk 77, 100, 115, 149, 153
Mittlerer Flammpanzerwagen Gerat 916 Ausf C (Sd Kfz 251/16) 22
Mittlerer Funkpanzerwagen Ausf D (Sd Kfz 251/3) 41
Mittlerer Gepanzerter Beobachtungskraftwagen (Sd Kfz 254) 68, 110, 125, 134
Mittlerer Kommandopanzerwagen (Sd Kfz 251/6) 40, 50, 91
Mittlerer Panzerkompanie K.St.N.1175 47
Mittlerer Pionierpanzerwagen Ausf D (Sd Kfz 251/7) 34
Mittlerer Schützenpanzerwagen (Sd Kfz 251/1)
  Ausf A 16
  Ausf B 55, 110, 161
  Ausf C 40, 50, 126, 138
  Ausf D 51
  Ausf D (Sd Kfz 251/9) 33, 151, 156
  Ausf D (Sd Kfz 251/22) 80, 145
  M3(a) 104
Mius River 92, 118, 120, 124, 125, 137, 138, 172
Model, Field Marshal Walther 29, 36, 48, 87, 92, 148, 156
Montgomery, General Bernard Law 134, 163
Moravia 69, 87, 145, 146
Mortain offensive 31, 32, 182
Moscow 19, 27, 46, 47, 57, 66, 68, 77, 90, 91, 100, 101, 110, 146, 149, 153, 155
Motorcycle Battalions 23, 103
Munitionsschlepper auf Panzerkampfwagen I (Sd Kfz 111) 38, 90
Mussolini, Benito 26, 84, 178

Nachtrichten Abteilungen 15, 48, 69, 98
Naples *137*, 139
Nashorn 93
Nikolaev, Russia 137, 172, 179
Nis, Yugoslavia 54, 108
Normandy 31, 32, 34, 94, 166–8, 185
North Africa 97, 100, 102, 104, 128–9, 130, 131–6, 157–65

Oder, River 145, 168, 180
Ohrdruf 23, 176
operations
  Bagration 87, 156
  Battleaxe 129, 130, 157, 159
  Cobra 94
  Crusader 130, 157
  Goodwood 166
  Lichtschlag 86
  Luttich 182
  Nordwind 168
  Seelöwe 146
  Sommernachtstraum 157
  Torch 102
  Typhoon 90
  Uranus 169
  Wacht am Reich 114, 187
  Zitadelle 69, 79, 92, 148
  see also Barbarossa; Fall Blau; Fall Gelb; Fall Weiss
Orel 46, 47, 58, 87, 91, 92, 117, 142, 143, 144, 146, 148, 150, 155

PaK40 7.5cm (Sf) auf Geschützwagen 39H (f) 166
PaK43/1 (L/71) 8.8cm auf Fahrgestell Panzerkampfwagen III/IV (Sf) 'Nashorn' 93
Panther *see* Panzerkampfwagen V
Panzer-Abteilung (Fkl) 301 34, 95, 96
Panzer artillery regiments
  27th 144
  74th 23, 29
  76th 68
  78th 80
  89th 176
  92nd 155
  102nd 95
  103rd 50
  115th 165
  116th 58
  119th 110
  see also artillery regiments
Panzer battalions
  2nd 86
  7th *Ersatz* 153
  10th 149
  11th 149
  18th 148
  21st 156
  25th *Ersatz* 149
  33rd 73, 88
  35th *Ersatz* 153
  51st 92, 94
  65th 65, 69
  67th 81
  504th 148
  508th 117
Panzer brigades
  1st 12, 36
  3rd 157
  4th 97
  7th 43
  8th 52
  101st 171
Panzer divisions
  first 11, 12, 61
  organization 17, 28, 37, 47, 71, 83, 93, 105, 109, 140, 143, 173
  see also individual divisions
Panzer-Jäger-Kompanie 'Nashorn' (8.8cm PaK43) K.St.N 1148b 93
Panzer-Kompanie (Fkl) 315 167
Panzer Lehr Division 185–7
Panzer Lehr Regiment 130 185, 186
panzer pioneer battalions 34, 38
panzer regiments 90
  1st 12, *13*, 14, 15, 17, 18, 19, 20–1
  2nd 12, *13*, *14*, 15, 16, 137, 140
  3rd 23, 25, 26, 27–8, 29, 31, 35
  4th 23, 24, 26, 118, 119, 120, 121, 142
  5th *37*, 39, 157, 158–63, 164, 165
  6th *37*, *39*, 41, 42, 146
  7th 98, 99, 100, 101, 102, 103, 104, 105
  8th 98, 100, 128, 129, 130, 132–3, 134, 136
  10th 84, 85–6, 86, 87
  11th 64, 66, 67, 69, 70–1, 72
  15th 47, 52, 108, 109, 111, *112*, 114
  16th 183, 184
  18th 146, 147, 148
  21st 153, 154–5
  24th 176, 177, 178, 179

INDEX

25th 75–6, 77–8
26th 181
27th 149, 150
28th 146
29th 115, 116, 117
31st 52, 54–5, 56–7, 59
33rd 27, 29, 89, 90, 91, 96, 142
35th 43, 44, 46–7, 48–9, 51
36th 43, 44, 45, 46, 123, 124, 125, 126
39th 142, 143, 144, 145
201st 171, 172
202nd 181
204th 169, 170
Panzerarmees
  1st 40, 79, 92, 127, 138, 144, 151, 169, 171, 172, 179
  2nd 29, 47, 48, 58, 87, 92, 117, 148, 150, 155
  3rd 29, 57, 155
  4th 21, 29, 57, 69, 79, 112, 144, 151, 155, 171, 176
  5th 35, 95, 102, 183, 187
  6th 187
  Afrika 128, 134, 136
Panzerbefehlswagen III
  (Sd Kfz 266-267-268) 17
  Ausf D1 44
  Ausf E 15, 45, 57, 66, 100
  Ausf H 68, 132
  Ausf K mit 5cm KwK39 L/60 79, 150
  Tauchpanzer 147
Panzerbefehlswagen V (Sd Kfz 267) 173
Panzerbefehlswagen 35(t) 65
Panzerbefehlswagen 38(t) Ausf B 75, 85
Panzerfunkwagen (Sd Kfz 263) 8-Rad 15, 48, 75, 98, 163
Panzergrenadier battalions 122
Panzergrenadier divisions 19, 112, 114, 134, 136, 182, 184
Panzergrenadier Regiments 89
  2nd 29
  12th 50
  33rd 51
  112th 168
  115th 133
  304th 29
  891st 178
  insignia 51
Panzergruppen
  1st 90, 108, 111, 118, 124, 137
  2nd 39, 46, 90, 142, 146, 147, 149
  3rd 16, 66, 68, 77, 115, 116, 149, 153, 154
  4th 16, 27, 66, 84, 110, 153
  Guderian 101
  Kleist 54, 89, 99, *100*
  West 31
Panzerjäger 38(t)
  fur 7.62cm PaK36(r) (Sd Kfz 139) 19, 101, 133
  mit 7.5cm PaK40/3 (Sd Kfz 138) Marder III 22, 92, 96, 101, 173
Panzerjäger battalions 93, 120
  18th 29
  33rd 133
  37th 19, 22
  38th 19
  41st 67
  49th 50

50th 92, 93, 94, 96
90th 101
128th 173
228th 183
Panzerkampfwagen I (Sd Kfz 101) 13, 28, 109
  4.7cm PaK(t) (Sf) Ausf B 67, 159
  Ausf A 38, 76, 99, 158, 159, 160, 162
  Ausf B 14, 24, 39, 44, 45, 53, 76, 124, 160
  Ausf B 15cm sIG33 (Sf) 18, 26, 55, 76, 89, 100
  Ausf B Ladungsleger 18, 76
  Ausf F Vk 1801 21, 117
  Kleiner Panzerbefehlswagen (Sd Kfz 256) 26, 28, 46, 109, 158
  Kleiner Panzerbefehlswagen (Sd Kfz 265) 160
  Munitionsschlepper (Sd Kfz 111) 38, 90
Panzerkampfwagen II (Sd Kfz 121) *10*, 19, 28, 29, 39, *73*, 109
  7.5cm PaK40/2 auf Fahrgestell (Sf) (Sd Kfz 131) Marder II 50
  15cm sIG33 (Sf) Fahrgestell 133
  Ausf B 44, 47, 98, 99, 116
  Ausf C 15, 25, 38, 53, 63, 67, 77, 78, 85, 91, 130, 147, 158, 162
  Ausf D 82, 85
  Ausf F 67, 102, 111, 119, 129, 164
  Ausf L (Sd Kfz 123) 48, 49, 94
  Flammpanzer II (Sd Kfz 122) 85, 150
Panzerkampfwagen III (Sd Kfz 141) *12*, 19, 28, 29, 37, 79, 105, 109
  Ausf A 24
  Ausf E 27, 54, 99
  Ausf F 17, 27, 45, 57, 119
  Ausf G 27, 101, 129, 159, 160
  Ausf H 18, 27, 39, 90, 101, 111, 124, 147
  Ausf J 27, 28, 39, 56, 125, 129, 132, 133, 164, 177
  Ausf L (Sd Kfz 141/1) 102, 104, 132
  Ausf M (Fl) (Sd Kfz 141/3) 70, 71, 141, 177
  Ausf M (Sd Kfz 141/1) 30, 69, 70, 126, 148
  Ausf N (Sd Kfz 141/2) 30, 70, 104, 126
  Tauchpanzer 46, 142
Panzerkampfwagen IV (Sd Kfz 161) 28, 29, *47*, *60*, 94, *115*, 152
  Ausf B 14, 53, 99
  Ausf D 17, 19, 38, 54, 64, 111, 158, 161, 164
  Ausf E 19, 65, 77, 89, 109, 116, 130, 147, 155
  Ausf F 55, 130
  Ausf F2 (Sd Kfz 161/1) 21, 126, 134, 163, 164, 165
  Ausf G (Sd Kfz 161/1 und 161/2) 49, 103, 136, 140, 165
  Ausf H (Sd Kfz 161/2) 30, 32, 41, 42, 51, 59, 96, 117, 166, 178, 186
  Flakpanzer IV 2cm Vierling *Wirbelwind* 35, 113
  Flakpanzer IV 3.7cm *Möbelwagen* 113, 152, 183
  Infanterie Sturmsteg auf Fahrgestell 38
  Jagdpanzer IV (Sd Kfz 162) 35, 122, 145, 173, 183

PaK43/1 (L/71) 8.8cm auf Fahrgestell (Sf) 'Nashorn' 93
Panzerkampfwagen V (Sd Kfz 171) 71, 72, 87, 101, 127, 152, *175*
  Ausf A 31, 42, 51, 121, 186
  Ausf D 120
  Ausf G 22, 59, 114, 179, 181, 184
  Jagdpanther (Sd Kfz 173) 187
Panzerkampfwagen VI (Sd Kfz 181) 31, 95, 102, 127, 151
  Ausf E 72, 96, 105
  Sturmmörser Tiger 38cm RW61 184
Panzerkampfwagen 35(t) 63, 64, 65, 66, 67
Panzerkampfwagen 38(t) 19, *81*, 149, 153
  Aufklärungspanzerwagen 38 (2cm) (Sd Kfz 140/1) 42, 186
  Ausf A 82
  Ausf B 75
  Ausf C 85, 116, 170
  Ausf E/F 78, 154, 170
  Ausf G 154
  Ausf H (Sd Kfz 138/1) 15cm SIG33 (Sf) 32
  Ausf M (Sd Kfz 138/1) 15cm SIG33 (Sf) 122
Panzerkampfwagen KV 1a 20, 86, 170
Panzerkampfwagen T-34 747 (r) 101
Panzerkorps 52
  II SS 151
  III 79, 124, 144, 151
  IV 179
  VIII 52
  XIV 90, 108, 137, 138
  XV 53, 74
  XVI 13, 16, 43, 44, 92
  XVIII 24
  XIX 14, 25, 36, 97
  XXII 14, 97
  XXIII 87
  XXIV 46
  XL 179
  XLI 29, 64, 66, 83
  XLVII 29, 31, 95, 127
  XLVIII 21, 79, 91, 112, 144, 172
  LI 178
  LVI 66
  LVI 172
  LX 171
  LXI 144, 168
  LXVII 144, 146, 187
  LXVIII 90, 137, 152, 156, 176
Panzerwerfer 42 15cm auf Sf (Sd Kfz 4/1) 80
Paulus, General Friedrich von 112, 138
pioneer battalions 18, 76, 81
Poland 26, 27, 51, 87, 108, 141, 152, 172, 179, 180
  6th Infantry Division 53
  invasion of 13–14, 24, 36–7, 43–4, 52–3, 62–3, 74, 82, 88, 97
  Narew Corps 97
Prague *10*, 36
Pripjet Marshes 48, 58
Prokorovka, Russia 112, 151

Radom, Poland 63, 74, 82
Reconnaissance Battalions
  2nd 29, 33
  3rd 42

191

INDEX

4th 12, 48, 49, 51
5th 23, 25
6th 94
7th 80
11th 25
12th 116
19th 151
20th 156
33rd 131
37th 76
92nd 155
Reichenau, General Walther von 13, 43, 63, 74, 82
Reinhardt, Generaloberst Georg-Hans 43, 64, 83
Remagen Bridge 96, 114, 187
reserve Panzer divisions
  155th 94
  179th 182
  273rd 113
Rhineland 23, 182
Romania 54, 87, 108, 118, 121, 156, 169
Rommel, Generalmajor Erwin
  France 53, 73, 74, 75, 166, 167, 183
  North Africa 77, 102, 128, 129, 131, 132, 134, 157, 162
Roslavl 27, 115
Rostov-on-Don 40, 118, 119, 124, 138
Ruhr Pocket 96, 183, 187
Rundstedt, Field Marshal Gerd von 25, 52, 63, 124, 166
Russia
  III Soviet Tank Corps 72
  Third Guards Tank Army 79–80
  counteroffensives 27, 29, 40–1, 47–8, 58, 66, 69, 79–80, 86–7, 92, 112, 115, 117, 120, 121, 124, 127, 138–9, 148, 151, 156, 172, 179
  invasion of 16–21, 27, 29, 39, 46–7, 56–7, 66–8, 77–8, 84, 90–1, 100–1, *106*, 110–11, 115, 118–19, 124–5, 137, 142–3, 146, 149
Rzhev 19, 20, 29, 57, 66, 77, 79, 92

Salerno *137*, 139, 141, 178
Sarajevo 84, 123
Saucken, General der Panzertruppen Dietrich von 43, 50
Schürzen side skirts 41, 177
Schützen brigades 62
  1st 12, 16
  2nd 23
  5th 52
  11th 108, 110
  12th 115
  14th 126
  22nd 169
  24th 176
Schützen regiments
  3rd 40
  5th 55
  112th 155
Schwere Infanteriegeschütz abteilung
  701st 89

702nd 18
703rd 18
704th 55
705th 76
707th 133
Schwere Panzer Abteilungen 93
  501st 102, 104, 105
  503rd 72, 105
  504th 102
  organization 105
Schwere Panzergruppe Bake 72
Schwere Panzerhaubitze auf Fahrgestell Panzerkampfwagen III/IV 15cm (Sf) (Sd Kfz 165) 29, 50, 58, 72, 144, 152
Schwerer Ladungstrager (Sd Kfz 301)
  Ausf A 34, 167
  Ausf B 95
Schwerer Panzerfunkwagen (Sd Kfz 263)
  6-Rad 69
Schwerer Panzerspähwagen
  (5cm) (Sd Kfz 234/2) 8-Rad 33
  (7.5cm) (Sd Kfz 233) 8-Rad 49, 103
  (Sd Kfz 231) 6-Rad 25, 69, 76
  (Sd Kfz 231) 8-Rad 113
  (Sd Kfz 232) 8-Rad 55
Sedan 14, 25, 98
Seine, River 74, 182
sFH13/1 15cm auf Geschützwagen Lorraine Schlepper (f) (Sd Kfz 135/1) 135, 165
Sicily 139, 181
Silesia 74, 82, 118
Skopje 54, 90, 108
Slovakia 87, 172, 179
Smolensk 29, 46, 77, 87, 100, 115, 142, 146, 149, 150, 153
Somua S-35 45
SS units
  1st SS Panzer Division *Leibstandarte* 118
  2nd SS Panzer Division *Das Reich* 108, 172
  II *Panzerkorps* 151, 178
  3rd SS Panzer Division *Totenkopf* 74, 75, 152, 172
  5th SS Panzer Division *Wiking* 119, 152, 172
  XIII Corps 114
Stabskompanie
  65th Battalion 65
  einer Panzer-Abteilung K.St.N.1150 17, 28
Stalin, Josef 139, 143
Stalin Line 66, 118
Stalingrad 40, 69, 86, 112, 119, 125, 127, 138–9, 143, 144, 169, *169*, 171–2, 176–7
Stalino 92, 120
Strachwitz, Hyazinth Graf von 148
Stumme, General der Kavallerie Georg 73, 82
Sturmgeschütz Battalions
  200th 166, 167
  276th 29
Sturmgeschütz III 40 7.5cm (Sd Kfz 142/1) 127
  Ausf F/8 103
  Ausf G 34, *62*, 140, 167

Sturminfanteriegeschütz 15cm 33B 172
sIG33 (Sf) auf Panzerkampfwagen 38(t) 32, 122
sIG33 (Sf) auf Panzerkampfwagen I Ausf B 18, 26, 55, 76, 89, 100
sIG33 (Sf) auf Panzerkampfwagen II 133
Sturmmörser Tiger 38cm RW61 184
Sturmpanzer IV (Sd Kfz 166) 178
Sudetenland 13, 36

T-34 42, 59, 67, 101, 119
Taganrog, Russia 118, 124, 138
Tarnopol, Russia 80, 87
Thoma, General der Panzertruppen W. Ritter von 62, 142, 153
Thuringen Panzer Brigade 35
Thuringia 74, 82, 114
Tiger *see* Panzerkampfwagen VI
Tobruk 130, 131, 132, 159, 162
Tula 46, 142, 146
Tunisia *97*, 102, 134, 136, 163

Ukraine 21, 41, 69, 87, 110, 127, 140, 141, 144, *149*, 151, 152, 172
Uman, Russia 41, 90, 110, 137

Valentine Mk III infantry tank 104
Vienna 88, 118
Viettinghoff-Scheel, Generalleutnant Heinrich von 52, 139
Vistila, River 52, 80, 141, 152, 180
Volga River 40, 47, 91, 138, 169, 176
Volksgrenadier Divisions 114
Voronezh 91, 112, 176
Vyasma 27, 57, 58, 100, 150, 153, 155

Warsaw 13, 37, 43, 44, 51, 52, 63, 74, 82, 152, 180
Wavell, General Archibald 129
Wehrmacht
  expansion 12, 61, 62, 107, 108
  Panzer divisions, first 11, 12
  tactics 43, 47
Weichs, General der Kavallerie Maximilian 12, 84, 123
Wespe 10.5cm self-propelled guns 29, 95, 144
West Prussia 48, 51, 59
Westwall 114, 182
Wirbelwind see Flakpanzer IV
Wurzburg 23, 43

Yugoslavia 26, 54, 84, 90, 108, 123, 124

Zagreb 84, 123
Zhitomir 21, 79–80, 87, 110, 137, 151, 152, 180
Zitadelle 69, 79, 92, 148
see also Kursk, Battle of